The Diplomacy of Independence

The Diplomacy of Independence

Benjamin Franklin Documents in the Archives of Spain

Edited by *Thomas E. Chávez*
With *Russ Davidson, Genoveva Enríquez, Patricia Kurz,* and *Celia López-Chávez*

American Philosophical Society Press
Philadelphia

Copyright © 2024 American Philosophical Society Press

All rights reserved. Except for brief quotations used for purposes of review or scholarly citation, none of this book may be reproduced in any form by any means without written permission from the publisher.

Published by
American Philosophical Society Press
Philadelphia, Pennsylvania 19106-3387
www.amphilsoc.org

Printed in the United States of America on acid-free paper
10 9 8 7 6 5 4 3 2 1

Library of Congress Cataloging-in-Publication Data
Names: Chavez, Thomas E., editor. | Davidson, Russ, editor. | Enríquez, Genoveva, editor. | López-Chávez, Celia, editor.
Title: The diplomacy of independence : Benjamin Franklin documents in the archives of Spain / edited by Thomas E. Chávez ; with Russ Davidson, Genoveva Enríquez, and Celia López-Chávez.
Other titles: Benjamin Franklin documents in the archives of Spain
Description: Philadelphia : American Philosophical Society Press, [2024]. | Includes bibliographical references. | Summary: "This book includes documents pertinent to Benjamin Franklin found in the archives of Spain. These documents speak to the relatively unknown history of Spain's early relationship with and aid to the fledging American colonies during their struggle to win independence from Great Britain"—Provided by publisher.
Identifiers: LCCN 2023046621 (print) | LCCN 2023046622 (ebook) | ISBN 9781606188958 (hardcover) | ISBN 9781606188972 (paperback) | ISBN 9781606188965 (epub)
Subjects: LCSH: Franklin, Benjamin, 1706-1790—Archives. | Statesmen—United States—Archives. | United States—Politics and government—1775-1783—Sources. | United States—Foreign relations—Spain. | Spain—Foreign relations—United States. | Archives—Spain.
Classification: LCC E302.F82 2024 (print) | LCC E302.F82 (ebook) | DDC 327.73046—dc23/eng/20240212
LC record available at https://lccn.loc.gov/2023046621
LC ebook record available at https://lccn.loc.gov/2023046622

Hardcover ISBN 9781606188958

Ebook ISBN 9781606188965

Paperback ISBN 9781606188972

*Dedicated to the memory of
Manuel Méndez García, Jr.
(20 January 1948–28 July 1967)*

A friend, born the day after me, who grew up in El Sereno, a suburb of Los Angeles, and who died in the Vietnam War.

With the hope that he and people like him will never be forgotten and that our governments will stop sending people like him off to war needlessly.

Contents

Introduction 1

Chapter 1. Franklin and the Prince 15

   1. Francisco Escarano to the Prince of Masserano, London, 13 January 1774; main letter, four pages; original in Spanish 15

   2. Francisco Escarano to the Prince of Masserano, London, 1 February 1774; main letter, five pages; original in Spanish 18

   3. Francisco Escarano to the Prince of Masserano, London, 18 February 1774; main letter, six pages; original in Spanish 21

   4. Francisco Escarano to the Prince of Masserano, London 11 March 1774; main letter, four pages; original in Spanish 25

   5. Francisco Escarano to the Prince of Masserano, London, 18 March 1774; main letter, six pages; original in Spanish; receipt included, Madrid, 11 April 1774 27

   6. Prince of Masserano to the Duke of Bexar, Madrid, 6 April 1774; summary note, one page; main letter, two pages, attached financial statement, one page; original in Spanish 31

   7. Francisco Escarano to the Prince of Masserano, London, 10 April 1774; main letter, four pages; original in Spanish 33

   8. Francisco Escarano to the Marquis of Grimaldi, London, 21 March 1775; main letter, three pages; original in Spanish 36

   9. Francisco Escarano to the Marquis of Grimaldi, 31 March 1779 copy (no. 469); main letter, one page; original in Spanish 38

10. Francisco Escarano to the Marquis of Grimaldi, London, 31 March 1775; main letter, three pages; original in Spanish 40

11. Benjamin Franklin to Don Gabriel de Borbón y Sajonia, Philadelphia, 12 December 1775; main letter, three pages; original in English 42

12. The Prince of Masserano to the Marquis of Grimaldi, London, 27 June 1775; main letter, five pages; original in Spanish 43

13. The Prince of Masserano to the Marquis of Grimaldi, London, 19 September 1775; main letter, two pages; original in Spanish 46

Chapter 2. Franklin the Diplomat 47

14. The Count of Aranda to the Marquis of Grimaldi, Paris, 28 June 1776 (no. 753); main letter, five pages; original in Spanish 47

15. The Count of Aranda to the Marquis of Grimaldi, Paris, 14 December 1776 (no. 83); partial letter, five pages; original in Spanish 50

16. The Prince of Masserano to the Marquis of Grimaldi, London, 17 December 1776; main letter, three pages; original in Spanish; summary note, one page; original in French 52

17. The Prince of Masserano to the Marquis of Grimaldi, London, 20 December 1776; main letter, three pages; original in Spanish 55

18. The Count of Aranda to the Marquis of Grimaldi, Paris, 4 January 1777; main letter, three pages; summary note, one page; original in Spanish 57

19. The Count of Aranda to the Marquis of Grimaldi, Paris, 13 January 1777 (no. 938, no. 4); summary note, one page; main letter, thirty-three pages; originals in Spanish 59

Attachment A, Aranda to Vergennes, Paris, 28 December 1776 (no. 5), one page, original in French 70

Attachment B, Aranda to Vergennes, Versailles, 28 April 1776, two pages, original in French 71

Contents • ix

Attachment C, Benjamin Franklin, Silas Deane, and Arthur Lee to Aranda, Paris, 28 December 1776, one page, original in Spanish translated from English 71

20. The Count of Aranda to the Marquis of Grimaldi, Paris, 13 January 1777 (no. 939, no. 6); main letter, thirty-eight pages; original in Spanish 73

21. To the Count of Aranda, El Pardo, 4 February 1777; main letter, four pages; introductory note, one page; original in Spanish 86

22. Benjamin Franklin, Silas Deane, and Arthur Lee to the Count of Vergennes; Paris, March 1777 (no. 35); main letter, four pages; original in English..88

23. Franklin to the Count of Aranda, Paris, 1 April 1777 (no. 23); main letter, three pages; original in English 90

Attachment, John Hancock, Congressional Commission, Baltimore, 2 January 1777 (no. 21); one page; original in English 91

24. The Count of Aranda to the Count of Floridablanca, Paris, 13 April 1777 (no. 1011, no. 20); main letter, twelve pages; original in Spanish..93

25. Memorial of Lord Stormont to the government of France. Sent by the Prince of Masserano to the Count of Floridablanca, London, 22 April 1777, two pages, original in English (and Spanish) 98

26. Committee for Commerce by the Congress to Bernardo de Gálvez, Philadelphia, 12 June 1777, three pages, original in Spanish..99

27. The Count of Aranda to the Count of Floridablanca, Paris, 22 June 1777 (no. 1055), nine pages, original in Spanish...........101

Attachment, paper of Franklin, June 1777, seven pages, original in French 104

28. The Count of Aranda to the Count of Floridablanca, Paris, 23 June 1777 (no. 1067, no. 28), main letter, three pages; original in Spanish..109

29. Benjamin Franklin Memorial, July 1777 (no. 29), seven pages, original in French 111

Attachment, poster in Loyd's Café, 3 July 1777, one page, original in French 115

30. Copy of a letter from the Count of Vergennes to Misters Franklin and Deane, Versailles, 16 July 1777 (no. 92); main letter, five pages; original in Spanish 117

31. The Count of Aranda to the Count of Floridablanca, Paris, 20 July 1777 (no. 1079, no. 28); main letter, twenty pages; original in Spanish 119

32. The Commissioners of the United States of America to the Count of Vergennes and the Count of Aranda, Passy, September 1777 (no. 34) Memorial with budget, nine pages; original in English 127

33. The Count of Aranda to the Count of Floridablanca, Paris, 27 September 1777 (no. 1139, no. 33); preliminary note, one page; original in Spanish 133

34. The Count of Aranda to the Count of Floridablanca, Paris, 27 September 1777; summary note, one page; draft letter, six pages; original in Spanish 135

35. The Count of Aranda to the Count of Floridablanca, Paris, 27 September 1777 (no. 1136, no. 32); main letter, three pages; original in Spanish 137

36. Francisco Escarano to the Count of Floridablanca, London, 3 October 1777; letter of introduction, one page; main letter, ten pages; original in Spanish 139

37. Robert Morris and William Smith to Bernardo de Gálvez, York in Pennsylvania, 24 October 1777; main letter, four pages; original in Spanish 145

38. The Count of Aranda to the Count of Floridablanca, Paris, 26 November 1777 (no. 1178); summary note, 23 October 1777, one page; main letter (draft), twelve pages; original in Spanish 148

Attachment A, Memorial of Benjamin Franklin, Silas Deane, and Arthur Lee; Paris, 23 November 1777 (no. 4612-156); three pages; original in English 153

Attachment B, congressional document signed by John Hancock, no date, one page, original in English..155

Attachment C, letter [Floridablanca] to the Count of Aranda, 9 December 1777 (no. 4612, No. 158-I, rough draft; preliminary letter, two pages; main letter, five pages, original in Spanish......156

39. The Count of Vergennes to Count of Montmorin, Versailles, 2 January 1778 (no. 199); extract of a letter, two pages; original in French..159

40. (Floridablanca) to the Count of Aranda, El Pardo (Spain), 13 January 1778 (no. 69); summary note, one page; main letter (draft), twenty-two pages; original in Spanish...160

Attachment, Montmorin to Vergennes, 13 January 1778 (no. 198), two pages, original in French..167

41. The Count of Aranda to the Count of Floridablanca, Paris, 19 March 1778 (no. 87-I); main letter, eleven pages; original in Spanish..168

42. Francisco Escarano to the Count of Floridablanca, London, 14 April 1778 (no.71); main letter, five pages; original in Spanish..173

43. Francisco Escarano to the Count of Floridablanca, London, 29 May 1778 (no. 12); main letter, five pages; original in Spanish..176

44. Graciano Sieulanne to Benjamin Franklin, Santa Cruz de Tenerife, 30 July 1778; letter book copy, four pages; original in French..179

45. Benjamin Franklin to Mister Grand (copy sent to Floridablanca), Passy, 3 November 1778 (no. 52); main letter, two pages; original in French; introductory letter, one page; original in Spanish..181

46. The Count of Aranda to the Count of Floridablanca, Paris, 9 September 1778 (no. 51); main letter, two pages; original in Spanish..183

47. The Count of Aranda to the Count of Floridablanca, Paris, 19 July 1779 (no. 126); main letter, three pages; original in Spanish..184

Attachment A, introductory note, the Count of Aranda, half page, Montgomery to Franklin, Alicante, 26 June 1779; main letter, three pages; original in French; summary note, one page; original in Spanish 185

Attachment B, J. Williams to Franklin, 13 July 1779; main letter. two pages; original in French...187

48. J. Williams to Franklin, Nantes, 22 July 1779 (translation); main letter, one page; original in French 188

Attachment A, Translators' certificate, 20 July 1779; main document, one page; original in French 188

Attachment B, Certification of Signatures, 22 July 1779; main document, one page; original in French 189

49. Juan Cólogan to Tomás Cólogan, Ostend, 27/31 December 1780; letter book, abbreviated letter, one page; original in English 191

50. The Count of Aranda to the Count of Floridablanca, Paris, 9 April 1781 (no. 1930); main letter, three pages; original in Spanish 193

51. The Count of Aranda to the Count of Floridablanca, Paris, 12 April 1781 (no. 1931); main letter, two pages; original in Spanish 195

52. Tomás Cólogan to Juan Cólogan, Tenerife, 6 June 1781 (partial letter); letter book, 1777 to 1782, two pages; original in English 197

53. Tomás Cólogan to Robert Morris, Tenerife, 7 June 1781, letter book, 1777 to 1782; four pages; original in English 199

54. Tomas Cólogan to Juan Cólogan of Cólogan, Pollard & Co. in London, Tenerife, 1 August 1781; letter book copy, four pages; original in English...201

55. The Count of Aranda to the Count of Floridablanca, Paris, 18 May 1782 (no. 2191); main letter, two pages; original in Spanish 202

56. The Count of Aranda to the Count of Floridablanca, Paris, 6 July 1782 (no. 2523); main letter, two pages; original in Spanish..203

57. The Count of Aranda to the Count of Floridablanca, Paris, 23 July 1783 (no. 2487); main letter, one page; original in Spanish 204

Attachment [Floridablanca] to the Count of Aranda, n.d., one page, original in Spanish 204

58. The Count of Aranda to the Count of Floridablanca, Paris, 3 September 1783 (no. 2523); main letter, one page; original in Spanish, attached to no. 37 205

Chapter 3. Postwar Franklin **207**

59. Minutes from the Board of Directors meeting of the Real Academia de la Historia, Madrid, 9 July 1784, main document, three pages; original in Spanish..207

60. Miscellaneous Dispatches and other notes, Wednesday 12 October 1785; Friday, 14 October; five pages, original in Spanish 209

61. Benjamin Franklin to Pedro Rodríguez, the Count of Campomanes, Philadelphia, 4 December 1786; main letter, one page; original in English 212

62. The Count of Campomanes to Benjamin Franklin (draft letter with Corrections), 24 May 1787, main letter, three pages, original in Spanish 213

Chapter 4. Spanish, French, and Latin Transcriptions **215**

Franklin y el Príncipe 215

Franklin el Diplomático 246

Franklin de la Posguerra 384

Notes *393*

Bibliography *435*

Index *439*

Acknowledgments *455*

INTRODUCTION

At first glance, the title of this book does not make sense because most people do not connect Benjamin Franklin to Spain, much less suspect that documents pertinent to him exist in the archives of Spain. Although he never set foot in Spain, from as early as 1774 until his death in 1790, he corresponded with Spanish royalty, officials, and intellectuals.

As the research in this project progressed, another bow to reality came into focus. The initial goal of publishing all the documents in the archives of Spain dealing with Franklin became illusive. More archives potentially containing Franklin documents constantly surfaced. Some of these proved fruitless, others contained one or two pieces of interest, and others hinted at still other archives. Eventually, it became obvious that we had set for ourselves an unrealistic goal. This extended to the archives that we researched, for there is no doubt that some documents were either overlooked or since have been newly accessioned. Nevertheless, what is presented here is a major source of information based on the majority of this invaluable resource material.

These papers, in turn, speak to another relatively unknown history, that of Spain's early relationship with and aid to the fledging American colonies during their struggle to win independence from Great Britain.

Benjamin Franklin is arguably the most affectionately remembered Founding Father of the United States of America. He personifies everything people from the United States see in themselves: He was a self-made man, very independent, a philosopher, an inventor, a businessman, and a public servant. In addition, he was the very image of Horatio Alger, whose philosophy he pretty much expressed in his *Poor Richard's Almanac*. He wrote that he inserted proverbs in the almanac that "inculcated industry and frugality as the means of procuring wealth and thereby securing virtue."[1] No wonder the sociologist Max Weber later used Franklin to exemplify the Protestant ethic or, as Weber called it, *modern capitalism*.[2]

On the other hand, Franklin dedicated much of his life to public service. Although "procuring wealth" is self-explanatory, "securing virtue" is a whole different matter. From his youth, Franklin sought ways to benefit the general good. No project was too minuscule or too large, so long as it benefited the public. From "the Franklin stove," to negotiating the peace treaty that secured the independence of the United States of America, Franklin sought to improve humankind.

By the time he was thirty-two years old, Benjamin Franklin had been in the printing and publishing business for over thirteen years; started his own newspaper; established the first subscription library in North America; formed his first junto of like-minded individuals; established the first public "fire company" in America; was appointed the postmaster of Philadelphia; and had lived in London, where he also printed and published, and wrote the first edition of *Poor Richard's Almanac*.[3] He also had married and started a family.

A little more than ten years later, at the age of forty-two, he retired from business to spend the rest of his life experimenting, inventing, writing, and, above all, trying to serve the public.

In 1757, when he was fifty-one years old, the Colonial legislature of Pennsylvania sent him to London as their spokesman in a dispute with the proprietors of their colony. While there, he took a trip to Flanders and Holland and returned to London in time to attend the coronation of George III on 22 September 1761. He returned to Philadelphia the next year.

Two years later the Pennsylvania legislature reappointed him as their representative in London. This time he was sent to petition the new king to terminate Pennsylvania's proprietary status in favor of making it a royal colony. This assignment grew into an eleven-year sojourn, during which Franklin, who left his family in Philadelphia, became the unofficial Colonial spokesman against what the Americans perceived as unlawful legislation. The first action criticized was the Stamp Act, in 1765, which Franklin originally did not oppose. The legislatures of Georgia in 1768, New Jersey in 1769, and Massachusetts in 1770 joined Pennsylvania in making him their official agent.

Franklin continued to write, correspond, and invent. He very much became a part of London's society and adopted a second family, with whom he lived. Mostly because of his work in science, especially electricity, he received honorary degrees from Saint Andrews and Oxford Universities and became an international celebrity.

While in London, he was given credit for inventing the glass armonica, although he credited another person for developing this device. Suffice it to say, he refined and popularized the instrument, which used glass bowls of different sizes that rotated on a spindle to make sounds when moist fingers rubbed against them. Franklin described the instrument's eerie sound as heavenly.

In 1774 the Spanish embassy contacted Franklin on behalf of Don Gabriel de Borbon, the youngest son of Spain's King Carlos III. The infante wanted to secure a glass armonica.[4] Don Gabriel was one of thirteen children and the third son to the king. He was born on 11 May 1752 and had not reached his twenty-second birthday when the embassy approached Franklin on his behalf. He spent his youth with the royal family in Naples, where his father was King Carlos VI of Naples, before ascending the throne in Spain in 1759 as Carlos III. Don Gabriel was a willing product of the Enlightenment. He studied literature, Roman history, music, art, and science, and played the clavichord. He translated from Latin, wrote, and published. His interest in the famous American inventor and his glass armonica could not have been more natural. The American statesman and the young prince would exchange gifts of a glass armonica for a translation of an early Roman history.

Franklin returned to Philadelphia in 1775, where he became a delegate to the Second Continental Congress and accepted an appointment to a committee with Thomas Jefferson and John Adams to help write the Declaration of Independence. During the subsequent war, the Continental Congress appointed him the senior member of the Secret Committee of Correspondence. Along with Silas Deane and Arthur Lee, who were other members of the committee, he received instructions to travel to Paris, where they were to secure alliances and aid for the rebelling colonies. By late 1776 he had embarked from Philadelphia to represent his aspiring young country in France. While there he dealt with Spain as the committee's composition, as well as its assignment, changed during the next eight years.

Because of delays in transit, his semi-secretive arrival in Paris in late December of 1776 created a controversy.[5] He immediately met with Charles Gravier, the Count of Vergennes, who was the French minister of foreign affairs, and sent a letter to Pedro Pablo Abarca de Bolea, the Count of Aranda, Spain's ambassador to France.

On behalf of the whole American Commission, Franklin requested a meeting with Aranda. The ambassador, anxious to hear from the Americans, arranged for the meeting to be held the next evening at his own sumptuous residence. That get-together was the first of many meetings Franklin would have with Aranda and was the beginning of the aspiring nation's contact with the Hispanic world.

At the time of their first meeting, on Sunday, December 29, Aranda had served a long, distinguished diplomatic career. At fifty-seven years old, he was thirteen years Franklin's junior. He was a very intelligent, opinionated, well-traveled, and, at times, a difficult and stubborn man. Yet he had a sense of position, forthrightness, and confidence. He could turn an obscure point into a time-consuming ordeal or brilliantly cut to the point. His own king referred to him as "more obstinate and stubborn than an Aragonese mule."[6] That the same king kept him in influential positions points to his value. His appointment to Paris was, at once, an exile from Madrid and recognition of his influence and talent. Vergennes soon found occasion to comment on him. He wrote, "I have never seen anything like this ambassador."[7] It is important to note that Aranda had a decidedly pro-American attitude.

In the process of their meetings, Franklin presented some paperwork that, at first, Aranda refused to accept. That paperwork, along with Aranda's cover letter, is now housed in Spain's national archives. One of the documents is an oversized certificate from the Continental Congress that names Franklin the minister to Spain whose assignment was "to communicate, treat and conclude with his most Catholic Majesty, the King of Spain ... a treaty ... for the just purpose for assistance in carrying on the present war between Great Britain and these United States."[8] John Hancock, the president of the Second Continental Congress, signed the document in his usual oversized script. Charles Thomson, the secretary of Congress, attested to the document. The latter hired Timothy Matlack, the scribe who wrote the Declaration of Independence, to write this document.

In the letter accompanying the certificate, Franklin explained that he had been named the "Minister Plenipotentiary" to Spain, but, given Spain's neutrality, he would stay in Paris and work with Aranda.[9] Franklin, Aranda, and the French would work together for the next six-plus years, through the final signing of peace in 1783. During that time, Franklin was in charge of the finances for himself and his colleagues, as well as raising money for the cause of independence. This included dealing with American privateers who, on occasion, violated the rights of allied or neutral shipping.

After the Treaty of Paris was signed, Franklin asked to be relieved of his duties, but he had to wait two years before he could return home. Once back in Pennsylvania, he was quickly elected the president of the Executive Council of Pennsylvania. He served in that capacity for the next three years. He also was selected to be a delegate to the Constitutional Convention in 1787–88. He retired from public life in 1789 and died on 17 April 1790. He was eighty-four years old.

Of all the country's founders, Franklin became the most internationally respected, even beloved, personage. For fairly long periods, he lived in England and then France. He corresponded with scientists and thinkers from all over the world. His direct effect on his contemporaries, much less subsequent generations, is still being discovered. For example, both Ludwig van Beethoven and Wolfgang Mozart wrote music for the glass armonica. In the distant city of San Juan, in western Argentina at the base of the Andes Mountains, a young Domingo Faustino Sarmiento (1811–88) established and named the city's first public library in Franklin's honor. Sarmiento would go on to become a great man of letters as well as the president of Argentina (1868–75). Franklin, of course, is given credit for establishing "subscription libraries" in North America. Franklin's idea of a junto—a nonpartisan think tank—evolved into the American Philosophical Society, which is the oldest American learned society today. No wonder, then, that his name is found in the membership rolls of other similar organizations in Europe, including Spain's Real Academia de la Historia, to which he was admitted on 9 July 1784.[10]

Benjamin Franklin had a rough edge about him. But these imperfections, although known, have been overlooked through the years.[11] As a teenager he violated the terms of his indentured service to his older brother and ran away from home. Although he married once, he had affairs with other women, and as an elder statesman in France, he, as one writer put it, "made his spiritual home in two of the great salons of the day."[12] His oldest son, William, was born of an unknown woman. One of his three children, named Francis, died at the age of four from smallpox. William became estranged from him, and only his daughter, Sally, welcomed him into her house, which actually belonged to Franklin, for his last years.

He is remembered in the United States for his *Autobiography* and *Poor Richard's Almanac*, whence comes his connection to the concept of the Puritan ethic and, some argue, the basis of capitalism.[13] But it was in public service where he achieved his greatest success and his greatest disappointment. Despite his work, many of his co-patriots loathed him in his day. Because of his many years abroad, some people suspected his loyalty to the colonies. During the peace negotiations, John Jay questioned his bias toward France. The US Senate refused to thank him for his service during his lifetime. When he died, the Senate, under the leadership of John Adams, Richard Henry Lee, and Ralph Izard, among others, refused to memorialize him.[14]

Time would overcome the pettiness of his contemporary rivals, for Franklin's public career was long and fruitful. Although he represented the colony of Pennsylvania and then many other colonies in London for many years, he considered himself a staunch Englishman, and, despite the protestations of his wife, whom he left in Philadelphia, he even considered making London his permanent home. However, when it became obvious to him that the rift between the colonies and the English government could not be repaired, he returned home, attended the Second Continental Congress, and became a true patriot.

The US public still knows little of his connections to Spain or, for that matter, Spain's connections to the United States during the latter's formative years. For all his long life's activities and many trips, Benjamin Franklin never went to Spain. In his many biographies, his work and connections with Spanish officials and others are barely mentioned. So why compile a book subtitled *Benjamin Franklin Documents in the Archives of Spain*?

He did indeed meet and correspond with Spanish officials. From Spain's point of view, he, along with Deane and Lee, were the initial faces of the rebelling colonies. Much of that correspondence exists in Spain today and has yet to be gleaned by US historians. While in Spain doing research on the role of Spain in the birth of the United States, I came across documents to and from, as well as about, Benjamin Franklin. These documents were housed in various Spanish archives. Although not specifically researching Franklin, I saw enough to realize that these documents provided additional information and a view of Franklin and Spain heretofore unknown. For example, "Dr. Franklin's" diplomatic mission and meetings with the Spanish ambassador in Paris are detailed in the Spanish archives.

The correspondence pertinent to him spills over to information heretofore not considered in the history of the birth of the United States. The specific impressions of Spanish officials and their philosophical as well as strategic motives in dealing with the rebelling colonies can now move beyond the realm of conjecture. The written English-language record of this critical time has never included the Spanish point of view regarding the cooperation, suspicions, and overall relationship between Spain and France.[15]

These insights into Spanish and French relations add to the knowledge of their respective relationship to the colonies. Spain and France had common as well as different attitudes and concerns. The documents shared in this collection provide an interesting insight into these key European allies. Franklin represented the Continental Congress, so, if nothing else, these documents provide more detail of what was requested from Spain.

The American needs range from specifics, such as twenty thousand pairs of shoes, eighty thousand pairs of socks, quinine, and pistols, to generalities such as friendship, trade, and protection for American ships in Spanish ports. Aside from satisfying the many students and fans of Franklin worldwide, these documents should interest every student of the Revolutionary War, for they add to an already interesting history. Moreover, they represent the very beginning of the United States' diplomatic relations with the Hispanic world.

An encounter with these initial documents raises the question of how many more Franklin-related documents exist in Spain. For example, the matter of his correspondence with Don Gabriel de Borbon, King Carlos III's youngest and favorite son, as well as his membership in the Spanish Royal Academy of History, necessitated a search in two new archives.

To date, Benjamin Franklin documents have been located in eight Spanish archives: the Archivo de Simancas (AGS) in Valladolid; the Archivo Histórico Nacional (AHN) in Madrid; the Archivo General del Palacio Real (AGP) in Madrid; the Biblioteca Nacional (BN) in Madrid; the Archivo del Real Academia de la Historia (RAH) in Madrid; Fundación Universitaria Española also in Madrid; the Archivo General de Indias (AGI) in Seville; and the Archivo Zárate-Cólogan in the Archivo Histórico Provincial de Santa Cruz (AHPTF/AZC), in Tenerife. Although documents have been located in these archives, as mentioned, the search is by no means complete.

This is especially true of the Archivo Zárate-Cólogan. This extensive archive deals mainly with the correspondence and activities of the Cólogan Valois family beginning with Juan Cólogan Blanco (White) and his sons. The Cólogans ran a large international mercantile operation, Juan Cólogan e hijos, which did business with the British colonies before, during, and after their struggle for independence. Franklin also placed personal orders for some of the Canary Islands' highly prized wine with Juan Cólogan e hijos.[16] The war affected the family in various ways. Benjamin Franklin is evoked through the documents, especially in a letter book written in minuscule handwriting. Research pertinent to Franklin in this archive has just begun. The Tenerife-based company, Juan Cólogan e hijos, called on Franklin to help resolve issues when its ships with their cargo were captured and taken as prizes by American captains. At first, this was a breach of Spain's neutrality and, after Spain declared war on Great Britain, such an activity was an affront to a country helping in the struggle. Franklin not only had to deal with American naval captains, but also privateers, whose ships were referred to as *corsairs,* who sometimes acted like pirates.

Not all research is fruitful. A wise professor once said that research is ninety-nine percent finding out where things are not. A search through the privately held records of the Basque banking firm of Gardoqui e Hijos (Gardoqui and Sons) in Valladolid surprisingly revealed nothing dealing with Franklin. Moreover, research in the Archivo del Ministerio de Asuntos Extereores (MAE) in Alcalá de Henares proved futile. However, some of the potential *legajos* (bundles) of documents could not be opened because of their bad condition. The papers of Francisco Saavedra in the Jesuit archives held on the campus of the University of Granada also came up empty. Document number 62 in this book came from a private archive, previously unexplored.

Then there is the question of the Conde de Aranda's private papers. Aranda died in the town of Épila, in the Province of Zaragoza in Spain in 1798 without a direct descendant. His extensive library, papers, as well as property passed down through the years until a collateral descendant married into the family of the Duke of Alba, at which point the Aranda name disappears, while his library, papers, and property remained with the family and descendants of the Duke of Alba. In 1987 and 1988, some of the property was sold off and some donated to local governments, including a portion of his papers, which were donated to the Province of Aragón.[17] These papers do not include any of Aranda's personal letters, rather they contain legal documents dealing with his properties. However, a portion of the library and papers remained part of the Alba family collections—with a possible exception. Although today the extensive Archivo de la Fundación de Alba de Tormes in Madrid holds Aranda's official papers also dealing with property, family heredity, and so on, his personal correspondence is missing. We know that Aranda was a prolific writer and can only image what private correspondence dealing with Franklin could have existed at his death. What became of those letters, if they existed at all, remains a mystery.

Why has the existence of Franklin documents in Spain not been investigated before? This point has been raised in a more general context as a result of the publication of *Spain and the Independence of the United States: An Intrinsic Gift* (2002).[18] It is not easy to arrive at an answer, for it implies conclusions that are not true; for example, that US historians cannot read Spanish or do not care to divulge this information. Historians in Spain and the United States have known that Franklin had something to do with Spain for years.

The real point of this inquiry is to understand why this story of Spain's involvement in the American Revolution, much less Franklin's connection, is barely known in the United States. More to the point: Why have US historians generally not seen, much less used these documents?

US historians have been working with Spanish documents and archives for over a hundred years. But they have concentrated on the history of Spain, the history of Spanish Latin America, and the history of Spanish maritime trade during the seventeenth and eighteenth centuries. The field of Spanish borderlands studies concentrated on Spanish expansion and settlement in what is today the southwestern United States and northern Mexico. The idea that papers relative to Benjamin Franklin existed in the archives of Spain was beyond their consideration as well as their scope of investigation. Until recently, historians of Hispanic subjects concentrated on other themes.

Franklin's many biographers have ignored or glossed over his work with Spain. Many of these biographies do not even list *Spain* or *Spanish* in their indexes. None of them use Spanish sources. Generally, in their view, Spain was dealt with through the French.[19]

If anything, Franklin's connections to Spain should have been noted by the legions of Franklin specialists because there are sources in English that point to Spain. Franklin's connections to Spain can be gleaned in English from among his own published papers. In addition, other published collections like the papers of the Continental Congress bring up the subject.[20] Once established in English, the natural investigative process should have turned to Spanish archives.

Basically, then, we are left with the explanation that the subject has been overlooked. The idea of Franklin and Spain has never attracted the interest of the many students of Franklin and, therefore, has remained an untapped archival resource through the years.

There are some small exceptions. For example, the archives of the Real Academia de la Historia in Madrid reveal that in 1956, the 250th anniversary of Franklin's birth, scholar Hayward Keniston (1883–1970), a professor emeritus of Romance languages at the University of Michigan, wrote a letter in Spanish to the institution's director suggesting that the Real Academia join in the celebrations because Franklin was one of its members. This resulted in a speech and presentation of a congressional medal by US ambassador John Davis Lodge. Lodge's speech, along with Professor Keniston's correspondence, is in the archives of the Real Academia.[21]

Spanish historians have written more about this subject. Within eight years of Franklin's death, a Spanish author, Pantaleón Aznar, wrote and published a biography of him. In justifying his book, Aznar wrote that he wanted to "present the life of Benjamin Franklin so he is not forgotten among the geniuses that have distinguished Europe" during the eighteenth century.[22] Modern Spanish historians have published and written about Franklin's relationship to Spain since at least 1925, when Juan Francisco Yela Utrilla wrote his seminal *España ante la independencia de los Estados Unidos*. The book was republished in 1988. Yela Utrilla's work not only shares an accurate narrative history about Spain's involvement in the birth of the United States, but it also contains an appendix of letters to and from American patriots, including Franklin. Yela Utrilla published the letters in their original language. In other words, he did not translate Spanish correspondence into English or vice versa.[23] Some of his work is included in abbreviated form in the published collection of Franklin's letters that Yale University has compiled. However, it appears that the editors of the latter mined Yela Utrilla's work without actually consulting the original sources in the archives of Spain. For example, the Yale edition notes that the document is included in Yela Utrilla's book and, like him, lists the general archive without specifics. In addition, the few Spanish letters, specifically written by Aranda, are extracts, thus losing most if not all context.[24] A few of the documents included in this volume have been published, in whole or in part, in both Yela Utrilla and subsequently in Yale's seminal work. The particular histories of these documents are indicated in the Notes.

The question arises: Why publish such a document again? Primarily because the current team has had the opportunity to work from the original document and note any differences that time or subsequent copies have accumulated. Following this method, the contextual information surrounding the document cannot be overlooked. The previously published documents have been updated, published in entirety, and included with the newly encountered unpublished documents, thus providing a more comprehensive understanding of their significance.

Between 1977 and 1985, the Spanish government published an eleven-volume bibliography describing and listing documents in Spanish archives that are pertinent to US independence. This important publication was compiled in honor of the United States' bicentennial in 1976. Again, many documents related to Franklin are identified. The title of this series is *Documents relativos a la independencia de Norteamérica existentes en archivos españoles* (1977–85).[25] Every serious library and archive in the United States should have copies of this set as well as Yela Utrilla's book.

El Conde de Aranda y los Estados Unidos (1987), by Joaquín Oltra and María Angeles Pérez Samper is an important publication in Spain. As

Franklin's Spanish diplomatic counterpart, Aranda knew Franklin as well as anyone. This book documents Aranda's diplomatic mission as the Spanish ambassador in Paris during the Revolutionary War. Aranda reported the details of his encounters with Franklin to Madrid.[26] Two more recent publications are also pertinent. The first deals with the Gardoqui family, who funneled money to the colonies; the second is about Juan de Miralles, who worked with the Continental Congress on behalf of Spain.[27]

Even general as well as popular publications in Spain have dealt with Franklin and Spain's role in US independence. The *Enciclopedia general ilustrada del País Vasco* revealed Franklin's role in arranging refuge for American naval captains, including John Paul Jones, under the care of the Spanish banker Diego de Gardoqui in the Spanish port of Bilbao.[28]

The popular *Yo solo: Bernardo de Gálvez y la toma de Panzacola en 1781* (1986), by Carmen de Reparaz, is a heavily illustrated and very good book about the battle of Pensacola, in which the Spanish defeated the British. In it a Franklin document is reproduced in miniscule type but original form.[29]

Mention should be made of historian Juan Martínez Cuesta, the painting curator of Spain's Patrimonio Nacional (National Patrimony). Before he unexpectedly passed away in 1999, he published an article and wrote an unfinished biography of the infante Don Gabriel de Borbon in which he wrote about Franklin's relationship to the prince.[30]

This project adds to the body of knowledge about Benjamin Franklin and throws more light on a critical period of US history. This volume presents a compilation of sixty-two documents, some with attachments, and is organized chronologically so that the general reader can make some sense of the letters, while historians can utilize them in their full provenance. For simplicity's sake, each document contains the name of the collection and archive in which the collection is kept. In their original form, those documents represent 280 original handwritten pages. Twenty-eight pages are written in English, fifteen in French, and 237 in Spanish.

When Franklin lived (1706–90), French was the diplomatic language. Nevertheless, it was common for participants to write in their own language. Franklin wrote in English both publicly and privately. Normally, while in Paris, documents written in English would be translated into either Spanish or French. Spanish internal documents were usually but not always written in Spanish.

The Count of Aranda was fluent in both Spanish and French, whereas the American delegation, as divulged by Aranda, was not fluent in French.[31] As a result, many of the Spanish and French documents are translations from documents originally written in English. Some of the latter documents still exist in various US archives. If located and/or known, the archival locations of the English originals are noted. In addition, when available, the English original has been compared to the subsequent translations.

Each document is preceded by a brief, formalized heading that includes the document's original language and how many pages it was in its original form. The French originals have been transcribed and translated into Spanish and English. The Spanish originals have been transcribed in their entirety before translation into English. The Spanish and French transcriptions provided here are the ones the team used to translate documents into English. The reader should note that letters were written by various sources and for various reasons. The legibility of handwriting is even more varied, from size to scribbling to use of actual print. Some were written in a very formal and educated hand, others in legalese, and still others use poor syntax; some even appear in draft form. The transcriptions are not exact in that some punctuation has been added to make the text understandable. In addition, some old phrases, if incomprehensible today, have been modernized.

Although the handwriting and text of eighteenth-century Spanish parallels the English of the same period, as always there are individual particulars, reflective of the writer's personality. Many times, this personality is expressed through long, one-sentence paragraphs. These paragraphs reflect a continuous thought process rather than a thought conveyed using coherent syntax. As the editors of the Yale edition of the Franklin Papers wrote about the translation of one of Aranda's reports, "The Spanish ... leaves the translator the alternatives of reproducing circumlocutions or vague constructions or taking liberties with the text to bring out the meaning [;] we have chosen the latter course."[32] This comment is equally true for this publication.

Rather than a direct word-for-word translation, this is an effort to translate the Spanish and French documents into readable English. The habitual capitalization of words for emphasis also is maintained. In addition, the letters are annotated with explanations of people, places, and some events.

A word about the process of translation is in order. A team of scholars was assembled to compile and process the documents. Translation requires that each document pass through many filters, as no two individuals will translate the same document alike. Each document was considered by three scholars, who reviewed and/or translated them. The scholars met and/or corresponded to resolve questions or differences.

The mailing systems constantly referred to in the documents should be mentioned here. Letters sent with noncompromising information were sent by "ordinary" or "official" mail, including even the French mailing system. Mail that needed to remain confidential, meaning it was not to be opened in transit, was sent in secret, entrusted into the hands of persons of confidence. This last type of mailing is sometimes referred to as *expedited* or *special*.

Every document is fully identified so that historians will be able to go to the originals with minimal effort. Ultimately, this simple format and its information will be a tool for subsequent investigators of history. This is not a revisionist or a postmodern attempt at reinterpreting a known body of knowledge, but an effort to make more information available. We hope this compilation allows others to glean new information for their own histories. In the process, historians and, eventually, the general public will learn more about Franklin's life and times as well as Spain's key role in the independence of the United States.

Today, more than three centuries after Franklin's birth, there is more to learn about this great and interesting man. Franklin's contact with the infante Don Gabriel de Borbon and his subsequent diplomatic work with Spain are two points from which to begin the search for and dissemination of Benjamin Franklin in the archives of Spain.

1

FRANKLIN AND THE PRINCE

🏵 Document 1
Legajo 7016-5, Estado, AGS
Francisco Escarano[1] to the Prince of Masserano,[2] London, 13 January 1774
[Main letter, four pages]
Original in Spanish

Sir:

El Pardo's response is given on 7 February 1774[3]
    The commission for the grand piano that Your Excellency saw fit to give me in your last letter could not have arrived in more timely fashion, because the Spanish ship *San Bernardo*, captained by Antonio de Revilla, was almost ready to set sail. I believe that it will leave tomorrow, and with it the shipment of a grand piano to Don Luis de Ventades[4] from a German, Mr. Pohlman,[5] from whom My Lady, the Duchess de Villahermosa,[6] has obtained one and whose services were used by the ambassador of France. It was only with considerable effort that I was able to persuade him to let me have one that he had made for a gentleman at a cost of 16 Guineas.[7] The one that Don Miguel de Ventades[8] has sent for the Marquesa de la Torrecilla has cost 16 and

nine schillings, and I believe that it is not as good. The Duchess de Villahermosa's cost twenty, because it required something more than the one I am sending to you.

Would that I should be able to discharge as promptly the other task of the armonica that His Excellency the Infante Don Gabriel desires.[9] As soon as I received Your Excellency's instructions I went to see Mademoiselle Davis,[10] who is the woman that Your Excellency saw play this instrument on occasion, and having told her that I would like to have a similar one for a sister of mine, she responded that she only had two, the one here that she uses, and another that she had left in Florence, where she planned to return shortly. She went on to say that her father, the inventor,[11] had just passed away and that I would certainly not find in England someone who could make me one like it. I made a thousand promises to her so that she would let me have the one she had in London, but there was no way to follow through on that.

I heard that the famous Doctor Franklin, who Your Excellency knows, had one. I went to see him and expressed to him my wish that he let me have it. This Philosopher, who is the finest man in the world, confessed that he has two of the instruments that I wanted. One is in America, for which he was soon to set out, and the other is in London. By the same token he told me what a pleasure it would be to give me the one in his possession were it in perfect condition and did not have four or five broken glass bowls; that to mend it was a very difficult task, and so the only thing that he could do was to suggest a man who at one time used to work on such instruments, but he warned me that he would ask for more than fifty pounds sterling if he should decide to do it. I thanked him profusely for his advice and, in taking leave, I almost managed to get out of him that if the man in question did not agree to fix the armonica for me, he would give me his for what it had cost him. Since I could not find the said artist at home yesterday, and being caught up with much to do, I shall not able to look for him until tomorrow, for which reason I will await the next dispatch of mail to inform Your Excellency of the results of my endeavors. I will do everything possible to fulfill His Lordship, the *Infante*'s charge, and it will gratify me to have the joy of that accomplishment.

As concerns My Lord North,[12] I have nothing to report to Your Excellency. I have not seen him again since he told me in the palace that he would send someone to meet with secretary of customs, Mr. Stanley, and consult with him about what could be done on Your Excellency's behalf.

Yesterday was the opening of Parliament, where the King delivered the oration that I include for you in French translation.

The country house of Steven Cox, the oldest child of My Lord Holland,[13] burnt down. The fire broke out during the night, and everyone had to vacate in his or her undershirts.

Nothing else occurs to me to report to Your Excellency, from whom I anxiously await news, to find out if you have recovered from your last attack of the gout.

I submit with the deepest respect to the obedience of Your Excellency and pray that God may keep you many years as I desire.

London, 13 January 1774
Most Excellent Sir, I am at Your Excellency's feet,
Your most humble and devoted subject
Francisco Escarano
[to] Most Excellent Lord, the Prince of Masserano

Document 2
Legajo 7016-7, AGS
Francisco Escarano to the Prince of Masserano, London, 1 February 1774
[Main letter, five pages]
Original in Spanish

Your Excellency
The response from Madrid was given on 24 February 1774[14]

Sir:
    Continuing to inform Your Excellency of the results of my endeavors to obtain the armonica that the Infante Don Gabriel desires, I can tell Your Excellency that having ventured to the house of the artisan whom the famous Doctor Franklin recommended to me, the former only with great difficulty brought out for me, as an exceedingly rare thing, the instrument that he had; and asked if he would want to sell it to me for a sister of mine, he replied that he would not get rid of it for any amount of money. All my entreaties to persuade him to let me have it were useless, as were those, less involved, to convince him that he should make another similar one for me, persisting all the while in telling me that he would not undertake the task for even a hundred guineas. Knowing that it is almost impossible to overcome the obstinacy of an Englishman, I went on to recount what had happened to Dr. Franklin, who, after similar resistance, offered to give me his armonica for what it had earlier cost him to get it fixed. As an honorable, good man that he [Franklin] is I felt that there should be no secrets and I confided in him that the armonica was meant to the Infante, which has impelled him even more to give me his instrument in good repair, though it cannot be before a month. I do not know exactly what it will cost. I am inclined to believe that it will not come to twenty-five pounds sterling, or forty *doblones*. I will be supremely happy when I managed to carry out this commission on behalf of Your Highness, and will as my duty demands employ great zeal and take every action.
    I have received with appreciation Your Excellency's letter on the 27th of December that consoles me with the good news that your health

has improved very much from your last attack of gout; [the] news has [also] been greatly celebrated by this Sovereign, who is continually informed about the details of Your Excellency's health.

Don Miguel de Ventades[15] must still send to Your Excellency an explanation of how to place the screws on the locks that he has sent; and, moreover, agrees to buy the pendulum according to the details that Your Excellency has seen fit to explain to me.

Don Josef Constant,[16] who places himself at Your Excellency's feet, says that there is no problem in utilizing an empowered representative in Barcelona to collect your Government's salary, if Your Excellency encounters difficulties from the Ministry of War, from which you were paid in London. I hope that Your Excellency conceals this option.

It is certain that the Duke of Gloucester[17] has been incognito in Paris for a few days and apparently has written to Your Excellency. This Monarch [England's king] who does not have the slightest indication that his brother wanted to make this escape has not taken it badly. If it were not for the Duke of Cumberland,[18] he would already have reconciled with the Duke of Gloucester, to whom he professes true affection.

I am happy that the Count of Fuentes[19] has gone to Aragon because the trip will have served to correct his sadness for his past misfortune. I beg Your Excellency to see fit to place me at the feet of My Lady, the Duchess of Villahermosa, and to the obedience of the Marquis of Mora, as well as of the Lord Duke.

We remain in the same state with My Lord North; the day before yesterday I sought to speak with him in the Palace. He knew and went off to look for Lord Mansfield,[20] who was in a corner of the King's reception room. The gentleman Porter has had the gout for a month and is not to be seen. My Lord Rochford will not receive us until Thursday, at which time I will urge him to persuade My Lord North to relieve me of the uncertainty that we are in. No doubt, Your Excellency, we will achieve some success, but to say to what type of small success is to expose ourselves to fail.

I have not done anything yet concerning My Lord Harcourt's[21] house because I am waiting for you to answer the letter in which I described it. I flatter myself that this response will arrive between today and eight days from now, and then we will timidly proceed to a settlement in which he will get the better sale. I suspect that Your Excellency will be anxious because I am not making progress in an aspect of your business, and that you will blame me, but I assure Your Excellency that what has not been completed is not my fault.

Puskin[22] assures that they have taken Silesia, and they have set fire to it, but at the same time he says that the entire army was to regain the Danube, which is clear proof that it has been destroyed.[23]

That Englishman Lloyd, who was an Abbot and librarian for the Duke of Montealegre[24] in Venice, a scribe in Madrid, an ensign of the artillery in Barcelona, and a middling camp adjunct to the Prince of Brunswick in Germany, is today a Major General in the service of the Czarina.[25]

These Ministers desire it because they know your good qualities. The beautiful My Lady, who lives very well with her husband, will come to London in the month of March, if a certain person does not cross the Straights. If she passes her so, the poor woman will stay in her country house. I refer to the Duchess of Villahermosa who sent me a letter for her husband, which I include via Your Excellency in the one that I am writing.

I have seen My Lord Grantham's[26] chaplain, who has come to me on the recommendation of Don Bernardo del Campo.[27] He appears to be a very learned and agreeable man. He said to me that he had visited Your Excellency the evening of your departure, and at that point you had almost recovered from your last attack of gout, which I rejoice with all my heart.

This queen has not recently appeared in public, given that she is expecting to give birth to a child very soon. His British Majesty always asks me about Your Excellency and is happy to hear that I am sure of your return to this Court. The entire diplomatic corps sends, as they should, their best wishes to Your Excellency, who I devotedly implore will see fit to keep me under your protection and honor me with your orders. May God keep Your Excellency many years, as I desire and and pray.

> London, 1 February 1774
> [note] The armonica is being repaired. They will deliver it to me within three weeks.
> Most Excellent Sir
> I am at Your Excellency's feet
> your most humble and devoted servant
> Francisco Escarano
> [to] His Most Excellent Lord, the Prince of Masserano

Document 3
Legajo 7016-6, Estado, AGS
Francisco Escarano to the Prince of Masserano, London,
18 February 1774
[Main letter, six pages]
Original in Spanish

Most Excellent Sir
The response from El Pardo was given on 8 and 10 March 1774

Sir:
Before answering the letter with which Your Excellency saw fit to honor me on the 24th of last month, I will tell you that having gone yesterday to see Doctor Franklin, he promised without fail to hand over to me next week the armonica entirely repaired, and we can count on him as a man of his word. I asked him to explain to me how to play this instrument, to which he responded that in his translated and printed works in French there can be found a letter of his to the celebrated Father Beccaria of Milan[28] in which everything that I wanted is explained, but, that nevertheless, if after looking over the letter I should find the instructions still are not very clear to me, he would put together and furnish me with an extremely clear set of instructions. Your Excellency can see that Doctor Franklin could not have acted more graciously, and we should be grateful to him.

Don Miguel de Ventades has told me that within a month a ship will leave for Bilbao and another could possibly sail to San Sebastián before that.[29] I can take advantage of the first of the two to send the instrument. I assure Your Excellency that I am upset that it has not been possible for me to be of service to His Lord, the Infante Don Gabriel, as promptly as I should like. I see to my misfortune that perhaps two months will pass before His Highness has the armonica there, but this considerable delay was not because of me.

If the China dishware and the silk damask fabrics that Your Excellency is thinking of sending through Bilbao will arrive before Your Excellency, I will go speak with My Lord North and will do what lies within my power so that they let everything come in without payment of duties. I have no doubt whatsoever that after so many fine words they

will get something done. It was necessary that these gentlemen would
not be so shameless as to go back on what was promised. I do not say
that they have specified to me how far their considerations will extend,
but they have repeated to me many times that they will keep all that are
possible in view of the esteem that they have, and have had, for Your
Excellency.

In keeping with your forewarning, the two carriages will continue to
be paid for, so that Your Excellency need not have to think about this
debt upon your arrival. [Josef] Constant has already received his
Governor's salary from [Miguel de] Ventades. He puts himself at Your
Excellency's feet and entrusts me to express to you his expression of
humble recognition.

The King has already paid the rent for the house. It cannot be
occupied until the end of July, so Your Excellency will have time to
look for another house in which you can live, if My Lord Harcourt has
not offered his [first], whose agent still has not received any reply to the
proposals that I made.

When your four Guias de Forasteros[30] that Your Excellency
intended to deliver to the Count of Priego[31] reach me, I will furnish two
to My Lord Bristol,[32] so that he gives one to his Sovereign and keeps the
other for himself. I will give the third to My Lord Rochford,[33] and I will
hold on to the fourth for myself, giving Your Excellency my respectful
thanks.

On Sunday, I expressed to His British Majesty the pleasure that
Your Excellency had in returning to this court and moreover informed
him that having obeyed him in asking Your Excellency if the Lord
Marquis would be exempt before Your Excellency should leave, he
answered that the King proposed not to advance anyone who had not
earned some personal merit in His service. His British Majesty saw fit to
tell me that this was very fair, but that perhaps there could some special
grace [extended]. The Count of Sernafis[34] asked me to tell you that he
will be infinitely sorry not to be here for your arrival but that having
already delayed his departure [by] four months more than what he
anticipated, he does not yet know if he will be able to extend his stay
for a while longer. We do not know if the matter that has given rise to
the threats [made by] gentleman Linch has been cleared up.

The Count of Pignatelli, he of Haslang, Garnier, and all those in
the diplomatic corps are constantly telling me their desire to see Your
Excellency again, and I pass along to all of them the normal sentiments.

Don Bernardino Delgado has written me asking that I request of Your Excellency that you recommend him highly to the Marquis of Grimaldi,[35] who can arrange something good for him, and I am doing that to please him, while at the same time asking a thousand pardons of Your Excellency for the liberty that I take, trusting that your goodness will overlook this on my part.

A brochure has come out titled "The Partition of Poland." It is the most terrible satire that could be written against the King of Prussia,[36] the Empress Queen, and the Czarina. Its author, it is believed, is Mr. Lind, a Scotsman, whom Your Excellency observed here as a tutor to the little prince, Poniatowski.[37] Owing to an opportunity that will present itself the day after tomorrow, I will send it along to Don Bernardo del Campo, and if it were also in French, I will send it to Your Excellency. Everyone admires it for the grace and spirit with which it is written. Lind likewise is the author of four letters about Poland that have created quite a stir. In said brochure there is a dialogue between the King of Russia and a Jew named Ephraim, his counselor, and Minister of State in which the king speaks these words:

"I have already told you, Ephraim, that I wish it thusly. I have given the order, so that they send me four hundred thousand ducats from Holland: You will have them melted down and minted again but with a certain alloy so that we can gain 25 salaries out of each one. Write to the Count of Maltzan[38] and tell him (if by chance his schemes in the funds are not keeping him too busy) to obtain some guineas for us, from which we will make the same use.

When he knows what we want to do, he will redouble his zeal in carrying out this assignment. I recently had proof of the talents of this Count, when packing all of his furniture, and played the role of a Minister who is summoned to his Court, so that his conduct should have an influence on the funds, and to be able to fish in the murky waters of the currency exchanges."

In another passage there are the following words.

The King of Prussia is speaking with the Empress:

"The prescription's long-held possession proves nothing against an ancient claim, provided that we can uphold it; nor can any ancient right be erased by any treaty, provided that we can violate that treaty with impunity."

The Empress Queen:

"Is this not carrying things too far? According to that way of reasoning I can again reclaim Siberia whenever I want, despite treaties that still exist between us."

The King of "Prussia:"

"No, madam. Not whenever Your Majesty wishes, but whenever Your Majesty can, I confess; but I will take care to stop Your Majesty from the temptation of making use of my maximums,[39] etc. etc.

It is the Czarina to whom it makes an easy target and with reason."

Moving on to another matter, I will tell Your Excellency that the Count of Guines[40] has sent here a person in whom he confides to take various declarations that he believes can work in his favor, and having come to the aid of Garnier, has answered him that he need not be involved in this matter. I am shocked that he acts with such ingratitude toward his boss, but I have known for a while that he does not think well. I plead with Your Excellency to keep these matters to yourself.

The doorman had a problem the past month when he badly hurt his hand when a glass window fell on top of him. Since then he has been in the hands of a surgeon, who has requested four guineas from him for the treatment. The doorman has approached me to make the payment, and I have declined to do so. He will write to Your Excellency, and I have told him to do as he wishes. If Your Excellency finds it convenient to extend the charity of giving him half, this amounts to two guineas, or whatever you wish, it would serve to tell me your answer, or the matter can be left for when you are here.

There is nothing new that merits writing about to Your Excellency, and there is more here to see compared to the little that I relate regarding matters of an official nature. For this reason, I will cease to bother you, but devotedly plead for your continued protection and orders. May God keep Your Excellency many years as I desire and it must be.

London, 18 February 1774

The attached [letter] is from the beautiful My Lady for her friend My Lady, the Duchess of Villahermosa, at whose feet I ask Your Excellency place me.

Most Excellent Sir

I am at Your Excellency's feet, Your
Humble and devoted servant
Francisco Escarano
[to] My Lord, the Prince of Masserano

Document 4
Legajo 7016-9, Estado, AGS
Francisco Escarano to the Prince of Masserano, London, 11 March 1774
[Main letter, four pages]
Original in Spanish

Most Excellent Sir
The response in Madrid was given on 14 April 1774

Sir:
    Yesterday Doctor Franklin sent me the armonica accompanied by his works translated into French, asking me to remit them to His Lord, the Infante Don Gabriel, and humbly ask His Highness to have the honor of receiving them, as you can see on page 209 of the second work the method of playing this instrument. With a ship that will depart in a few days from Bilbao I will remit the armonica to Don Luis de Ventades, entrusting it to his utmost care, along with the two books that I will put in oilcloth so they do not get wet or mishandled.

    I have thanked Dr. Franklin, telling him not to entertain any doubts that His Highness would read his works with great pleasure, and I have paid for the cost of the instrument and its repairs, whose expense, with that of its sailing, and other costs, will amount to some twenty sterling pounds with little difference. I will send Your Excellency the bill in the coming week as well as the knowledge of the ship's captain who is anxious to be in Spain. Your Excellency believes that the delay for not having fulfilled this commission was not my fault.

    As Your Excellency will be able to see in the letter that I write to the Boss:[41] The Parliament is beginning to deal with the difficult issue of the American colonies. Charles Fox's post has been given to My Lord Beauchamp,[42] the son of My Lord Herdfort. The gentleman Meredith has been made the King's comptroller in place of My Lord Pelham, who has been named first Judge of the Royal Forests, which they call a sinecure here,[43] and we call a simple donation, that the Duke of Leeds,[44] who has been given a pension, will naturally pass after his death to his son the Marquis de Carmarthen.[45]

    My Lord Rochford told me yesterday that if Your Excellency takes My Lord Harcourt's house he would pay you many visits. The best part is that this nobility desires that Your Excellency reside there, but Your Excellency knows what is best.

We have had bad weather this week, and it is not strange that the mail has not arrived today.

I am improved from my fluxing[46] of my eyes, but even if not freely understood. I imagine that this letter, and the one that I will have the honor of writing to you in the next posting, will find Your Excellency still in Madrid; and I will subsequently await your orders in whatever method that you direct them.

I know that Your Excellency has danced in the boss's house, which gave me such satisfaction, because it is proof of your good health, in which I am concerned in all my life.

I ask Your Excellency to honor me with your orders and that you be ever assured of my gratitude. That God give Your Excellency many years as I desire.

> London, 11 March 1774
> Most Excellent Sir
> At Your Excellency's feet
> Your humble and devoted servant
> Francisco Escarano
> [To] His Excellent Lord, the Prince of Masserano

▇ Document 5
Legajo 7016-10, Estado, AGS
Francisco Escarano to the Prince of Masserano, London,
18 March 1774
[Main letter, six pages]
Original in Spanish

Answered from Madrid on 14 April 1774

Sir:

The ship *Santo Domingo*, and the *Good Fortune* of Captain Cotarro, is the one bringing the harmonica, whose cost comes to twenty pounds sterling, as Your Excellency will see on the attached [statement of] account. Don Luis de Ventades will pay the freight up to Bilbao, and will take care of sending it to Madrid, with the greatest care, as I advised him. I have told him to wait for Your Excellency's orders or those of his Lordship the Marquis of Grimaldi, and that he [Ventades] should try to do as much as he can to make sure this instrument reaches the court as soon as possible.

Three days ago, My Lord Rochford sent me a package that he had received for me from Paris, and in which I found a letter from Your Excellency with four travelers' guides.[47] I immediately took two to My Lord Bristol so he could place in the hands of His British Majesty the one that came in a case and keep the other for himself, which he did. He has asked me to extend a thousand thanks to Your Excellency for your remembrance and on Sunday the day after tomorrow this sovereign will perhaps speak to me about what he owes to Your Excellency.[48] My Lord Rochford has likewise appreciated the gift from Your Excellency as proof of your friendship, and I repeat to you my humble gratitude [or, and I again voice to you my humble gratitude] for that [traveler's guide] you gave to me.

I have received the letter of 24 February with which Your Excellency deigned to honor me, in which I note with consummate sorrow the grave illness of his Lordship the Marquis of Mora. I cannot weigh up for Your Excellency the grief caused to me in considering that [grief] of his poor father. I hope that God must console with the health of a son, whomever he has so many reasons to love in the extreme. I beg [that] Your Excellency place me at the complaisance of one and another and at the feet of My Lady, the Duchess of Villahermosa, whom I contemplate [as] terribly afflicted. Your Excellency knows how many duties I owe to all in this respectable family, and as such you will understand the interest that I have in all things pertaining to them.

Constant has already collected here his salary as governor, about which Your Excellency need not inconvenience you in taking any action. Don Miguel de Ventades has already received 130 bottles of Celse water,[49] and has notice of the wine from the Marquis of Vanmark, everything that keeps coming in will be collected and cared for until Your Excellency arrives.

The carriages are ready. I spoke yesterday with Wright, and according to what he has explained to me he has not, nor will he have the least concern over the interest on the money that hasn't been paid to him, nor for the rental of the carriage depot. Two hundred pounds sterling, on the account, will be delivered to him the day after tomorrow. A hundred are from the January and February savings, and the rest are those that I had to collect the last day of March. With what he has gone on saving from the 50 pounds that I give him every month Constant has enough for the April expenses: When Your Excellency comes you will see the accounts from January 1st of this year, and if you like I will send them to Paris for you: I have tried [to make sure] that everything proceeds with the greatest exactitude, and on that score, I have done no more than what is my obligation.

As concerns of dwellings, I cannot think of what to say: I've sent Your Excellency the lists of furniture that are needed for Harcourt's and for General Clarc's;[50] I have set out for you the condition of the two; thus, with that, nothing remains for me but to await Your Excellency's decision. I heartily desire that Your Excellency not make any until seeing with your own eyes what suits you most.

Referring to any income I have also written to Your Excellency about what happened to me recently with My Lord North: From that I deduce that he will facilitate something for us, if not everything that we wish. Before I forget I will tell Your Excellency that His British Majesty saw fit last week to tell me that he hoped that the King, upon saying his goodbyes would give you the patent of exemption for his Lord Marquis. *Believe me, this will be the gift of the departure,*[51] were his formal words. It would delight me that His Majesty might have guessed it.

I have not talked again to Your Excellency about the new Russian Major General because nothing has occurred to me to add to what I have presented. He still finds himself here, and whenever he goes to the Palace this sovereign receives him very affably: he's eager to join the Army of the Danube if peace is not made this winter. Regarding the Count of Guines nothing for sure is known, but everyone believes that he will not return to this Embassy. His legal action has still not begun and it will be a lengthy process. I feel in my soul that he has as enemies, or at least as indifferent, those persons to whom he has done good, and to whom he has given such special treatment. Your Excellency understands me without having to explain myself further.

If the Count of Fernán Núñez comes I will pay my respects to him as is called for. He is a young man of very considerable merit. Magallón has also suggested that I hold out hopes of his coming to England, but I still don't believe it.

The Marquis of Cordón has arrived. He seems an excellent man and will be liked in this country because of his natural and straightforward ways. He presented himself to the Court with a wig in the style of Foresta,[52] [or, styled after that of Foresta] but better groomed, and with its bows of simple batiste. The Count of Searnafis[53] is getting ready to leave at the end of this month.

Resolutions have already started being taken in Parliament with respect to the American colonies. The House of Commons has consented to My Lord North's proposal, that the Customs House in Boston be sacked, moved to another site, its port be blockaded, and all import and export trade be stopped until they accept what is their duty, and begin by compensating the East India Company for all the harm that they have caused it.

There is nothing else new that merits Your Excellency's attention. I fear that this letter is not going to find you now in Madrid, but Your Excellency will of course have given instructions that they send it on to Bayona. I wish Your Excellency a most pleasant trip and assure you that my deepest desire is to again place myself at your feet. Until I achieve this satisfaction I beg that Your Excellency extend me that of rendering you obedience and attention. May God keep Your Excellency many years as is necessary. London 18 March 1774.

I'm told that the beautiful My Lady has come to London, but I have still not seen her.

[left marginal note]

> Most Excellent Sir
> At the feet of Your Excellency your most humble and trustworthy servant.
> Francisco Escarano
> [Statement of account attached]

Pounds Sterling Shillings

For the cost of the harmonica 17 17

For the container and packaging 01 05

Costs of transporting to the ship, and for customs .... <u>00 18</u>

.... 20 00

Total cost: 20 pounds sterling.

[Note of receipt of payment signed by Masserano]

The instrument called the harmonica was for his Lord the Infante Don Gabriel, from whom I have received this sum, in Madrid 11 April 1774. Masserano

[Additional note at the end of the letter]

Sir:
    I don't know if you would agree that his Lord, the Infante Don Gabriel should repay the gift of the books from Doctor Franklin with his own. May Your Excellency pardon this suggestion.

Document 6
Legajo 501, Infante Don Gabriel, AGP
The Prince of Masserano to the Duke of Bexar,[54] Madrid, 6 April 1774
[Preliminary note, one page]
Original in Spanish

                Serene Infante Don Gabriel

Letter from the Prince of Masserano and a bill for the cost, packing, and customs taxes for the instrument called an armonica, submitted for Your Highness by the secretary of the Embassy in London.

    A draft has been issued for its value to Hermenegildo Vasques to be delivered to him on the 7th of this month by special mail.

[Main letter, two pages]
Original in Spanish

Most Excellent Sir:

    My dear Lord and Friend. I have just received notice from the Secretary of the embassy in London, Don Francisco Escarano that he has dispatched the armonica for Infante Don Gabriel, for which His Highness [the infante] instructed me to arrange. After sending to me the enclosed invoice with costs, I forward it to you so that, as you prefer, [it might be] sent either directly to him or to me to deliver to him, and proceed to order the payment for the cost of 20 pounds sterling as indicated. With this motive, I renew my friendship and affection, wishing ever to be of service to you, and may God keep you for many years.

    Madrid, 6 April 1774
    Most Excellency Sir
    I kiss your hands
    Your friend and trustworthy servant
    [Signed] The Prince of Masserano
    [To] His Excellency, The Duke of Béjar

[Attachment, one page]

Original in Spanish

Glass instrument called an armonica

	Sterling Pounds	Shillings
For the cost of the armonica	17	17
For the crate and packing	1	5
Expenses for transportation and Customs	0	18
	20	00

The total amounts to twenty pounds Sterling.

Document 7
Legajo 7016-11, Estado, AGS
Francisco Escarano to the Prince of Masserano, London 10 April 1774
[Main letter, four pages]
Original in Spanish

Most Excellent Sir

Answered from Paris on 18 May 1774

Sir:
   Although I find myself [afflicted] with constant watering eyes I shan't leave off from answering, today, holy Friday, the letter that Your Excellency undertook to begin writing to me on the 7th of the past month and concluded on the 10th. The terrible news of the death of our *Infante* has filled me with sorrow: I was thunderstruck upon reading the official notice of it through which I was informed of this misfortune. It has been a loss for the entire Nation and our sorrow can be alleviated only by the hope that our Lady the Princess puts it right by giving us other *Infantes*, as I beg of God.
   The boss[55] has written me directing me to thank My Lord Rochford for the good news of the vacating of the Gran Malvina and on complying with this order it seemed advisable to me to deliver to said Minister [a] translation of his Lordship the Marquis's letter, in which due praises are made of this Secretary of State who *has been very pleased by the way the Marquis talks about him.*[56]
   I am reporting today what the stated Lord has told me, that he has gone off to spend Easter in the countryside, like Mister Sufolk [sic][57] as well.
   The ship that is carrying the [glass] harmonica has still not departed. Your Excellency already know about the vagaries of the winds:[58] it was fifteen days ago that you told me it was going to set sail. I am beside myself because I know his Lordship, the *Infante* will be anxiously hoping to see this instrument. I beg Your Excellency (if by chance my letter finds you in Madrid) to place me at the feet of His Highness, and submit humble thanks to him for the book that he has

been so kind to present to me, [and] which I will keep as the greatest treasure for my entire life. I have no doubt that Doctor Franklin will appreciate such a magnificent gift: Both he and I fully acknowledge that it is Your Excellency who has brought it about.

I imagine that in the first letter that Your Excellency writes me you will respond to the one that I had the honor to direct to you, reporting to you on the conditions set by My Lord Harcourt. Even if Your Excellency decides to take it[59] I will endeavor not to conclude anything until you find yourself in Paris, and if it can be until Your Excellency arrives in London, well that way you will be able to see what most suits you.

The proposals made to Your Excellency by the Count of Guines seem reasonable to me: For this reason, I will also continue day by day to drop in on My Lord Harcourt's agent.

I'm sorry that the Ambassador of France puts Your Excellency in the embarrassing position of giving explanations: I do not know to what purpose all this [is] when your innocence is so proven. Malicious funds have created so much regret. Your Excellency cannot loath them more than I [do]. Fortunately, in the time that I have been in charge of business no matters to deal with have arisen, and thus I've been freed of the calumnies that I could have met with. I am quite sure that any private secretary that Your Excellency brings will come persuaded that he is not permitted to deal directly, or indirectly, with any trader. I know, time and again, that they are loathsome people and that a man of honor must avoid [them].

I very much doubt that the coaches can be fully paid for when Your Excellency arrives, if you come as I wish, at the end of May. 200 pounds [sterling] have already been given, and we still need to hand over 150, give or take a little. Whatever can be saved in April, and May will be reduced to some 120. Do believe Your Excellency that the finances of this, your house, is one of the points over which I have taken most care.

If on receipt of this [letter of] of mine Your Excellency is still in Madrid you will see what has officially been written, and thus that there is no point in relating to you the very little that is taking place around here; and if you are in route this letter will reach you so belatedly that it will not be worth the trouble of reading it. Furthermore, my eyes are affecting me so badly, that I cannot go on.

I beg Your Excellency to keep me ever under your protection, and you honor me with your orders. May God keep Your Excellency many years, as I desire and is necessary. London 10 April 1774.

The Count of Haslang[60] who puts himself at the obedience of Your Excellency has charged me with imploring of you that bring him a gown from Paris, which the Count of Guines should have brought. He says that the matter of gowns will not cause Your Excellency any difficulty and I have responded to him that it will cause him a good many, even though I do not believe so.

At the feet of Your Excellency your most humble and devoted servant.
Francisco de Escarano

Document 8
Legajo 6989-33, Estado, AGS
Francisco Escarano to the Marquis of Grimaldi, London,
21 March 1775
[Main letter, three pages]
Original in Spanish

Sir:

The House of Lords should today read for the third time the Bill[61] by which the Province of New England is prohibited from fishing in [the waters] of Newfoundland, about which matter the debates took place on the 16th of this month, concerning which I reported to Your Excellency in one of my previous letters. Having later been able to have an extract of the eloquent speech given that day by Lord Camden[62] [sic] in favor of the Americans I send it on to Your Excellency translated into French.

The famous Doctor Franklin, a native of Philadelphia, has set off for his country the day before yesterday, and since he finds himself complaining mightily toward the Ministry for having removed him from a highly lucrative job that he had with that Province, there is a fear that he will stir that antipathy [of the colonists], and persuading them to continue in the spirit of resistance which they have shown up till now. Those who know in depth the English colonies in America fear that the fire that has been set there will go on growing, and that the Ministry cannot put it out when so ever it wishes to. The gentleman Blaquier, Secretary of the Viceroyalty of Ireland, who finds himself here with permission, said a few days ago to a friend of his that it was a great good fortune for England that Spain should think only of war with the Moroccans. I would not name the person if this letter were not to go in the hands of a French official, who has promised me to place it in those of my counterpart in Calais.

With the mail from Holland that arrived yesterday the news has spread that an English war frigate destined for America had paid a visit to a Dutch Merchant Ship [in the] estuary of Texel, that armaments had not been found on board, nor war munitions, but indeed only several letters and papers [meant] for Philadelphia, which the captain of the frigate had immediately remitted to this admiralty.

It is likely that the Republic registers a complaint, if the event is certain, and it is likewise so that it will not be given any satisfaction. This East India Company has lost off the coasts of Africa its ship the Middleton, which was returning interested[63] in eighty thousand pounds sterling.

The younger daughter of the Duke of Gloucester has died: they say that this Prince desired that she be laid to rest in the vault that this Royal Family has in Westminster Abbey, but His British Majesty not have consented to it so she is to be buried in Windsor Cathedral. My Lord Bristol has also died from a paralyzing accident in Bath, the same [Lord Bristol] who was Ambassador to this Court: his brother, the Head of the Harvey Squadron, succeeds him. My Lord Stormond [*sic*][64] has arrived from Paris with license my lord Ormond.[65] It is believed that he has come to marry a daughter of My Lord Harrington.

> May God keep Your Excellency many years as I desire. London 21 March 1775.
> Most Excellent Sir
> I kiss the hand of Your Excellency your most humble and trustworthy servant.
> Francisco Escarano

Document 9
Legajo 7016-53, AGS
Francisco de Escarano to the Marquis of Grimaldi, 31 March 1779
[1775] (copy), no. 469
[Main letter, one page][66]
Original in Spanish
Copy of the letter of Don Francisco de Escarano to the Excellent
Marquis of Grimaldi with the incorrect date of 31 March 1779; the
correct year is 1775.

Most Excellent Sir

Sir:
As the news has for certain had it, and as I advised Your Excellency in my letter of yesterday, no frigate has arrived from Gibraltar. The person who has come is Mr. Stott, Captain of the ship called the *Allarme*, who, leaving his ship in Toulon[67] and making great haste, has arrived in London in just a few days. It has been vouched to me, and in great secrecy, that he comes from Algeria, whose Dey (ruler)[68] has given *cart blanche* to conclude a Treaty of Peace with this court. My Lord Rochford is overjoyed, and is preparing to extract the greatest advantages from the propitious leaning, which that Regency is demonstrating. The aforementioned Stott will depart again very soon with the Treaty, and as a reward he will be named general consul in that Port with a salary of five Pounds sterling per day, in addition to that of Captain of the Frigate, whose command he maintains.

At a time like the present, the English Ministry, although it says the opposite, fears that we will take advantage of the critical circumstances and make war on them, or, at the least, to fan the flames of the American colonies. The suspicion occurs to me, perhaps ill founded, that trying to persuade the Algerians to undertake the siege of Oran to get us to distract ourselves might be a part of the secret instructions for Mr. Stott. The Count of Maltzan,[69] [acting] with very mysterious airs, has confided in me that he has received a letter from Holland telling him that it was England that has incited the Moroccan King to declare war on us. I have never put much stock in the news from this Prussian Minister and in the above-mentioned instance much less because I am persuaded that, via this means, he like those ministers of Russia and Denmark would like to see a break with this Court.

Believing it opportune that [the information in] this letter reaches the hands of Your Excellency as soon as possible, so that it go by safe conduct up to Calais,[70] I am sending a copy to His Lord, the Count of Aranda, asking him to send it to you if the use of expedited mail is offered.

May God Keep Your Excellency
To the reverse[71]

40 • The Diplomacy of Independence

Document 10
Legajo 6989-39, Estado, AGS
Francisco Escarano to the Marquis of Grimaldi, London
31 March 1775[72]
[Main letter, three pages]
Original in Spanish

Sir:

In the meeting that I had yesterday with My Lord Suffolk[73] he began by telling me that he was in admiration of the heroic Resistance of Melilla,[74] adding that, as it seemed from the great preparations that were made in Spain's Ports, that our Lord the King was resolved to put an end to this war with a vigorous blow, which they could not fail to approve. I replied that Your Excellency had not written anything to me about this matter but that it was no surprise that His Majesty should want to teach a lesson to the Moroccans' King for his audacity, who, without considering the great advantages which had accrued to him from his peace with us, had dared to break it.

To this followed [my] question to him whether the reports that had reached them from America were as good as I wished; he answered me [by] saying that they were favorable and gave them to conceive solid hopes that the colonies might yield to reason. Making a show of giving him credit, I said to him that on this basis they would perhaps suspend sending troops, and ships; to which he replied that they would not be suspended, since it was necessary to make the Americans see that there was a way of bringing them to their duty by force, and that despite knowing that the government's side had made great progress in those Provinces some time would transpire before reestablishing complete tranquility in them.

The man in charge of France's business affairs has told me that My Lord Suffolk, speaking to him about our maritime preparations, had high praise for the King's determination, characterizing it as wise and prudent. I believe that in this case this Ministry has no other position to take, since it would be rash to ask explanations of us regarding our armaments when we do not ask them about what they are preparing for

America. Besides this I imagine it does not weigh on them to see us tied down by expenses, and occupied with the Moroccans.

Almost all the Foreign Ministers have been amazed at hearing My Lord Suffolk say that they had received favorable reports from Boston, when they have constantly been extremely bad, such as I have communicated to Your Excellency in my letter number 468 which I sent yesterday by secure means to Calais. Until now we have found this Secretary of State [to be] very sincere, but he must have in these days a reason to put it about that affairs in America are going well [when], rightly, it's the other way around.

His British Majesty came into Parliament yesterday to approve the Bill[75] prohibiting the residents of New England from fishing in Newfoundland's [waters]. Once it is printed I will try to send it to Your Excellency so that you may observe the terms on which it is conceived. Those who know that country well are of the opinion that it can't have a good effect: they will end by stirring up their passions, and they will come to a shock of desperation. It is with very strong feelings that the Ministry has seen the famous Doctor Franklin take leave from here. Resentful as he was against this government for having removed him from a highly lucrative job that he had in Philadelphia, it is likely he might make considerable do much harm in that Province, where they look on him as the Father of the country. I repeat to Your Excellency that one cannot foresee [that] they can resolve the differences with the colonies without the fall of the current Ministers; and the majority of them believe it thus. If this Sovereign makes the colonists see that to please them he has changed Ministers it could be they might be brought to obedience, negotiating beforehand an agreement [for] their privileges: In all cases it seems to me the Americans will come to win.

May God keep Your Excellency many years as I desire. London 31 March 1775.

Most Excellent Sir,
I kiss the hand of Your Excellency your most humble and trustworthy servant.
Francisco Escarano

Document 11
Legajo 501, Archive of the Infante de Don Gabriel, AGP
Benjamin Franklin to His Excellency Don Gabriel de Borbón y Saxoria,[76]
Philadelphia, 12 December 1775
[Main letter, three pages]
Original in English

Illustrious Prince:

    I have just received thro' the hands of the Ambassador of Spain, the much esteemed Present your most serene Highness hath so kindly sent me, of your excellent version of Salust.[77] I am extremely sensible of this Honour done me, and beg you would accept my thankful Acknowledgements. I wish I could send from hence any American literary Production worthy [of] your Perusal; but as yet the Muses have scarcely visited these remote Regions. Perhaps, however, the late Proceedings of our American Congress, just published, may be a Subject of some Curiosity at your court. I therefore take the Liberty of sending your Highness a Copy, with some other Papers which contain Accounts of the Successes wherewith Providence has lately, favoured us. Therein your wise Politicians may contemplate the first efforts of a rising State, which seems likely soon to act a Part of some Importance on the Stage of Human Affairs, and furnish Materials for a future Salust. I am very old, and can scarcely hope to see the Event of this great Contest: but looking forward I think I see a powerful Dominion growing up here, whose interest it will be to form a close and firm Alliance with Spain, their Territories bordering; and who being united will be able, not only to preserve their own People in Peace, but to repel the Force of all the other Powers in Europe. It seems therefore prudent on both sides to cultivate a good Understanding that may hereafter be so useful to both; towards which a fair foundation is already laid in our Minds by the well-founded popular Opinion entertained here of Spanish Integrity and Honour. I hope my Presumption in hinting this will be pardoned. If in any thing on this side of the Globe I can render either Service or Pleasure to your Royal Highness, your Commands will make me happy. With the utmost Esteem and Veneration, I have the Honor to be,

    Your serene Highness's
    Most obedient
    and most humble Servant
    [signed] B. Franklin

Document 12
Legajo Estado 6990-15, AGS
The Prince of Masserano to the Marquis of Grimaldi, London, 27 June 1775, no. 25
[Main letter, five pages]
Original in Spanish

Most Excellent Lord

My good Lord:
Very bad news continues arriving from America. The letters from Boston confirm that the rebels have blocked that capital; that as the result of an assembly that was held its residents have expressed to General Gage,[78] that after the cruelties committed by his troops, they could no longer recognize him as [their] governor, nor obey him in any way; that having requested permission from him to withdraw from the city he responded to them that he would accede to that provided they left unarmed, a condition to which they did not agree; that the garrison lacked every kind of fresh provisions, that they could not last for long except with salted meat; and that they have found themselves in the greatest consternation.

I am told it has increased with an unfortunate event that occurred on the first of the month before last.[79] In one of their barracks, some soldiers were given a batch of cartridges that one of them accidently ignited, setting off a chain reaction and burning down not only the building that they were in but also several warehouses close by that belonged to different private citizens, a loss that some calculate will come to twenty thousand pounds sterling and others [estimate] twice that much.

It is known through the letters from Cambridge, in New England, dated the 18th of May, that the Rebels, without losing one man, have taken control of Ticonderoga, a fort of major importance in that Province. The event is described in this way. Two hundred forty militiamen, commanded by Colonels Allen and Easton,[80] made their way to the lake near Ticonderoga, some eighty of whom, crossing it, reached the fort at dawn. The sentry on watch fired [at them], but the militiamen subdued him immediately and, passing through on a covered road, penetrated as far as the parade ground, where they found the garrison's [soldiers] asleep in their beds. They formed up in a square shape and after a light skirmish trapped them in it. Upon approaching the officer in command of the fort, Colonel Easton called on him to surrender in the *name of America*.[81] The officer had to yield before such a force and order his men to hand over their arms. The rebels took all of them prisoner and took possession of that sizable fortress, in which they found more than one hundred cannons of different calibers, some mortars, and not an insignificant amount of gunpowder and other munitions.[82] Afterwards, two rebel detachments left to reinforce the two castles known as *Crownpoint* and *Skenesborough*.[83] They discovered in the former many cannons and, in the latter, they found some small artillery pieces. In this last one they took prisoner Sergeant Major Skene and everyone in his family.

Also, there are letters from Philadelphia that report the arrival there of the famous Doctor Franklin, who has been received in a manner little short of triumphant and that, likewise, report that he has been given a post of equal weight to the one that this [the British] government relieved him of. [The letters] add that the General Congress wanted to issue a manifesto begging for the protection of foreign powers, which, if it this were indeed the case, would indicate that those entities are in no way disposed to reconcile with the government of Great Britain.

In confirmation of the news that I gave to Your Excellency last week regarding the idea of sending some frigates to America, as the most suitable way to patrol the coasts and cut off commerce to those colonies, I can tell you that today the order was given to arm four of them, these being the *Milford*, the *Acteon*, the *Solebay*, and the *Lizard*.[84] Without question they will set off for Boston once they are ready.

An order also has been issued to arm another frigate, the *Aretusa*, which will go to the Mediterranean.

The squadron to carry out maneuvers, commanded by the Gentleman Parker, already has left Portsmouth for the Biscay Sea.

The City of London has decided to present to this Sovereign a second petition in favor of the American cause. Tomorrow the sheriffs will go to the Palace to learn on what day His British Majesty will want to receive the Lord Mayor, who is the person, accompanied by the rest of the magistrates, who has to hand the petition to him. This petition will not be looked upon any more than the first petition.

I have not seen My Lord Rochford in recent days because he is in the country, and thus do not have further news to communicate to Your Excellency, whose life may God keep, as I desire, for many years.

London, 27 June 1775
Most Excellent Sir
I kiss the hands of Your Excellency
Your best Servant
The Prince of Masserano
[to] His Excellency the Marquis de Grimaldi

Document 13
Legajo Estado 6991-26, AGS
The Prince of Masserano to the Marquis of Grimaldi, London, 19 September 1775, no. 88
[Main letter, two pages]
Original in Spanish

                    Most Excellent Sir

My good Lord:
   Following Manchester's example, the cities of Leicester and Liverpool have through Lord Dartmouth[85] presented some very sincere requests to His British Majesty, asking him to enforce respect for his Royal authority in the American colonies, and offering to contribute to this cause as many means as might be at their disposal.
   The general Congress of Philadelphia has named the celebrated Doctor Franklin as Postmaster for all of America. He had been director of the mails for Pennsylvania, and other administrative areas close by, but the Ministry relieved him of this position last year,[86] having come to understand that he upheld the Americans' cause with too much enthusiasm. This same Congress has resolved to collect a million pesos to continue funding the costs of the war, and do not doubt that they will have war.
   General Gage's wife has arrived; according to what I am told, she left from Boston on the 20th on the month before last. It is known from some who have accompanied her that the two armies remained out of action, and that the rebel army, hugely superior to that of the Royal troops, was in a defensive mode and disposed to resist, with advantage, any attack.
   No other matter comes to me to report to Your Excellency, whose life may God keep for many years, as I desire. London, 19 September 1775

   Most Excellent Sir
   I kiss the Hands of Your Excellency
   Your Best Servant
   The Prince of Masserano
   [to] His Most Excellent Lord, the Marquis of Grimaldi

2

FRANKLIN THE DIPLOMAT

■ Document 14
Legajo 4603, AGS
The Count of Aranda to the Marquis of Grimaldi, Paris, 28 June 1776, no. 753[1]
[Main letter, five pages]
Original in Spanish

Most Excellent Sir

My Dear Sir:
    In Marly,[2] on the day before I came to this capital, I received a letter, a copy [of which] I include for Your Excellency, signed by Barbeu DuBourg,[3] and I responded verbally to its bearer, his servant, that if his master wished to speak with me, he would find me in Paris, where I have been resting for four days. Accordingly, he came to see me yesterday and explained that he was authorized by the English Colonies of America and was an informant of Doctor Franklin, one of the principal members of the general Congress of Philadelphia, [and] that having taken different steps with this Ministry to obtain certain forms of assistance, and having secured means for the purchase and shipment of different items, came to implore the same means from Spain, directing himself to me, given that we both find ourselves at this court.

I replied that I could not enter into his dealings, because my authority pertained to no more than Spain's private affairs with France and did not extend to inserting myself into other, foreign matters, above all, going against a Power with whom the King, my Sovereign, was on known peaceful terms, the consideration of which, it seemed to me, would persuade him of the correctness of my reason for refraining from dealing with him [and] entertaining his proposals.

This notwithstanding, as a private interchange, and out of personal curiosity to know about the current state of the Colonies, their forces, their mood, and the ideas that they may have formed for sustaining their separation, I entered into a conversation with him, and he told me that, in general, all of the thirteen colonies thought in agreement about throwing off the yoke of the English and only some had deviated in resisting the idea of making a formal declaration of their intended independence, all of them resisting as one body to gain it, but deferring publication of this declaration until things were more secure; but they had in the end proclaimed open trade with all the world's nations, with the exception of the subjects of the British crown.

[Moreover], that the maritime forces that the Colonies were readying were remarkable in their size because the colonists are so given to navigation, and this had been their strength, by means of trade, to experience the growth that they had, and although the English have impressed many men, still they [the colonies] had surmounted their losses, those being greater in number and of greater consequence [for the English] than the losses that the insurgents had sustained.

That he [DuBourg] had managed from this Court to have 15,000 muskets taken from its stores, by way of purchasing them from their contracted supplier, who would replace them, with six thousand of them now found on board in Nantes, to set sail at the first wind.

That, in due course, their attempt to secure arms was directed at getting 300 cannons of different caliber, and made of bronze, that choosing them from 1,200 pieces now held in different places did not pose an obstacle for him, but that the discomfiting thing consisted in the fact that all of them [the colonies] are in possession of French arms, which, although they can smooth it over, would produce public notoriety here that would be difficult to hide. So that it occurred to him that if Spain claimed to have purchased them, thereby effacing the connection of the arms to France, they could later be transported while hiding their point of origin, whether in the use of said artillery after reaching, happily enough, its destination, or in case the English intercepts it in the preparatory stage. He wondered if this Ministry might have already spoken to me about the matter, and so also spurred my interest, on behalf of those he represented, to deign to support this measure that would facilitate getting them the arms that they needed.

I told him that the Ministry of this Court [the French] had not been in contact with me in any way regarding that which he recounted to me, and that all I knew was to repeat to him that my authority did not extend beyond the affairs of my Embassy.

He again asked me, if this Ministry were queried, if I would agree to the proposal. I told him again that on no subject could I assume for myself powers that I did not have, that if it were presented to this Ministry I would see on what terms it did so, and on which of them I should need to respond.

With this our conversation concluded, and we left unsettled the matter of whether he would come to see me on occasion.

I report this to Your Excellency in order that you can inform His Majesty and I pray that God may keep your Excellency for many years.

Paris 28 June 1776
Most Excellent Sir
I kiss the hand of Your Excellency
Your trustworthy servant
The Count of Aranda
[to] His Most Excellent Lord, the Marquis of Grimaldi

Document 15
Legajo 4605, Estado, AGS
The Count of Aranda to the Marquis of Grimaldi, Paris,
14 December 1776,
no. 83
[Partial document, five pages]
Original in Spanish

He [DuBourg] changed subjects to give me the news that he had just received word from Nantes that the famous Dr. Franklin, a member of the American Congress, had arrived in that port in a well-armed frigate that seized two English vessels while in transit. He planned then to move on to Paris, bringing with him three children[4] in order to see to their education.

He related that the Americans found themselves in a better state than the one in which they have been pictured here and had now resolved to assemble for the next campaign more than eighty regiments of eight hundred men in each one. [Moreover], that at the time of his departure a corps of troops from Carolina had marched off to occupy the Floridas. [And] that there was no need to think of compromising.

[Furthermore], that while up to this point there had not been any great desertion of English troops, the latter had now begun, and the Hessians[5] were glad to be among the insurgents. They had unleashed a sudden attack on Staten Island, and had inflicted considerable damage on the English who still remained there.

I told His Excellency, the Count de Vergennes,[6] that Franklin's name will alarm the English and that it was natural that he should come here fully empowered by the now independent Congress to make some overture. He [Vergennes] responded to me that it was necessary to wait for his arrival.

I also asked him if the ships loaded with aid for the Americans had left? He answered that he believed that they already had set sail but was not positive about this. I said to His Excellency, fine, but if the English should intercept them because they heard about their destination, what would this Court do? He told me that they would claim that the ships were going to Santo Domingo. I replied, but if the public notoriety undercut this claim, wouldn't the English have a pretext to hold on to them? His rejoinder was that he hoped that this would not happen.

I also saw His Lord, the Count of Maurepas,[7] and enlightened him on matters relating to Your Excellency's work bearing on the profitable compensation for the defeats and rescue operation of Mahón and Gibraltar. He did not appear happy about entering into a discussion, for, at the same time, he changed the subject with a question about whether I had heard that England is negotiating with Russia on behalf of troops for Portugal. I responded that I had not, but that yes, the Hanoverians were disposed toward that. Did it not appear to me, he said, that both seemed to be happening? I responded that, as concerned the Russians, I doubted it because the Czarina[8] [Catherine II] would look twice on clashing the Bourbon Powers, and that Russia did not concern me a great deal, because although their troops were much superior to the Hanoverians, they [England] could not count on them until the Baltic ice thaws, which would take time. [I added] that navigation in those waters was slow, in which case there would be the option of our intercepting them with naval forces. With respect to the Hanoverians, it was public knowledge that they had enhanced the composition of their troops both by enlarging the older forces and by introducing new ones numbering up to thirty thousand men, including those garrisoned in Gibraltar and Mahón. They had an easy passage to England, and from there to Portugal also was a short voyage, and under English flag, such that the Russians could never embark, because the English have just enough for their American undertaking.

> God keep Your Excellency many years,
> Paris, 14 December 1776
> Most Excellent Sir,
> I kiss the hand of Your Excellency
> Your trustworthy servant
> The Count of Aranda
> [to] His Excellent Lord, the Marquis of Grimaldi

Document 16
Legajo 6995-77, Estado, AGS
The Prince of Masserano to the Marquis of Grimaldi, London, 17 December 1776
[Main letter, three pages]
Original in Spanish
[Note attached, one page]
Original in French

Most Excellent Sir

My Dear Lord:
With the intention of causing trouble the opposition party has put it about these days that the famous Doctor Franklin, taking leave of the Congress in Philadelphia, has gone to Paris, upon learning that at last the royal troops will triumph over the Americans, who lack the forces to oppose them. Since the replies [made] by the representatives of said Congress to General Howe indicate no intention of accepting the peace that he proposed to them I strongly doubt the news of the journey to France of the person in question.

It is known that the Emperor must have set out on his trip to Paris the 8th of this month via Austria, and Munick [sic]; that he will be in that capital at the beginning of February; that he will take the title of Count of Lickestein;[9] as he does not want parties, nor visits; and that only his head of the palace and a favorite General of his will accompany him. He [the Count] has written to his Minister the Count of Belgioioso, telling him that it is a long time since he has seen him, and that he can find himself in Paris at the beginning of February, in order to spend two or three weeks together, being eager to return by way of Vienna without passing through Flanders before the month of March is out.

To this news [the following] are added: that he has ordered that thirty thousand recruits be ready in his states at the beginning of April; and that the King of Prussia has given a similar order so that around that time his troops will find themselves ready to be on the march. Since this latter sovereign is not so accustomed to have his troops in a position to put themselves on the move, being accustomed, [rather], to get on the march [only] at the call to arms I don't give much credit to these rumors, which if they were true the King would have known about them directly through normal channels. To give credit to [the rumors] here [people] lean on [the fact] of the great buildup of armaments that England is preparing, and which understandably causes everyone to be suspicious, despite the protests that the Princes of Europe make of unanimously desiring peace. War nonetheless being able to break out when we least expect it, it behooves [us] to be alert for any occurrence; and for that matter there is also the just motive of the King's recovering what against all good faith the Portuguese have usurped at a time when the Court of Lisbon was assuring him of its wishes to preserve the greatest harmony.

Taking advantage of Parliament's holidays and of the mildness of the season, these ministers have gone off to spend some days at their country houses.

I had written up here when I had been told, as an assured thing, that urgent mail dispatched by My Lord Stormond [sic][10] arrived the day before yesterday with the notice that Doctor Franklin, and another member of the Congress of Philadelphia, had disembarked in Nantes and that they were being awaited in Paris.

The Ambassador from France dispatched a letter to his court tonight, and I am taking advantage of it to send this letter to my counterpart in Calais, in which I have nothing more to tell Your Excellency but that the causes that I have given you, to believe that there is some Discord among those who comprise this Ministry, are intensifying, for which reason I will not be surprised if there is some change.

>May God keep Your Excellency many years as I desire.
>London 17 December 1776.
>Most Excellent Sir
>I kiss the hands of Your Excellency
>Your greatest servant
>The Prince of Masserano

[Note attached in French]
London 17 December 1776

The 12th of this month, the Commons[11] did not occupy itself with matters of any importance, and on the 14th the two chambers met only to attend religious services on the occasion of a fast observed for the reestablishment of proper order in America. After this, the *Pares*[12] arranged to meet on the 23rd of next month, and the Commons on the 21st of said month.

🕸 Document 17
Legajo 6995-80, Estado, AGS
The Prince of Masserano to the Marquis of Grimaldi, London, 20 December 1776
[Main letter, three pages]
Original in Spanish

Most Excellent Sir

My Dear Lord:
I extend the greatest thanks to Your Excellency for the important notice that you saw fit to pass on to me in letter of the 2nd of this month, of the King, our Princes, our Lady the *Infanta*, and the remaining persons of their royal family having relocated in robust health from the site of San Lorenzo el Real to their Madrid Palace.

I have not learned anything regarding Canada after informing Your Excellency of the news publicized here by General Burgoyne on his arrival from Quebec, with whom I have spoken, has confirmed for me that he appears with no more license that that of General Carleton, and that he [General Carleton] does not sit well with him, accusing him of slowness in the expedition to Lake Champlain, which is what the entire campaign has been reduced to. He has told me that the Rebels are maintaining themselves well entrenched in Ticonderago [sic],[13] that to attack that [fortified] town is impossible, there being no more road for the Artillery than an impenetrable forest, and that it can only draw close to [the fortified town] by water doing a disembarkation of troops, but that from the beginning of November such an operation is impeded by ice. There are those who say that this General has come [here] with the aim of proposing a new plan for the next campaign, but I doubt of its acceptance, since it has not been well received by this Monarch.

There is a great deal of talk here and has caused a decrease in the funds[14] the arrival in France of the famous Doctor Francklin [sic]: many objectives are attributed to this prime mover of the Congress of Philadelphia. The first is to deal with the Americans' advantages with France; the second that of wanting to deal with England from a personally secure site; and the third that of distancing himself from the congress because great major disagreements having [arisen] among the grandees who compose it. He has invoked the pretext of bringing his sons to France to educate them: Time will make the truth clear.

The Nobleman Horta who is going as Minister to Holland has arrived from Lisbon. He is a young man twenty-two years of age who has finished his studies: he took off from that Court with the *paquebote*[15] the first of this month: He says that the King his master was somewhat better, and that he pronounced some words with difficulty: Adding that when he wasn't understood he wrote [down] what he wanted with a pencil, and that in this way he ordered that his Ministry should be obeyed in full. I imagine that the Marquis of Pombal will have guided his hand in that.

These ministers display hope that if that Monarch is gone our disputes with that court will be resolved.

According to what is said Mister Suffolk has gone off to his country house to convalesce from his latest attack of gout, and for that reason did not hold a meeting yesterday with the Foreign Ministers.

I end telling Your Excellency that I understood the terms of your letter of 30 of November about whose content I do not need to respond.

May God keep Your Excellency for many years as I desire. London 20 December 1776.

P. S. My Lord Dunmore,[16] Governor of Virginia, has arrived.

> Most Excellent Sir
> I kiss the hands of Your Excellency
> Your Best Servant
> The Prince of Masserano

✳ Document 18
Legajo 4609-5, Estado, AGS
The Count of Aranda to the Marquis of Grimaldi, Paris, 4 January 1777
[Summary note, one page; main letter, three pages]
Original in Spanish

[Summary note]
Paris, 4 January 1777
The Count of Aranda
(By French special mail)

    He offers a letter of his within a few days and meanwhile remits two memorials which that Ministry has delivered to him, one concerning the project for a treaty with the English colonies presented by them and another reflecting on a current situation with England and the measures that it suits both Spain as well as France to take very soon.

[Main letter]

Most Excellent Sir

My Lord:
    I am taking advantage of the opportunity of this Court dispatching the mail to its Ambassador the Marquis of Ossun; furnishing you the two documents, of which the attached are copies that His Lordship the Count of Devergennes has passed on to me.
    One is the proposal that Doctor Franklin has delivered for a Treaty of friendship and trade of the colonies with France. The other is a memorial composed by His Lordship the Count of Devergennes, and approved by the most Christian King, to be transmitted to your uncle the Catholic King about the probability at present of a possible rupture with England.
    With the Lintillac mail and dated the 14th of December I advised Your Excellency of Doctor Franklin's arrival in these Kingdoms: and I am told that as of the 21st of the same month that he had not arrived in Paris. [On] the 28th he had his audience with His Lordship the Count of Devergennes during the morning, because according to what the said Count told me he had believed that since no one would doubt that

Franklin would have been heard by this Ministry, he had found it least problematic not to manufacture any mystery, and in the audience handed His Lordship the document, or idea of the Treaty of friendship, and trade, as though it were his only commission.

At night on the 22nd Mister Franklin came to see me with his companions Dean [sic], and Lee, telling me that they had been in Versailles, that His Lordship the Count of Devergennes had assured them of the close union that reigned between the Courts of Madrid and Paris; that they could explain themselves before the Ambassador from Spain; that, consequently, he began by extending thanks for the good treatment that the colonies colors had been received in the dominions of the Catholic King: that he would pass another proposal on to me, with respect to Spain, in alignment with that presented to France, to be directed to my Court; but up to this day he has not reappeared.

Since the Villa mail has to leave within a few days with the commissions that Your Excellency has carried out for me, I will leave it there and will not add anything more to my dispatch since I did not have much time to prepare more communications; and while Villa [mail] is on its way Your Excellency will be able to find out more news from the documents that I send along and from what the Ambassador might express to Your Excellency.

> May God keep Your Excellency many years. Paris 4 January 1777
> Most Excellent Sir
> I kiss the hand of Your Excellency
> Your trustworthy servant
> The Count of Aranda

Document 19
Legajo 3884, Estado AHN
The Count of Aranda to the Marquis of Grimaldi, Paris, 13 January 1777,[17] no. 938 and no. 4[18]
[Summary note, one page]
Original in Spanish

The Count of Aranda
[By] Special Mail
    His conversation with those Ministers relevant to the matters of the English Colonies and Commissioners residing in Paris and [in reference to] the ideas that they had about an inevitable conflict soon to happen.

[Main letter, thirty-three pages]
Original in Spanish

Most Excellent Sir

My very good Lord:
    With the express mail of the 14th of last (month), and in letter no. 911, I told your Excellency about the arrival of Doctor Franklin in this Kingdom, about whom His Lord, the Count of Vergennes,[19] and I had spoken. Word then had it that he would set off immediately to Paris, and also, it was said, that through some disposition of this Ministry he would linger without making an appearance at the Court, reservedly explaining himself beforehand in writing, or through some intermediary, about the idea of his trip.
    On Tuesday, the 17th I asked the Count of Vergennes how we stood with respect to Franklin's arrival, and he answered in what seemed to me ambiguous terms.
    The *Amphitrite*, which is the principal vessel carrying officers and goods to the Americans, sailed from [the port of] Le Havre on the night of the 16th; there arrived at the same port correspondence dispatched from this Ministry to the Naval Commissary, Mr. Mistras, ordering that, if this shipment of supplies had not left, it should be detained, and if it had left, he should send another ship carrying orders for it to return to

port. The Commissary immediately assembled the most reputable pilots, and they unanimously told him that it would be fruitless, since after three days the *Amphitrite* would have already reached the open sea, neither would it be possible to overtake it during the course of its voyage, since a considerable number of days would go by before a ship could be prepared and provisioned for that purpose. I learned of this for certain on the 19th, and it seemed appropriate to me to get to the bottom of this development.

I went to Versailles on Friday the 20th and addressed the matter with His Lord, the Count of Vergennes, who admitted it to me, with certain excuses about the action taken, but not realized, that left me in no doubt either regarding the timidity that reigned, or that he was not being altogether plain and clear in relating to me how matters stood with the Insurgents.

I again asked His Excellency about Franklin and following his reply that he did not know when he [Franklin] was to arrive, I said to him that I wondered whether he had been cautioned not to present himself in Paris and only to secretly reveal the purpose of his coming, so as to better conceal from the public the purpose of his mission. But, in an embarrassed tone, he repeated to me again that he was waiting for him. I expressed to him my personal opinion that since Franklin's arrival, as of the 6th, in Quiberon, near Nantes, was well known, it seemed to me that too many days had gone by for such an important thing still to remain in the dark.[20] To which he replied that I was correct and that he was assured that Franklin would not be delayed in reaching Paris.

On the 21st I reviewed your Excellency's letters of the 9th sent by regular post, among them the one that dealt with the Queen of Portugal's Regency with the reply of the King our Lord, and the other one, in your Excellency's hand, concerning the idea of Spain directly aiding the Americans, which would be communicated to me. On the 22nd I went to Versailles for the purpose of sharing the first letter and of making use of the second, depending on the lay of the land, because I had concluded that I was being spoken to in a guarded way about Franklin, and that it suited Spain even more than France not to lose sight of the Insurgents' endeavors. I went there very early because, it being Sunday, there would be countless other people who could interrupt. I began with Your Excellency's letter concerning the Regency of Her Most Faithful Majesty, the Queen of Portugal.[21]

After covering this ground at great length, I came to the matter of Franklin, whom His Lord, the Count of Vergennes, told me that he had not yet met. I repeated to him that time was being lost in determining if his coming [to these shores] was for nothing else than avoiding those disturbances or represented an actual commission. He answered that he already knew the answer, but without being able to hide his discomfiture. Then I decided to tell him that I could only discharge [my duties] as Ambassador by requesting of His Excellency that one or the other had to be clarified, and that Spain had the right to learn definitely whatever was true was concerning Franklin's arrival, since at this request, the French Court had taken up the idea of aiding the Insurgents, [and] Spain had contributed a million Tours pounds (*livres tournois*),[22] and France had even again proposed that the Insurgents be aided in the response given me in writing at Fountainbleau at the beginning of November. That my Court, clearly as the result of these encouragements by France, and by working in concert with her, was thinking as to how to aid the Colonies by different means, [and] that the letters that I had received the day before said the same to me. And, finally, both by the actions already taken and for those intended, the Catholic King[23] wasn't to be kept in ignorance about anything that came to France's notice, nor should news conducive to the fulfillment of his resolutions be delayed [in reaching him].

Pressured as such, His Lord, the Count of Vergennes, told me that Franklin had arrived in Paris on the day before Saturday; that on Friday afternoon he had entered Versailles, where Mr. Deane,[24] an old representative of the Colonies, was waiting for him; and that he had not wanted to see them, but only to arrange their transfer to Paris. Then he would be able to recall the pretense with which he could learn from them what they wanted and would communicate to me the results without delay. At this point, I cut short the conversation, taking great care in the confidences of friendship on the part of both Courts, and so forth.

Having returned to Paris I received news on Monday the 23rd that gave me reason to conclude that Franklin had arrived in Paris some days before, having managed with the greatest modesty to keep his identity unknown. These comments were highly probable, so that the suspicions that I myself had were only augmented.

On Tuesday, the 24th I entered once more into conversations with His Lord, the Count of Vergennes, since he did not tell me anything else but only repeated to me [the story of] Franklin's passage through Versailles on Friday afternoon and his overnight stay. He implied that I was accusing Franklin of having been hidden in Paris days before, and that he must have intentionally gone from this Capital to Versailles on Friday, and not simply made a stop on his trip. I told him that it had come to my notice that days before His Excellency had expressed to me that Franklin had passed through Versailles [and that] Franklin had been in Paris wholly incognito. He did not agree with this, assuring me that it could not be so, that Mr. Deane had come to meet him in Versailles—and of this I could be sure.

I stressed again to His Lord, the Count of Vergennes, the urgency of knowing Franklin's purposes, making him see that, whatever they might be, if no time was lost here through an eight-day difference, an inquiry about them in Madrid, where the news should be sent, would be considerably delayed in light of the distance, [and] that this circumstance required attention in order to be relieved of doubt as soon as possible.

Then he told me that he had forewarned Mr. Deane through Mr. Gerard,[25] the First Commissioner of State,[26] that neither he nor Mr. Franklin should speak with anyone concerning the intended purpose of the Franklin's coming, keeping this well apart from the physician Mr. DuBourg and from Beaumarchais,[27] who until now had been confidants of Mr. Deane. That they should put in writing Franklin's Commission along with the proposals he had to put forth, and then he would communicate the contents to me; that since this was an undertaking that demanded a great deal of care, it was normal that they should take time in carrying it out. To this I replied that he should forgive me if I did not perceive the delay as quite so normal; rather, a thorough man like Franklin, who would have his instructions for his initial set of proposals clearly delineated, as well as for altering them according to how the negotiations proceeded, who had come by ship for such a long voyage without distractions that might preoccupy him, and who already had been in France half a month, did not need many hours to set forth his request, nor was it necessary for him to lose time so long as Your Excellency should give him the means to accomplish his task. Thus was [the discussion of] this matter terminated on said day, and I remained greatly in doubt whether some secret review might have already taken place, or [whether] this Court wished more speedily to avoid entertaining the Colonies' proposals.

Showing confidence toward me, he told me that he had already begun a determined initiative with England, [it] being indispensable to break with her based on how things were developing, and that England was arming herself, which he wanted to make clear to me, that although he had not finished writing it, he read to me what he had [thus far] produced; and we looked it over, partially complete as it might be.

Rather than returning to Versailles during the week, and so as to have some token explanation about Franklin from His Lord, the Count of Vergennes, as well as to the document he had begun to read to me, I preferred to compose a note to him on Saturday the 28th in the terms of the attached document A,[28] effectively fulfilling my objective on both counts, in light of his reply B of the same day.[29]

He informs me that on that same morning he had been paid a visit by Franklin, who had commented, briefly and exclusively, on trade, referring to the Memorial that he presented, and [to the fact] that he would need several days to get it translated, etc. With regard to the initiative about which he had confided in me, he says that he had finished it and passed it on to be seen by His Most Christian King[30] to gain his approval, that it would be communicated to me and my Court, [and that he was] thinking of dispatching a mail at the start of the year to his Ambassador so as to learn the opinion and modifications of the Catholic King,[31] who in similar fashion would be made aware of what transpired on the same day with Franklin.

On the night of the same Saturday I got the attached document C[32] from Franklin in which he requests an hour to see me. Since at that time I still had not received the reply of His Lord, the Count of Vergennes, I told the bearer that I would respond. A short while later it reached me, and perceiving from it that Franklin had already presented himself to His Lord, the Count of Vergennes, along with the rest of its contents, I advised Franklin by message on the following Sunday that I would receive him at seven at night; to wit he came with his two companions, Deane and Lee, whom I invited into my residence without the rest of the Family noticing them.

Franklin speaks very little French, Deane much less, and Lee nothing at all; whereby they labored to understand us, but in the end, we managed it. Franklin told me about his going to Versailles the day before, that he presented His Lord, the Count of Vergennes, with a Memorial on productive interchange and Commerce; that his Excellency had described to him the close connection between the Courts of Madrid and Paris, and that he could explain himself to me with all assurance; that in that spirit of understanding he sought first to give thanks to my Court for the asylum that the colors[33] of the United Colonies of America had experienced in its ports; that he would deliver to me a copy of the document presented to His Lord, the Count of Vergennes, which he asked me to forward it on to my Court, to which I responded that I would do so when he gave it to me.

It seemed to me convenient to learn more. I asked him if he carried full powers from the Congress in all matters. He assured me that he did. [I asked] if the Memorial that he had presented was entirely done when he brought it, or had he worked on it since his arrival? He told me that the Congress itself arranged it.

I explained to him that I was surprised that it did not comprise anything other than productive interchange, when in the difficulties in which they found themselves anyone would judge that his coming would be aimed, foremost, at quickly looking for aid and requesting it with other proposals welcome to the Courts which they sought out, and not to deal with good relationships when they were still not peaceful masters of their [own] freedom. He replied that he still had more to present in another Memorial, and that he was making a copy of the one presented for dispatching it to the Ministry of Spain through my own conveyance.

I asked him about the present state of the Colonies with respect to their forces and their hostility against the English. He answered that as concerned forces they need have no fear, nor, owing to the general feelings of embitterment, need they fear about keeping up their determination. He wished to learn from me if Spain's ports would allow their corsairs not only shelter and refreshment that they might need, but also to enter there with their spoils and sell them.

I told him that, as to the first matter, they should have seen that their banner had entered our ports, and had even been protected notwithstanding the contrary efforts of England. But as to the second matter, regarding spoils, I could not satisfy him, both because I did not know what the thinking of my Court would be, and because I had not been apprised of what rules had been invoked in similar cases, since they depended on particular treaties between the Powers.

I did everything possible to discover if, before having presented the Memorial, he had received some preliminary explanations from this Ministry or someone acting under its commission; but with the difficulty of language, along with some hesitation that I could not comprehend, the answer was not entirely clear to me.

I asked him if Congress had invested him with open power to deal with everything that might arise. He replied that he came with his instructions, and his powers were ample.

On Tuesday, the last day of the year, I went to Versailles in the afternoon with the intention of engaging His Lord, the Count of Vergennes, that night for a little while. I managed it, in part, for we were interrupted. He told me that he had won approval from his Majesty for the document that he had finished.

His Lord, the Count of Vergennes, indeed read to me what he had presented to the King, and I noted that it was the same that he earlier had confided to me. He told me that on Saturday the 3rd of January he would send it to Madrid and, at the same time, send a copy of Franklin's proposal for a Treaty of Friendship and Commerce, which he now had translated. He would also furnish me with a translation of both pieces so that I could knowledgably write about them, should I wish to take advantage of his dispatch. I answered him in the affirmative [and] thanked him for the offer, and I only said to him that I was astonished that, based on what he told me, the American Congress's petition came down to wanting a Treaty of Friendship and Commerce even when it still was not independent and confirmed in its self-rule. I also expressed that, since its great difficulties were so well known, it should not start out by calling for protection and aid from the Crowns with whom it sought friendship while extending them some more advantageous offers.

With respect to the content of his document, I told His Lord, the Count of Vergennes, that I did not see in it a proposal for entering into a contest, but, rather, [it] substantially concentrated on preparatory moves and threats [while] waiting to be insulted in order to form a strategy. With regard to lining up ground troops, he found those of France quite sensibly allocated, but not those of Spain in El Ferrol and Cádiz. Not in El Ferrol, by way of posing a threat to Ireland, because if His Excellency recalled our former conversations, neither His Majesty [the King of France] nor the rest of the Ministry had believed that in any instance should an attempt be made against Ireland but rather to foment unrest among the natives, assisting them in other ways, and distracting England's forces on other fronts. Anything more than that, even if taken as menacing, would be fruitless, for the English would recognize it as just that, because they would see it as not accompanied by the trappings of reality, which would demand the preparation of an enormous quantity of transport supplies, artillery trains,[34] war ammunitions, and firearms with all their loud reports to prove that it was a decisive enterprise, and attainable from the start. So that, for Spain to make such outlays in vain, and purely to make an impression, when she was involved in other projects so costly, would be money ill-spent. Worst of all, without exercising due caution with the English as concerns ground forces, in any case, they would deploy forces of their own against the naval forces of El Ferrol to observe and counteract them. This would be to their advantage if ours had to set out in a convoy of such magnitude, since providing cover would cause more trouble for its escort's warships. Only the naval forces as they set out, and engaged in combat, would cause them to suffer considerable losses.

That even though the English could swallow up the expedition to Ireland, it would have no other results but to make them accept foreign troops in order to garrison that Island. And, in this case, the act might get the disposition of its natives stirred up, would serve to frighten them, as opposed to moving them to action if the island were not garrisoned.[35] The English would rejoice at a similar waste of troops destined to El Ferrol for embarkation, since naturally they would judge them as lost for any other objective-considering that Portugal herself would not be frightened by a force of twenty thousand men, since that approach is not frightening for so few people unless there are superior forces going by another route.

Nor could a threat be raised in Gibraltar from Cádiz, because the English know full well that the site cannot be attacked by land, and they would breathe easy in the face of such a notion. Neither [would it work] as an interesting strategy toward Portugal, since the approaches to the Algarve[36] also would not cause them alarm. That to come to the aid of America in some points, in unusual fashion from Andalucía and Galicia, there were always troops in both Provinces to be employed.

That for France to take action on her coasts for landing in England was greatly subject to shifting circumstances, since this operation in whatever break of relations was suitable by nature, the English knowing well the inevitability of wanting to put it into action, that it is an obvious mortal blow, plainly obvious, and which admits of no chances, so long as France played her part and utilized her options and possibilities in such a way that she alone, well disguised, could do more than all. Since instead of augmenting her American troops, they would be drawn down, in order to return them their own homeland, against the risk of leaving it defenseless if they did not do so. And from this fact, the Colonies already realized as much as they could wish for to weaken their enemy and draw encouragement of their own. The same threat by land would oblige England to form another strong fleet just for the Channel[37] and impede the passage that never should be made with warships from France, and, consequently, to oblige England to maintain ships at sea and battalions on the coast would be a signal revelation for France and Spain.

I had substantially the same discussions with His Lord, the Count of Maurepas. It seemed to me that while the explanation that this Court has offered through its latest dispatch appeared indecisive, there is within it a considerable leaning from which the Catholic King could benefit; for I understand that there is a struggle between the knowledge of what a Power like France ought to do versus the constrictions of her present state of mind, which is sustained by the hope of private conveniences.

Figuring that France will gain infinitely by the independence of the Colonies alone, this idea has been the rule up until now on the part of the Ministry. [This is] because they promised that, once in route with France's traffic, they will come to her for all the goods with which she abounds and which they lack, bringing those that this country lacks. The French would do the same directly, her islands serving as intermediaries, and the empire of trade would be closer at hand, and as a result these islands would flourish as well as France itself, believing that England, oblivious, would fall into decay once the separation of her Colonies is effected, and the commerce she had with them diminished, leaving to her the heavy burden of a National debt and the scarcity of funds stemming from the expenditures of this war.

Even if this outcome soon proves to be the case, England might get back on her feet once she had enough time to look after her own affairs, and on some occasion, sooner or later, France found herself immersed in some war on the Continent and thereby was overcome. Up until this point France has been viewed with indifference, since in such a case France has counted on Spain's assistance as a fine ally, in the belief that with the latter guarding her rear flank, the two Powers together would be enough to confront and handle the expressed risk. But it is being realized that the true course would be to destroy England once and for all, since this would be to guarantee us security from the dangers to come, and reinforce the same idea that I have brought up. Above all, when in centuries will another opportunity arise to bring down England for the afflictions in which she has placed herself?

Who would believe that France would come to invoke the phrase: "It is by lassitude and exhaustion that one aspires toward defeat rather than combat, or there would be with the advantage that knowledge and experience provide."[38] And all in all, it seems that the premise of the Memorial promises a plan of *lassitude* and *exhaustion*[39] that we feel could be prudent and good instead of furthering it by those same means, Spain and France being active parties to a considerable degree, it turns out; it will depend on England's will on whether she backs out or not. If she is not keen on bolstering her vigilance until she finds the most propitious moment, [then] she need not fear the preparations and immense sums that remain unused will have been expended on them, and, moreover, a singular occasion lost. When she comes to explain herself with her *knowledge* and *experience*,[40] little caution can be taken.

If this Memorial is compared with those of September and November with regard to the suspicions of a revolution between two Continental Powers, one will see that in the first Memorial they were not given credence, and in the second one, they hold themselves infallible. In this third one, it is as if there is no awareness of the existence of Austria and Prussia, only mentioning Russia, Denmark, and Holland, even setting forth considerations to assuring themselves of them.

The [French] Court is chagrined to appear indolent, while at the same time it looks toward preparing itself for when it is set upon. It is trying to dissuade Spain from the indifference it accuses her of and likewise not communicating this to her in order to keep Spain in such state as to take advantage of her for its own purposes and urgent needs. Therefore, we see the disconnection between her earlier proposals with the latter ones, the confusion with which it presents its ideas. It does not want, nor will want, losses by Spain because these would rebound to the benefit of her enemies, and would weaken her ability to be an effective ally of France. But neither does it want, nor desire, that Spain should extend one finger, so that she does not rise above those greater than she or resist its orders, or [take issue with] the profit that it disposes so handsomely. One discovers that the times enlighten things, the relationships grow distant, the disillusions multiply themselves; its own interest is the first obligation of each Monarchy, and that Spain will calculate like any other. Therefore, to keep the pressure on is the preservation of everything, and France's organizing principle; and, as his faithful subject, I beg the King to keep in mind this truth in choosing which sides to take.

Let us not speak about Portugal, concerning which his Majesty has seen what has taken place. Let us focus on England, from whom Gibraltar or Mahón[41] can be rescued, at the same time laying low her power for what comes next. This is a common cause with France, apart from her aims on Spain, and it depends from day to day on whether the latter has an active or passive voice. If one waits for France to be insulted, Spain will passively come forward to aid her; if both Powers, taking advantage of England's embarrassment, truly move to take her on, Spain, on an equal footing, has the right independently to secure its own interest free of the shadow of France. And this depends on impelling her to carry out forthwith the very thing that would have happened at another time and not wait for her to be provoked. Once explained, I do no doubt that France will make use of all her abilities, and these are what Spain needs against England, besides that of making themselves masters of the actions or depending on incitements of her adversary, [and] will entirely change of fortunes of armed conflict. England, without the practice of naval battles through the science as well as experience that the Court of Paris attributes to her, can arrive at the agony of her affliction and then see that she needs to recover her health, although weakened by loss of blood or dismemberment, not having become altogether gangrenous.

Spain has many possessions to guard in America and cannot ignore them either now, at this moment, or in what lies ahead. One should not doubt that England shall go after Spain at all times throughout those parts, and with many options will direct herself to the most exposed; in the face of which, what would be the radical remedy to avoid these risks if not to so take England down that she can never raise again?

If the present straits in which said Power finds herself offers the appropriate occasion to bring her down, if as time passes another moment presents itself that is even more problematic for her; if Spain then would be at liberty and in a better state than now; if France also could join the enterprise more or less at liberty, with more or fewer motives of resentment and interest, with its naval forces in a better or worse state, when at present she has already positioned herself as she had never been, which is more than enough for the purposes of the

Bourbon sovereignties once united. These are considerations that deserve to be probed more deeply to respond to the pending explanation of this Court, and for taking the side that should be most convenient.

Because of the historical connection underlying matters that this official communication contains, I have included in it Doctor Franklin's first overture;[42] and insofar as later steps now constitute a point that merits separate consideration, I refer to the communication that follows this one, in which I will take up what concerns the Commission and the purposes of those in charge of the English Colonies of America.

Paris, 13 January 1777

> May God keep your Excellency many years
> Most Excellent Sir, I kiss the hand of Your Excellency
> Your most obedient servant,
> [Signed] The Count of Aranda
> [to] His Most Excellent Sir, the Marquis of Grimaldi

[Attachment A, one page]
Aranda to the Count of Vergennes, Paris, 28 December 1776
Original in French

The letters from my Court today do not bring me anything. My Lord, the Count insists on inconveniencing you to see if you have anything else to tell concerning Mr. Franklin, because if so, I shall go to Versailles tomorrow, and shall be at your disposal; otherwise, I planned on calling on Your Excellency Tuesday evening, on the eve of the new year, since the Ambassadors are postponing from Tuesday to Wednesday to present themselves before His Majesty, and to seize the opportunity that evening to speak with you for a few moments about the article that, in your wise foresight, you so kindly let me read. At the beginning of next month, I will have to send my letter to Madrid, and it would be important for my Court to be informed of the Insurgents' ideas with which Mr. Franklin should have been instructed. I hope that you will think so as well, and that you will be willing to give me some explanations on that subject.

I have the honor of being, with most perfect affection = Sir = Your Excellency, your very humble and very obedient servant, The Count of Aranda = [to] His Excellency, the Count of Vergennes.

[Attachment B, two pages]
Vergennes to Aranda, in Versailles, 28 December 1776
Original in French

Since I planned, My Lord, on having the honor of seeing you tomorrow, I did not write you today to inform you that Dr. F. ... and his colleagues visited me this morning. The visit was neither long nor very interesting; he only spoke to me of trade, and it was brief, referring to a project that he gave me, which will require a few days to translate. He avoided relying on his memory to give me an exact account of the state of his country, and of its state of mind; he wants to inform me about it in writing. He seems to be an intelligent individual, but very wary; that does not surprise me. He promised me that he would not be questioned by anyone, Your Excellency being the sole exception, if he has the chance to meet with you. He has been informed that the most perfect unity of views and interests exists between our Courts. As things stand, Your Excellency only needs to come here by Tuesday; tomorrow I will not have anything more important to tell you than what I am writing to you at the moment. The project, whose beginning Your Excellency read, is finished, [and] has passed before the King, who approved it and who has authorized me to convey it to Your Excellency and the Court. At the beginning of the year, I intend to mail it to our Ambassador [in Spain] in order to obtain His Catholic Majesty's opinion and corrections. I shall enclose the details of my conference of this morning, and the copy of the project, the content of which I am not yet aware.

I have the honor of being His Excellency = De Vergennes

[Attachment C, one page][43]
Benjamin Franklin, Silas Deane, and Arthur Lee to His Excellency the Count of Aranda, Ambassador of Spain, Paris, 28 December 1776
Original in Spanish, translated from English[44]

Sir:
We desire to inform Your Excellency that we are directed or sent by the United Provinces of America to cultivate the good will of the Courts of Spain and France. For this purpose, as well as to pay our Respect personally, we propose that you will be able to see our

proposals tomorrow or whatever day would be more convenient, and whichever hour that would please Your Excellency to dine with us.

>We have the honor to be your most
>Obedient and humble Servants of Your Excellency,
>B. Franklin = Silas Deane = Arthur Lee
>Plenipotentiaries of the Congress of
>The United Provinces of North America

Document 20
Legajo 3884, Estado, AHN
The Count of Aranda to the Marquis of Grimaldi, Paris, 13 January 1777, no. 939 and no. 6[45]
[Main letter, thirty-eight pages]
Original in Spanish

Most Excellent Sir:

My Very Good Lord: As a consequence of the preceding communication, I will tell your Excellency that upon seeing that Dr. Franklin did not explain himself to me in spite of his promise, I made known to him that I would like to speak with him, and he indeed came accompanied by Arthur Lee on the night of Saturday, the 4th of the current month.

Because of the difficulty in understanding one another, it seemed to me that it would be very helpful to avail myself to [the services of] the Count of Lacy, the King's Minister Plenipotentiary Minister at the Court of Petersburg[46] and [at present] lodging in my house, who knows the English language, so that he should make clear to Franklin and Lee the meaning of the points that should be addressed, if they did not understand them well, and likewise [clarify] for me their explanations.

I asked Dr. Franklin when he would deliver the document for Spain, with its proposal considering that there had been an opportunity to furnish it.

He replied that he already had it prepared, that he only needed to compare it to his copy, but a delay had ensued because Mr. Deane had been somewhat indisposed.

[I asked] if the document in question contained anything different from the one given to France.

He replied that it did not, that it was identical, conforming to the orders that he had from the Congress.

[I asked] if there was not some necessary difference, taking into account that the location of Spain's dominions and their names always required a context, that it had to vary from the one [presented] to France.

He replied that he was authorized by the Congress to treat with each of the two Courts according to their interests, and with full powers, in the face of whatever should come up.

[I asked] him how it is that, without yet finding themselves assured of their independence, nor being recognized as yet by these Powers, the colonies came proposing treaties when everyone believed that Dr. Franklin's arrival was more immediately directed at requesting aid until they secured their separation.

He replied, that through such a treaty they would see the Power that desired to be their true friend, and that until they had assured themselves of this condition, they had not believed it opportune to deal with the matter of need, all the more so since their situation was still not such that would immediately require direct assistance.

[I asked] if it was certain that they already had received help from this Realm [France], if the *Amphitrite* had left port, and if two other shipments of supplies that were supposed to follow it had done so, or were being held up.

He replied that they had not received any aid from this Power; that through a Company[47] they had been furnished different merchandise, arms, and munitions; that they had also received the services of officers; and that in all these affairs, France had done nothing else than to not oppose them and to allow the freedom to carry them out; that the *Amphitrite* had sailed, and that he believed that the departure of the other two ships had been suspended.

[I asked] what would be the aid that was most urgent for them at present?

He replied that [that would be] bronze cannons and warships, considering that the vessels that they possessed up until now were inferior in fighting power to the English, and while they had many privateers and had made a number of seizures up to the sum of a million and a half pounds sterling according to the calculation made in London itself, since they could not confront the English warships, this put them into an inferior position that they needed to redress, all the more since the English with their many warships protecting their many transport ships were capable of carrying their troops and provisions to any part of that continent.

[I asked him] why he had not proffered right away all the explanations he might have for the Court of Madrid, considering that because of the [physical] distance, he did not have the opportunity to present them from one day to another, as could be managed in Versailles, from where, of course, he would learn as well their responses.

He responded that, in consideration of this, he would tender another document that would contain whatever had been indicated to him; that if it were agreed that one of his fellow representatives should go to Madrid, of course it would be done.

In response to this, I told him that they were free to do this or not; but it would not progress all that much, because they would have to come to grips with it among themselves through [the use of] the regular mails; and the Court of Madrid, so far as any proposal that it might receive, would want to consult about it with the Court of Paris. [Thus] the better course was to put forth the explanations here, because they then would be communicated to Madrid with this Court's opinion. I repeated to him that if they wished, so it would be proposed to Madrid. Both [Franklin and Lee] for this reason made many demonstrations of respect toward the Catholic King and claimed that their principal purpose was that of convincing [others] that they earnestly hoped for his protection.

[I asked] if they had any commerce with the Spanish dominions of America?

They replied that before, while under British rule, they had carried out some by way of Jamaica, but that, in these times, they were not carrying through with it.

[I asked] if they had many foreign officers?

He responded that the greater number consisted of Frenchmen; there were some Germans, and a Pole; that at first some had come through Santo Domingo and others had transited from French ports. There had been the thought of raising three regiments in Canada, but this came to naught because of the English occupation. [He added] that they maintained said officials on salary even when not deploying them.

[I asked] if the members of Congress were not the recipients of wrong information?

He replied very succinctly that they were not.

To raise their spirits a bit, and so they should not wonder about the questions that I had put to them, I told them that enlightening moments were waiting for them based on the state in which they found themselves; and that, in turn, they could ask about what came to mind for them, for insofar as I could answer them, I would do so candidly, just as I would [let them know] if I did not find myself in a position to answer them.

They proceeded to ask me if there was a likelihood that Russia would reach an accord with England for a body of troops against the Americans, so as to foster this suspicion in them, and I told them that public reports in the gazette[48] had touched upon it, but beyond that nothing else was known.

They explained that the Congress had sent to Cádiz six shipments of cargo to the English House of Buick and Company, which withheld its payments; this sum of money was urgently required because the Congress had allotted it for making the purchases in France that it needed, and they asked what means there might exist to obtain such justifiable satisfaction from the aforementioned House, given that it refused to answer any queries regarding the matter.[49]

I told them that there could perhaps be some kind of reprisal made, because it was an English House, from overdrafts that other merchants had in place with the Americans. To this they replied that this was not possible, for the correspondence with individual businesses had never been cut off. On the contrary, the Congress was most vigilant that it should be scrupulously maintained, so that indeed various letters of exchange had come in its own vessel from London for such transactions. It was therefore explained to them that the way to solicit payment from the House of Buick would be to present a specific case with the evidence of the company's debt, and the necessary powers of attorney, requesting before the proper tribunal the payment of what was owed to them. In this instance, support could be sought from the authorities, so that justice could be done without delay.

On Tuesday the 7th, during the regular conference of Ambassadors, His Lord, the Count of Vergennes, asked me if Franklin had furnished me with his documents. I replied that he had not yet done so, although on the night of the 4th, when I saw him, he had indicated to me that he would soon do so. In telling His Excellency the substance of the conversations that we have had, they seemed to him quite proper. We agreed that once they were passed on to me, if they were in English, His Excellency would take it upon himself to have them translated for me, which I found most agreeable, since in any case I had to understand them.

On the night of Wednesday, the 8th, I reviewed the documents from Dr. Franklin, which he brought himself, accompanied by Lee, and I remitted them in the original to His Lord, the Count of Vergennes, who received them for translation on Thursday morning; and these turned out to simply entail the act of Confederation, and the Memorial concerning their present situation, [both of which] are enclosed.

On Friday, the 10th, I went to Versailles. His Excellency told me that the version [in Spanish] was being prepared, and he gave me a copy of Franklin's later proposal requesting that France furnish warships at its expense as Your Excellency will see per [document] no. 1, and per that of no. 2, the response of His Most Christian Majesty offering them other [forms of] secret aid. His Lord, the Count of Vergennes, told me that this response would be read to Franklin, Deane, and Lee by his First Commissioner, Mr. Gerard, letting them have the substance of it so that demonstrable document would never come out. [Vergennes added] that the King had granted two million of Tour pounds (*livres tournis*)[50] which they could convert into six [million] in the purchases they needed by using the terms of trade,[51] and many merchants would take part in providing the Americans with what they should need. He also told me that the *Amphitrite*, which had arrived in the ports of France because of the bad weather it has suffered thereby, would set out again, and that the two other supply ships held up in le Havre would likewise set sail, although measures would be taken so that everything might be carried out with greater secrecy than up until now.

The Americans propose nothing more than warm friendship and reciprocal trade, but if it were enough for France, it would not be adaptable for Spain without the understanding that it be limited solely to its realm in Europe; because if the concession should also be extended to its dominions in America, National Trade would wind up being lost. It is quite credible that the United American Provinces should be aware of this consideration, satisfying themselves with confining their interchange and trade to Spain's presence in Europe. And, if they should remonstrate by asking for access to our Islands as they would have to those belonging to France, the counterclaim could be made to them that our islands are linked with that continent [Spanish America], from whose rules they are inseparable, when the French have nothing on it [the South American land mass], and Spain's Islands are considered as totally united to these Realms even though located in those parts. They clamor as well for other particulars that would lead to securing the success of their resistance, and France is aiding and abetting [the effort] within the terms she believes possible, in one or another way, as the attached documents disclose.

But I will set aside all these incidents helpful to the Colonies for [achieving] their independence, and I am going to explain to the King the present posture of his Monarchy, and that of his future interests.

Four European Powers ruled the American Continent: The Spanish in their possessions; France in Canada, which it lost; the English in the northern colonies that have separated from them; and Portugal in her Brazil, which has unmindfully doubled it with usurpations from Spain.

While this division lasts, Spain's aim needed to be directed toward conserving her own, seeking an equilibrium with the other competitors, and even coolly making use of each of them to contain the one that would transgress itself; but the system is already changing, [and] other political considerations are now indispensable.

Spain alone is going to remain, hand in hand with another Power in all that is terra firma in North America—and which Power [is that]? A stable and territorial one that already has invoked the ancestral name of America with two and a half million inhabitants descended from Europeans, which, based on the rules that operate population growth, will double its people every 25 or 30 years, and in 50 or 60 years can reach eight to ten million of them; the immigration will mainly continue from Europe itself because of the appeal that the laws of the new dominion will exert.

To conserve its own possessions in America, and with the purpose of distracting them from the example of the English colonies, bereft of their support, and to stop these from helping them [Spain's American possessions], it is vital that Spain assures and locks in [the loyalty of] that new power by means of a solemn treaty, by meritoriously freeing it of its urgent situation.

If, before the uprising of the Colonies, it had been Spain's choice whether it should take place or not, there undoubtedly would have been strong reasons for vacillating, because in the end the difference between having as a neighbor a State firm in its own domain, or merely provinces of a distant Crown, is open to question. A State that grew as a Colony would do so more slowly. However, free of its vassalage and dedicated progress, it will rapidly expand the means to attain high importance.

But these considerations are of no use now, nor is the difference in this theater so great for Spain, because England had remained alone in North America, and joined its possibilities in Europe with those it was nurturing in America; if indeed one reflects, it would likely deduce that Spain could be faced with fewer countermoves in those places that she can now supply, if it were resolved to consummate a considered plan, piecing together all the details that the current situation offers.

England's objective in blocking the insurrection is none other than securing its downfall and triumphing completely over the rebels, in which case the cure [for Spain] would be worse than the disease. The British Crown would then be indomitable and far more fearsome than ever to Spain. Let it be seen if in this contrasting set of circumstances a less harmful measure might be operative [aiding the rebels], which would protect the possessions of Spain in America and put a better face on her position in Europe.

It appears that necessity now demands assuring to the new Power of America recognition of its own long-standing possessions, joining [with them] on behalf of a mutual guarantee and, setting down, through a solemn treaty, the rules of beneficial reciprocity for the future. If this should be deferred to when she has survived her difficulties, neither would her good will be so well disposed, nor would the urgencies of her situation serve to help us in obtaining better prospects.

If anyone is to find himself at an advantage, it should not be through the hidden means of secret and insufficient aids, since they neither have any great worth nor serve the purpose of attracting the other party to accept a serious and formal meeting.[52] The time would pass in pleasant discussion, and nothing of importance would have been assured.

Of course, offering openly avowed assistance for achieving independence, when its fortunes still hang in the balance, and it lies within sight of enormous efforts that England will make to prevent it, would be the means to come to an agreement on what is wished for with the Colonies. This truth is undeniable, and it only remains to debate whether a rupture with England would be a mistake or not, and if its consequences could turn out to be bad after thinking that its results would prove beneficial.

To effect a break, the first consideration must be that of calculating the enemy's resistance and its forces, their own and those of its allies, that could be raised in opposition.

England, at present, is reduced to a third of her natural old forces, according to an indisputable calculation.

The Colonies allotted a third of their maritime crews to their navy. I have heard Dr. Franklin say that the number of American sailors who in earlier wars served in British fleets amounted to 25 or 30 thousand men. Since the revolt, this third no longer exists; England has fewer men now and remains with only the other two-thirds.

The separated third, having taken up arms, has, at least, one of the two residuary forces fighting against it, the result being that England is left in a state of having only one-third remaining to dispose of at her will.

It is known that to assemble the forty-five warships and a number of frigates that she wants to have in a state of readiness, neither an extreme enforcement of the levy nor the worthy inducements that she has offered will suffice. Even greater reason, then, that providing a crew for sixty ships and the accompanying frigates is out of reach, [despite] England's wanting to settle on that number, so as to avoid the criticism that her forces are being earnestly drawn down, with the assumption of relying solely on a voluntary force.

If to this reduction one adds to the rest, for which her economic interest suffers, thinning out maritime trade to complete her armament; the decay of her skilled crafts and manufacturing resulting from the break with the Colonies; the taxes and assessments required to meet unavoidable current expenses; the increase in her national debt; and, finally, the oppressiveness from which, with each passing day, she further suffocates herself, destroying the interior and exterior of her Realms, it will have to be agreed that, truly and down to the physical element, England at present finds herself at the point that has been posited.

Our forces and the allied ones that could oppose her consist of eighty ships-of-the-line, and frigates in a proportionate number, according to the reports of the Courts of Madrid and Paris. From this, one can definitely see the notable superiority that results, [on the condition] that these forces are effective and that those granted to England are without factual bases and spun out of fantasy.

England would therefore see herself compromised at just the moment of her worst disposition since she forfeited her maritime predominance, for she would suffer it passively, with fewer forces and with enemies whom she never had faced in a better state.

Spain cannot forget Gibraltar and Mahón. Their loss would be one of the major blows for England and a deserved forfeiture because their loss is justifiable and because making restitution for an usurpation by returning the territories to Spain would save them from more severe penalties exacted by Spain through an eventual Peace Treaty.[53] France would play an equal part with Spain in procuring the dismemberment of

England; and however much she resists other ideas of Spain in regard to Portugal, the reintegration of said ports would be [no more than] her partial concern.

France cannot help recognizing how much it now suits her, as it does Spain, to break with the English. [This is] because the British Crown is France's biggest natural enemy, because if she does not bring England down, she will have England over her as long as her trade flourishes or until France wishes to reestablish her Navy. And as long as through inescapable circumstances France finds herself intertwined with other Powers on the Continent, England will take the advantage of the opportunity to trample on her. The insulting subjection of Dunkirk[54] is likewise not redeemed except through a similar opportunity, so that France must at all times fear England if she should not now pay attention, cutting off her wings forever.

The treaty proposed by the Americans, which this Court lately remitted through its mail, is conceived with considerable skill, and makes observations about what needs to be done.

They propose friendship and trade as if they were already a consolidated Power. Under Article 7 they only offer to France, in case of war with England, not to assist the latter with men, money, ships, etc.—and under Article 8 they demand the renunciation of whatever possessions she might claim by virtue of her old rights, according to how they are expressed in it, agreeing to the fishing grounds of Newfoundland.

In this same Article they incorporate Florida, which can only correspond to Spain. Hancock, the President of the Congress, signs its original so its emissaries have not done anything more than make a copy of the original.

Your Excellency will observe that I do not send the separate proposal for Spain, although Franklin offered it to me, for he has not yet brought it to me. In his visit on the 8th, when he submitted the other documents, he questioned whether I could excuse him, since they found themselves anxious without persons in whom to trust, and [with] Mr. Deane suffering recurring fevers,[55] which indeed he has, for I sent the good quinine that I happened to have with an acquaintance of his.[56]

I am instructed through a source—an apparent confidant of theirs whom they do not watch closely—that the Congress had no wish to take part by humbly begging, or demonstrate any excessive needs, in order not to be struck by a harsh law that it feared would be imposed upon it. So one sees that in the last Memorial, requesting warships, they also offer remuneration and want nothing for free.

Hence all of this depends on just one operation, which would be that of openly declaring war on England by offering the Colonies to carry it out if by means of a favorable treaty they should render themselves deserving of it. They undoubtedly accept the offer in order to hasten their establishment, to alleviate their burdens, not risk their lot, and, further, would oblige themselves to continue supporting their allies until a general peace should be agreed to by all.

This declared war does not require a vast operation, nor taking risky actions, since its management, as will be shown, would bring about the total outcome desired.

Of course, the plan that France has proposed as a precaution, in case she is insulted, would entail all that is needed with slight variations in its delivery, subject only to verifying the declaration of war.

Thus, the English would see themselves in the condition of shrinking their efforts against the Insurgents, and the latter in that of resisting these efforts and of vanquishing the English.

Through it trade maintained by the British Isles would be totally ruined, since they would be unable to maintain what is left to them, and this would be a decisive battle to seize the possibilities without [the threat of] risky combats having to preceded it.

Through it, expenses would increase, which will weaken England.

Through it her fleets, if they went out to sea, would have to expend themselves, [with] those of Spain and France remaining in their ports awaiting opportunities.

Through it they would have to split themselves up over different objectives and into different squadrons; those that amount to sixty ships covering various goals could not possibly be as numerous as those that would comprise eighty ships. They would have to choose of failing with greater force on the former, targeting those that seem most vulnerable.

Thus, the Spanish, French, and American seaborne campaign would be superior in the extreme to what the British Isles could do, with the supreme advantage of their positions to sail out, and to shelter their outfitters.

Through it civil discord would necessarily be kindled in England herself, which would undermine her efforts and would oblige her Ministry to save her [from] total ruin by accepting the sacrifice of some losses, sensitive as they might be.

Under this scenario, the consequences—from the human perspective—should not turn out to be harmful, but, rather, beneficial.

One of Spain's greatest precautions would seem to be that of guarding against not letting itself have two natural enemies, either one of which could be problematic, as doubtless the American colonies would be, [if] not having secured good reciprocity [in benefits] with her; and as England would be, in restoring herself to power after her American enterprise, even though diminished by a third.

If Spain should secure the destruction of England so that it could no longer hold up its head, Spain would manage to have one less of its two enemies. Spain will have gained so much for the future and its interests in Europe by remaining hand in hand with those of America, if the latter should become a free state.

The acts of union clearly demonstrate the purposes for which they have resolved to form a free State, and that their objective is to give it a firm base on which to flourish in agriculture, the arts, and commerce; that its system is a peaceful one and is consistent with the way of thinking of those who conceived it, most of whom are Quakers by way of religion. This observation is important for understanding that any measure that leads them faster to a more tranquil State, and lends a hand to the functioning of their system, will be well received by the Colonies, and for that will lend them to whatever may be arbitrated.

Out of this also arises the fact that Spain must fix her borders, inland, and to the rear of the Colonies, to avoid problems in the future and because she has not settled them with the English. If this is not forestalled, as they go on growing in population and expanding at their own will, they will be able to penetrate toward our possessions along the back flank of Louisiana.

One must keep in mind that the St. Lawrence River runs through Canada all the way to Lake Ontario, and this lake connects with Lake Erie, or Oswego. Furthermore, near to this place the Ohio River originates, which flows into the Mississippi, which goes down to New Orleans. Lake Erie also connects with Lake Huron, and this one with the others called Superior and Michigan, beyond which the Mississippi comes running.

I am not getting into determining which boundaries would be suitable; rather, I am limiting myself to setting forth that all of them are important, that the makeup of that country, so crossed by rivers and lakes, will be of considerable value to a population that will increase beyond sight for the cause of freedom and the right treatment of their laws as well as for agriculture, arts, and commerce, upon which they will base their happiness. I will conclude that securing a favorable treaty from said United Provinces will depend on openly getting them out of their troubles, and on taking advantage of this opportunity to come to agreement with them.

What is more, through the break with England in the formal treaty with the Colonies, [Spain] would also gain the reintegration of Florida, which England acquired during the last peace [treaty],[57] and which by right belongs to Spain once and for all, and the Colonies would not dispute it as of now, but they will later as a conquest over some other means, because said Province does not yet form one of those [belonging to] their confederation. It also is extremely important that that new power does not take control of that strategic location, which is the one that precisely forms the Bahamas Channel and reaches to the Mississippi River and to the gates of New Orleans, with the notable port of Pensacola[58] inside the Gulf of Mexico. Spain certainly needs no extensions [of new lands], since those that she has are more a burden than are useful to her, but, in the present case, losing the opportunity of restoring to her the use of the Bahamas Channel along both coasts and letting that stable Power [the new United States] penetrate into the Gulf of Mexico would be harmful.

Spain could also acquire a portion of the Newfoundland fishing grounds and secure some piece of its coast for her own use.

If France should want to possess Canada again, she would actually manage to do so without any recrimination on the part of the Colonies owing to the simple fact of their alliance, and break with England; and that would be to Spain's advantage because the United Colonies of America would remain fastened on both sides, and there would be a counterbalancing of forces between Spain and France if they should seek to expand; besides which, a mutual guarantee of the two Powers [Spain and France] with the new one would also be more natural and solid if France reinstates herself in her old dominions.

France has indeed had this idea, and even that of forming another Republic out of Canada itself, as I related to Your Excellency in my letter no. 853 on the 10th of October. If she now strays from it, it will be because of the new idea she has formed, that apart from other considerations her commerce is the greatest advantage that can come to her from the separation of the Colonies. Nevertheless, it would always be advantageous to recover Florida.

Spain and France need to be persuaded of one thing, and it is that the English will not return to her Islands whether victorious over or defeated by the Americans without taking advantage along the way of the forces and armament they have on those seas. I have in my earlier correspondence repeatedly spoken about these suspicions of what we must expect will happen, and I therefore avoid repeating them.

In America, Spain's expressed motives with respect to the Colonies; in Europe to Gibraltar and Mahón, some existing commercial treaties detrimental to that of Spain and their usefulness there in formulating them anew in a more equitable arrangement; the demotion of England when she is more submerged than ever so that she never again holds up her head; a good naval situation in which the two Bourbon Crowns find themselves; [and] a way to effect a break, which, without risky actions, would yield the desired fruit of war with the British Crown on this occasion, are the reasons with which I sum up explaining to His Majesty that this point would merit his keen consideration and listening with due consideration to the sentiments of his wise Ministers, for the most tested resolution.

Regarding the Memorial of France, I will also say that, while indecisive, I judge that France itself shall want the Catholic King to urge it on and can base this opinion on what I have perceived on the part of the [French] Ministry, which desires it. I firmly believe that it does not deal with Portugal, which has always been the touchstone, but only with England, whose downfall is of such importance to France, [and that] the latter will proceed with vigor and in good faith in declaring herself; and I believe that everything depends on the resolve of the King our Lord and on the conditions under which this endeavor is directed.

May God keep Your Excellency for many years, Paris, 13 January 1777
Most Excellent Sir
I Kiss the hand of Your Excellency
Your Trustworthy Servant
The Count of Aranda
[to] His Most Excellent Sir, the Marquis of Grimaldi

Document 21
Legajo 4069-47/48, Estado, AGS
To the Count of Aranda, El Pardo, 4 February 1777
[Letter of introduction, one page; and main letter, four pages]
Original in Spanish

[Letter of Introduction]
El Pardo 4 February 1777
By Special Mail with number 2

Responding to several different matters from your dispatches for being obliged not to mention in the prior letter what is evident.

[Main letter]

Most Excellent Sir:
Since the previously numbered letter comes down to pointing out the King's way of thinking with respect to the two essential matters of the day and with the aim that Your Excellency can deliver a copy of it to this Ministry, it did not behoove me that I touch on some particular things from your earlier dispatches.

In letter number 939[59] Your Excellency referred extensively to all the [illegible] that had occurred since Doctor's Franklin's arrival in France was learned of up to the [?] of various meetings with him and his associates taking effect; but one was inclined to believe that on the part of His Lordship the Count of Vergennes that he had proceeded with some air of mystery, not relating to Your Excellency all of the comings and goings as they were occurring. There is really no [reason] to come to doubt the facts that Your Excellency himself with your understanding has been able to observe; but not discovering on the other hand a true interest of using a estrangement with Your Excellency (because at present France's outlook on the colonies cannot be different than Spain's) it seems more natural to attribute it to another innocent cause or to [the fact] that that Minister of State[60] was avoiding speaking on that matter until being able to do so based on a greater understanding of the Deputies' ideas.

In the same letter Your Excellency expounds at length about the questions that you put to Franklin with the motive of plumbing all of his ideas, right up to what point his powers reached. This caution of Your Excellency is proper to your perception and the King has judged it as such. Your Excellency adds a good many thoughts so as to persuade that at that time that Ministry of course found itself quite inclined to embrace the rupture if some impulse was given it from here. But in this particular, while in their daily and regular discussions with Your Excellency there will perhaps be comments made in favor of that position it is necessary to observe that in all the documents that you submit to us and in your frequent dispatches to the Marquis of Ossun you do not manifest it: and in any case the reasons on which the King up till now has founded his determination, are solid and carefully weighed, so that France herself recognizes them as such and has indeed been inclined to the proper course of waiting some time more until perceiving the direction that the Americans' negotiations take next Spring.

It is not possible for me to go into detail about the remaining combinations and discussions that Your Excellency brings up in the already cited letter and other successive ones, nor do I judge it necessary having carried out the main part which has been to read them to His Majesty so that he is aware of the length to which your conscientiousness and your loyalty go; but I will repeat that [your zeal] has been prized a great deal.

May God keep Your Excellency.

Document 22
Legajo 3884, AHN
Benjamin Franklin, Silas Deane, and Arthur Lee to his Excellency the Count of Vergennes, Paris, March 1777, no. 35[61]
[Attachment to no. 6 above, four pages]
Original in English

Sir:

We have lately received an express from the Congress containing some new instructions to us, the purpose of which it is proper your Excellency should be acquainted with, viz:

The Congress, tho' firmly determined to maintain as long as possible their Independence, whether assisted or not by any other Power,[62] yet, for the sake of Humanity, wishing universal Peace they would not for the Advantage of America only, desire to kindle war in Europe, the extent and duration of which cannot be foreseen. They therefore as well as for Reasons of Respect to the King, who's [sic] Character they venerate, do not presume to propose that France should enter into a War merely on their Account.

But if France to obtain satisfaction from Britain for the injuries received in the last War commenced by that Nation in a manner contrary to the Law of Nations; or for any other just causes, should think it right make use of the present Occasion in declaring War against Britain, we are directed (to induce, if it may be the more early making of that Declaration) to offer the following advantage in addition to those of Commerce already proposed.

That[63] the object of the War be to obtain for France satisfaction for the injuries aforesaid, and for the United States the establishment of their Independence with a Reduction of the British Power for the security both of France and America; to which ends it is proposed that the Conquest of Canada, Nova Scotia, Newfoundland, St. John, the Floridas, Bermuda, Bahamas, and all the West India Islands now in Possession of Britain, be attempted by the joint force of France and the United States, and in case of success half the fishery of Newfoundland together with all the Sugar Islands shall hereafter appertain to France, the rest to the United States; and the trade between the King's Dominions and the United States shall henceforth be carried on by the ships of the said Dominions of France and Spain and the United States only.

That in case it is agreed that the Conquest of the British Sugar Islands[64] be attempted, the United States shall on timely notice furnish Provisions for the Expedition to the amount of 2,000,000 of Dollars, with 6 frigates manned with not less than 24 guns each with such other assistance as may be in this Power and as becoming good allies.

That as a close connection is understood to subsist between France and Spain, and that their interests are the same, it is also proposed by the Congress, that in case Spain shall enter with France in the said war, the United States, if required, will declare war with them against Portugal (which has already insulted the commerce of the States) and continue the said war for the total conquest of that Kingdom to be added to the Dominion of Spain.

That a Peace shall not be made but by mutual consent.

But if it be determined by his most Christian Majesty to remain in Peace with Britain, the Congress do them pray that his Majesty would be pleased to use his influence in Europe for preventing the further transportation of foreign troops into America to use against the United States, and to obtain a recall of those already there. And having an unbounded confidence in the King's goodness and wisdom they pray his advice in their present circumstances whether to apply to any of the other Powers of Europe for auxiliary aids, or to make offers of Peace to Britain on conditions of their Independence being acknowledged. In neither of these points would the Congress take a step without consulting his Majesty's Ministers, and we hope for a favorable answer.

P.S. The Congress and the People of the United States continue unanimous in their Opposition to the Claims of Britain and are fully determined to assert their own Independency to the last.—There is no doubt but Britain would on certain Terms acknowledge their Independence—if the United States can have no Aid from France directly and if no Encouragement can be given to receive support in a short space of time; as the United States wish for nothing so much as Peace & Liberty, they wish and ask for advice whether under those circumstances they should not thro' the friendly interposition of his most Christian Majesty, or other way [sic], make offers of Peace to Britain on the condition of their Independence, or pursue the War & risqué [risk] the event.

Document 23
Legajo 3884, Estado, AHN
Benjamin Franklin to the Count of Aranda, Paris, 1 April 1777, no. 23
[Main letter, three pages]
Original in English

Sir:

I left in your Excellency's Hands to be communicated, if you please, to your Court a Duplicate of the Commission from the Congress appointing me to go to Spain as their Minister Plenipotentiary. But as I understand that the Receiving [of] such a Minister is not at present thought convenient, and I am sure the Congress would have nothing done that might incommode in the least a Court they so much respect. I shall therefore postpone that Journey, till Circumstances may make it more suitable. And in the mean time, I beg leave to lie before his Catholic Majesty, through the Hands of your Excellency, the Propositions contained in a Resolution of Congress, dated Dec. 30, 1776, vis.

"That if his Catholic Majesty will join with the United States in a War against Great Britain, they will assist in reducing to the Possession of Spain the Town & Harbour of Pensacola; provided the Inhabitants of the United States shall have the free Navigation of the Mississippi, and the use of the Harbour of Pensacola—and they will (provided it shall be true that the King [sic] of Portugal has insultingly expelled the Vessels of these States from his Ports or has confiscated any such Vessels) declare War against the said King [sic], if that Measure shall be agreeable to and supported by the Courts of Spain and France."

It is understood that the strictest Union subsists between those two Courts; and in case they should think fit to attempt the Conquest of the English Sugar Islands, the Congress have further proposed to furnish provisions to the amount to Two Millions of Dollars and to join the Fleet with 6 Frigates of not less than 24 guns each, mounted and fitted for Service; and to render any other Assistance which may be in their Power as becomes good Allies, without desiring for themselves the Possession of any of the said Islands.

These Propositions are subject to Discussion and to receive such Modifications as may be found proper.

With great Respect, I have the Honor to be
Your Excellency's Most obedient and most humble Servant
[Signed] B. Franklin
To His Excellency the Comte d Aranda

Attachment
Legajo 3884, Estado, Folio 1, Expediente 3, AHN
John Hancock, Congressional Commission, 2 January 1777, no. 21[65]
[Main document, one page]
Original in English [oversize]

The Delegates of the United States of New Hampshire, Massachusetts Bay, Rhode Island, Connecticut, New York, New Jersey, Pennsylvania, Delaware, Maryland, Virginia, North Carolina, South Carolina & Georgia to all who shall see these presents send greeting.

Whereas a friendly and commercial connection between the subjects of his most Catholic Majesty the King of Spain and the people of these states will be beneficial to both nations, know ye therefore, that we confiding in the providence and integrity of Benjamin Franklin one of the delegates of Congress from the State of Pennsylvania and a commissioner from these United States to the Court of France have appointed and deputed and by these presents do appoint and depute him the said Benjamin Franklin our Commissioner, giving and granting to him the said Benjamin Franklin full power to communicate, treat and conclude with his most Catholic Majesty the King of Spain or with such person or persons as shall by him be for that purpose authorized of and upon a true and sincere friendship and a firm inviolable and meaningful peace for the defense, protection and safety of the navigation & mutual convenience of the subjects of his most Catholic Majesty and the people of the united states,[66] and also to enter into and agree upon a treaty with his most Catholic Majesty or such person or persons as shall be by him authorized for such purpose for assistance in carrying on the present war between Great Britain and these united states, and to do all other things, which may conduce to those desirable ends and promising in good faith to ratify whatsoever our said commissioner shall transact in the premises. Provided always that the said Benjamin Franklin shall continue to be possessed of all the powers heretofore given him as commissioner to the Court of France from these states so long as he shall remain and be present as said court. Done in Congress at

Baltimore the second day of January in the year of our Lord one thousand seven hundred and seventy-seven. In testimony whereof the president by order of the said Congress hath hereunto subscribed his name and affixed his Seal.

Attest [Signed] Chal Thomson,[67] Sec.y   [Signed] John Hancock

❋ Document 24
Legajo 3884, Estado, AHN
The Count of Aranda to the Count of Floridablanca,[68] Paris, 13 April 1777, no. 1011 and no. 20[69]
[Main letter, twelve pages]
Original in Spanish

Most Excellent Sir:

My Very Good Lord;

Mr. Arthur Lee reached this court on a Thursday afternoon, the 3rd of this month, and immediately advised me of his arrival by a note, requesting that I receive him accompanied by his associates. I sent word to him, giving them time on Saturday the 5th after nightfall, in case the letters to be received via normal delivery at two or three in the afternoon on that same day conveyed something to me concerning this Lee, and if not, to limit myself to listening, as I was unprepared to answer him.

As it happened, three letters from your Excellency dated the 24th of the past month reached me at that time and among them letter no. 2 relating what had occurred with Mr. Arthur Lee about his interview with His Lord, the Duke of Grimaldi,[70] and its results, and the King's intentions for the management of my affairs.

The three Representatives of the American Colonies, Franklin, Deane, and Lee, came around at the indicated time and, after the customary courtesies were exchanged, I asked them what they had to share with me.

Lee began by asking me if I had in my possession some bills of exchange remitted to Holland in their favor. I replied that I did not and asked on what basis he thought that they might be in my possession. He told me that, having set out for Madrid, he arrived in Burgos, where he encountered His Lord, the Duke of Grimaldi, who persuaded him not to proceed but, instead, disclose to him all his petitions, with which the two of them would deal. His Excellency would give an account to the King, and the resolve of His Majesty toward them would be received; and to agree that by acting thusly the good intentions that the Catholic King had in favor of the Colonies could be advanced without obstacles coming in between that naturally would result when the arrival of an

American representative in Madrid came to be known. [Lee continued] that while his intention had been to get to the Court, thinking that his presence there, entirely incognito, would be to the mutual advantage of Spain and the United Provinces, in order not to lose time in dealing with whatever matters that might come up between them, he had yielded to the efficacy of His Lord, the Duke of Grimaldi, due to the fact that the Duke had been authorized by the King to conduct that interview, and had expressed to him [Grimaldi] the present urgencies experienced by the Insurgents, which were their resolute intention to not lend themselves to any party to a reconciliation with the British Crown.

The efforts of the latter to overpower them based on the probability that their [the British] land forces would not be victorious, and if they [the colonists] were more powerful by sea, by cutting off trade and the arrival of aid and assistance that, up until now, they had maintained to some degree to provide for their needs. That the English had as many as 86 warships of under 50 cannons [each], and some were being increased in size to accommodate a row of 50 to 74. That the Colonies did not as yet have more than small privateer vessels and lacked larger ships to be able to counter the British. That while they were engaged in constructing frigates and did not lack laborers, timber, and iron, they lacked artillery, sails, rigging and tackle, and some other things that they had earlier received from England in exchange for the produce from their continent, which they had not yet begun to produce. The interruption of their trade and the costly outlays to form an army exhausted the Americans' wealth. That the perseverance of England, as feverish as it was, would force such efforts as to put the Colonies in great risk of surrendering to them, and that if they [the British] secured it, they would not allow the Colonies to develop economically, except that they would make use of them in that part of the world [as a force] against Spain, and in this manner persist in smothering their aspirations, for it had always been the case to attack Spain in the Americas, [in which] England principally had used the forces which it had deployed in its American possessions. That the Colonies would remain so grateful to the Catholic King for having contributed to their independence that His Majesty could count on them in whatever England might attempt against his dominions. There were many other reasons that he alleged to me and I was unable to keep them clearly enough in mind in order to recount them.

Mr. [Arthur] Lee conjectured to me that His Lord, the Duke of Grimaldi, posted mail from Burgos and that he had him turn back to

Vitoria[71] to await there the response form the Court; that the same had arrived, and His Lord, the Duke of Grimaldi, personally conveyed it to him, [and] it came down to repeating to him the considerations that he had presented to him at Burgos, [namely], those considerations that Spain could not completely embrace but that Spain, nonetheless desired the colonies' independence. Spain had adopted some measures to come to their aid with goods useful for continuing their war, not only for the ports in Europe but also those in America, in particular by Louisiana, to whose Governor, General Lee, [he] had already explained himself last year, when he commanded troops of those Provinces that border it. That the King definitely agreed to a financial subsidy (though Lee did not express to me its amount) that he would receive through bills of exchange [monetary drafts] remitted to Holland, [and] in this case they would be given to him as if they were merchants, without Spain figuring in the matter. Since the said Arthur Lee had to immediately return to Paris, where he and his companions could avail himself of his Majesty's Ambassador and the Ministry of the Most Christian King, with whose cognizance Spain had always to act in everything. As a consequence of said offer he wanted to know the orders that I might have to make the promised bills of exchange effective.

Since Your Excellency in your aforementioned letter does not mention if either the bills in question, or the amount agreed upon, are to come through my hands, it seemed better to me, for now, to pretend not to know what has taken place. I confined myself to what Your Excellency also indicates to me, insofar as guessing, through my particular communications, the King's good disposition. So, my response to him was that he could be sure that whatever His Lord Grimaldi had offered him he could be sure that it would be accomplished. Because, beyond what he would have done about it according to the good will of the Court, I had understood through my private communications that His Majesty tilted in his thinking in favor of the Colonies; and that I knew from experience that his Royal word was firm and constant, and a pledge whose value was as worthy as the most solemn document. [I asked] that he should be at ease and believe that on the day and hour least expected he would find himself with the bills of exchange, to make use of them in the manner that they had been promised to him.

This discussion with Arthur Lee ended, [and] Dr. Franklin stated that he had just received an order from the Congress to go to Spain, and presented the formal credential[72] to me with different instructions for his commission, by virtue of which he found himself in the condition of having to obey his superiors.

I explained to him that I could do no less than persuade him not carry out his commission for now, since the same reasons applied that had detained his companion [Lee] along the way [to Madrid] were still in effect, and, for its being so recent, the Catholic King would be annoyed by an insistence that did not differ from the step taken by Lee, even if he, Franklin, had more formal credentials. That he should be aware of the caution with which Spain needed to proceed while it remained at peace with England [i.e., neutral] and that he should consider that Spain also found itself with a considerable deployment of forces committed to her possessions in South America, whose success needed to be realized, and that it would take some months from this point before that could be apparent. That above all, Spain had first to prepare, and it was common knowledge that it was preparing for whatsoever could happen. All these things required waiting for a favorable moment, which they must presume that the Catholic King would consider with great care. They should lend themselves to enjoying the favors that they had obtained and wait for the right time; that whatever he [Franklin] had to propose on behalf of the Congress, he could do in writing, and this would be passed on to my Court, and it would suffice for both parties to have understood each other, on which matter I could not think differently from that which I was advising him, nor do I agree in any way to his journey.

Dr. Franklin acquiesced, providing that he would pass on to me a written Memorial that contained all the points that were sent to him to propose, and returning to him the credential that he had placed in my hands, as it seemed to me it was an original document he insisted that I should keep [in order] to send it with his Memorial, since he had it copied, and wanted it to be seen in its proper form, as Your Excellency will see from one and the other piece that I include for you, having sent me the second one in a sealed packet on the evening of Tuesday the 8th. I had warned them that the most prudent course would be to not frequent my house, even though it be in the dark of night, but, rather, that they make clear to me their wishes in writing, with the understanding that I would not be able to answer back in the same manner, for when I had to forewarn them of something, I would contact them by message.

I have communicated to His Lord, the Count of Vergennes all that has been covered, and even asked him to have the credential and the

Memorial translated for me, in view of the fact that I do not find myself with a confidante to whom I could entrust the task. This is why I can pass on to Your Excellency the originals in English and their translations in French.

I note in the proposal of the Colonies that the benefits [that] they offer provide no recompense for what they ask to be done on their behalf and that Franklin adds, for his part, that the proposal is subject to such modifications as might be appropriate.

So that the King may have a clear idea of the move that French trade is making with the Americans, I direct to Your Excellency's attention the plan that a Company of merchants has formed among themselves, without which the commercial activity that is taking place in these ports cannot be explained.

> May God keep Your Excellency for many years. Paris,
> April 13, 1777
> Most Excellent Sir
> I kiss the hand of Your Excellency
> Your Trustworthy Servant
> The Count of Aranda
> [to] His Most Excellent Lord, the Count of Floridablanca

Document 25
Legajo 1452-47, Estado, AGS
Memorial of Lord Stormont to the government of France. Sent by the Prince of Masserano to the Count of Floridablanca, London, 22 April 1777
[Manuscript, two pages]
Original in English[73]

Copy of a Memorial lately presented to the Minister of France by Lord Stormont, the English Ambassador at the Court of Versailles

Independent of what Sovereign States[74] owe to themselves according to the Sacred Laws of Nature, and of Nations in cases where any of their Provinces may rebel; and not to mention, that should the efforts of the English American Colonies prove successful, the Provinces appertaining to other States might be induced to make a similar attempt; the subscribing party is instructed to represent to the enlightened Ministers of France, that our Colonies have nearly formed themselves into an independent, and formidable Empire. Should they not be timely prevented, it will by no means be difficult (considering their powerful resources of every kind) for them to attempt the conquest of other Provinces in America richer, and better situated. France and Spain have therefore, everything to apprehend for the safety of their colonies, should those of Great Britain succeed in their designs.

The subscribing party hopes that these reflections may induce his most Christian Majesty, not only to continue his pacific intentions at this particular juncture, but also, that he may so far extend his neutrality and friendship, as to prohibit the merchants in his Dominions from affording those of America (with whom they now trade openly) such vast succors as have hitherto been finished. Above all it is hoped, that Misters Deane and Franklin may be restrained in those measures, which have been gradually unfolded so as to become less and less equivocal. The papers annexed to this memorial will so amply display the nature, and the progress of Mr. Deane's negotiations, that after perusal it might reasonably be expected that he should be delivered up.

  Stormont

Document 26
Legajo 2596, Santo Domingo, AGI
Committee for Commerce by the Congress to Bernardo de Gálvez,[75]
Philadelphia, 12 June 1777, no. 168
[Three pages]
Original in Spanish[76]

Philadelphia, 12 June 1777

Sir:
We are informed through Mr. Oliver Pollock[77] of the very favorable disposition that has been shown for the advancement of the interest and cause of the citizens of the free and independent United States of America, on each of the occasions that have been presented to you after Your Excellency assumed the governorship of New Orleans and Louisiana. And Mr. Pollock assures us in particular that you are inclined to afford all the protection that you can to encourage us to send to the Mississippi those ships and boats that we want to use for commerce.

Since we, the undersigned selected members of Congress, are tasked and entrusted with overseeing and directing the public commerce for these States, we consider it to be our duty to convey to you our great gratitude for the friendly action that you have taken, and we pray for the continuation of the same.

Those with influence and authority in the affairs of these States are equally disposed to promote friendly communication and a mutual correspondence of agreeable actions between the subjects of His Most Catholic Majesty and their own. The Congress has sent a commissioner, charged with its powers, to the court in Madrid to enter into a treaty of trade and friendship, and we have every reason to believe that Court fully disposed to assist us with its friendship. We have received notice from our commissioner that on his way to Madrid he encountered in a place called *Gastos*[78] a person of consequence,[79] who assured him that they would be furnished with blankets and clothing, as well as military supplies, that will be ordered from Havana to New Orleans and deposited there for our use, where they must remain until we send for them. Nevertheless, we have waited to hear more regarding the matter before taking any action in procuring these items, but if some similar goods arrive during the interim, we have no doubt that Your Excellency will notify us of it.

It is very likely that you find it agreeable to know our present situation.

Time will not permit us to give you all the details, but one can relate in brief that General Howe[80] continues on with the bulk of his army in Brunswick in New Jersey inside the stronghold that he erected last winter when General Washington forced him to retreat behind Trenton and Princeton. He has been gathering his forces there for quite some time and making preparations to open the campaign. We have not been idle on our part, and so all that we await is that Mr. Howe starts marching at any instant and directs his objective towards this City. General Washington already has positioned himself in a very strong location in this area behind Mr. Howe and very near to him, prepared to defend or attack according to what the cause of the war requires. The armies are nearly equal in numbers; but they [the British] have the advantage of being better disciplined and armed and uniformed. Ours are more active and are better marksmen and fight for a better cause. Also, they will be supported by the country's militia should it be urgently needed, a militia that has already participated in the glory of inflicting defeat on such a formidable enemy.

Our army in Ticonderoga under General Gates is equally prepared to receive General Sir Guy Carleton and General Burgoyne.[81] In sum, we are moderately prepared, but we fear, once the campaign gets underway, that our soldiers, being new, may turn against us, although we have no doubt that it will conclude with much honor and advantages for America, and in the end we will firmly establish our freedom and the independence such that no human power will ever be capable of depriving us. We have the honor of remitting to you some gazettes [newspapers], which we will do again, in further correspondence, on the occasions that present themselves. We are Your Excellency's most obedient and very devoted servants.

> In commission for Commerce by the Congress
> Duplicate
> York in Pennsylvania, October 24, 1777

※ Document 27
Legajo 4611, AGS
The Count of Aranda to the Count of Floridablanca, Paris, 22 June 1777, no. 1055
[Nine pages]
Original in Spanish

Most Excellent Sir

My Very Good Lord:
At mid afternoon on Wednesday the 18th the Uribarri mail arrived with Your Excellency's dispatch of the 11th of the current Month, consisting of two separate numbered documents, the first public, and the second confidential, both concerned with the suspension of hostilities in South America that the King has just agreed to with the Court of Lisbon.

I immediately sent Your Excellency's letter and the one from that Ambassador to His Lord, the Count of Vergennes, as well as Lord Grantham's to Lord Stormont, and to Portugal's Ambassador the one from his brother.

I went to Versailles on the following morning and read the dispatch numbered 1 to His Lord, the Count of Vergennes, to fully instruct him on the terms in which it was conceived; and since the confidential letter number 2 gave me as much clarity as necessary to guide my explanations, I modified them accordingly, concealing the good understanding that has privately been reached between the King of Spain and his niece Her Faithful Majesty [the Queen of Portugal].

His Lord, the Count of Vergennes, was curious to understand why the resolution of the Catholic King [to suspend hostilities in South America] had come about so quickly and peacefully. I told him it was the simplest thing in the world: because His Majesty, satisfied with how his dignity was compensated by the good effect of his arms, in the meantime with the death of His Most Faithful Majesty[82] and thus separated from the Marquis of Pombal,[83] both of whom had disrespected him, providing an immediate opening for the Most Faithful Queens, His Majesty's [the king of Spain] sister and niece, who desired to make amends for the wrongs that they had disapproved.[84] That the Catholic King, using his natural generosity, and not wanting to deprive Portugal from what was legitimately theirs, [and] aware of the good faith of the two Princesses, had demonstrated his moderation, helping set them at ease. That this was a noble act, and inherent in the character of the King, and this was the reason for such a rapid demonstration of composure [on their part]. For which the King My Lord would not have succeeded with his pretensions had it not been for the opportunity provided by the death of the King of Portugal and retirement of his Minister.

Afterwards, I went to His Christian Majesty's[85] Court, who said to me, "It appears that things are getting settled,"[86] and I responded that since the King my liege found himself with two respectable Ladies, and of his own blood, that they had already shown him their desire for reconciliation; he undoubtedly wanted to show them his noble way of thinking.

Later I went to see His Lord, the Count of Maurepas, whom I found with the Lords Vergennes and Sartine;[87] I had the same discussion, and because Maurepas is a prankster, we followed along with Spanish gallantry, so if these ministers have not acted with such reserve in not displaying their suspicions to me, I would believe going on appearances that they do not suspect such good inside intelligence as Your Excellency indicates to me had been established.

I was surprised by seeing there Mr. de Sartine because the day before he had told me in Paris that he would not return to Versailles to dine until Friday and had even proposed that I accompany him if I was going to Versailles that day, as I indeed promised him because I was thinking of going.

It occurred to me whether, by virtue of having received the news of the suspension of hostilities the previous afternoon, His Lord de Maurepas would have made an appointment with him, [Sartine] as well as with Vergennes, to discuss the effects. I observed, while the four of us were together, that the three Ministers agreed that Spain's reconciliation with Portugal would be very sensitive to the English, since it not only would free up the Spanish forces sent to oppose Portugal, but they would no longer have Portugal to employ as a diversionary tool. I asked them if they were satisfied with the step taken in light of the results that they attributed. They said that they were, but asked if I believed that it would simply go no further than Portugal's neutrality. I replied that this alone would always be an advantage, that to demand that Portugal return to being an enemy of England would be difficult;

that for this it should have been necessary for Cevallos,[88] after having recouped all the Kings claims, to enter the Portuguese possessions and place them under the arms of the Catholic King, in this way binding Portugal to ally with the Bourbon Courts[89] as a condition or returning their lands to them. If those two Ministers had recognized Spain's successes, they would have said to Spain that it was going to shake up the entire world, and instigate a general war when they had no desire for any such disturbance. Since the second confidential letter makes clear to me that the propitious thing would be to downplay [the importance of] the close understanding that had been established between Madrid and Lisbon, to avoid the interference of any foreign elements, it seemed to me that it would be good to create the impression that while things were coming together nicely, they had not reached such a degree of closeness as to undertake projects difficult to execute, while no other existed except that of distracting this Ministry from pressuring the Spanish over such matters. So much more credible for me was this way of thinking, based on the results of the position taken by the King, of clearly lending himself to the suspension of hostilities, since I had earlier shown myself, to this Ministry, as being partial to the separation of Portugal from England.

I thought of sending to Your Excellency a letter on the 19th, having prepared the communiqué that follows this one, and while the news about some matters can arrive belatedly given the state of things, there are others that will let Your Excellency know this Ministry's way of thinking these days, with all the information that it contains about the present state of affairs, I send it on to Your Excellency just as it was when I already composed it.

I note isolated words on the part of these Ministries that persuade me that they find themselves convinced that the war with England is inevitable; they made these arguments even when we were together on Thursday the 19th. To better sound out His Lord, the Count of Vergennes's, inner thoughts on this same morning, as well as from our first meeting, I asked him if he had seen a paper, newly put together by Franklin. He responded that he had not, and that it would please him to see it, if I had it. I showed it to him because I had just received it the day before. He read it carefully and asked me for a copy. I asked him to read it again, until he got a very good idea of it, in view of the fact that a conscientious person, upon entrusting it to me, had demanded my word not to give a copy of it to anyone, and I had interjected to him that it would be natural, seeing as it was put together directly for France, that it should reach her through one or another channel. He [Vergennes] asked me if some associate of the Duke of Choiseul[90] had given it to me, since that party had been very vocal with the requests of the Colonies, in order to support them. I truthfully responded that it is a foreigner who had confided in me. Sizing up how it appeared to him, I saw that he was confused. For my part I abstained from getting drawn into discussion, only saying that he would well remember those same reasons, about which we had spoken on different occasions, even going back a year. As I am recognized as being a part of my Court, I am not being untrue to my word in submitting to you a small portion of said document.

When I saw Sartine in Paris on the morning of the 18th, he told that he was disposed to send to Santo Domingo and Martinique five frigates that with some other boats were deployed in those waters; they would amount to ten ships and that in September they would transport troops to Santa Domingo and some ships-of-the-line. I responded that if they left from here in September they would not arrive there until the end of October or into November, and that if they arrived late, what purpose would they serve. He did not answer but said that by the end of the year His Most Christian Majesty could count on fifty ships-of-the-line and frigates in a proportionate number, and that right now the navy has forty-three ships in condition to sail. I said to him in a joking way, that it appears Your Lordships are more suspicious now than before, to which he replied that there was a good deal to fear, and the English let themselves plunge ahead, without observing any respect. I brought our conversation to a conclusion [by saying that] he should keep in mind that, with its publicly known support for the Insurgents, France had done plenty to give the English reasons to complain, and had done very little to reassure them and get them out of their troubles.

> God keep Your Excellency many years, Paris, 22 June 1777
> Most Excellent Sir,
> I kiss the hand of Your Excellency
> Your Trustworthy Servant
> The Count of Aranda
> [to] His Most Excellent Lord, the Count of Floridablanca

Attachment, Paper of Doctor Franklin, June 1777[91]
[Seven pages]
Original in French

It seems that the present decision by the French court (which many believe is wise) is to avoid, at least for the time being, playing any part in the present dispute between Great Britain and the United States of Northern America, under the assumption that the English Power will exhaust itself to the point of offering France, in the near future, more favorable conditions to start the war at an advantage. However, this policy is too subtle, too fragile, and too disadvantageous to remain that of a wise government for long. It is based on two assumptions, each of which is not only uncertain, but also quite implausible.

The first one is that Great Britain will in fact become much weaker and less able to resist the advances of a European power than it is at present, and this is not at all likely. No doubt England's public debt will increase, but that increase will not make it any less powerful. As long as it can enjoy a peaceful Europe, England will not immediately experience a weakened condition resulting from its national debt, because it will always be able to borrow as much money as it sees fit. It will not cease to daily increase its troops and its warships: by using them against the United States of America, Great Britain will strengthen considerably the courage, the discipline, and the experience of its forces on land and on sea, while those of France, maintained at an almost equivalent cost, will languish in idleness and inexperience! Great Britain, although more burdened by debt today than it was last summer, is nevertheless more prepared to wage war now than it was then, just as it was in the previous war; even though its debt increased by close to eight million sterling, it was more powerful at the end of the war than at the beginning.

The second assumption is that the present war between Great Britain and the United States undoubtedly [will] last a considerable time without France's intervention, an even less probable assumption than the first. The British government has everything to lose and nothing to gain by pursuing the war beyond the present campaign. Thus, it plans, and wisely so, to exert its last and greatest efforts to recover its sovereignty over America. The Ministers hope that the outcome of the war will be somewhat successful and, in conjunction with the hardships and the suffering [of the colonies], will cause the latter to retain, with some limitations, their dependency on Great Britain.

They [the Ministers] believe that, if the course of this campaign cannot bring about anything decisive towards America's submission, [then] nothing more can be expected from further efforts; that extended hostilities can only increase and prolong the risks of a war in Europe. Their plan, therefore, having tempted fate in this campaign, is to put an end to the war, regardless of its outcome, in the best obtainable terms, and if it is absolutely not feasible to reduce the Americans to the status of subjects, to then immediately recognize their independence, and to ensure, through a treaty of alliances, their friendship and the benefit of their commerce. This clear and serious decision by the British Ministry was fully evident in the last debates in the Chamber of Lords, when Lord Chatham[92] made his proposal. One can be the more certain since this course of action is the only reasonable one. Moreover, this certainty is bolstered by private and reliable information.

France therefore can only prevent a prompt reconciliation between the Colonies and Great Britain, be it as subjects or as allies, by immediately drawing up with the former such agreements that, shutting out any other alliances, the Colonies may find the assurance of assistance and of trade that they need and thus be able to repel Great Britain's attacks and reject its offers.

It should not be forgotten that the first purpose of the Colonies' resistance is not to gain independence, but only the redressing of their grievances, and that even now several of their inhabitants would be content to remain subjects of the British Crown, albeit with some limitations. The great majority of them, it is true, have declared themselves in favor of independence, but they have chosen this course of action primarily with the trust that France, aware of and pursuing its own interests, would soon support them openly and effectively. When, their expectations dashed as they see that several European states actively assist Great Britain in their subjugation, that another state has publicly forbidden and proscribed trade with them, and that even the most sympathetic content themselves with remaining idle spectators of the quarrel, and even deny them a verbal acknowledgment of their independence, it is quite possible that, despairing of any outside assistance, and urged by an awareness of their own needs and domestic difficulties, they would lean toward an acceptance of the terms that the British government will be prepared to offer them in its own interest.

Lord George Germain[93] recently declared in the House of Commons that hopes to end the American war in the course of this year were mainly founded upon the discouragement and the despair that would be felt by the Americans when they learned that France would not offer them any assistance. The emissaries, and the supporters of Great Britain, will spare no effort to diffuse and to intensify that despair and discouragement. They have already started to hint that France, a foe of both parties equally, foments the present dispute with the sole reason of using them as tools for their mutual destruction, without a wish to see the Colonies ever becoming independent.

If by dint of these subterfuges, or similar others, Great Britain succeeds in isolating the Colonies from France, and to attach them to itself, the French Crown will forever lose the most favorable opportunity yet presented to any nation to increase its own wealth and power by humiliating and weakening the most formidable, insolent, and inveterate enemy—an end that no human prudence could have brought about, and that the most zealous French patriot could hardly have hoped to witness in the century. Quod nemo divum promittese auderet, en tempus attulit ultro.[94]

However, it is not only the opportunity to enrich itself and to humiliate Great Britain that France will lose by continuing to remain passive: it will also endanger the security of all its American possessions. The British Ministry knows, or believes, that France already has secretly aided the Americans in their resistance, and not only the Ministry, but also the King and the British nation are already stirred against the French as if war had indeed been declared. In truth, France already has done too much if its intention is not to do more. Since it has not given the United States any really effective assistance, it would have been better not to give any. The English nation, a natural enemy of France, contemplates and longs for the return of peace with America in order to turn its arms against that Kingdom and to satisfy both its desire for revenge and its own interests. It is truly determined to cause the war with France to immediately follow the reconciliation with the Colonies.

Such is the universal expression of the nation, and in particular that of its leaders, or what in England is called *the minority*.[95] The calm, wise Lord Camden himself a few days ago concluded a very long and widely applauded speech in the Chamber of Lords by fervently wishing *peace with America*[96] and war *with the rest of the whole world*.[97] In truth the Ministry prudently avoided to elaborate openly on these designs. But whoever reflects on the preceding considerations, and on the extreme feelings that we know the King of Great Britain to harbor, will not be able to doubt that, as soon as peace is concluded with America, regardless of its terms, all the forces that Great Britain has now stationed on the American continent will henceforth be transported to the West Indies and deployed to conquer the French sugar islands in order to compensate England for the losses and the expenses incurred in the present war, and as revenge for the encouragement and assistance that it assumes France secretly afforded the Colonies against their mother country. There certainly remain no other means for the British Ministry to calm angry spirits and to cause the nation to tolerate the loss of its hopes dashed by the American war. It has been promised that America would compensate for all the expenses incurred in its subjugation; but such promises can never be fulfilled, since America, should it be reduced to the lowest degree of enslavement, could never in the long run provide any revenues to Great Britain. Hence the British government must find other ways to recover from this war's expenses and at the same time to squelch the hatred and the resentment of the nation by using against the French possessions in America the very foreign troops whose obligation England must discharge, unless it informs their respective sovereigns with much advance notice.

The spirits of both nations, French and British alike, are not too irritated, and too many subjects of dispute will arise daily, so that war between the two Crowns cannot be avoided before too long; it seems therefore that it is in France's interest to start it without delay, before Great Britain has time to prepare and strengthen itself, and while the Colonies, not being subjugated yet, have both the power and the will to give the French armies the most effective and most decisive assistance.

Document 28
Legajo 4611, Estado, AGS
The Count of Aranda to the Count of Floridablanca, Paris, 23 June 1777, no. 1067 and no. 68
[Three pages]
Original in Spanish

Most Excellent Sir

My Very Good Lord:

Dr. Franklin has come to my house today to express his gratitude to me for the aid received for the American colonies, not only in money but also in supplies and equipment, and the transport route through Bilbao.

On this basis, he has insinuated to me how important it would be for his colonies to have ships-of-the-line, and that if Spain and France could grant them some, they would manage with these to take themselves to another level of resistance, obligating themselves to always fulfill that on which they should be judged. I answered him that on this matter I could not tell him anything positive because, although our fleet is substantial, it always needs surplus ships to replace those that are left unserviceable, along with the many other items to which it is necessary to attend.

I availed myself of this conversation with Mr. Franklin to ask him about the probability that the English held advantages over the Insurgents, also what level of credence does he give to the rumors that were spread around that England was better disposed to attract votes in the Congress in favor of its cause. As concerned the advantages, he assured me that they never came to as much as they made them sound. With regard to the other matter, he did not believe in any way that there might be disunity in the Congress, because there was no reason [for such], nor even intimations of persuading the Congress of it, since this year the Colonies have found themselves in a much better situation than in the past, well provided with arms and munitions; and he added as evidence of what he was assuring me, that a ship had subsequently reached them in Boston with twelve thousand muskets,[98] and more ships with the same supplies at various ports, in which *The Amphitrite* was not included, and other ships, though he had yet to receive news of them.

I share this with Your Excellency so that you give this news to the King, Our Lord.
God keep Your Excellency many years
Paris, 23 June 1777
Most Excellent Sir
I kiss the hands of Your Excellency
Your Trustworthy Servant
The Count of Aranda
[to] His Excellent Sir, the Count of Floridablanca

Document 29
Legajo 3884, Estado, AHN
Benjamin Franklin, Memorial, July 1777, no. 29
[Seven pages]
Original in French

In July of 1777 = From Doctor Franklin[99]

Memorial

In a preceding Memoir, it was said that according to the power of reason, according to very authentic information, and in the general opinion of people from all parties in England, the war against the United States will be over this year, [and] that if Great Britain fails in making them submit to its domination, it would lose hope of ever succeeding, and would decide to make an alliance with them in order to regain as much of their friendship and trade as possible.

Likewise, strong reasons and trustworthy opinions make us think that once Great Britain has made its peace with the United States, it will immediately enter into a war with France. That is the current wish of the opposition party in London, and the Ministry itself will soon judge such a war necessary for its own preservation. The people of England allowed themselves to get drawn into this American war because they were promised that the Colonies would soon be subjugated and that considerable revenue could be gained from it. The first part of this promise has already vanished, and the same will happen to the latter, because if the colonies are not subjugated, no revenue at all shall be had from them, and if they are, it is certain that they will be too drained to pay any subsidies for a long time. The English Ministers know this all too well, but each time that they seemed to acknowledge this sad truth, and [said] that they wanted to abandon the idea of gaining any revenue from America, the House of Commons, and in particular the landowners in this house, took fright and spread the fear of a widespread revolt. Therefore, there will be an outbreak of discontent and animosity in the English Nation once it finds out for sure that it has been tricked by its Ministers, and that it can expect neither revenue nor any other profit that can compensate for the blood and gold squandered so terribly in the current war. It is thus clear that in order to divert the public vengeance away from their heads, the current Ministers will have to seek a way to give it free rein through other means, and to attribute their failure to the encouragement and secret aid given by France to the Americans; this will surely be published and proclaimed very loudly, as much to excuse their own mistakes as to turn the people's resentment against the Nation. The English Ministers' intention to follow this course has already appeared in several proceedings and publications. This animosity, which has so easily stirred up the English against the French nation, has already broken out on several occasions recently. Now, the care with which the Government stirs up this animosity is even more certain proof of its inclination toward war than any increase it may make in its naval armaments or the twenty new Regiments that are known to be ready to be conscripted in Great Britain and Ireland.

Whenever Great Britain does decide to start a new war, it will infallibly start like the last one, meaning by some sudden and unexpected hostility, which would ensure its definitive success in the war and weaken its enemy. Its current situation would greatly favor such an enterprise. Its German auxiliaries are not enlisted to be transported to America, but they are there; its land and naval forces are already assembled there, and they make the most formidable army; if they fail in this campaign, will the English Ministry hasten its own downfall and shame by bringing them back to Europe? Would not it rather give orders to its Plenipotentiaries to make the best peace possible with the United States and use its terrifying forces to suddenly attack the American possessions of the French or Spanish? Most of these would be conquered before the people here even found out about the English plan. This conduct would offer the British Ministry the means to provide for its own security, and would maintain them in their possessions, as it would also satisfy the nation's avarice and resentment. This fortunate beginning, and a war undertaken in this way, would prevent a considerable decrease in English funds and would probably allow Great Britain to pursue it vigorously, while France, having received the first defeat, would encounter the greatest difficulty in finding money. To start it in this way, the English Ministry would only need the pretext of the secret assistance that France has supposedly given the United States.

They are flattering themselves in England that France's finances are in such bad order that it cannot enter into a war, but whatever degree of truth there may be in that assertion, no reason can be seen that would delay the process of deciding under what circumstances the English Ministry must start the war; on the contrary, that is what will rather encourage it to do so. France's insensibility and its indolence will not repair its finances, if they are really in such disorder, and will not prevent England from attacking it. Real difficulties and dangers should be prevented with promptitude and confidence. *Obsta principiis*[100] is a wise maxim. It is only by making war promptly that France can ensure permanent peace for itself. If Great Britain is attacked at the present time, while a large part of its forces are employed against the United States, it will be judged incapable of ever troubling the Powers of Europe. A simple declaration of war from France against Great Britain in the present circumstances will make the loss of the United States inevitable for the English in the eyes of the whole universe, and consequently will make it impossible for them to take out any grants whatsoever. Necessity will thus make them surrender immediately. The war would thus not only be very short, but not very costly. At a time when Great Britain is so occupied with America, France would not need to make any other effort than that which it is currently able to make through a vigorous use of its land and naval forces. All of the necessary money would easily be found before the beginning of the hostilities, whereas if England is left to first make its peace with America and then to attack France, much more considerable sums will be needed, and grants will become unfeasible.

Great Britain appears to have no ally from whom it can hope to receive any considerable aid if it were attacked at the present time. Even Russia itself would probably remain inactive, especially since it is too far away to do any damage to France or Spain, and besides, it probably will have enough on its hands to deal with at home. A war with Great Britain at the present time would certainly be short and successful, and appears to be the only economical, wise, and infallible means to prevent the bloodshed and immense loss of money that would result from a long and sustained war, once Great Britain had made its peace with America.

England's current dispute with America appears to have been designed by providence for the elevation and glory of France: in the order of human affairs, Heaven has rarely offered a nation such a favorable opportunity to elevate itself and to humiliate its adversaries; and so glorious a moment does not appear a second time. It is to those living at this time to whom it is offered; and if they do not know to seize it, their negligence or blindness will bring down on their memory the complaints and reproaches of posterity.

If one objects that France does not have just motives for making war on England, the response will be that men have so many reasons that they are never lacking any in order to do whatever they please. Nations are always skillful at imagining special pretexts for the wars they want to engage in for motives of interest or for even more reprehensible reasons. But people are not to be duped any more, and very few pay attention to the reasons States use to plead their cause and justify their conduct: people take even less trouble to find out about it [conduct] abides by strict, ethical rules.

If a war is undertaken according to strict, political rules, and its operations succeed, it is always praised as being just and glorious. The nations who allied against Louis XIV had never had, nor claimed to have, any just cause for complaint against him. They only proclaimed that they feared the excessive increase in his power. Such a warning would justify a similar alliance to separate America from Great Britain, and to make free a trade of which it would have the sole monopoly.

But after the inexcusable manner in which England started the last war, will it ever lack good reasons to start another one? By seizing as it has done, against all rights and justice, French ships and sailors, in large part it has ruined France's navy, consequently making it impossible for it [France] to defend its possessions; it has for all time invested France with not only the right, but the obligation to do its utmost to recover them as soon as the opportunity arises, and the time has surely come.

But if one thought it not proper to plead the cause of past grievances, it would be easy to find even more recent causes for a quarrel. The English navy officers' arrogance and that of their sailors has already manifested itself in different places, through acts of violence, which through means of just reprisals on the part of France would be multiplied and aggravated by the English to the point of more than authorizing France to go to war.

If, despite all that, the Government of France prefers to establish its security on future contingents rather than by making it stable through a short and successful war, the best thing to do in these circumstances would be to get a few of the Powers of Europe to commit to recognizing the independence of the United States. There might be a way to convince the Emperor of Germany, the Kings of Spain, of the Two Sicily's, of Sweden, and of Prussia, as well as the Grand Duke of Tuscany to take this concerted action with France. Supposing that there would only be a certain number of these States consenting, they would still be too great in number for Great Britain to declare war on all of them at the same time. And if this declaration was made in the same way and at the same time by these Powers, their offenses would be so identical that Great Britain would have no pretext to attack one more than another. Such recognition would rekindle the United States' courage, to the point of making them reject any of Great Britain's proposals for a compromise. All of Europe would thus see that this Power has lost forever all of its former trade and possessions in America, and consequently would eventually find itself incapable of paying even the interest on its national debt. It would see its credit ruined; it would not only find itself powerless to start a war in Europe, but also to continue the ongoing one in America. This declaration would therefore endanger none of the Powers agreeing to it, but on the contrary, would contribute to their security; and since it would not cost anything but words, the United States are certainly entitled to expect aid as little as this from those who will benefit so greatly from their separation from Great Britain.

But if we decide otherwise, and if we allow Great Britain to be the first State to recognize the independence of the United States, it will be natural for them (the United States) to think that they are only weakly bound to the other Powers, and will once again give to Great Britain a greater part of their trade and friendship than to the interests of France and Spain, whose prosperity and even security could be compromised by such an agreement.

[Attachment, one page]
Poster in Lloyd's Café, 3 July 1777
Original in French

Note: (This café is the place where all of the ships' insurers and captains meet daily.)[101]

Merchants, ship-owners, and insurers, noticing that the French, against the law of nations, allow American Privateers not only to bring their British ships and cargo into their European and American ports, but also to sell them, although it is well known that number of these

Privateers belong to the French, and that the crew comes from the same nation; and the continuation of such conduct can only lead to the ruin of Trade, and of the interest of this Kingdom. The owners of such ships and cargo that have been seized, or that may have been seized, and sold either in French or American Ports, are most particularly requested to give the details thereof to Lord Viscount Weymouth,[102] Secretary of State for the Department of the South, also to the Lords of the Admiralty, so that the Government may be informed in detail and made aware of the extent and the alarming consequences of these depredations.

Document 30
Legajo 4611-92, Estado, AGS
The Count of Vergennes to Benjamin Franklin and Silas Deane,
Versailles, 16 July 1777
[Main letter, five pages]
Original in French

Copy of a letter from the Count of Vergennes to Misters Franklin and Deane[103]
Versailles, 16 July 1777

You cannot have forgotten, sirs, that in the first conference that I had with you both, I assured you that, in France, you would personally enjoy all the security that we show to foreigners, and that for your ships and your commerce you would have all the facilities compatible with the strict observance of our treaties with England that our King has taken, on principle, to comply with religiously. In order to prevent any misunderstanding about the type of vessels that could enjoy the favors we grant to friendly nations in our ports, I had you read the article in the Treaty that prohibits us from allowing privateers free access to our ports, unless it is out of urgent need, as well as to the off-loading and sale of their seized goods. You, sirs, promised to uphold it.

After such a pointed explanation, we did not press for the departure of the ship, *La Représaille*, which had brought Dr. Franklin to France, because we were assured that she was meant to return as a merchant vessel. We lost sight of this ship and believed her to be in America, when to our surprise we learned that she had entered L'Orient[104] after having made several seizures. An order was immediately issued for her to depart within twenty-four hours, and to hand over her seized goods to those officials of the Admiralty who alone can be authorized to decide on their validity. Captain Wikes [sic][105] excused himself, alluding to damage in the hull of his ship. [After] a visit conducted by the designated authorities his claim was recognized as legitimate and accepted, [and] he was permitted to make the needed repairs and [then] ordered to head out to sea.[106]

After so many repeated warnings, whose purpose had been explained to you, we did not expect that this Mr. Wickes [sic] would continue his raids on the seas of Europe, and we cannot but be singularly astonished because, having joining forces with the corsairs, the *Lexington* and the *Delfin*, to carry out incursions along the coasts of England, the three have then come to seek refuge in our ports.

You, sirs, are too well informed and too knowledgeable not to understand the extent to which this behavior hurts the dignity of the King my Lord; at the same time it offends the neutrality to which His Majesty professes. I therefore hope for your fair-mindedness that you will be the first to condemn conduct so opposed to the duty of hospitality and propriety. The king cannot conceal it [his vexation], and on his express order I warn you, sirs, that directives have been sent to the ports where these corsairs have managed to come in so that they be seized and held, until there can be sufficient assurance that they will return directly to their country, without exposing us to [the chance] that because of new hostile actions they come back to seek asylum in our ports.

In regard to the seizures they may have made, if they have brought them into our ports they will face the order of immediate removal, and this will be done with every captor or seizure, whatever nation may be involved. Such are the obligations of our treaties in agreement with our Naval ordinances, which the King cannot in any way disregard. It would behoove you to make this order known wherever you deem it appropriate, so that new ship owners, attracted by the example of the abuses that those against whom we have been obliged to act with severity took the liberty of committing, do not expose themselves to the same difficulties.

That which I have had the honor of making known to you, sirs, about the dispositions of the King, changes nothing with respect to the assurances that I am authorized to give you upon your arrival, and that I renew for you for the security of [the duration of] your stay and of all those of your nation whom it pleases to live among us, as well as for that sanctioned trade that, on our part, will be facilitated so far as our laws and our customs allow it.

I have the honor of remaining with the most perfect consideration, etc.

Document 31
Legajo 3884, Estado, AHN
The Count of Aranda to the Count of Floridablanca, Paris, 20 July 1777,
no. 1079 and no. 28
[Main letter, twenty pages]
Original in Spanish

Most Excellent Sir

My Very Good Lord:
On Tuesday the 8th of the current month, the usual day for official visits of Ambassadors, it seems that England's ambassador presented a vigorous complaint to His Lord, the Count of Vergennes, over the safe refuge that the American corsairs had in France's ports, it being so injurious to England that even the maintenance of ordinary shipping traffic along its coasts suffered, for even the coal barges found themselves under attack. That in France's ports the spoils were publicly being sold, which was contrary to the very treaties of both Crowns concerning similar cases; that this and many other things did not correspond to the reciprocal statements of understanding that had operated since they [the English] found themselves at war with the Insurgents.

His Lord, the Count of Vergennes, did not relate anything else to me during the week, aside from the fact that Lord Stormont[107] was much agitated, and in discussions with confidants still expressed resentment. I replied to him that it also had come to my notice, and, since he did not tell me the [names of the] persons he knew about, neither did I want to mention to him [the names of] my informants.

Drawing on some of their more tried and true ways of figuring out this type of situation, these [people] were concluding that it was a maneuver on part of this Court [the French], dissembled by the tint of free trade, that under this rubric there was an open traffic with the Americans in the ports of Dunkirk, Saint Malo, Nantes, La Rochelle, and Bordeaux, these wharves [being] covered with war goods that were publically loaded as much on French as on American ships, under the guise of being the kinds of things permitted for sale in this Realm. He already had clearly exposed it and did not understand how he still found himself in Paris, since from one day to the next he found himself ready to leave [be withdrawn].[108]

From such expressions by the Ambassador of England, some deduced that he already was laying the groundwork for complaints for the British Ministry to put to use the ideas formed, for good or ill, thus nullifying the objective of the Colonies. Others thought of them as having been made to create rumors, so that the Court of Paris should at least modify the efforts, of which it was being accused, of sustaining the rebels albeit underhandedly.

On Tuesday the 15th, His Lord, the Count of Vergennes, spoke to me personally, reading to me the reply he had prepared for Lord Stormont when the occasion should arise, and then he told me about the vigorous exposition that he [Lord Stormont] had made the previous Tuesday. Since I viewed it as put forth by way of an official communication, which lacked only a signature, and it seemed to me that it would be highly indicative of intent once released, I made an observation, asking if Lord Stormont had presented him with a Memorial, since he was answering him in writing. He replied that everything had been passed on between them verbally, and that the said document was nothing more than something to read to him because all the dots were connected in it, without risk of forgetting any one, or of explaining them in different terms than what was suitable. He would send a copy to His Lord d'Ossun so that he should convey it to Your Excellency and take advantage of my special mail, of which I had duly advised him in case he had to avail himself of it.

Since His Lord, the Count of Vergennes, did not do more than rapidly read his memorandum to me, the points it stressed did not stay with me with any exactitude. I only recall that there are many offers to resolve the issue of the abuses by the corsairs and the sales from the spoils, so that ultimately, complaints also were raised to counter the insults that the French colors suffer. These are the searching of their ships and the detention of some under the pretext of [locating] goods that are passed on to the Insurgents, the abrupt assault on the American Captain in Cherbourg whereby France also wants satisfaction, and some pompous statements about showing strength at the right time, and that there is recognition of those matters on which English appeals could be justified.

I quickly made the observation to the Count of Vergennes that all of that would merely serve to buy time because the English were already so heated concerning the refuge of the Americans in the ports of France, that whatever small thing should happen, they would revive the earlier indictments that the Insurgents were so much at home in the French ports, and the merchants of this Realm are so caught up with them because of the immense profits that came to them. So it would be impossible either to avoid such opportunities or conceal them. That, in order to eradicate all the incidents that would occur because of the Americans, there would be no other measure but to forbid them transit and confine them to arrivals for provisioning themselves with food or getting repairs.[109] That, if this should be done, not only would it deprive the Insurgents of the means of sustaining their war, but it would also, in time, lead to their being declared enemies. The Colonies alleging that they had been abandoned to their fate, after France let them feel confident in the aid and resources that were provided to them and that from whatever aspect he looked at the present state of things, [I continued,] he could see that France was already in a crisis that could not end well. Only the fortunate one would prevent the other's action by striking a consequential blow. That he should remember my entreaties to cover the points expressed without wasting time, preparing for everything that could happen.

His Lord, the Count of Vergennes, told me that for sure in this month of September, six veteran battalions ready for campaigning would set out, three for Santo Domingo and the other three for Martinique and Guadalupe, with 600 artillerymen to be distributed among them, and 200 dragoons to be mounted in the first one. That another six battalions were already on these islands, plus the regular corps, for which four thousand recruits were being sent to get them equally ready for war. Thus, including what is there, one could count on eleven thousand men.

After this conversation, the copy of a placard circulated around here that was posted in public places in London by order of the British Ministry, the translation of which is included for your Excellency, who will see it is aimed at fomenting awareness about the affronts supposedly received from France. Should this be certain, it would indicate quite a lot; and presuming [it is done] by some individual person assuming the Government's name, it can be seen that it is meant to exalt the Nation, and to pressure the Ministry itself, accusing it of enduring affronts without applying any remedy. It thus is opening the door by this means so that at one and the same time endless complaints go about that actively stir up the Cabinet and the Nation. One clearly sees coming, in one form or another, [that] the Court in London will petition the Court in Paris to make up for the damages caused by the sheltering of the American corsairs. It will cite the sales made in her ports, which are several and considerable; and France without dishonoring herself will not be able lend herself to a similar request. Your Excellency will see that the English will base their claim in the Treaty of Navigation and Commerce concluded by Louis IV with Queen Anne in the year of 1713.

I am stunned to have observed that this Court recognizes the risks to which it is exposed. Many of its members have thought quite carefully, and, all things considered, the Court's manner of acting does not correspond to the risks because hope and consideration had prevailed that the English would remain extenuated, owing to how much they suffer, and would think only of recovering themselves.

I confess that I am not partial to this opinion and fascination because England, so displeased with France, will not be halted in her ambitions, to which the entire nation will lend itself with pleasure, the people working together to contribute them against her great enemy that she had been reluctant to invest them on those whom she considered her brethren and compatriots. It may be added that English talent and courage will not lose the real and true condition of finding themselves armed at the end of their war with the Colonies, whether they defeat them or not. Since this is the most essential part of the efforts, we will have to agree that if England's resilient and ardent character recognizes things thusly, for it is clearer than day, and if her great preoccupation is to assure herself of the preservation of superior naval power over the other nations, she will not stop in providing aid if it will serve to keep her current forces useful and proves the remedy for her misfortunes.

Another of the reasons that have calmed the temper of this Court has been the consideration that the English and Insurgents were mutually destroying themselves. That the British Crown was becoming weak and it would be better to take advantage once it is debilitated. I will not part from this political reflection. Rather I will ask whether it is known how many years will pass and be lost while waiting for the last of them to decide and take over England while she is still enmeshed with her adversary. That is the great operation, if a rupture were to occur, to pounce on the wound when it is opening and from the start radically destroy the enemy, without waiting for it to remain a hand-to-hand matter, in which case it would be a mouthful harder to swallow.

The varied tones in which I hear these Minsters converse for weeks, for days, and even hourly, sometimes animated, at other times tempered, and still others sounding confident, does not allow me to form an unambiguous judgment about their ideas. Nonetheless, I have observed that since our armistice with Portugal they count on said Power not to take sides with England in the future; nor will Spain have to deal with this distraction and, as a consequence, will remain whole for what might occur. That assured of one less enemy, and understanding that perhaps next year would be the last one for England to find herself embroiled, they are already agreeing more among themselves about what the opportune moment could be to affect a break, once the English have begun the risky campaign against the Insurgents or even before they launch it while occupying themselves with the preparations and convoys, and by capturing them as they embark.

The principal concern that has prevailed in this Court from the beginning up until now, to avoid a war, has been the misgiving over its duration and the lack of funds to sustain it if it lasted long. I concede that they may be prudent reasons, and understandable, if avoiding it was the Court's will alone, and without the risk that England might think differently for now and later on. But even with this assurance, it was necessary that France's conduct needed to have been so indifferent toward the Americans that it in no way disgruntle the English, nor give them an excuse to become displeased with some settlement of accounts and grievances to be repeated. It was also necessary to be assured of the current Ministry's stability, to whom the honorable gesture should have to have been made of not hindering it any more during its endeavor with the Rebel [ships], so as to come out of the episode with glory. And it was indispensable for France to be a Power that in the future should have no reasons to quarrel with the British Power because of their understanding and disposition as states, the good harmony of a peaceful spirit between them depending on an absence of unforeseen incidents, or interests that might cross each other to upset it. [Yet] neither has their conduct been thus, nor can the objectives of both Crowns keep from producing a thousand disputes, except in the case that one of the two should remain so inferior to the other as not to be unable to provoke disputes out of the sheer inability to deal with their consequences. In which case the intention alone is of little use.

If today it is well examined, the insupportable duration [of the war] stemming from lack of funds, which in all cases is a concern worth having, would not happen because the total ruination of England depends on the first campaign if in it is realized what keeps leaping before one's eyes. So that to topple her, would be done in the first instance, and [the goal of] securing her final subjection would be managed solely by keeping our feet over her so that in her extreme distress she would mercifully be subject to the law that one should wish to apply to her.

It is the pure truth that with the separation of the Insurgents, a third of her former forces have been detached from England. She has deployed, at least, another third against insurgents, and only one-third remains for employing against the powerful House of Bourbon, which, even if Britain's three-thirds were still together, would have enough forces to counter them. It is undeniable that it [the House of Bourbon] finds itself with one more enemy at present, whose presence alone represents a constant preoccupation by land and sea—and Spain and France could never entertain the hope of having her as a partner.

If [Spain and France] with middling naval forces would just pounce at once on those forces that the English have spread [across] North America, they would sweep them away as though with a broom, and the Americans would then come to Europe to augment England's disarray.

If the English naval forces were swept from America, those on land would be left cut off from all support, and perforce would dissolve like salt in water. Those on sea would not be able to return to Europe in a condition to substantially reinforce the armaments that the British Crown could muster in these parts. For certain all of our apprehensions that the English might be able to descend upon any of our points in America would be dispelled, and leave Spain and France forming an integral unit for all that might happen.

If there were added to this the interruption of commerce, and the great number of Spanish, French, and American corsairs that would fall upon it, who will deny that with this alone England would be rendered helpless? That the rupture would turn out costing less, and consequently, the funds for its duration would be bearable for the Royal House of Bourbon? Who in good faith will refrain from agreeing that with the rupture alone, English credit would plunge with regard to loans, and the national fund to supplement them would be exhausted?

These considerations in and of themselves can decide the possibility or impossibility for England, as well as the risks to the fortune of the House of Bourbon. If this should deliver a mortal blow to the British Crown, it [the House of Bourbon] remains master of the action, and its enemy without recourse to men, ships, or wealth or funds; the English Nation will be afflicted; the parties in opposition to each other, enfeebling her, would consume one another, and she would find herself in the greatest distress from within and without. If she is left free, without our taking advantage of the opportunity, England will preserve her credit and will find funds with greater or lesser benefit that she solicits. England's national pride will persist, and, as long as this endures, she will easily lend herself impossible [missions].

By forestalling such action, one becomes free from worries for the present time, and forever. Expenses are reduced, and one cannot only secure their compensation, but [also] the recovery of valuable goods of interest to Spain and France, the improvement of Trade agreements, the dominion over the seas, and respectful consideration among all the other Powers, so that the Bourbon influences seem like mandates.

By disregarding the opportunity, everything is lost. A never-ending disquiet will remain; expenses will be higher and longer lasting; there will not be an opportunity to repay them, or grounds for reintegrating usurpations [of territory]. Commerce, the use of the seas, will continue with the impediments that they suffer, and the concept of Europe will derive from the manifest laxity and negligence of its Courts.

France in particular will in time have to pay for the consequences of leaving her greatest enemy standing. Within a year France will necessarily see herself obliged on land with all her power due to different occasions on which she will necessarily have to involve herself. Then she will see how the neglected enemy, prompted by others, and absent this, by itself alone, and already reestablished, will catch her with her arms tied because of her other adversaries. Spain will have to sally forth on the imperative of covering its ally's back and, at best, the game can turn out a draw, each side remaining as it was until next time.

Spain cannot help but foresee this predicament, because it is in the natural order of things. And, if she has to avoid it, how much better would it be that she take advantage of the present circumstance in tandem with France after having convinced her to decide, to put England in a state whereby she could neither attempt to disrupt France, then obliging Spain to protect her ally; nor leave Spain alone, so that the latter would have no cause to fear her, or depend upon the will of another, which, although it might be quite sympathetic, could at the same time cause difficult circumstances on different sides, and would need all that she had for herself alone.

If this common enemy does not remain incapable of restoring herself, the precaution [taken] during peace has always had to be like the blueprint for a war. Can the kingdoms flourish that live with these woes, and with continual expenses under the pain of abandoning themselves to their enemies, and why? Because of having wasted the opportunity that will not return in many centuries. We lost the one of 1770, in which England found herself in a troubled state, unable to quickly provide for her urgencies, according to what individually and jointly His Lord, the Prince of Masserano, and the Marquis Caraccioli [*sic*],[110] at the time Ambassadors of Spain and Naples serving in the Court of London, had on repeated occasions told me. The whole world knows that what they cried out about with respect to action in the Malvinas[111] was for the purpose of concealing their unhealthy condition, knowing the way of thinking of the Ministries of Madrid and Versailles, on whom they would impose their threats.

In letter no. 1055 of the last dispatch of June 22nd, I included for Your Excellency a paper by Dr. Franklin about current affairs. Now I remit a second one that he has prepared, which seems to have been prompted by this Ministry in order to keep him busy, and he does not know that I have it [the second one].

>God keep your Excellency many years
>I kiss the Hands of your Excellency,
>Your Obedient Servant
>[Signed] The Count of Aranda
>[To] Most Excellent Lord, the Count of Floridablanca

Document 32
Legajo 3884, Estado, AHN
The Commissioners of the United States of America to the Count of Vergennes and the Count of Aranda, Passy,[112] September 1777, no. 34[113]
[Memorial with a budget, nine pages]
Original in English

To his Excellency the Count of Vergennes, Minister for the foreign Affairs of France, etc., etc. and to his Excellency the Count of Aranda, Ambassador of Spain, etc., etc.—[114]

A Memorial from the Commissioners of the United States of America

The Congress, some Months since acquainted us, that 80,000 Suits of Clothes will be wanted for their Army next winter. Also, a Number of brass Cannon, Fusils, Pistols, etc. and a large Quantity of Naval Stores.

To pay for these, they informed us that they had purchased great Quantities of Tobacco, Rice, Indigo, Pot-Ash, and other Produce of the Country, which they would forward to us as soon as the great difficulties of procuring Ships, and Marines for the Merchant Service, with Convoys of Force sufficient could be surmounted.

They also directed us to borrow two Millions Sterling in Europe on the Credit of the United States; which Sum, if the Loan could have been effected here, would have been, as the most profitable Way of transmitting it, laid out by us chiefly in the Manufactures of these Kingdoms, greatly to the Advantage of their People, not only encouraging and energizing their present Industry, but, by introducing the Knowledge of their Manufactures and Produce, and the Taste for them, would have been the Source of great future Commerce.

The Loan was found to be, in our present Circumstances, difficult; and without the Aid of Some Credit from France and Spain seems impracticable.

And the Ships bringing the Products of America to us, have been intercepted, some by the Treachery of the Seamen, but chiefly by the Enemy's Ships of War, which, with the Difficulty above mentioned of finding Ships, and the Blocking up of our Ports, has left us hitherto disappointed of the expected Remittances.

But France having actually furnished us with some Money in regular Payments, and kindly promised us a Continuance of them; and Spain having given us Expectations of considerable Aids, Though without specifying the Quantity, the Commissioners conceiving it would not be less than what France was giving, and impressed with the Urgent Necessity of the Clothing [sic], etc. ventured to order 30,000 Suits; and have also sent or contracted for considerable Quantities of Arms and other Necessaries for which they are indebted.

Spain after furnishing us with 187,500 *livras* in Money, and some Naval Stores sent directly to her Ports (the Value not yet known to us) has desisted.

And the Commissioners find themselves extremely embarrassed by their Engagements, and Likely to be discredited with their Constituents by the Expectations they have given of effectual Aids from France and Spain, if not a Diversion that might be favourable to the States: But the worst is the Prejudice their cause and Country must buffer by the Disappointment of Supplies.

The Commissioners received soon after their Arrival, kind assurances of the Amity of France and Spain, and substantial Proofs of it, which will ever be remembered with Gratitude.

They by Authority from the Congress, offered Proposals for a Treaty of Commerce, and for uniting the Force of the States with that of France and Spain, in Conquering for those Crowns the English Sugar-Islands, with other Advantages & Stipulations, in case Britain should commence the War on Account of the Aids granted to us; which Proposal the Commissioners hope were not disagreeable, and have long expected with Anxiety an Answer to them.

Some late Proceedings in France relating to our armed Vessels and their Prizes, and to the Exportation of War like Stores, and the cessation of Supplies from Spain, might occasion a Doubt that the Disposition of those Courts towards the United States is changed, if the Commissioners had not the fullest Confidence in those Dispositions as being well-founded in the true Interest of these Kingdoms, and as it is conceived no Cause has been given on the Side of America for their Diminution.

They therefore ascribe the late Strictness in France to the Circumstances of the Times; and the Stoppage of Supplies from Spain to the Inattention occasioned by Occupation in other great Affairs.

And they hope that a little Time will remedy both the one and the other.

In the mean while, they request a present Supply proportioned to their Wants, which will appear by the annexed Estimate.

France and Spain (as they have represented in a former Memoir) will be greatly Gainers by the American Commerce, in Vent of Products and Manufactures, Increase of People by furnishing more Employment, Increase of Shipping and Seamen and of course Naval Power, while Britain is diminished and weakened in proportion, which will make the Difference double. But they offer these Advantages, not as putting them to Sale for a Price, but as Ties of the Friendship they wish to cultivate with these Kingdoms.

And knowing that after a Settlement of their States in Peace, a few Years will enable them to repay the Aids that may now be lent them. They with the more Freedom ask greater Assistance by way of Loan, than they would presume to ask by way of Subsidy.

But if those Powers apprehend that the Granting such Aid may be one means of occasioning a War between them and Britain, and the present Circumstances render such a War not eligible; and if they there decline the same, and would advise the Americans to make Peace; it is requested that these Courts as Friends of the United States, would assist them with their Advice and Influence in the Negotiation, that their Liberties with the Freedom of Commerce may be maintained.

And they further request to the explicitly informed of the present Intentions of these Courts respecting the Premises, that they may communicate as much of the same to the Congress as may be necessary for the Regulating of its Conduct, and preventing the Misapprehensions that the late Proceedings above mentioned may otherwise occasion.

They can assure your Excellences that they have no Account of any Treaty on foot in America for an Accommodation, nor do they believe there is any: Nor have any Propositions been made by them to the Court of England, nor any the smallest Overture received from thence which they have not already communicated: The Congress having the fullest Confidence in the Goodwill and Wisdom of these Courts, & having accordingly given us Orders to enter into no Treaty with any other Power inconsistent with the Propositions made to them, if those Propositions are likely to be accepted; and to act with their Advice and Approbation. And the Commissioners are firmly of Opinion that nothing will induce the Congress to accommodate on the Terms of an exclusive

Commerce with Britain but the Despair of obtaining effectual Aid and Support from Europe.

But as it is probable that England is not yet sufficiently weakened or humbled to agree to any equitable Terms of Accommodation; & as the United States with an Aid much less than would be spent by France and Spain in case of their entering into the War, will be enabled to continue it with England as long as may be necessary, the Commissioners request that those Powers would resolve upon Granting such Subsidy as may be sufficient for the Purpose; or otherwise and to the said States the Sum they desire of Two Millions Sterling at the Interest of Six Per Cent—which they have all reason to believe they shall be well able to pay after a happy Finishing of the War, and which they mean punctually to perform.

[Dated and signed] B. Franklin, Silas Deane, and Arthur Lee

Estimate & expenses

Balance of M. Grand's[115] Aud.t rendered June 10, 1777		66,417.1.1
Payments to August 14, 1777	170,196.11.1	
Drafts since that time by the Commissioners & By M. Williams—suppose—	30,000.0.0	
Agreements are made for 30,000 Suits of Cloths Suppose them to Cost 35 livres each	1,050,000.0.0	
Ditto ... for 1000 Fuses	18,000.0.0	
Ditto ... 100,000 ld. Copper & Tin for Casting Cannon	150,000.0.0	
Ditto ... 100 Tons Salt Petre	110,000.0.0	
Ditto for shoes, for Pistols & engaged by Mr. Williams including also the Ship for Carrying out the Goods	250,000.0.0	
Repairs of Several Vessels ... suppose	50,000.0.0	
Paid Mr. Delap with Aud.t	40,000.0.0	

Cordage Anchors & for a 64 Gun Ship	200,000.0.0	
To Compleat & load the Ship in Holland the least sum will be	550,000.0.0	
Mr. Grand received July 10th		500,000.0.0
Balance against the Commissioners by Their Estimate		1,454,018.10.0
	2,618,196.11.1	2,618,196.11.1
Balance as above 1,454,018.10	1,454,018.10.0	
To be received in October		500,000.0.0
Balance against the Commissioners After receiving the Sum of 500,000 will be 954,018.10		954,018.10.0
	1,454,018.10	1,454,018.10.0
Balance as above 954,018.10 is Carried over to the next Page	954,018.10.0	

Estimate and expenses Continued

Balance against the Commissioners Brought from last Page	954,018,10.0	
Blankets, Shirts, Tent Cloths, Brass Cannon & many other Articles essentially necessary are not reckoned, that will amount to a very considerable Sum		
For instance		
80,000 Blankets at 7 livres	560,000.0.0	
80,000 Shirts ... 4 ...	320,000.0.0	
20,000 Pairs shoes ... 3 ... 10...	70,000.0.0	
10,000 Pairs stockings already bought	15,000.0.0	
70,000 ditto wanted	105,000.0.0	
100 Tons Powder ... wanted ...	200,000.0.0	

Brass Cannon cannot be estimated at present
The Sum which the Commissioners will be indebted in October

                                          2,224,018.10.0

The Commissioners Orders are for 80,000 Suits of Cloaths compleat, but only 30,000 are ordered, to compleat this order they will want	1,750.000
To give each soldier shirts	320,000
6,000 pair of Shoes	210,000
Furniture for 3000 Horse	450,000
Brass Cannon ordered Will at least amount	2,000,000
Adding the Charge and Transportation & Expenses of every kind, these Goods must be sent in Armed Vessels. The Congress have ordered Eight War Ships of the Line to be purchased which will amount to	3,000,000
	7,730,000.0.0

    The Ships of War may now be Purchased & probably for the Money they are estimated at; They are absolutely necessary as well for the Carrying out the Goods & Stores engaged as to open the Commerce & bring back the productions of America for Payment of the Sum wanted.

    The estimate does not include many necessary Articles; as the Congress could if Eight Ships of the Line protected their trade, procure them in Exchange for their Productions.

Document 33
Legajo 3884, Estado, AHN
The Count of Aranda to the Count of Floridablanca, Paris, 27 September 1777, no. 1139 and no. 33
[Preliminary note, one page]
Original in Spanish

The Count of Aranda by his Excellency[116]
He relates to his conversation with an Agent of the American Representatives about the way on our part to continue the remittances to the Colonies, [by their] paying for them in products from their country.

[Main letter, two pages]
Original in Spanish

Most Excellent Sir

My Dear Sir:
The day before yesterday this Court's banker, Mr. Grand, who has dealings with the American Representatives, came to see me and to bring me the enclosed document, which he took to be the duplicate of the one that they had passed on to His Lord, the Count of Vergennes, so that I should likewise direct it to Madrid. Due to it's being in English, and my not understanding it, I avoided trying to read and answer it. And, while Mr. Grand wanted to translate it to me verbally, I contrived that he not do it by assuring him that he should send it in its original form at the first opportunity.[117]

Mr. Grand told me that the terms of this document were called for by the fact that there was no response by this Court to the advantageous proposals that the Representatives had made last winter, offering various things to France as payment for the favorable stance that the Bourbon Crowns should take relative to them—and unable to assure myself that none of these Ministers had spoken to me about the said matter, I implied that I would be glad to see its contents, and he having offered and passed on a copy to me, I likewise include it for Your Excellency.

I cannot reflect on either of the two documents, because I lack knowledge of the English language, and as far as translating them, although there would be numerous people in Paris to interpret them, I would not know how to answer for the discretion of such translators.

When Your Excellency finds himself informed by the faithful version that you might have ordered done, you will be able to tell me if, regarding the said document of offers, you have acquired knowledge through my correspondence regarding said paper of proposals, or by communication from that Ambassador of France [in Madrid], or if this Ministry has kept it from you.

> God keep your Excellency many years,
> Most Excellent Sir,
> I kiss the hand of Your Excellency
> Your Trustworthy Servant
> The Count of Aranda
> [To] Most Excellent Sir, the Count of Floridablanca

Document 34
Legajo 3884, Estado, AHN
The Count of Aranda to the Count of Floridablanca, Paris,
27 September 1777
[Summary note, one page] [118]
Original in Spanish

Paris, 27 September 1777

To the Count of Aranda (by express mail)
Referring to the visit that the American Representatives have made and including two documents that they delivered, consonant with those that they gave to that ministry, about the present state of their [businesses][119] and assistance that they need.
The Count of Aranda to the Count of Floridablanca, no city, no date. A rough draft.

[Main letter draft, six pages]
Original in Spanish

Most Excellent Sir:
In your letter of September 27th, marked with number 1139,[120] Your Excellency notes that Mr. Grand arrived and delivered to you a document equal to that which the American Representatives had placed in the hands of that Ministry. Although, as it was in English, Your Excellency made use of that circumstance to excuse yourself from entering into polemics or discussions over the points with which it dealt.
A short while after receiving the cited letter from Your Excellency, and when I already had translated same document into Castilian, the Marquis de Ossuna[121] delivered another copy to me in French with the extract of what they wrote to him from his Court with said purpose.
Since Your Excellency was unable to read it, I begin by directing its translation to you, so that you are for certain aware of the Americans' requests and the reasons with which they try to bolster them, which they have explained with considerable artfulness and sagacity.
The Ministry of Versailles shows much inclination to adopt the Representatives' ideas and to pass on to them increased sums of money

as it appears through the dispatch written to this Embassy, and also I include for Your Excellency its copy in order that you have greater cognizance of it.

On the part of that court they have not afforded us more openings than those which are known to Your Excellency, and one clearly sees that they have done so on the occasion that called for it without subjecting themselves to the detail of instructing us of each incident or conversation with the Representatives, as would perhaps have our way of managing our affairs.

In my earlier dispatches, I have explained myself sufficiently to be convinced of the true value and importance of every kind of aid that we have been giving for two or three years, to this date, to the Colonists, and of which Your Excellency has made the corresponding use. But it should be noted that in their writings the Representatives and even the very Court of France do not show themselves to be convinced of this truth, without also being aware that the greater part of the aid and assistance that has been given by our hand to the American Provinces has come to be converted into donations to French trade, as happened with the first two millions in *reales* that we gifted through the channel of this Ministry, which were invested in munitions and clothing purchased in France, and [as] has been done again with the aid supplied in bills of exchange to the same Representatives.

Neither are they much aware of the value that should be given to our armaments, and because of the spirit of moderation it does not behoove us to detain ourselves much in comparing them with those that, until now, the Court of France has given. But it has appeared convenient to call the attention of one or another and make them understand the King Our Lord's way of thinking and that of all in Ministry in the present circumstances, both in the point, that stands indicated, of competently helping the Colonies, and in that of calculating our steps and dispositions so that war is not hastened to our detriment. With this view they have prepared the document, from which also I attach a copy, which had been delivered a few days ago to this Embassy in response to the dispatch confided to us by His Lord, the Count of Vergennes.

Your Excellency will carefully examine it and with your customary precision adjust to these ideas your argumentation and persuasions with the Ministers of His Most Christian Majesty.

[May] God keep Your Excellency

Document 35
Legajo 3884, Estado, AHN
The Count of Aranda to the Count of Floridablanca, Paris, 27 September 1777, no. 1136 and no. 32
[Main letter, three pages]
Original in Spanish

Most Excellent Sir

My Very Good Lord:
In letter no. 4 of the dispatch of the 11th of the current month, Your Excellency replies to my letter numbered 1113 of August 26,[122] in which I reported the explanation of Mr. Grand on behalf of the American Representatives with respect to the demand made upon them by the Merchant of Bilbao, Gardoqui.[123]

Aligning myself, then, to what your Excellency communicates to me, I have seen Mr. Grand and told him that the aid furnished up to now, and for which Gardoqui insisted on compensation, is generously recalled, [but] without [such] accountability, as with several other extensions of aid that have been furnished through different channels.

I have brought up before you various considerations concerning the excessive expenses that Spain had noticeably borne, and still does, [and] the considerable amount that Spain [spent] indirectly to the advantage of the Americans with her armaments and preparatory measures, for which reason the best thing would be to formalize an adjustment to continue remittances in agreement with what had occurred with the farmers-general.[124]

With Mr. Grand cognizant of everything, we have decided that the Representatives should respond to Gardoqui, telling him that the *friends*[125] who commissioned him for the shipment should show themselves disposed to his compensation, there only remaining the arrangement of what comes next, that Gardoqui himself [should] take charge of similar shipments while taking pains to anticipate their cost. Concerning the reimbursement of the quantities he should supply, it will be well for him to be in agreement regarding the kinds of goods that it should suit him to receive [in turn] for his trade and that these be products of the Colonies by adjusting their prices to accommodate their operations and deliveries in payment for the advances.

I have told Mr. Grand that as a consequence of this the Representatives should come to an understanding with Gardoqui and with a merchant as their agent, and that they instruct him as to the effects that he should dispatch, that they fix their prices with him, and that they take up with him the kinds of payment and their value as well as the schedule of payments, and whatever else that might occur to them in this matter.

This appears to me as being the spirit of your Excellency's letter, that, in short, there should be a third party acting as their merchant who intervenes in facilitating for the Colonist the goods that can be conveyed to them to meet their needs, and that they satisfy payment for the consignments made to them.

I hope that Mr. Grand will have understood without fail all that I have told him; and in view of what is here transmitted to Your Excellency, I believe that it would be good to forewarn Gardoqui so that he maintains his relationship in line with the idea expressed [above].

> God keep your Excellency many years, Paris, 27 September 1777
> Most Excellent Sir
> I kiss the hand of Your Excellency
> Your trusted servant,
> [Signed] The Count of Aranda
> [To] His Most Excellent Sir, the Count of Floridablanca

Document 36
Legajo 6998-9, Estado, AGS
Francisco Escarano to the Count of Floridablanca, London,
3 October 1777
[Letter of introduction, one page; main letter, ten pages]
Original in Spanish

[Letter of introduction]
England 1777
Confidential letter of Don Francisco Escarano
In London 3 October 1777

Conveyed by Spanish ship to Bilbao and received on 7 November, the notice of which was given surreptitiously.[126]

It deals with his conversation with Lord Mansfield relative to the Americans, the present state of England and our Lord the King's way of thinking.

[Letter]

Most Excellent Sir

Sir:
   Twelve days after his Lordship the Prince of Masserano's departure from this Court, the Consul Don Miguel de Ventades delivered to me a sealed document that the Captain of one of our Ships from Bilbao had placed in his hands. Having opened it I found inside a personal letter from Your Excellency written on the 7th of July of this year to that Ambassador, in which you alerted him to how he should deal here with the ministers or persons of his confidence regarding the circumstances in which this Court finds itself, and we find ourselves with respect to the affairs of America.
   Your Excellency's Instruction is so precise, so clear, that to carry it out well it has left me with nothing to wish for but the good guidance of the cited Ambassador, and his connections, or friendship with the

Dignitaries of this Country. Lacking one or the other I tried, necessarily, to avail myself of one of the few means that are in my power, that being Lord Mansfield. Your Excellency knows that this Magistrate, so responsible owing to his age as well as to his high talents enjoys in this way [and] for many years the full confidence of this Monarch; that his British Majesty and his Ministers of State consult him on the most difficult political matters; that his vote is of great influence in the Cabinet; and that scarcely any or no business is concluded with taking his advice beforehand. It seemed to me, then, that if I had the good fortune of getting him to adopt my ideas [then] those of Your Excellency would have managed to take effect and thus I did not dally in going out to his country home a few miles away from the capital. Not finding him in it he came to my residence the day before yesterday in the morning, and in more than an hour's conversation [we] covered what I am going to convey to Your Excellency.

I began [by] telling him that I had gone alone to look for him, to give him news of how happily his Lordship the Prince of Masserano was going about his journey, knowing how pleasant such news would be for him [Lord Mansfield].

He expressed himself to me as very pleased; asking me to notify him whenever I should receive letters from his close friend, and he offered the greatest praise for his manner of operating while he resided in England.

Moving on afterwards to extend congratulations to him for the advances of the Army that General Bourgoyne [sic][127] commands, and answering me that it was not doubted here that they would soon be followed by others still more favorable because of dissension now among the rebels, that in the end they could not but lead to their total ruin, I explained to him it did not seem advisable to me to brag overly, since to subjugate such vast territories was not easy, [nor] to win over the hearts of more than three million inhabitants spurred by an enthusiasm for freedom, and deeply resentful against the slights that they claim to have received; adding for him that according to my feeble way of thinking the efforts against the Metropole[128] would increase, or decrease in proportion to the greater, or lesser hopes of a rupture of the latter with those Powers, from whom, perhaps in vain, they hope for aid and protection.

He then told me that if all the Princes should think properly they would not [risk] exposing themselves to a war by lending aid to some ungrateful subjects; to which I responded [that I was] almost of his opinion, persuaded that the advantages of peace, as little as they might be, were always preferable to all those which could result from a war; but that it was also [the case] that his would not conclude all that soon, even though the rebellious colonists should not have the least [amount of] aid from the Foreign Provinces, but, rather, lost all hope of England being set on a rupture with some of them. Deducing from his silence that my thought carried force with him, I went on telling him: My Lord: perhaps I deceive myself, but I am given to understand that if a way should be found to persuade those Powers with whom the Americans brag themselves that this Court can break up, [and] that they be advised to accede to the proposals that are made to them from here, it would be a device so effective that we would see them very ready to bow to their duty. Upon hearing this he told me that I was quite right and that I thought skillfully, but that in France they were lending an ear to as many Americans as presented themselves, and that Mister Lee and Mister Sayre, contemptible individuals, had just arrived in Paris from Berlin;[129] adding for me with a kind of satisfaction that the first of these had lost self control in the latter of these two Courts. I then asked him, why could the Court of Madrid not be sounded out; to which he responded [with] these formal words. The King of Spain has a [certain] character: I know that we can put our trust in him: Yes, My Lord, I immediately said to him, and the best character in the world: His Good faith is quite well known everywhere. [Having] given his word he would sacrifice all his interests to fulfill it.

I then recalled for him a conversation that I had had with him three years ago, finding myself in charge of the King's affairs, in which having told me that His Majesty, never forgetting the audacity that Captain Martin had shown in Naples, wanted no more than to make war on England in satisfaction of that insult, I had evidently demonstrated the opposite to him, and that the King yearned anxiously for the continuation of peace; that true Father to his vassals he thought only of the means of making them content, increasing the Population, advancing Agriculture, encouraging foreign Trade, and facilitating internal Commerce with new roads, and canals in his Kingdom; works that interested his noble heart, and that even if not completely stopping [the works] they would always suffer some loss, if His Majesty should be seen as needing to invest in a war part of the considerable funds that [the works] absorb. He assured me of keeping in mind my then conversation [with him], and confessed to me that since I had disabused him of the error he was in, he lived remained fully persuaded that the King was a great one for peace. In that instant, the wise reflection that I have encountered in the cited letter of Your Excellency came much to mind, of Spain being an estate from which England extracts the fruits, and appropriating it myself I told him that this Country, having a real interest that ours should flourish through the lucrative trade that it [England] had with it, ought to contribute to prolonging the tranquility that we enjoyed; which in my understanding depended on the British King. He showed me he firmly believed it using this expression himself [:] It would be of benefit to England that for each man there is in Spain there were thousand [men]. After a short pause, he asked me if I knew how Your Excellency thought on the matter of the Americans, adding for me that it was said now to be a sure thing that Doctor Franklin was going to Madrid, and that if [this] was true he would believe that a man so astute would not undertake such a journey without the certainty of being very well received. I responded that Your Excellency longed no less for the continuation of peace than the King our Sovereign; that I did not doubt [that] whatever proposals that should have its prolongation as their objective would be very pleasing to [Your Excellency]; that I knew that [Your Excellency] wanted to contribute with all his force so that his fellow citizens might experience the greatest benefits that can result from it [peace]; that I could all but assure him that this Ministry would find Your Excellency very ready to work to ensure that the colonists yield themselves up to due obedience; and that as concerned to Doctor Franklin perhaps one would not want to deny him entrance to Spain if only because he was a man of wisdom, whose works grant such honor to the Republic of Letters, and whose reputation is so firmly set in that Kingdom. I told him in addition to this that certain as his journey to Madrid was supposed to be, England would be able to take advantage of it, notifying to our Court, so that through its means the general Congress of Philadelphia should come to know how far the King was from breaking with this Nation, and how much he would celebrate the reconciliation between the Colonies, and England; to which he made no answer but to tell me that it would be felt deeply if the trip to Madrid of the indicated Franklin should be confirmed, because it would produce a great ferment in this Country, where there is no one whose eyes are not open regarding our conduct vis-à-vis the Americans.

This was followed by giving him to understand that the present situation of this Monarchy, the increase of the national debt, the interruption of its shipping, and the sizeable decline of its manufactured goods was not hidden from the King, to which he responded to me that nobody knew better than he the damages [wrought by] the current war; and switching then from that matter he confided to me they wrote to him from Paris, that our Treaty with Portugal was now arranged; by virtue of which we ceded the Island of Santa Catalina, and preserved forever the Colony of Sacramento. I expressed the greatest thanks for his confidence, at the same time offering him the thought that this itself should serve as proof to England of the King's preference for a partial peace to all the advantages that he could draw from a war, since at the moment at which his armaments encounter no obstacle to advance his triumphs he renounces the enormous benefits that they could obtain for him in order to avoid shedding the blood of humankind, and to allow those [benefits] of peacefulness to bring enjoyment to his vassals, on which [point] he agreed.

Upon bidding him farewell I told him that I would not speak to any of Secretaries of State about the ideas that I had confided to him for not having instructions to make them any proposal; and only if [at] some time it should be furnished to me to see Lord North, I would communicate my thinking to him, remembering that two years ago he told me, in the Palace, that following the tenets of the sage Minister Walpole, who in the Council of State always expressed it to be very advisable for this Kingdom to distance itself from war with Spain, he would try to preserve peace with us to the extent that he could. He put an end to the conversation praising Lord North's way of thinking, and assuring me to depart persuaded that the measures that I had proposed to him would be utterly effective in perpetuating peace between two Monarchies, and in removing any notion of lack of confidence.

I do not doubt that Lord Mansfield will have given an account to this sovereign of what passed between us, but it is not easy for me to ascertain what the results will be. It is likely that if they should be as we desire he [Lord Mansfield] will seek me out to continue [pursuing] the matter. For now, nothing remains for me but to wait some days, and to go afterwards to pay him a visit of friendship at his country house in order to see how he explains himself.

I will also try to find some pretext to approach Lord North, with whom it is very difficult to speak at length because of the many, and grave, affairs that he has under his watch. He is a man of very good intentions, quite candid, and nobody has a greater personal interest in the preservation of peace, nor in the subjugation of the insurgents, since his difficulties in locating funds to continue the war grow as a consequence of the little progress that the English Army is making in America. It was he with whom the Minister Plenipotentiary of France, Mister Francés,[130] dealt during the tricky negotiations over the Malvinas, and in his abilities, and good heart were evidenced those qualities, which could not be found in the hard manner, and guardedness of Lord Weymouth. Knowing that I should not show great interest in getting these Ministers to adopt my proposals and above all that I should endeavor that they consider them purely as an effect of my good intentions that the present harmony between Spain and England be continued, I will proceed with supreme care and prudence in this negotiation, but, grounding its success only on the superior clarity of mind of Your Excellency I beg of you that you be so kind as to continue [offering] them to me, with which I shall assure a prudent decision.

Though meaning to explain clearly what transpired in the cited conversation I [know I] have been too vague in this letter, that the Captain of the Spanish mail boat San Sebastián, which will not be delayed in setting sail, is carrying to Bilbao. I hope that attending to my good wish Your Excellency will understand [the good intention] and that you will remain convinced that I will take great care in assuring in this [case], as in any other affair, my zeal on behalf of service to His Majesty. May God keep Your Excellency many years as I desire. London, 3 October 1777.

>Most Excellent Sir
>I kiss the hands of Your Excellency your most humble and trustworthy servant.
>Francisco Escarano

Document 37
Legajo, 2596, Santo Domingo, AGI
Robert Morris and William Smith[131] to Bernardo de Gálvez, York in Pennsylvania, 24 October 1777, no. 169
[Main letter, four pages]
Original in Spanish[132]

Sir:

On the 12th of last June, we had the honor, through Captain Jaime Le Mere, to direct to Your Excellency the same letter that is contained in the copy attached to this letter, in which Your Excellency is referred to what we are requesting. Of course, we have been gladdened to receive your letter on the 22nd of last June, but it is our misfortune that in this place [York][133] to which we have been obliged to withdraw, there is not a single person well enough versed in the Spanish language who can produce a correct translation of it. Nevertheless, we have gathered from it, and from the letter of Mr. Pollock,[134] the part regarding the supplies that they had advised us needed to be sent from Spain, for our use, [which] had arrived in New Orleans, and that others would arrive monthly.

Recognizing that Your Excellency is in charge of them, and will deliver them on our request, we therefore take the liberty of including for Your Excellency a certification signed by the President of the Congress, which will make clear the business that has been commissioned for us to administer. And since it is not our intention to divert you from your own affairs, and motivated, so far as possible, to cause you the least amount of difficulty, we have employed Mr. Oliver Pollock, who resides in New Orleans, to serve as our agent, and we instructed him to charter or purchase ships suited for transporting these supplies along the coast, until whenever they can reach one of our ports or estuaries where they can be unloaded, and he has been advised to consult with Your Excellency on this matter, and we request your favorable attention to protecting him [as well as] guide him in all that is appropriate, and [in] protecting our ships and cargoes that Mr. Pollock has reason to request.

We find ourselves compelled to further extend our requests, likewise asking you, should he need it, to furnish money to him [Pollock] to underwrite the costs and expenses that may arise in transporting the goods. Pollock issued receipts for what is given to him for these deliveries, and we shall repay them in full value through our Agent at the court of Spain.

We do not know if perhaps you will find yourself already informed of this in order to provide similar supplies, but whatever the case, we are very sure that in all that is transacted in this, it will henceforth have your approval. We should not be subject to this or any other necessity if our ports were open and able to make shipments of flour as before. But, at present, the English warships are so numerous and so strong along our coasts that they have effectively blocked all the ports from where the shipment of flour could take place. Nevertheless, we have formed a plan, and we are executing it, for it is probable our enemies will find another objective in which to make use of many of their ships. And when this is confirmed, we will embrace with pleasure the opportunity of sending supplies of flour to New Orleans, [if] informed in advance that there is a need for them.

The campaign was opened in this area as well as in the north, about which we lately wrote, and it continues with more intensity. Many battles have been won and lost by both sides, but at the present General Howe and the Royalists are in possession of the city of Philadelphia, which has caused us to be here [in York], but they have not been able to bring their ships up to this city, since we possess the forts and passes of the river.

General Washington has the city surrounded and will soon force them, because of hunger, to abandon it, and then he will attack them, and we have every reason to believe that he will emerge victorious. In the north, we have had the most favorable fortune, since all the battles between Burgoyne and our General Gates have ended in our favor, and we have just received news that they have heard of the complete surrender of Burgoyne, with his entire army [taken] as prisoners of war through capitulation.[135] So now we have no enemies to inconvenience us in those parts. General Gates can rapidly reinforce General Washington, and, as we have related, there is very little doubt that the campaign will conclude in our favor, and that in the end we shall be able to establish that liberty that we so justly deserve to enjoy.

We are Your Excellency's
Most obedient servants,
Roberto Morris and Guillermo Smith

P.S. The notice of Burgoyne's surrender is confirmed, and we have his capitulation in hand.

This is a copy translated from the original.

Bernardo de Gálvez

Document 38
Legajo 4612, Estado, AGS
The Count of Aranda to the Count of Floridablanca, Paris, 26 November 1777, no. 1178
[Note with an earlier date written before the main letter, one page]
Original in Spanish
San Lorenzo el Real,[136] 23 October 1777
To the Count of Aranda (by expedited mail)

With number 11

Remitting various documents that give evidence of seizures made by the Americans prejudicial to the Spanish; that the King has been much offended and suspended the consignment of money that he was going to give them; that he spoke about this in all seriousness.

With number 12

That this mailing is dispatched believing he [Aranda] is back in Paris.

[Main letter, twelve pages]
Original in Spanish

Most Excellent Sir

My Very Good Sir:

In Your Excellency's communiqué of October 23rd that Don Ignacio Heredia received in my absence, numbers 2 and 11, which deal with matters pertaining to the Americans, in which are expressed the King's intentions to effectively help them, and in this His Majesty explains himself as justifiably offended by the excess committed by an Insurgent corsair seizing the French ship *La Fortunée* with a cargo of goods destined for Cádiz's market, solely for the reason of being English, and coming from those ports.

His Majesty ordered me to make the appropriate explanation to this Court; and Don Ignacio Heredia immediately fulfilled the task, with a copy of Your Excellency's letter that he delivered to His Lord, the Count of Vergennes.[137] The King likewise desired that I make the

Representatives understand that we want not only the restitution for the seizure with full compensation for the damages caused, but also some effective measures [taken] so that similar assaults are avoided in the future.

To comply with this part, after I returned, I called on Mr. Grand, the recognized spokesman, as Your Excellency knows. I communicated to him what needed to be [done], and, of course, he expressed to me how Franklin, Deane, and Lee felt about it, His Lord, the Count of Vergennes, having made the occurrence known to them and the total displeasure of the Catholic King. He [Grand] followed by passing along my explanation, and its requirements, to said Representatives, and returned on the following day to convey to me on their behalf the most submissive disposition toward what could satisfy His Majesty and aid in preventing similar disturbances from being repeated.

Mr. Grand assured me that on the first opportunity they will write to Congress for the restitution of the seized cargo, and compensation for their damages, and also that it [the Congress] should with the utmost rigor impel the corsairs [to observe] due moderation; and, still more, and insofar as possible, to remedy the situation they would right away transmit to their commercial agents in the different European ports an order, to be made known to all the American ships that might arrive, so as to instruct and advise that they should caution other vessels of their own Nation that they encounter about the conduct that they should observe, in order not to fall into actions of this kind.

On one of these past days Mr. Grand brought me a rough draft of a Memorial that the Representatives planned to pass on to me to direct to my Court in satisfaction for what had occurred to make clear their sentiments, and offering to undertake whatever should be feasible for them as evidence of their respect for the Bourbon Sovereigns. I asked him if His Lord, the Count of Vergennes, had seen it, and answered that he had not, I told him that he should take the same step with His Excellency (Vergennes) of showing it [the Memorial] to him, and that what His Lord, the Count of Vergennes, should approve or make corrections to, would be equally my verdict.

On the 21st I was in Versailles and asked His Lord, the Count of Vergennes, if the banker Grand had complied with my recommendation to show him the Memorial put forward by the Representatives, telling him at that same moment that I left it up to what His Excellency should settle on, and he assured me that, yes, [Grand had indeed done so], having also warned him that they [the Representatives] should suppress the proposal that they had made, [and] that, bearing the seized cargo, their corsairs should openly enter the ports of both Crowns, and that the Admiralties should, of course, duly judge those seizures that were made and those that were undertaken outside of the current rules, because to admit the ship owners outright with [their] seizures was to authorize their privateering; and for the Admiralties to take notice by themselves of those [seized cargos] that might be introduced [into the ports], they did not need the permission or consent of the Insurgents.

Mr. Grand came back to see me, and having agreed that I received the indicated Memorial through His Lord, the Count of Vergennes, he has brought me the one that I attach for Your Excellency.

Mr. Lee has been to see me to let me know that he had received letters of credentials from Congress that authorize him to deal directly with Spain and consulted with me about whether he should be off personally to provide such notice. I responded to him that in no way should he do so, for the reasons that earlier applied,[138] and because it was sufficient that my Court simply know of it in case of some necessity.

In the different conversations that I have had with His Lord, the Count of Vergennes, he has explained to me about the King's not cutting his aid as indicated in No. 11 because France had already agreed [to provide] three million pounds in one year in four installments of 750,000 every three months, and having said to me that he had already has written about it to that Ambassador of France, through him Your Excellency will know more precisely the terms in which this Ministry explains its position.

With this motive, we have spoken of the content of letter number 2 and have rectified the error that I observed in it, and also in the Memorial [that was the] answer that on October 17th Your Excellency forwarded to that Ambassador, of having on our part contributed two million *reales*, since they were actually four million. His Lord, the Count of Vergennes, had been persuaded that it was a carelessness of the pen, as His Excellency detected it.

On the 21st, led on by the conversation, His Lord, the Count of Vergennes, ended up confiding to me that the emissary of this Court was about to depart, being made to go in a packet boat without a suspicious cargo as if it was heading to the Island of Miquelon,[139] so that from this route he was to be left on the coast and could arrive without hindrance.

He showed me two instructions that he [the emissary] had to carry, one concerning his conduct with those General States, the other about the particular matter of trade that it would be beneficial to enter into for France's utility. He read to me the first but not the second.

In the [first] one it says that it is to be made known only to the main members of the Congress, entrusting them to uphold the greatest discretion with the public. That he has to attempt to persuade them not to be subdued by the English, because they would later place them in a form of slavery. That if by means of a peaceful resolution they could get the English to recognize their independence, they would never have to concede them prerogatives,[140] nor preferences in trade, or enter into some offensive or defensive alliance with them. Because if it were so, the colonies would lose the attractive objective of trading with the Bourbon Crowns, and in an indirect way they would remain reduced and pinned down to English trade alone, so that while recognized as free in name, they would not be in substance. That the great interest of the Colonies at the time of making peace with the English will be asking for the guarantee of the Bourbon Crowns. Because the British Crown, remaining in possession of Florida, Nova Scotia, and Canada, entrapping the new State from its two flanks, they will come to see when they should least think it, that England's rights were revived, and that their opportunity was lost [with] England taking advantage for its own purposes.

This is the substance of the general instruction for the emissary's handling, and I observed by a side-glance that the other one on trade was quite lengthy. By taking a certain tack, I introduced into the discussion the [subject of] the type of trade that we could engage in with them and that the trade from Spain was more difficult to arrange because of its possessions contiguous with the Colonies, when France's Islands were at a certain distance, [and] that they would only serve a port of call or storage.

His Lord, the Count of Vergennes, told me that, according to their ideas and temperament, the colonies would establish themselves as an agricultural State, without dedicating themselves to a manufacturing and craft industry, except for what was required for their daily needs. That on this footing Spain would be able to harness from them the products of the soil from that vast extension of land, and supplies of cod, because unlike France, Spain did not have a cod fishing industry; that during years of a shortage of grain in Spain, we would have that recourse for our peninsula, and for the American Provinces that need it; and since I perceived that he was trying to avoid the topic when addressing the articles pertinent to France, and even on those pertaining to Spain, [and] spoke evasively about the others, I desisted from making him uncomfortable.

In my private judgment, I do not agree with some of His Lord, the Count of Vergennes's, propositions, as herein recounted.

It is assumed in the instruction of conduct and matters that the emissary has to address that the British Crown can remain in possession of Florida, Nova Scotia, and Canada. Well, I consider it a difficulty if England does not hasten to concur in total independence and recognize the free States with the end of retaining the said possessions; because if the Americans come to destroy the English land forces, they will without losing time not stop at occupying them, adding to their confederation, and they must act accordingly, in order to forever be free of troubles.

Nor do I agree in that independent Colonies will confine themselves to being a State for farming, since they are populated with so many Europeans, who are bringing there the crafts introduced from the beginning by fine European workers.

I have an opinion as well on the business of fishing that France flatters herself on retaining in those seas of Newfoundland if the English should be thrown out of Canada, and I will only be in agreement [with Vergennes] in the event that they should manage to last; because the Colonies, not linked beforehand by a treaty [concluded] during their time of troubles, and coming to see themselves as removed from those, their enemies, expelled from the Continent, and in view of such an interesting object [such as fishing] in the seas of their own house, it could be that the element of a guarantee is not so valuable to them, believing that it is no longer necessary, and that the attraction of a total interest in a sector [fishing], which sooner or later Europe can obtain from their hands alone, comes to prevail.

I have expressed in several occasions in my correspondence that France does not think about anything else but the augmentation and extension of its commerce, because France believes herself to be possessed of such wealth, and to be abundant of so many items of industry, that they will always surpass and triumph over the balance, despite the goods that she takes in because she lacks them, such as tobacco, timber, linen, hemp, indigo, etc., and in my opinion [France] trusts that either with a treaty or without it she would continue as a natural and needed partner of the Colonies and would quickly accustom and cement them in their reciprocal trade.

May God keep Your Excellency many years.
Paris
26 November 1777
Most Excellent Sir
I kiss the hand of Your Excellency
Your Trustworthy Servant
The Count of Aranda
[to] His Excellent Lord, the Count of Floridablanca

Three attached documents[141]

[Attachment A]
Legajo 4612-156, Estado, AGS[142]
Memorial of Benjamin Franklin, Silas Deane, and Arthur Lee, Paris, 23 November 1777, no. 4612-156

[Main document, three pages]
Original in English[143]

 The Commissioners from the United States of America are extremely concerned to understand that the Courts of Spain and France are offended with said States, on account of the Taking of the French ship *Fortune* by an American Privateer, which ship was bound from England to Cadiz, and is represented to have had Spanish Property on board. The Commissioners are confident that nothing can be more distant from the Intention of the said States, than that their Subjects should profit by making such Prizes (as they have no War with those Nations but consider them as real Friends) and have moreover the greatest personal Respect for their most Christian and Catholic Majesties, with the strongest Desire of meriting and cultivating their Friendship. The Purpose of the Congress in commissioning armed Vessels, as well as the Measures taken in their several States by establishing Courts of Admiralty to prevent or remedy irregular Captures (in which Courts all Prizes brought there are to Suffer a regular Trial) appears on the Face of the Commissions granted, an authentic Copy whereof is hereunto annexed.[144] By which Commission also it will appear that the Congress have not authorized any Act that may be contrary to the Law of Nations. The Commissioners tho' they have no

Concern or Correspondence with the Captain who took the Prize in question, are of Opinion, that knowing it to be a Practice with the English Merchants to cover their Property in Ships bound to Spain under the Names of Spanish Subjects, he might conceive the Goods consigned to Cadiz from London in the *Fortune* were of that kind; and that it was therefore right to have a Trial on them by sending the Ship to Boston, where it is not doubted but that the Ship will be Discharged and her Freight and Damages Paid, as belonging to France, and the Goods reclaimed or their Value on the Proofs appearing that they belong to the Subjects of Spain, be delivered to the Claimers. By this means only the Irregularities and Inconveniences of such Captures (which in no War can possibly be entirely prevented) will be rectified and remedied. And in this Confidence the Commissioners hope the Displeasure conceived against their Country on the present Occasion will subside, and that the United States will obtain and preserve the Favour of their Catholic and most Christian Majesties which of all things is most earnestly desired. They also Submit it to consideration whether the Appointment of an Agent or Consul to reside in America, and take care of the Interests of the Merchants of these Nations, by making Reclamations where necessary, and Supporting such Claims in the Courts of Justice, would not be useful, not only in obtaining more speedy Justice but in preserving that good Intelligence between the People of the different Countries which may be advantageous to all. To prevent Misunderstandings for the future, we propose to write immediately to the Congress, acquainting them with this Transaction, and urging them to give strict Orders to all who act under their Commissions to respect the Flags of every neutral or Friendly Power, under severe Penalties for Disobedience. And in the mean time we shall recommend it to our Correspondents at the several Ports, to warn the Captains of American armed Vessels to conduct themselves as if such Orders were already given.

    Paris, November 23rd, 1777
    [signed] B. Franklin
    Silas Deane
    Arthur Lee

[Attachment B]
Legajo 4612-157, Estado, AGI, undated
Congressional document signed by John Hancock[145]

[One printed page]
Original in English

    IN CONGRESS. The DELEGATES of the United States of New-Hampshire, Massachusetts-Bay, Rhode-Island, Connecticut, New-York, New-Jersey, Pennsylvania, Delaware, Maryland, Virginia, North-Carolina, South-Carolina, and Georgia, TO ALL unto whom there Present shall come, SEND GREETING—KNOW YE,[146]

    THAT We have granted, and these Presents do grant, License and Authority to [blank] Mariner, Commander of the [blank] called the [blank] of the Burthen of [blank] Tons or thereabouts, belonging to [blank] mounting [blank] Carriage Guns, and navigated by [blank] Men, to fit out and set forth the said [blank] in a warlike Manner, and by and with the said [blank] and the Crew thereof, by Force of Arms, to attack, subdue and take all Ships and other Vessels whatsoever carrying Soldiers, Arms, Gunpowder, Ammunition, Provisions, or any other contraband Good to any of the British Armies or Ships of War employed against these United States. And also to attack, seize and take all Ships or other Vessels that belong to the Inhabitants of Great-Britain, or to any Subject or Subjects thereof, with their Tackle, Apparel, Furniture and Ladings, on the High Seas, or between high and low-water Marks, (the Ships or Vessels, together with their Cargoes, belonging to any Inhabitant or Inhabitants of Bermuda, Providence and the Bahaman Islands, and such other Ships and Vessels bringing Persons with Intent to settle and reside within any of the United States, or bringing Arms, Ammunition, Warlike Stores to the said States for the Use thereof, which said Ships or Vessels you shall suffer to pass unmolested, the Commanders thereof permitting a peaceable Search and giving satisfactory Information of the Contents of the Ladings and Destination of the Voyages, only excepted.) And the said Ships or Vessels so apprehended as aforesaid, and as Prize taken, to carry into any Port or Harbour within the Dominions of any neutral State willing to admit the same, or into any Port with the said United States, in Order that the Courts there instituted to hear and determine Causes Civil and Maritime, may proceed in due Form to condemn the said Captures, if they be adjudged lawful Prize, or otherwise according to the Usage of such Cases at the Port or in the State where the same shall be carried. The said [blank] having given-Bond, with sufficient Sureties, that Nothing be done by the said [blank] or any of his Officers, Marines or Company thereof contrary to or inconsistent with the Usage and Customs of Nations, and that he shall not excel or transgress the Powers and Authorities contained in this Commission. And we will require all our Officers whatsoever in the Service of the United States to give Succour and Assistance to the said [blank] in the Premises. This Commission shall continue in Force until the Congress shall issue Orders to the contrary.

    DATED at [blank]
    By Order of the Congress,
    ATTEST, Cha Thomson [signed]   John Hancock [signed]
    President

[Attachment C, preliminary letter, two pages]
Legajo 4612-158I
Letter [Floridablanca] to the Count of Aranda, main letter, rough draft, 9 December 1777
[Preliminary letter, two pages; main letter, five pages][147]
Original in Spanish

Excellent Sir:
    Your Excellency has directed your letter numbered 1178 of the 26th of November to points pertaining to the Anglo-American Colonies, and I am going to answer it after having informed the King of the various matters that it contains and after receiving his Royal orders with respect to each point.
    His Majesty has found very appropriate how Your Excellency has dealt with Mr. Grand, the intermediary for the American Representatives, concerning the restitution of the French ship *La Fortunée*, with commerce from Cádiz and seized by an insurgent corsair for the sole reason of coming from an English port with English goods.
    By virtue of the offers made to Your Excellency by these Representatives to write immediately to the Congress for the restitution for the seizure and redress of all damages, the measures that they are going to take to prevent assaults of the same kind from occurring in the future, the sentiment they have expressed, their compliant inclination to

do whatever might satisfy His Majesty, and the confirmation of these intentions in the document that they delivered to Your Excellency and you remit to me, His Majesty stands completely satisfied, and approves Your Excellency's acceptance of the Memorial, after coming to previous agreement [on accepting the Memorial] by Your Excellency, [and] after coming to previous agreement [on accepting the Memorial] with His Lord, the Count of Vergennes.

Your Excellency should now make manifest to the Representatives, for their ease, that their deference and decisive stand have earned the favor of His Majesty, just as the offense of the corsair caused him great displeasure, [and] that it is necessary that they recommend to Congress that it act firmly in seeing that its ship owners[148] comply with orders to respect the Spanish flag and in no way disturb its Commerce as His Majesty will not be able to tolerate the contrary, and in the present case, leaving aside the prompt restitution and full redress of all damages, for which His Majesty will not desist, they will experience as they have up until now the continuance of the results of the true generosity and compassion with which his magnanimous heart looks on them, and of which they will see no shortage of efficacious proof.

Your Excellency is to express the foregoing in all its aspects for His Lord, the Count of Vergennes, for his edification.

[The following paragraph is written in the left-hand margin.]

Purely as guidance for Your Excellency alone, I will tell you that the King's intention in whatever aid he provides to the Americans is to not bind himself with promises or contracts, due to many considerations that bear both on his [own] honor and on politics, linking all of the current circumstances in Europe with our interests and the situation of our commercial pursuits.

[end of marginal note]

His Majesty is informed of Mr. Lee's having received official letters from the Congress that authorize him [to proceed] directly to Spain, and he approves of the response that Your Excellency gave to his suggestion that he would personally come to present his credentials to the Spanish Court, since if he had come, not only would His Majesty neither have allowed him to be heard nor permitted him to deal with any matter at all, but he would have made him leave, [because] no American Representative needs to reside here,[149] in order that His Majesty continue [providing] his protection to the Americans.

Your Excellency demonstrates your conscientious accuracy in [your] report about the instruction that is being carried by the emissary whom that Court sent to the Colonies, according to what His Lord, the Count of Vergennes, has read [to you] in part relating to its [the French Court's] conduct with those General States, although Vergennes did not entrust anything to you pertaining to the particular commerce that it would be suitable to establish for the good of France. His Majesty values the observations Your Excellency makes clarifying this news and orders me to respond to you with the news that another emissary has already been sent from whose general instructions for conducting himself are largely in agreement with those that the French emissary is taking.

Document 39
Legajo 4612, Estado, AGS
Extract of a letter from the Count of Vergennes to the Count of Montmorin,[150] 2 January 1778, no. 199
[Two pages]
Original in French

    I still have not, My Lord, been able to receive the King's orders regarding Spain's response and therefore am not in a position to inform you of His Majesty's decision. However, meanwhile I send to you the result of our deliberations. I believe that I must inform you that the Court of London is redoubling its activity and its entreaties with the American representatives. A Moravian[151] leader named Huston [sic] has just arrived on their behalf; [he is] a very wise man, an intimate friend of Mr. Franklin, and highly esteemed by the King of England. This new emissary had a secret meeting of more than an hour with His British Majesty before leaving London. Since his arrival he has had a first meeting with his friend that lasted more than two hours, and they are to have a second meeting tomorrow. Franklin alone was present; his colleagues were not invited along.[152] It is not through the Americans that I am informed of these facts; [rather] they came to my knowledge through an indirect source on whose trustworthiness I can rely. I request of you, My Lord, that you communicate these developments to His Lord, the Count of Floridablanca. I am refraining from adding any reflections to them; this Ministry is sufficiently enlightened to figure out all that of which that they give evidence, and to perceive their weight.

Document 40

Legajo 3884, Estado, AHN
(Floridablanca) to the Count of Aranda, El Pardo, Spain,[153] 13 January 1778, no. 69
[Summary note, one page, expedited mail]
Original in Spanish

The Count of Aranda (by Expedited Mail) with no. 1

Esteemed Sir:

Going into many reflections to deduce that we still do not find ourselves at the point of going to war and expounding various cases and doubts not only for that venture but also for the results or consequences.

Here are the 16 questions that the King termed the catechism; and at the end of the tenth one, Gibraltar, Menorca, etc. are expressly asked about. Look for the cold responses that they gave us, [which are] with the one that is missing.[154]

[Main letter, twenty-two pages]
Original in Spanish

Most Excellent Sir:

In my letter of the 23rd of December of the year just passed, directed to Your Excellency through the expedited mail that this Embassy of France dispatched, I set forth at length for Your Excellency the King's view, so that without abandoning or displeasing the American Colonists, we could take some time for ourselves during which we could see the position that England was adopting. We should [thus] have more clarity about their designs and could make our decisions without rushing.

Through subsequent news and through the information that Your Excellency communicates to us in your last letter of the 28th of the same month of December, we see that the English Ministry and

Parliament have also taken time to formulate their ideas, and that meanwhile their dealings and attempts to adjust themselves to the Colonies revolve around the motive of saving the sovereignty of the Mother Country and the navigation acts,[155] and sugarcoating these pretensions with soft and even ambiguous words.

In the same letter of Your Excellency the maneuverings of the two Court parties are unerringly referred to and the opposition argued by Dr. Bencroft [sic][156] to implement an adjustment with the Americans by means of three members of the same opposition whose news coincides with the direct notices that have come to us from London that, with the current Ministry being assured of its permanence by his British Majesty, it is wisely trying to compromise the said Members in a plan of adjustment that, by not taking effect, disillusions the Nation and will embroil it [the Ministry] in another Campaign, which that Monarch wishes to do to test fortune.

However, all this notwithstanding, since His Majesty wants to use the time that he judged we ought to take to be forewarned for whatever can happen and [because] the examination that is intended to be done in London on February 2nd, regarding the position which that Court finds it convenient to take, is already approaching. His Majesty had deemed it indispensable that, by means of Your Excellency, I get explanations from that Ministry [the French] about the various cases that can transpire if matters in England become curtailed. In this way, we may proceed in common agreement in all affairs, forming a plan beforehand and setting in order the means of bringing it to due effect with the assurances and preparations that correspond to it so as to promise a gratifying result.

Since these cases, more or less urgent or possible, can be many, as well as the points that we must tie together, it is His Majesty's will that I explain them with plain frankness without concealing any of our ideas, objectives, or apprehensions, which becomes the close friendship and union of the two Courts, and the mutual trust both of them must manifest in all their designs, situations, and possibilities, believing that nothing is lost by having it all foreseen and communicated, although not everything can be accomplished or prevented.

1. Assuming that the present English Ministry lasts[157] and that it contemplates undertaking another campaign against the

American Colonists, it behooves us to examine and agree whether it is advisable to divert it from such a project with negotiations and preemptive measures. Or, to the contrary, whether it is better and more prudent to let it so engage itself and to curtail our notions of sustaining the Colonists themselves with secret aid, offering only not to abandon them provided they do not give us ground to suspect that they are trying to adjust their position without our knowledge and join with our enemies to work against us.

2. My aforementioned letter of the 23rd of December made cursory mention of the case in which we would see the British Ministry changing and persons antagonistic to our Courts moving into it, and who, because of their character, past experiences, or from the measures they are seen to take, must arouse suspicion of a rupture. And, for such an occurrence, and after having explained ourselves circumspectly to the Court of London, it also behooves us to resolve whether we should initiate and carry out our negotiations with vigor for some agreement with the Colonies.

3. To come to this conclusion in the case that was just cited, the notices and instructions that the [American] Representatives resident in Paris have asked for from their Leaders in Congress would be needed, in order not to expose ourselves to dealing with individuals who do not rely on competent guidance, credit, or faculties based on the present state of the Colonies themselves. We wish to know if this can wait or if the said Representatives in Paris have already sent formal proposals to the Congress, as reported.

4. In addition to what has been referred to, one should consider it will also be in keeping with good policy to wait, to whatever extent the urgency allows, the notices of our emissaries who find themselves among the Colonists; so that among ourselves we have a morally assured knowledge of the state of those affairs and of what we will be able to count on regarding to the fidelity and forces of said Provinces,

[The letter continues here in different, more careful script, which is tiny and very neat.]

according to the negotiations that they have entered into with their Mother Country, the parties and propensities that might prevail there, and the advantages or interests they expect from one and another.

5. Since, during this negotiation, war can break out or, because the English might penetrate or suspect our dealings, or for any other reason, it is just and necessary to agree on the precautions and the Plan that we shall make to defend ourselves, and inflict harm on our enemies in any anticipated action, with specific measures that will have to be taken as of now. Concerning these preparations, we hope to be enlightened, since we must be suspicious and avoid evil consequences as much as we can.

6. Having to include in our defense the safe return of both the fleet and the land forces and sea forces that are coming from Buenos Aires,[158] it is deemed necessary to take some resolution to stop our enemies from delivering a fatal blow. We must determine whether we have to send out Fleets of greater strength than the English to defend those two targets. We must decide upon the number of vessels each Court will furnish, and at what time and place, combining and ordering their operations. Or, if another idea is preferable that can distract and occupy our enemies, so that it makes it impossible for them to attend to defending themselves and assaulting us at one and the same time.

7. Of course, there are other main targets that must be protected from an all-out invasion, such as the islands of Santo Domingo, Martinique, Puerto Rico, the Plaza of Havana, and the Coast of the Province of Caracas, without naming now many other places that the English could be thinking of. It is therefore incumbent on us to agree on and to know how and with what naval and land forces we will try to cover those sites from America to Europe, setting in place the preventive measures that we must undertake without losing time, or abandoning the rest of the targets indicated in the preceding article. We should always have our sights focused on the possible case that England wishes to avail herself of her troops and warships stationed in the American Colonies for an invasion against us that begins to take effect before reports have arrived over here, the credible suspicion of which [would] demand taking active and vigorous resolutions well beforehand to forestall it.

8. If we should have time to arrange a treaty with the Colonists, and without violating its secret, can designate the moment for its declaration or publication, it becomes necessary to arrange it now,

when this can be verified, making for the purpose a prudent calculation of the time when it shall be employed in taking and effecting all the measures and precautions conducive of assuring the return of the Fleet and Expedition from Buenos Aires, along with the **defense**----------------[159]

[Here the manuscript returns to the original handwriting.]

of the islands and important posts of the Spanish and French Nations. Regarding the fleet and forces of our southern America, we doubt that we can, until the month of July, count on having them in our Ports.[160]

Consequently, it will be necessary to formulate and agree on a plan about the manner and substance in which we must deal with the Colonists [and] what the terms of their alliance has to be, whether purely defensive or offensive as well, [and] if it will be better and more proper to call it protection and that the protecting Crowns stipulate not to abandon them while they are not recognized as an independent state. Also, what aid has to be given and received and whether specified or unspecified and what advantages would Spain have or compensation for the damages and expenses that she has to suffer, once trade with the Colonists, through our situation, relations, and Treaties, cannot serve her at all.[161]

9. It is equally necessary, when the time comes for the publication or declaration, to have thought about what we have to do and what plan of war we will follow that is useful to the two Nations and that preserves or, if possible, augments the glory of their arms. France will be able to indicate the objectives that she has so as to combine with ours, and gradually assemble the scale of the operations. The interruption or extinction of the English commerce can be an objective of the greatest importance for the Nation, and this fruit will be attained merely with the act of precipitating the war and making it last. But such an interruption is of no utility for us, never being able to dispute or compete for the advantages of trade with England, or with France herself. That Power [France] can also think about the conquest of the

English Isles or the greater [advantage] of a strong and free fishing [presence] in Newfoundland. Spain herself has no further objectives than to recover the humiliating usurpations of Gibraltar and Menorca, and to expel from the Gulf of Mexico, the Bay of Honduras, and the Coast of Campeche some settlers who cause her endless trouble. Therefore, it is necessary to agree on where we will begin and if it will be convenient for us to go about it separately rather than jointly, reciprocally supporting the undertaking and distraction by one ally through the plans of the other, [and] on which particular the number of forces that each one has to employ and the time or moment to act should similarly be determined.

10. Since all of this Plan cannot be executed in its different parts without counting on the aid that the Colonists will be able to give us, even though it be only the diversion of forces, it is opportune to consider whether they have to be entrusted, singly or not, with our ideas, and what things have to be demanded of them, specifically so that they help bring them about, and to know what risks can befall us from this candidness and communication of our secrets to People who have so many relations of Nationality, kinship, and even interests with Great Britain.

11. It is likewise behooves the two Courts to know, by a prudent rule, the number of campaigns that each will be able to undertake and both to agree on this point and on what is called for to be done to fulfill it, in their respective efforts. Otherwise, it would not be easy to attain the objectives that we should propose for ourselves for the war that ensues.

12. Considering what has been covered, it will be right to tell ourselves that in the event a rupture between Russians and Turks is confirmed and that the former, either by themselves alone or aided by other Powers, undertake the conquest of the greater part of the Ottoman Empire, especially in Europe, France contemplates finding herself in the condition of taking on everything and not abandoning the commitments to the war that we shall have begun with England. With this foresight we can avoid contingencies, for Spain could then see herself with some loss of her possessions,[162] and see herself obligated to a prejudicial and humiliating peace that we hope a Power as friendly and allied as France, on whom we count and will always count, does not want to allow.[163]

13. We say the same respecting the case in which the eventual succession of Bavaria, or other incidents pertaining to the territories of Germany and Flanders, should oblige that Crown to take part in such quarrels, such as the French Ministry around April of last year in a certain way insinuated to us. For such an affair, then, it will be well for both Allies to be sure of the way in which we conduct ourselves and to not run the risk of an untimely and prejudicial peace with the English.

14. Assuming that the Court of London will not miss any means of seeking distractions for France emanating from the [above mentioned] Continental matters, one wants to know if it would be opportune to anticipate some steps [to be taken] in other Courts, or to sound out the Dutch, who already show themselves discontented with England, so as at least to find resources and avoid fortuitous damages and increasing for said Court [England] the number of its enemies.

15. Finally, for the same purpose we would like to know if it would behoove us to encourage other Princes to take actions to recognize the Independence of the Colonies, even if it were only through demonstrations and events that one provokes. And if the British Cabinet is displeased with the King of Prussia[164] for having impeded the passage of recruits along the Rhine, some move with that Monarchy would be useful unless such a move would be incompatible with other relationships and considerations that the Court of Versailles has to uphold.

We would advance our view about each one of the points expressed if the lack of confidence that we have in our own knowledge did not hold us back. Thus, we draw on that of His Christian Majesty and his enlightened Ministry so that they communicate their own views to us, so that, with those, we can agree to proceed with a common understanding on a matter that is of the most importance to the two Monarchies, because stemming from it the consequences can be so beneficial or so fatal.

[Attachment]
Montmorin to Vergennes, 13 January 1778, no. 198
[Main letter, two pages]
Original in French

Sir:

I have the honor of sending to Your Excellency an extract from the response I received to the letter that I posted to Versailles on the 24th of last month. You will see, My Lord Count that circumstances are becoming more critical with each passing day, and there is little pretense that they are leaving to us the choice of what can be done. We will probably have to take a position or give up taking advantage of the most favorable moment in time that has ever been presented to the house of Bourbon.

Although I still find myself in more or less the same condition, I hope to be able to go on Thursday morning to reaffirm for you, My Lord Count, the assurances of the bond and the high esteem with which I have the honor of being Your Excellency's

most humble and trustworthy servant,
The Count de Montmorin

I enclose here a letter from His Lord, The Duke of Penthièvre,[165] for His Excellency, the Count of Floridablanca.

His Catholic Majesty has the parquet [flooring] that Your Excellency was good enough to permit me to send him through your courier?[166]

Document 41
Legajo 4616-87-I, Estado, AGS
The Count of Aranda to the Count of Floridablanca, Paris, 19 March 1778, no. 87-I
[Main letter, eleven pages]
Original in Spanish

Most Excellent Sir

My Very Good Lord:
    I am going to go on describing to Your Excellency the different matters, which have taken place since [the letter] number 1251 of the 10th of the present up to the first special mail.
    On Thursday, the 12th Monsieur Devergennes showed me the draft of the letter that the Most Christian King had written as part of his mail of the 10th to his uncle the Catholic King, to explain [the pressure of] the situation in which he found himself regarding the Declaration to England without time to consult His Majesty on the step that it was indispensable to take.
    Monsieur Devergennes told me that three mail packets had left in the same hour, one for Madrid, another for London carrying the declaration, and another for Vienna with two objectives, one to communicate to it the cited step taken with England, the other to make it aware of the King of Prussia's requests to this Court: especially the last one resulting from Baron Goltz[167] having received, on Thursday the 5th, mail from his Court in virtue of which he went to Versailles on Friday the 6th and told Monsieur Devergennes that His Prussian Majesty, considering that his alliance could be more secure, and useful to France, than that with the House of Austria, wished to formalize it with this Crown, so much more appropriate for her who could not desist from recognizing the Court of Vienna's ambitions, and France would not want to support it, but rather, cut it off in time. That His Lordship the Count Devergennes replied to him, that since a similar proposal was not awaited, he was not warned to respond to him, and could only tell him that the alliance between Paris and Vienna having been made for prudent reasons, and the reciprocal benefit thus taken into account, the stronger motive now was to maintain the friendship and the close tie that

had ensued between both Families, for which reason he believed it would be inopportune and useless to speak of a similar proposal.

That Baron Goltz, seeing that he found no disposition toward his first point, went on to propose that in the next dispute over the Elector of Bavaria's heritage, France should declare herself neutral; as the Court of Vienna was not in the situation of accepting that his hereditary properties be attacked, because if war came, the King of Prussia wanted nothing of it, but to bow out to protect a Prince of Germany worthy of consideration as the Palatine [168] to whom Vienna's violence had [been] imposed, and threatening him with the risk of greater harms, taking advantage of the superiority of its forces. That His Lordship Devergennes replied, that even though the pretensions of Vienna were not clearly perceived, so that he could assure him, that the Most Christian King professed a warm friendship for the Empress Queen, and would ever be for the observance of their alliance, unless something very odd and arbitrary should happen.

That Baron Goltz expressed to him as [a matter of] surprise that France should count so little on Prussia's King, and not value standing with him at present, beyond the reasons that would apply against the House of Austria, taking into account that France was going to enter into a war with England, which had looked up to the King of Prussia with many requests, and he had refused [it]; but seeing himself discounted he would take another side: that France could reflect, that a deviation of His Prussian Majesty would be awkward for France: that the Court of Petersburg was also in his hand, which [by] entangling itself with the Turk would distract France, who would find herself impeded [in] wanting to come to this one's aid: that the Czarina [sic] could also give assistance to England, that only the King of Prussia could distract her, and the same [with] Denmark. That Monsieur Devergennes replied to him, that His Prussian Majesty was a very enlightened Prince to take part in the disagreement between France and England; that France found itself without funds with which to finance the expenses that His Prussian Majesty should incur by aiding it, and that His Prussian Majesty would indebt himself by indulging a whim, making his troops cross through the Empire to come into the territory of France where he hadn't any claim [to be], it wasn't credible, making in vain all the hardship that would be expended for it: That he didn't understand the aid that the Czarina [sic] would be able to give the British King, since her land Army needed everything [it had] to counteract the Turk.

That Baron Goltz replied, that Russia would give maritime aid to England, and Monsieur Devergennes responded that as concerned ships they did not lack these, and would not make use of the unsatisfactory Russian ones, their having serviceable ones, and owning them: that Goltz replied to him, it would be in sailors, and Monsieur Devergennes countered that neither were the Russians effective for the actions of the English nor did the Czarina [sic] have enough of them to loan them [out], depopulating her country over what those in her very Empire would be clamoring against: that as regards Denmark his ponderings came late, because England had already taken out of her as many sailors as was possible. That Monsieur Devergennes added that if His Prussian Majesty looked to France as a mediator, so that in the current disputes of Germany each interested party should lend itself to desist to the extent possible for the good of peace, in this case France would exert every effort to contribute to a general rapprochement.

Monsieur Devergennes told me that taking this declaration of the King of Prussia as pretext, the good offices of communicating it to the Court of Vienna, and the difficulties in which France was going to find herself, should England take badly the declaration that was made to her; he also added, that the Court of Vienna's determined effort seemed aimed at doubtful acquisitions, that the Empire's chief Princes exposed [the acquisitions] in their writings, characterizing them as voluntary, and forced; for which [reason] France did not consider in this case lending the stipulated aid, nor would she be able to offer it as if she found herself rid of it, when everything was needed to defend herself.

Monsieur Devergennes told me that through the first regular mail he was going to inform Holland of the declaration made to England because they would be very gladdened there; since in addition to the terms in which it was conceived it shielded France from being the aggressor, and as a result freed Holland from granting its stipulated assistance to England, Holland wanted others to begin to recognize the colonies as independent, to facilitate its doing so as well.

Monsieur Devergennes told me that, as soon as London's reply came in, Franklin would present himself at the King's audience, that by agreement of the Ambassador of England with the rest [of the ambassadors] it would not be on Tuesday, nor would he [Franklin] attend the following audiences while Stormond [sic] was there; [but] take further days to speak with Ministers about what might be offered him.

I went to see Monsieur de Maurepas, I found him with Señor de Sartine, and Mister Gerard: this one [Gerard] took himself off, we spoke of the effect [that] the declaration would have in London. About Franklin he indicated the same to me as [had] Monsieur Devergennes.

He told me that Deane had received an order from the Congress to withdraw, believing it was gossip about disagreement among the deputies. That one of the Adams, famous partisans of independence, had come to take his place. That as soon as My Lord Stormond [sic] learned of Deane's withdrawal, believing him [to be] upset, he had begun to work through third parties to win him over so that on his arrival he might be partial to England with the Congress: but considering that [or better in the context, and as] Deane was [a] canny [man], he was given as a gift the portrait of the King in regal garb, as evidence of this Court's satisfaction [with him] during his residence, and that he would carry an official letter from Monsieur Devergennes recommending him to the Congress.

Monsieur de Maurepas asked me if Don Francisco Escarano had written me, that Lord Nugent, one of those who now speaks the most in Parliament, had told him that the effective thing would be to form a union of Spain with England, since this would be true friendship, whereas that of France [would] always [be] costly to Spain for all the family relations there might be. I responded to him that Escarano [had] not told me anything and he repeated, well, so it is, because this one [Nugent] has spoken of it to Noailles, who writes to us [about] it.

Speaking of the new aspect that things [have] taken, and so as to capture the spirit of Monsieur de Maurepas, as well as to unpack his ideas, I said, that if [things] turn out well as appearances indicate, this would be France's epoch of greatest power; for having opened a vast trade with the colonies, of which before it had [been] deprived; with their separation her natural enemy was left much reduced, and with only seeing to it, that it is not undone, France would live calmly, and with an influence as never [before] with the rest of the [Great] Powers; that His Lordship the Count of Maurepas could end his days with glory in leaving France as it had never been: He was very flattered by my compliment, and continuing the discussion told me, that up to 60 battalions would be placed on the coasts, and would form two camps of invasion: I, replying to him that thirty per camp was little, since each one would hardly make up 17 thousand infantrymen, and so would be small Armies to contend alone wherever they might make landing: he answered me that England was undefended; that for appearances they sufficed, and for the blow that he had preplanned, ten thousand would completely manage it. Asking him, what it was, he told me it was to pitch them onto the Isle of

Wight that shelters the Port of Portsmouth, with whose taking this [Port] would be rendered useless, and that establishment could be destroyed: that it was of such consequence for the English to rescue it, that the following day, peace was assured.

This is the only matter of interest that has happened in the interval between my last mail of the 7th of this month up that of today, which I dispatch for the [same] reason that the preceding number entailed.

> May God keep Your Excellency many years. Paris 19 March 1778.
> Most Excellent Sir
> I kiss the hand of Your Excellency
> Your trustworthy servant
> The Count of Aranda

Document 42
Legajo 7000-71, Estado, AGS
Francisco Escarano to the Count of Floridablanca, London, 14 April 1778 (no. 71)
[Main letter, five pages]
Original in Spanish

Most Excellent Sir

Sir:
If by chance Your Excellency's letters corresponding to the 30th of last month end up with our Vice Consul in Calais I am set on dispatching a servant tonight to that port so that he brings them to me, and by this secure means I will inform Your Excellency of the little that I have been able to learn and that seems to me worthy of your attention.

The Ministry has decided to send as soon as possible a squadron of five warships to the East Indies, to be commanded, they say, by Admiral Byron. As a result of this decision the Admiralty has stipulated that two hundred carpenters, to whom a double daily wage is to be paid, are to be employed in repairing the *Burfort*, which is one of the five [warships]; it is not believed, however, that it can be ready within the space of three weeks, as is desired.

Admiral Keppel has gone to Chatham to speed up the arming of the ship *Victory*, and having returned the day before yesterday to London had all his luggage sent off immediately to Portsmouth, from which it is inferred he shan't delay in setting sail.

In Spithead at present there are 31 ships-of-the-line, including two frigates. Because ten of them have provisions for eight months, and [have] their full crew, they find themselves capable of going to any part of America at the first notice. The ship *Protheus* has set off with munitions for Newfoundland.

The Dukes of Devonshire, and of Dorset, as well as these Lords of the high Nobility, among whom are some from the opposition party, have requested that his Sovereign give them command of the Militia Regiments of their respective Provinces, and having conceded it to them they have now kissed the hand of His British Majesty.

At the same time that all these preparations to launch an offensive are observed, defensively there is not the least doubt that the current

Ministers wish to avoid a war with France, if they can preserve the Nation's dignity, whether out of pure Patriotism, or out of private interest, because surely if a new war starts they will not maintain their offices, it being quite ordinary [that] His British Majesty wishes to give the handling of affairs to persons in whom the Nation has some confidence. Lord Chatam [sic] has hardly resettled himself for a short time [than] he has returned to his country house, telling his friends that if the King, his master, thinks that despite his constant ailments he can be of some service in England's current trials he will very gladly sacrifice the little health that remains for him for the benefit of the Fatherland.

The commissioners assigned to deal with the Congress will embark once the wind allows it, which is now much to the opposite. My Lord North has expressed in the House of Commons that he hoped they might for the public's benefit fulfill the charge they carried, but regarding the same, not take too much notice.

I know that even after the Ambassador from France, the Marquis of Noailles,[169] had left here, this Monarch has secretly sent a certain Mister Pultney [sic][170] to deal with Doctor Franklin, and that he has not come back very satisfied with his interviews with that American. This Court is testing out as many ways as are presented to it of reconciling itself with the colonies, and although the Ministers do not wish for now to consent publicly to their independence they will in the end have to recognize them as free, above all if they offer greater advantages to England's trade than to that of the other Nations.

In the past week, there have been several meetings of the leading Catholics, in which Lord Peter [sic][171] has presided, and in consequence of which they have resolved to offer the King their lives, and estates, and to raise at their own cost, if His British Majesty wishes, a Regiment composed entirely of people of our Religion. They curry favor in this way [so] that some privileges will be granted to them, and the penal Laws that exist against them will be revoked, but they certainly curry favor in vain, since neither will this Monarch accept their offer, nor will there be Ministers who dare to advise giving any disposition in their favor, which could never take place without the consent of Parliament. It is Lord Shelburne, known here for [being] as able as [he is] insincere, who has persuaded the stated Lord Peter, and My Lord Surry [sic],[172] first son of the Duke of Norfolk, to join together to deal with the expressed matter, getting them to believe that Lord Jorge Germain,[173]

My Lord Mansfield, My Lord Butte [sic],[174] and other members of the cabinet would sponsor their request, but this is a rope[175] that he has wanted to set on the Ministers to inflame the People against them, in case the Catholics are shown favor.

Parliament's vacation that will last fifteen days more or less, will start tomorrow. Before dismissing itself, the House of Commons has given permission to the Treasury Minister to seek a million and half Pounds Sterling from notes of the Exchequer.[176] Even this sum added to the new loan of six million will not be sufficient for the year's extra expenses, if war breaks out with France, in which case the National Debt will have to be increased, be it through [the issuance of] Notes for the Navy, or through some secret negotiation with the East India Company directors, to whom Lord North will offer certain advantages with the hope of getting them approved in Parliament.

It is said that a Proclamation will be issued shortly to the effect that each Parish in the Kingdom provide two men who will serve to form new Regiments, and fill in the current ones, which go on being very short-handed.

It is very likely that the Ministers are going to spend the Easter holiday at their country homes, as they do every year, and that for this, or another reason My Lord Weymouth will excuse himself from conferring with us the day after tomorrow.

This, my only letter, cannot but seem very insubstantial to Your Excellency, especially at a time in which very important happenings must lie ahead, but as much as I have tried to inquire whether there was something worthy of Your Excellency's curiosity I haven't been able to learn more than what I have referred to.

> May God keep Your Excellency many years as I desire. London, 14 April 1778.
> Most Excellent Sir
> I kiss the hand of Your Excellency your most humble and devoted servant.
> Francisco Escarano

Document 43
Legajo 7001-12, Estado, AGS
Francisco Escarano to the Count of Floridablanca, London, 29 May 1778, no. 12
[Main letter, five pages]
Original in Spanish

Most Excellent Sir

Sir:

On Tuesday last an inquiry into the conduct of General Bourgoyne [sic] in his expedition to Saratoga was proposed in the House of Commons. This General who attended the House with the purpose of voluntarily satisfying various questions that he knew his opponents had contrived to put to him, spoke for the space of two hours delving into some points that seemed to him to demand an immediate satisfaction, and he concluded saying that he himself wanted the House to set itself up as a special committee for the cited inquiry, and justification for its proceedings. At the same time, he complained about the Ministers who had advised the King that he should deny him entrance for now to the Palace: to which My Lord George Germain responded that cases the same as his had been looked for, so as to not inflict this unpleasantness on him; but that they had not been found. Lord Germain objected to the proposal of the inquiry stating that General Bourgoyne [sic] was not subject to the judgment of the House, finding himself as a prisoner in England; and although Bourgoyne [sic] tried to defend the opposite, he could not achieve it, he himself confessing that he had come from America with permission of the Congress: and so, after many debates the proposal was rejected. During these Mister Lutrell spoke in favor of General Bourgoyne [sic], and not content with praising his talent, courage and conduct, humiliated Lord Germain comparing his [conduct] in the Battle of Minden in which, he said, he [Lord Germain] had disobeyed the orders of his superiors, and abandoned the flags.[177] This expression stung My Lord to such an extreme that, lambasting Mister Lutrell with very insulting words, told him that he would know how to avenge himself from those that he [Mister Lutrell] had uttered. This altercation rocked the entire House, and despite the efforts that the

Speaker made to reestablish order, imposing silence on the offended [parliamentarians], he could not manage it for some time. Mister Lutrell, who was threatened that he would be arrested, said that he would circumvent that by not ceding the right to speak in the terms that he had been used: that he had not said something about My Lord that was not founded in public opinion and in a judgment made in the time of George the Second after a formal trial: and that My Lord had used epithets against him that offended his character and that he did not want to suffer. At last the Speaker forced on Mister Lutrell, that in this interval he wanted him to take leave of the House, that he should return to his post, and demanded of him and of My Lord that they should retract from all immoderate and insulting expressions, which they had broken into. They followed suit, My Lord being the first who began to apologize. My Lord Germain had not been the only person provoked. Mister Lutrell in his harangue shot some indirect barbs at My Lord North: and he [North], when Mister Fox shouted for order, said that he {Fox} was the most disorderly of all: but these outpours did not have any results.

Via the printed matter that I include for Your Excellency you will see the advantages that the Catholics of this kingdom are going to experience and the form of oath that they should swear to the King; although it could be that before the bill is published there is some expression changed in it that will not be very essential. These advantages are very great in their implications for the security of the Catholics' properties, for the acquisitions of other [properties] that they can make in this country, and for the regular order of succession in families, avoiding the misfortunes that would ensue, whereby a second one [successor], becoming protestant, could deprive the first born [male] of his natural inheritance. More so, regarding what pertains to the penal laws, the most horrible ones still exist in force against the Catholics (inasmuch as they are not revoked): and only those, the cited advantages, are celebrated today, because said laws are not applied at the moment, and because they [the Catholics] find themselves hopeful that in the next session of Parliament they will obtain at least an implicit revocation of the strongest [laws].

It has been proposed in the House of Commons that His Majesty be implored, in recognition of the need that exists to complete considerable pending business in Parliament, not to postpone [the session] according to procedure, but to keep it running for now, calling it [into session] from one day to the next until those [pending matters] are concluded: but this proposal has been rejected.

Another proposal has been made in the same House, and withdrawn by the one who put it forward owing to the demands of his colleagues of [considering] other writings [such]: that of a request of the House to the King expressing to His Majesty the wish that reconciliation with the Americans take place as soon as possible, and that the House will help His Majesty in [utilizing] all measures that he judges opportune to this end. The Court's party supported this proposal; but the opposition party suspected that by this move the ministry would be able to declare the colonies independent if it should seem necessary for reconciliation; and on [the basis of] this supposition expressed itself against the request.

The member of the House of Commons who has made these two proposals is a certain Mister Hartley who is in the opposition party (do not be surprised Your Excellency [by] the business of the Court's report with respect to the independence of the colonies, since on this point many individuals of both parties differ) and has returned not long ago from Paris where he had gone, I do not know if carried away by his zeal, or through a ministerial commission to deal with Mister Franklin on a means of reconciliation with the Americans. Franklin told him that England would not manage it if it did not concede them independence.

The Parliament has proposed to the King that he order a one-time issuance of 200 pounds sterling to the family of My Lord Chatham to pay the debts of the deceased; amount which will be satisfied to his Majesty by the national funds.

> May Our Lord keep Your Excellency's life many years as I desire.
> London, 29 May 1778.
> Most Excellent Sir
> I kiss the hand of Your Excellency your most humble and trustworthy servant
> Francisco Escarano

Document 44
Signatura 121, AHPTF/AZC[178]
Graciano Sieulanne to Benjamin Franklin, Santa Cruz de Tenerife,
30 July 1778[179]
Letter book copy
[Main letter, four pages]
Original in French

Copy of a letter from Mister Sieulanne to Mister Doctor Franklin
Santa Cruz de Tenerife, 30 July 1778 (with 137)

Sir:

I have the honor to inform you that Captain Cunningham,[180] in command of the American ship *La Revenge*, authorized corsair, having captured and brought the English brigantine The *Comtesse of Moreton* to the island of La Palma, one of the Canaries, proposed to me [that] I convey it to Martinique. After having obtained the permission of my consul [stationed] in these islands and having reached agreements with Captain Cunningham, I moved on to La Palma where I took possession of the said Brigantine. However, Sir, when I was at the point of getting the rigging set, the governor of La Palma sent an armed skiff [and came] on board to require me to speak with him, and having done so, told me that he had just received orders from His Lordship the Marquis of Tabalosos [*sic*][181] to detain my ship, and as a result had the sails and nautical instrumentation lowered to the deck. I asked him the reasons for such a forcible action. He answered me that he had an order to detain not only me, but also Captain Cunningham. He [Cunningham] had rigged out his ship a little before me and was still visible from the port. The governor added that I must speak with the commanding officer.[182] Consequently, I traveled to Tenerife and having presented myself to the said commanding officer he rained insults down on me, and Captain Cunningham, treating us as bandits. I responded to him that I had no idea what he could have against that captain, that my mission came down to taking the captured ship in question to Martinique, and that I wanted to know the reason for which he had detained me so ignominiously. He then told me to go in search of an English merchant, called Thomas Cologan, situated in the port of Orotava. Not knowing to what end this request would play out, I went to render an account of what had happened to my consul. He advised me to write to the said Mr. Cologan, who furnished me the reply, a copy of which I attach herewith. This letter, Sir, lays bare the entire mystery, and it seems that the cause of my detention is by way of retaliation, and that it was Captain Cunningham who should have been detained. I shall not reflect further on such a forcible action on the part of the commanding officer of the Canaries; I will limit myself only to beg you that you use your good offices so that the Court of Spain obliges the Commanding Officer to pay me all of the expenses that this delay has caused me and which can be assessed at five hundred *piastras*,[183] understanding that my agreement with Captain Cunningham is for the crossing, with eight men for crew, and that I will see myself obliged to sell at a loss a portion of my cargo, which consists of wine from Catalonia, in La Palma.

This sum can be sent to the consul of France, who will transfer it to where I find myself, in agreement with the request that I have made of him, and the notices that I shall give him. I also think, Sir, that in all fairness this Commanding Officer should be obliged to answer for everything that can happen to me until my arrival in Martinique, since he has caused me a delay of almost three weeks. The cargo and the ship are estimated at sixteen thousand *piastras* or sixty-five thousand pounds.

With respect, Sir, to the insult made to the flag, I am persuaded that you will obtain satisfaction and that it shall never again be endangered in these parts by similar aggressions. I also hope that you [will] pardon my inopportuneness, but I believe that I would have failed in respect to what I owe Captain Cunningham, who would entrust his interests to me, if I had omitted to give you word of this situation.

I have the honor of remaining respectfully yours, Sir, Your, etc. Sieulanne

Document 45
Legajo 4618-52, Estado, AGS
Benjamin Franklin to Mister Grand, Passy, 3 November 1778, no. 52
Main letter, two pages
Original in French
The Count of Aranda, 9 November 1778
[Introductory note, half a page]
Original in Spanish

Includes the response of the American representatives concerning the complaints leveled by the privateer Conyngham.
For his part, the American representative complains that as retaliation we seize [or, arrest] an American and take him to the Canaries.
Reply in 23 with No. 2

Franklin to Grand, Passy, 3 November 1778
Original in French

Notified, and that the second point go unanswered until taking notice of this prior incident of the ship that was conveyed to the Canaries.

We must thank the person, Sir, who through you has furnished us with the note that we have received against Conyngham; and we must assure you again that, replete with respect toward His Catholic Majesty, nothing saddens us more than the complaints on your part against our compatriots.

His majesty will have seen through the documents that you earlier sent on our part to His Excellency the Count of Aranda, all of the measures that the Congress had taken to prevent whatever wrongful conduct on the part of our ship owners and seafarers, and in this respect nothing proves their precautions more that the Proclamation that has just been issued, of which copy N. 2 is herein [included], to which we attach the copy of its [the Congress's] Resolution on preserving the property of a ship, even though it belongs to nation from which we cannot lease them.[184]

Yet if one pays attention to the barbarous actions of the English towards all nations, without distinction, it would not surprise us that their annoying example finds supporters among some individuals of a nation that they have offended against so strongly, but this does not excuse Conyngham. In our eyes it is a crime to have attacked a nation for which the Congress feels respect, although she may have done justice by herself [by] having captured, in retaliation, the English vessel that Conyngham had taken to Tenerife in order to get it sent on to Martinique. We will not inform the Congress of the reasons for the complaint that this ship owner has made to His Catholic Majesty. It will doubtless be a new reason to extend to your flag all the honors and respect that it merits.

I dare to hope that from the wisdom, as well as the justice of His Majesty, he will have faith in this expression of our feelings toward him and that he in turn will deign to show us their fruits.

I have the honor of being, Sir, your very humble and obedient servant.
B. Franklin
In Passy, this 3rd of November 1778
M. Grand

Document 46
Legajo 4618-51, Estado, AGS
The Count of Aranda to the Count of Floridablanca, Paris, 9 November 1778, no. 51
[Main letter, two pages]
Original in Spanish

Most Excellent Sir

My Very Good Lord:
In [a] letter of 14 September number 3 Your Excellency informs me of the atrocities that the American corsair Cunningham was continually committing along our coasts; and pointedly of the capture that he had just made of a Swedish ship, [its cargo] loaded in London at the expense of Spaniards; and Your Excellency alerted me to the King's order, that it should be made known second hand to the American representatives, demanding that they should make arrangements [as suits them] for due restitution; and for making amends for Cunningham's conduct. I duly took care of it through the Banker Mister Grant, as I told Your Excellency in a letter of the 2d of the past [month], number 1348. And as a result, Grant himself has brought me the letter that Doctor Francklin [sic] has written to you about this matter, accompanied by the Congress's Proclamation regarding the treatment of neutral Flags; and its resolution concerning a captured Portuguese [ship], with their translations into French. All of which I pass along into the hands of Your Excellency so that you can notify the King of the response of these representatives to our complaint, and of the state in which this matter [currently] finds itself.

    May God keep Your Excellency many years. Paris
    Most Excellent Sir
    I kiss the hand of Your Excellency
    Your Trustworthy Servant
    The Count of Aranda

Document 47
Lejajo 4620-126, Estado, AGS
The Count of Aranda to the Count of Floridablanca, Paris, 19 July 1779, no. 126
[Main letter, three pages]
Original in Spanish

Most Excellent Sir

My Dear Sir:
The letters from England come very irregularly as much from the delay in passage from Downes to Ostende, quite different from the narrowness of that [strait] of Calais for managing it in moderate time, as from the risk of the Privateers that chase the Packet Boats, which are detained in Downes itself, whenever some suspicious ship is known to be found in the Canal. For that reason, the last letters that have reached this place are from the 9th, and say only that Admiral Hardy's flotilla had been in the Bay of Torbay, from where it had sailed [and been] reinforced by up to 40 ships-of-the-line.

Your Excellency wrote to me, on the dates of the 2nd and 17th of May, about attacks attributed to the American Flag against the Spanish Packet Boat, that came from Tenerife to La Coruña, and a Catalan ship around the waters of the Island of Santo Domingo, so that it should be made known to the Representative of the Americans in this Court, in the terms that are judged helpful. Consequently, I called upon the Banker Mr. Grand, and furnished him the basic details of said occurrences translated into French, so that he might make them known to Doctor Francklin [sic]; and today [itself] he has brought me by way of response that which the American Commissioner in Nantes has set forth, which I include for Your Excellency.

Mr. Grand has likewise delivered to me the other item that accompanies [this], of a plea that a merchant established in Alicante [and] named Montgomery, who purports to be an American, has made to Francklin [sic] himself, and who withal has been treated as an Englishman in the [context of the] orders that have been laid down after

the rupture; requesting of me that I should pass it along to Your
Excellency affirming that he was a person in favor of the States.

It is said that the orders to embark go forward actively in Saint
Malo, and Havre de Gracia [sic][185]; and that the Field of Dunkirk is
building up infantry, and cavalry.

I acknowledge receipt from Your Excellency of your four numbers
of the 5th of the current month, which do not require [any] particular
answer.

>May God keep Your Excellency many years. Paris, 19 July 1779.
>Most Excellent Sir
>I kiss the hand of Your Excellency
>Your Trustworthy Servant
>The Count of Aranda

Attachment A
Legajo 4620-127, Estado, AGS
The Count of Aranda, Paris, 19 July 1779[186]
[Introductory note, half page]
Original in Spanish

Montgomery to Benjamin Franklin, Alicante, 26 June 1779
[Copy of the main letter, three pages]
Original in French

It includes the response that he has given to the American
representative regarding our complaints against three privateering ships
named the *Resolution*, the *Plymouth*, and the *Petite Resolution*,
confirming his disbelief that such privateers exist or that they have left,
as is supposed, from the ports of France, since there would be reports.

It accompanies the objection of an American named
Montgomery,[187] resident in Alicante, who complains of being treated
full-blown as an Englishman and whom [the authorities] wish to eject
from the kingdom.

Responded to on 2 August with Number 2

That information will be gathered over the business concerning
Montgomery to learn whether up to now he has passed for an
Englishman and now intends to be looked upon as an American. That

with respect to the embargo it was an order that the authorities gave in Alicante, breaking with a mistaken premise and putting [in place] an alternative solution once it was known here.

[Copy of a letter from Mister Montgomery of Alicante to Mister B. Franklin, 26 June 1779]
Original in French

I find myself in the painful necessity of importuning your excellency to inform you that despite my truthfulness in declaring and subscribing myself as a citizen of the 13 United States of North America, at all times that foreign merchants established here have been convened by the Governor to come [forward] to declare which country they are from, yesterday, under a declaration of war made against England, they have seized me, personally, [and] my possessions, and some soldiers who came in great numbers invaded my house. I immediately presented the certificate and passport that you together with Misters Lee and Adams had given me when I had the honor of offering my respects to you in August during my passage through that city.
But those documents have not been of use to me in recovering them [his possessions], which caused me to ask if Spain had declared war against America. Although they answered me in the negative, they did not treat me better nor do I even have the hope that they will do so.

Having a conscience of being totally innocent in conscience and not having more against me than a physical appearance as English as [I am] opposed to that so far as sentiments are concerned, I beg of your excellency that you be so good as to write immediately to the Count de Ricla, the Minister of War, so that in consequence of my status as a person in support of the Allies, he is so good as to order that what they have taken from me is restored to me, and that all my rights are reinstated.

I also request that you tell me who is in charge of Commercial Affairs in Madrid, if there is someone already named, with the purpose of addressing myself to him in the future in case, this repeats itself.

I trust completely in your benevolence and fairness to deliver me from the state of distress in which I find myself. Nor do I doubt that you will not deny me a response, without which it would be quite difficult for me to be get out of this lamentable situation, salvage my credit and avoid the loss of the same etc. etc.

Attachment B
Legajo 4620-129, Estado, AGS
J. Williams to Franklin, Nantes, 13 July 1779
[Main letter, two pages]
Original in French[188]
Translation of a letter of 13 July 1779, written from Nantes by Mister J. Williams[189] to Mister Doctor Franklin.

In reply to the documents contained in your letter of the 9th of this month. The first, an account of the insults[190] made against the Spanish flag by three American warships: The *Resolution*, the *Plymouth*, and the *Petite Resolution*, that supposedly left [port] in Nantes. The second, an account of the insults made against the same flag by other American ships in the Antilles.

I must assure you that I have never had notice of the existence of American warships with the above-cited names, and neither do I have knowledge that [ships] with those names have ever left any port of France. These particulars and still others lead me to believe that some English privateers have come aboard Spanish ships under the American flag, declaring themselves [to be] citizens of the United States[191] with the intention of passing themselves off as subjects of this nation and all of us as pirates.

I will not spare anything to secure the most accurate reports about this matter, and if some time I discover an instance of similar conduct on the part of some American, I will believe that it is my duty to denounce him and do all that is in my hands to deliver him up to the rigor of the laws, the honor and the reputation of my right-minded compatriots being so strongly threatened.

Document 48
Legajo 4620-130, Estado, AGS
J. Williams to Franklin, Nantes, 22 July 1779
[Main copy of translation of a letter in English, one page]
Original in French

Translation of the letter from Mr. J. Williams to Mr. Doctor Franklin, dated 22 July 1779.

Since I had the honor of writing to you on the 13th of this month to inform you that the privateering vessels about whom the Court of Spain complained cannot be Americans, I have made the widest investigations with the purpose of clearing [things] up, beyond a shadow of doubt, with my Lord the Ambassador. I remit to you the documents that he got me accompanied by a testimony of the commercial agents here, who declare that privateering vessels with those names have never appeared in France.

I cannot affirm anything about the matter of the Antilles, but I am thoroughly convinced that all of these attacks have been made by Englishmen and not by Americans.

I remain with all respect.

Attachment A
Legajo 4620-131, Estado, AGS
Nantes, 20 July 1779
[Certificate signed by the translators, one page]
Original in French

We, the undersigned sworn translators of Foreign Languages and all royal [of the King] trading agents, certify that all of the frigates or privateering vessels belonging to the United States of America which have docked in this river have received assistance from and been served by us in [our] capacity as aforementioned translators and trading agents, and that since the war that currently exists between the said States and the kingdom of Great Britain, no frigate or privateering vessel of said nation or belonging to said States has docked in this river. With their names and captains [as] cited they would the following:

The frigate *Resolution* armed with 26 canons and 120 crew members, at the command of Captain Jean Gran; the *Plymouth* of 20 canons and 100 crew members at the command of Captain Ning; the privateering vessel the *Little [Petite] Resolution* of 14 canons and 40 crew members; and the frigate the *Terrible*, captained by Samuel Ayers. Mr. Jon [sic] Williams of this city, having presented us a memorial with complaints against the said frigates and privateering vessel, saying that they came from Nantes, [and] that [without provocation] had attacked on the 30th of last March, under the flag of the United States, the Spanish mail boat called the *Bird*,[192] voyaging from Santa Cruz de Tenerife to La Coruña, required certification from us to prove that said frigates and privateering vessel had never come up this river, and that since the month of January of this year up to the aforementioned time no more than a single American privateering vessel, named the *General Washington*, of Alexandria in Virginia, at the command of Mr. Francis Speake, bearing 16 or 18 canons, had sailed out of this port or river, [it] was rigged out toward the end of last March and voyaged to Brest to join a convoy. That consequently it can be presumed that the attack made against the Spanish mail boat was the work of the English under the flag of the United States of America. In testimony of which we set forth the present document in order that it can be used and be of value for whatever is needed.

Nantes, 20 July 1779.
Odiette de la Bauche, J. B. Duchesne, and F. M. van Neunen.

Attachment B
Nantes, 22 July 1779
[Note of Certification of Signatures, one page]
Original in French

I, Marie Pierre Charles Bascher,[193] adviser to the King, lieutenant, civil and criminal adviser[194] in the royal site of the Admiralty of Nantes, certify before whomever it concerns that the signatures Odiette de la Bauche, F. M. Van Neunen and Duchesne recorded on the other companion part are the true signatures of the master[195] René Odiette de la Bauche, master François Maximilien van Neunen and master Jean

Baptiste Duchesne, all of them sworn and royal translators of foreign languages and trading agents in this city; and that be used for all [cases] and all [legal] situations, in faithful testimony in witness to which I have signed the present document with the regular seal of the jurisdiction.

> Given in my house in Nantes, 22 July 1779
> Bascher
> Received for legalization and seal, 25 soles.[196]

Document 49
Signatura 779-75-1R, AHPTF/AZC
Juan Cólogan to Tomás Cólogan, Ostend,[197] 27/31 December 1780
[Letter book of copied letters, 1777 to 1782, abbreviated letter, one page]
Original in English

Dear Brother:
    I wrote [to] you my last 13/14 instant via Coruña with duplicates via Cádiz. Yesterday sailed the [illegible] Captain Dane to your address with a fair wind that continues in the same point. I am in hopes that what she carries will be of your approbation. We were too far engaged when your letters came to hand to assist. I must indeed lament to have been great part of this year deprived of your letters, they being sent to Ghent. I say the same with regard to the *Province of Flanders*.[198] We must therefore conclude the expeditions of these two ships and wait your further orders for what we are to do. The rupture of England with Holland has just taken place. War is actually declared and many Dutch ships stopped. What will be the end of all this? Some will have it that Peace is at hand, others will have the Northern Powers first in combustion [to become suddenly angry]. May God help us. Russia must come in the dance by the treaty she has signed with Holland.
    Annexed you will find Mr. Brand's answer with respect to your property at Philadelphia.[199] When I see him next month it will not be in my power to come to determination. The object is of too great consequence to take it upon me and I dread you being displeased. I am of opinion that although it must be a tedious negotiation, it must be done from you to him, unless you empower me with proper instructions and tell me how far I can act without incurring your [approval]. Said Grand is no doubt the properest [sic] and only person to whom your funds can come to. If he does not know the reduction of Pounds Currency into Dollars, I do not know it. Mr. Morris must explain that. When I see Mr. Grand I may be tempted to value on said Morris to his order for part of said funds. This war with Holland must make a sensation in America and better [improve] their funds. You must in consequence get a better

price for your currency. The 6% interest allowed by Congress on money lent is paid in Paris by Mr. Grand. He is the man through whose hands pass the American money matters. He pays the Bills drawn by Congress or others accepted by Doctor Franklin. What I say of the currency bettering in America may be the reverse if England gets any advantage in that quarter especially if they take possession of [illegible]. The *Province of Flanders* is here and will begin to load as soon as she will be able to come into the Bason.[200] This little port is so crowded with vessels that it is with the greatest difficulty [that] I can get anything done. The Bason is too small for the number of vessels and it is a matter to get [a] wharf to load, first come, first served. There was some delay with *the Valon* on that account. Yet I hope that *the Province of Flanders* will be under sail in about fifteen days. She would have been here two months ago had it not been for the accident at Boulogne and Dunkirk. She is a strong staunch brig that will take all the goods that are here and maybe not fill her. I am expecting 80 barrels [of] Red Herrings from Woodhouse at Liverpool but they came by a Dutchman and I am afraid that she will be carried into some English port. If that is the case Mr. Bowens will claim them and in all probability, will get them back. Said Woodhouse wants to send 1000 barrels [of] Herrings to your island and take *Vidonias*[201] in payment delivered at the Isle of Man.[202] This cannot be done at this time of the year. Such expedition should be taken in hand so as to be with you before winter. Besides, I do not think it would be agreeable to you. I am [in] treaty for the wines remaining at Guernsey[203] or else I could supply him from that Island ...

... You will have it that we knew of the War when yours and other people's goods were ordered and bought. I cannot help it if you will not believe. It is true we ordered part of yours without your positive orders came to hand as we had done on other occasions and more so then as there was a better prospect and we wished to have you provided in case of a war with Spain as it happened at the time of our late father.[204] Even when the war was declared nobody thought that the Prohibition would be as it is, but only as it was [in] the last war. I mean the long war, when English goods were admitted clandestinely and even openly without certificates and the difficulties there is now ...

Document 50
Legajo 4624-71, Estado, AGS
Count of Aranda to the Count of Floridablanca, Paris, 9 April 1781, no. 1930
[Main letter, three pages]
Original in Spanish

Most Excellent Sir

My Very Good Lord:
Yesterday Dr. Franklin sent to me the document from Your Excellency that arrived in the mail from that Representative of the American colonies, Mr. Jay, with the date of 28th of March, and it includes the letter [written] by the Administrator of the Burgos mail over the French mail, regarding the mental breakdown that had afflicted [the Frenchman].[205] And, since I see from Your Excellency's subsequent letter of the 30th sent by the mail of Cabarrús[206] that the delayed documents have appeared, I will limit myself to informing His Lord, the Count of Vergennes, tomorrow of such an incidental occurrence, it being normal that you have been informed about everything from the Ambassador of France.

Favorable news from the East Indies are circulating here, on the assumption that Hyder Ali Khan[207] has defeated the English; and, also, from New York, that Washington has defeated Clinton, and although some gazette from Holland also reports it as a postscript of the letters from London of the 30th, I am suspending my judgment until the first news from England.

Mr. de Grasse[208] sent a corvette on the 27th from the 42 degree of latitude, and 16 degree west longitude of the meridian of Paris, around 60 leagues west of the Cape of Finisterre,[209] and since it left, the said ship had sailed on for three days, enjoying the northeast wind favorable to the navigation of the convoy, so that I did not doubt that it will have reached upon coming into the breezes, or trade winds, and that it will comprise a sailing rarely seen.

In his last letter, of the 30th, Don Matías de Gandásegui[210] tells me that a seized French ship called the *Sartine*,[211] coming from Havana with documents for the two Courts, had arrived in Limerick in Ireland, but that the packets with which it came loaded had been tossed overboard in time, and he asks that I communicate this to Your Excellency.

>May God keep Your Excellency many years, Paris, 9 April 1781
>Most Excellent Sir
>I kiss the Hand of Your Excellency
>Your Trustworthy Servant
>The Count of Aranda
>[to] His Excellency the Count of Floridablanca

Document 51
Legajo 4624-73, Estado, AGS
The Count of Aranda to the Count of Floridablanca, Paris, 12 April 1781, no. 1931
[Main letter, two pages]
Original in Spanish

                                   Most Excellent Sir

My Very Good Lord:
    I received Your Excellency's letter of the 28th of March through mail from Mr. Jay to Dr. Franklin, which he delivered to me by a person from his residence, [and which] relates what occurred with the French correspondent who suffered a mental breakdown on the outskirts of Burgos. I advised His Lord, the Count of Vergennes, about it the day before yesterday, Tuesday, having him read the notice from the Burgos postal Administer to the Directors of Madrid, and he was fully aware of everything, and what is more, had also received the same news through that Ambassador.
    Upon leaving from my presence, Dr. Franklin said to me that the same mail would return today, and if I wanted to write I should send my letter to him by ten in the morning. I accepted this offer. This is to forestall that I write three letters to Your Excellency today, to wit: this one;[212] another through the French mail that His Lord, the Count of Vergennes, told me he would dispatch tonight, or early tomorrow; and the main one [to be sent] through Don Francisco Cabarrús, who will set off at midnight and will carry it to Irun[213] with a caution from me to the administrator of the Irun mail that if the faulty[214] one comes through with a time difference of but a few hours that he send it along with my letter to Your Excellency, and if this is not the case, that he dispatch the mail by horseback.
    The matter treated is what was contained in Your Excellency's dispatch through Cabarrús's mail of March 30th. In the one that will go by French mail, I touched on it superficially and covered it extensively in the one coming via Cabarrús, but naturally it will be the last of the three that arrive, for which it will suit that even though that Ambassador[215] for his part proffers you the information, Your Excellency

should try not to answer him about anything until you have received my account; and because my letter will make reference to what he said, [Your Excellency] should take this into account when you report expansively on this matter. I believe that my letter [coming] through Irun can indeed reach Your Excellency by the 21st.[216]

> May God keep Your Excellency many years. Paris, 12 April 1781
> Most Excellent Sir
> I Kiss the Hand of Your Excellency
> Your trustworthy Servant
> The Count of Aranda
> [to] His Most Excellent Lord, the Count of Floridablanca

Document 52
Signatura 121, AHPTF/AZC
Tomás Cólogan to Juan Cólogan Valois, Tenerife, 6 June 1781
[Letter book of copied letters, 1777 to 1782, partial letter, two pages][217]
Original in English

Tenerife the 6th of June 1781

Dear Brother:
... We have seen the copy of the letters you received with regard to the accommodations that we required for the Court of Madrid in favor of Br T's[218] affair and really if we had depended on those you would send we would have been badly off. We repeat our desire [that] you should procure us all hope [that] you may be able and send them to Don Fermín Sánchez de Muniain[219] to keep by until the acts should go to Madrid. Once you are in Paris we believe that it will very easy for you to secure a letter from the Count of Aranda and the Viscount de la Herería, who cannot but have some friends in the Council of War, even from Doctor Franklin who must have connections in the Spanish Court. We have nothing to share with you beyond the essential points we request. Regarding this, we believe we forwarded to you about 20 letters of recommendation, and none of them could come from such high stationed people that you can easily obtain [from there].[220] We well comprehend that one of the three must go to Madrid on Mr. Lynch's inheritance, but surely you never could be of any great help, not being instructed in the affair and having a very superficial idea of the lawsuit, we don't deny all your expressions tend towards our welfare and come from a true desire of being of service to us but experience is wanted and knowledge of the affair what you are going upon. We confess to you that of the three, you can make the voyage with more ease and less danger, but whoever goes must have a thorough knowledge of the affair, as the contrary party has a very lively and keen agent that will do anything to obtain a sentence in his favor ...
... With regard to the produce of the half cargo [from] the *Good Boors* delivered to Mr. Robert Morris, from the beginning we wrote to him to remit the net proceeds to you at Mr. J. F. Batheda but though our letters went by triplicate we have had no answer. We will write him

again now telling him to take loan Bills payable by Grand with Doctor Franklin's acceptance and we will repeat the order several ways to see if we can come at them though you could even draw on Morris for a part though at a loss, etc. as that would be even more secure than to take anyone's bill's. We tell Morris of it also that he may put no objection to the acceptance of your bills. We are very desirous to have this stock at your side and you have said nothing. If you have recovered the 60$ you expressed some time ago from the insurers of the *Good Boor's* cargo, Mr Batheda [and colleagues] are very uneasy about their share and we comprehended from them you have made nothing good on their concern in such a manner that it is to be wished the vessel had not been retaken. Do all you [can] possible to recall these means though with great loss of the sum, the half Cargo produced in America. Hence, forward we will write Mr. Morris several ways to hurry him to make your remittances. He is very secure by all accounts but the insurers we think should be answerable to us for any deficiency we should suffer, the voyage of the ship being ended in Philadelphia by superior orders _____ it follows on the other side of this leaf.[221]

Document 53
Signatura 121, AHPTF/ACZ
Tomás Cólogan to Robert Morris, Tenerife, 7 June 1781[222]
[Letter book of copied letters, 1777 to 1782; beginning 21 October 1777; four pages]
Original in English

Robert Morris, Esquire   Tenerife, 7 June 1781

Sir:
We had the pleasure to write you the foregoing by triplicate covering the sundry vouchers to represent our property in the *Golden Rose's* cargo and seeing [that] we have received no answer to any of them and that our brother John Cólogan lately at Paris has received no remittances from you as he advised us by April 17th, we repeat to you our desire [that] you should procure to take bills in Europe if we may go receiving said funds. Said brother tells us you could purchase some loan bills payable by Mr. Grand in Paris with the acceptance of Doctor Franklin, to be sure the discount will be great, but we prefer it was being the quickest way to receive said funds and [that] are laying idle a long time indeed, we are assured Doctor Franklin uses this method for his own private affairs, as being the security, tho with great loss, an how you are only spot and we will conform to whatever may you will think more prudent to receive these funds of which we are very desirous seeing we cannot even know from you the state of the affair is in at your side. Nothing was done at Madrid with regards to the claim we ordered on a half of the cargo delivered to the recaptor [sic] as we were answered it should be done first at the Port where she was carried into, and with copy of the diligences, then to present ourselves in Madrid and if not justly sentenced then to apply for redress at the same time we knew it was just the delivery of half of the cargo to the recaptor [sic] and of course we dropped any representation on the subject. We have nothing else to say but wishing to hear from you on the subject and it frees us from care it being in your hands.
We remain very sincerely. We have wrote [sic] our brother John Cologan that if he could obtain from Doctor Franklin or any other

substantial person I would give him a sum of money, he could draw on you for it tho it should be with a disadvantageous. Excellence, if it should to happen we beg you will honor his drafts that you will be pleased to carry to the debit of our account, and it will be in payment of the produce of the goods [that] you have received our account of the *Golden Rose's* cargo, this method would be very secure if it could be obtained, tho we suppose it will not be very early. It would be equal to us if you could find good bills on Holland, Hamburg or Cádiz; and sending them to our brother he would negotiate them at Paris or where he should think more profitable.

Tomas Cólogan

Note of the lost merchandise in the inventory of goods belonging to the Cólogans.

Document 54
Signatura 121, AHPTF/AZC
Tomás Cólogan to Juan Cólogan of Cólogan, Pollard & Co. of London, Tenerife, 1 August 1781[223]
[Letter book of copied letters from 1777 to 1782, one partial page extracted from a four-page letter][224]
Original in English

In regard of the proceeds from the *Golden Rose*'s cargo[225] in Philadelphia, we don't see anything to do but wait [on] Mr. Morris for his advice or perhaps his remittances. If he does not remit, then you may draw [an] order from Mr. Grand or from Dr. Franklin, if they have ready money[226] or to receive it when they learn it was paid in America. The terms may be agreed upon accordingly. If they advance the money, you may allow them an interest and if not they must allow it to you, or pay the exchange accordingly.

But we must say to your government[227] in settling with the underwriters[228] that you must reflect if, in the end, there is any profit in half of the delivered cargo to us. The said underwriters are to account to us for the cost and changes of the other condemned half given to the recaptors [*sic*] and for the plundered part about which we have given you an account. If, on the contrary, there is a loss on the said half, it must be on their account or let it be at once decided that they pay the interest in case it remains for their account and running the risk of Remittances, etc. We suppose that Mr. Morris is to account with you for the Vintage Pipe[229] not comprehended in the Bond of [un deciphered company or person] and his wife; and please have it present.

Document 55
Legajo 4626-179, Estado, AGS
The Count of Aranda to the Count of Floridablanca, Paris, 18 May 1782, no. 2191
[Main letter, two pages]
Original in Spanish

Most Excellent Sir

My Excellent Lord:
    In letter number 2 of the 5th of this month sent by French mail, Your Excellency informs me about the spreading news that the Americans were going to issue letters of marque [reprisal] against the Portuguese house, under which they believe it certain that up to now the Spanish were carrying at risk much treasure and goods, the supposed authenticity of which I will look into with astuteness and discretion [to determine] if such a lot should be certain, and in that case I will urge Mr. Franklin to request of the Congress orders to save the goods that belong to the Spanish.
    As for some questions that I was asking about the matter, I elicited nothing, everyone being ignorant of it, for which reason, finding ourselves on Tuesday the 13th in the quarters of His Lord the Dauphin,[230] and with the diplomatic corps awaiting the royal entrance, I took advantage of the opportunity to approach Mr. Franklin and ask him what had taken place with regard to the [supposed] marque against Portuguese flag.[231] He responded in a natural manner that he neither knew about it nor believed it, for that for them [the Americans] having England as an enemy was enough without looking for others. I asked him, on this occasion, if the American colors were entering Portuguese ports, and he told me that since it was prohibited to them by decree of Her Most Faithful Majesty, they did not use them; that later they had been given to understand that under the French flag they would not be sent away, and that while this had been made known to the sailors of these waters, none have used such measures up till now. He told me that the said notions had come from London purely to sow confusion, and repeated to me that he neither knew of nor believed in such a thing.

>   May God keep Your Excellency many years, Paris, 18 May 1782
>   Most Excellent Sir
>   I kiss the Hand of Your Excellency
>   Your Trustworthy Servant
>   The Count of Aranda
>   [to] His Most Excellent Lord, the Count of Floridablanca

Document 56
Legajo 4615-49, Estado, AGS
The Count of Aranda to the Count of Floridablanca, Paris, 6 July 1782, no. 2487
[Main letter, two pages]
Original in Spanish

Most Excellent [Lord]:[232]

There is such a change in the weather around here that, following an excessive heat for two or three days that repeated three times, we have fallen into moderately October-like cold that has lasted six or eight days and brought on a huge number of colds, so it is incumbent to be very careful with one's chest. I find myself [down] with it, and having to write, or walk in one direction or another, has not sat well with me; but service to the King goes on, which is what matters. I see that Your Excellency's health is also affected, and since your sedentary and desk-bound life has to be more continuous than mine, it is necessary for Your Excellency to lessen it to the extent possible, because the strong enemy of health is the lady plume/pen.

I am responding by letter about what was communicated in the instruction that was sent to me, and I remain cognizant of the private letter from Your Excellency of the 27th of the past month, which I received yesterday.

Today Jay and Franklin will take a meal with me[233] in the style of this country, but without formalities, and for the sole purpose of getting them accustomed to seeing us informally for when we will begin to speak [more] familiarly.

A thick packet is going to Count Lacy that has some artillery treatises, that a general officer from here is sending to him, and that can be useful to him in Gibraltar, for which I ask Your Excellency that when there is mail service you will send it on to him, and, if so, by ordinary post, that it might be exempt from postage.

[I am] at Your Excellency's command
Your Trustworthy Servant
[The Count of] Aranda
I have already come away finding the funds, in keeping to my position, in which [matter] Your Excellency had a hand, and thus I thank you again.
[to] His Excellent Lord, the Count of Floridablanca

Document 57
Legajo 4630-187, Estado, AGS
The Count of Aranda to the Count of Floridablanca, Paris, 23 July 1783, no. 2487
[Main letter, one page]
Original in Spanish
[A note addressed to the Count of Aranda, regarding the copy of the Constitution given to him by Franklin]

Most Excellent Sir

My Very Good Lord:
Today without a document or anything more than a message on his part, and the name of his domicile, Dr. Franklin has passed along to me two copies of the constitution of the 13 united States,[234] one in a half-size booklet for Our Lord the King and the other in a quarter-size booklet for me, in consideration of which I send that one to Your Excellency on this occasion.

> God keep Your Excellency many years, Paris 23 July 1783
> Most Excellent Sir
> I kiss the hand of Your Excellency
> Your Trustworthy Servant
> The Count of Aranda
> [to] His Most Excellent Lord, the Count of Floridablanca

[Attachment][235]

[To] The Count of Aranda:
I remit a copy of the Constitution of the Thirteen United States that Mr. Franklin delivered for Our Lord the King.
Answered on the 23rd of August, I have presented this copy to the King, and he has ordered that it be kept in the Archive of the Secretariat, and insofar as they are sold, it will be convenient that for common use he sends three or four copies in quarter-size booklets.
Yesterday His Lord the Count presented Mr. Carmichael to the King as the person in charge of business affairs of the Thirteen States.[236]

Document 58
Legajo 4630-234, Estado, AGS
The Count of Aranda to the Count of Floridablanca, Paris, 3 September 1783, no. 2523
[Main letter, one page, attached to no. 37]
Original in Spanish

                Most Excellent Sir

My Very Good Lord:
  I remit to Your Excellency two examples from the Constitution of the States of America, and the rest of them that you requested from me in Number 8 of the document sent on the 23rd of the past month will go in another special mailing.

  May God keep Your Excellency many years, Paris, 3 September 1783
  Most Excellent Sir
  I Kiss the Hand of Your Excellency
  Your Trustworthy Servant
  The Count of Aranda
  [to] His Excellent Lord, the Count of Floridablanca

3

Postwar Franklin

Document 59
Minutes from the Board of Directors meeting of the Real Academia de Historia, Madrid, 9 July 1784, RAH[1]
[Main document, three pages]
Original in Spanish
Academy, 9 July 1784
[All the directors present are listed in the margin.][2]

    Mr. Don Ramón de Guerra informed [the Academy Board of Directors] that Dr. Benjamin Franklin, Minister Plenipotentiary of the United States of North America to the Court of Paris, had gifted a copy of his collection of works, the political volumes in particular, to his Excellency the Director,[3] writing him with this motive a letter in English that by request Mr. Guevara has translated, and which will be brought to the Academy with a copy of the original, the translation, and a draft of the reply given by His Excellency the Director. Mr. Guevara added that with the letter and copies of Franklin's works, Don Guillermo Carmichael, the person in charge of business affairs of these same United States to this Court [Spain], included a note that he had written by hand, which he [Guevara] read to the Academy in which Carmichael informed His Excellency [the director Campomanes] that the Academy of Sciences established in Philadelphia under the title of Philosophical

Society[4] had named him as a corresponding member [to the society] with the honorific accompaniments reported in the London chapter of the current month's issue of *Madrid Gazette*, sent from London.

Attentive to what was expressed, and of the wide fame justly acquired by Dr. Franklin as a celebrated politician and intellectual, and by virtue of his being a member of the major academies of Europe, and to correspond to the gesture that the Philosophical Society of Philadelphia has made, His Excellency the Director proposed that the Academy nominate him [Franklin] as an honorary member of the Academy. And it was approved by acclamation to admit him in such a category.

> [The minutes continue with other business.]
> [Recorded] by the Secretary
> [Signed] Josef de Guevara Vasconselos

Document 60
Legajo 8141-33, Estado, AGS
Miscellaneous Dispatches and other notes, Wednesday, 12 October 1785; and Friday, 14 October 1785
[Five pages]
Original in Spanish

Wednesday 12 October

On Monday Mister Adams received dispatches from America[5] [sentence crossed out on the draft but legible]

Many adventurers will go with the first ships to India to establish a new trading post in Negapatnam [sic][6] on the Coromandel Coast; given that it [money? trade posts? rights to trade?] will not be returned to the Dutch who have no equivalent to give in exchange.[7]

His Majesty's Ship *Assurance*, of 44[8] has been ordered to be fitted out immediately in Chatham for a far-away destination. It is believed that it will go to India.

Gravesend 11 October. The merchant ships *Belisario* and the one called *Juana and Isabel*, [captained by] Capitán Fraser, have sailed, [respectively], for the Mosquito Coast and for Piscataqua.

The Ship *Impregnable*, of 90 canons, that should have been launched in Deptford this month, will according to a new order remain on its stocks until next spring.

Nevis 30 July. The frigate *Boreas* has captured, with their cargos, 4 American vessels that carried out clandestine trade with this island, they were immediately confiscated by this expeditious Tribunal of the Admiralty.

Friday 14 October

As desirous as His Catholic Majesty is to close the Ports of his dominions to every class and kind of British and Irish manufactured goods; the Spanish Nation has yet to reach a sufficient state of maturity to be able to sustain such a measure. The vast consumption of stocks of wool and other merchandise from English factories (without taking into account the indispensable assortment [consumed] in Spain herself) necessarily impedes the issuance of a [royal] decree of said nature; since the twentieth part of wool fabrics needed is not produced in that Kingdom, neither within its confines alone, nor from another part of Europe would it be able to provision itself with very many things: One should thus look at the paragraph published days ago in some national Pamphlet "that a gentleman recently arrived from Cádiz had brought said news" as one of those fabrications done merely to cause unease to the nation without any foundation.

Wednesday afternoon letters were received from Gibraltar, brought on the Ship *Ana*, [captained by] Capitan Heachan [*sic*],[9] which arrived from Queensborough. They contain news of the Ship *Peace & Plenty*, [captained by] Capitan Robertson having arrived there from Cádiz, after having detained an Algerian privateer, and taking off it some barrels of salted beef and various other articles.

Next March all of His Majesty's ships deployed to the Mediterranean will have returned and will be replaced by others, except for the *Trusty*, of 50 canons, on which Commodore Cosby has set out.

While the Dutch were friends with this Nation they have enjoyed a long stretch, uninterrupted, of considerable peace and prosperity. They were content in their dwellings and respected outside of them; but once they formed new relationships and separated themselves from their former ones the House of Austria has taken control of a part of their territories, even obligating them to pay the costs of such revolution. Now Prussia has shown its pretensions, those which, one supposes, will follow new airs of superiority: And thus, through their ambition and perfidy they have lost, in two years, all those advantages to whose acquisition they had devoted themselves for almost two whole centuries.

It is noted in Letter from Copenhagen[10] that a group of traditional shipbuilders from the shipyards of Genoa had arrived there, having seen themselves in need of separating from that Republic owing to some disagreements that they had with some Magistrates relative to their payments. The King immediately employed them, continuing in his effort of placing his Navy on a footing with the most respectable in Europe.

The news that we have from Portsmouth in New Hampshire relate that last August the Americans launched in that port a new 50-canon ship, named the *Defender* and that the construction went on there of others of 74 [canons] which it seems are to be sold to the French.

Philadelphia 25 June. It is known for sure that Don Franklin's intention in visiting America at this juncture is for the purpose of contributing his enlightened views to the formation of a new code of laws for improving the government of the different States: It will resemble in some way that of England and will place particular care on being concise and thoroughly intelligible. This second Newton will also contribute to conciliating the sentiments of all parties and to consigning to perpetual oblivion the odious distinctions of Whigism and Toryism. It is believed that he will be given the presidency of the Congress in the next election since there is no person better qualified for it.

It is known from Nova Scotia that having [this incomplete sentence is crossed out on the draft but is legible]

New York 28 June. The State of Frankland has concluded a treaty of perpetual peace and friendship with the Cherokee Indians and a negotiation is pending to give that Nation a place among the representatives of the same State and it is hoped that the commissioners of the United States will manage similarly to pacify the Creek Indians and other western tribes that get in our way as well as those of Kentuky [*sic*].

13 August. The news is unfavorable concerning the negotiation by our commissioners with the 6 nations of the Indians [illegible] who insist on various concessions of territories which they purport belong to them, making reference to the stipulations of British officials regarding the strait of Niagara.

Document 61
The Gasset Family Private Archive (Madrid)[11]
Benjamin Franklin to Pedro Rodríguez, Count of Campomanes,
Philadelphia, 4 December 1786
[Main letter, one page]
Original in English

Sir:
It is with great pleasure I obey the commands of our Philosophical Society, in transmitting to your excellency the enlos'd Certificate of their having done themselves the Honour of electing you a Member, together with the second Volume of their Transactions, which I hope you will favorably accept. Wishing you every Felicity, and particularly that of constant Success in your continued laudable endeavours for the Service of your Country, I have the honour to be, with sincere & great Esteem, Sir,

Your Excellency's most obedient
& most humble Servant,
[signed] B. Franklin
[Attached is an oversized certificate of membership into the American Philosophical Society signed by Franklin, with a seal and a blue ribbon attached].[12]

Document 62
Legajo [file] 55-138, The Gasset Family Private Archive[13]
The Count of Campomanes to Benjamin Franklin (draft letter with corrections, 24 May 1787, main letter, three pages, original in Spanish [Introductory note, one page]
Original in Spanish

Certificate of Individual membership in the American Philosophical Society
Note-
Attached is the letter that Mister Benjamin Franklin addressed to him and the response of his most illustrious self.
[2- Presentation note (one page)]
Original in Spanish

Madrid, 24 May 1787

To Mr. Benjamin Franklin,
 Responding to his, which is included, of December 4th last, and sending him the first volume of Father Cañes's Spanish, Latin, and Arabic Dictionary, among other books that the Academy of History remits to him, the list of which accompanies [this letter].[14]

[Main letter draft, three pages]
Original in Spanish

Most Excellent Sir

My Dear Sir:
 I have received by the hand of Mister William Carmichel Your Excellency's esteemed letter of last December 4th, together with the valued title of membership in the American Philosophical Society, and the second volume of its Transactions, which contain the Society's statutes, the list of members and various experiments, observations and writings on matters relating for the most part to the natural and exact sciences.
 I am very indebted for all this, both to Your Excellency and to our Society, whose works interest me like my own for the honor it has

accorded me [by] adding me to its guild, [and] I am living up with great satisfaction to the wisdom, appreciation and intelligence of all the different topics included [in those works], which in my judgment, will contribute effectively to considerably advance useful knowledge [as the] object of the laudable institute of our Academy of Philadelphia, and to make it an equal, following the recuperation of its endeavors as a benefit of peace, of the most venerable and renowned of its kind established in Europe.

Amidst the continual business of governing the Council, this role assigned to me some years ago, that body and its distinguished President will always find me ready to contribute not only to their service and deference, but also to their undertakings, not wasting the opportunity to be of assistance in them as soon as circumstances [and] time allow it, and [illegible] things and cases come to my notice that I think appropriate to the purposes of the Society.

The books that our Academy of History sent to Your Excellency are accompanied by the first Dictionary of Spanish, Latin, and Arabic, printed here under my direction; at the beginning of which I contributed a piece on the usefulness of the study of the Arabic language, especially for Spaniards, considering [illegible] to dedicate to its [illegible] the brief intervals that studies and the affairs of my profession left free for me during my youth. I have still to send the volumes, which are in press, that remain to complement the work, as soon as they come out.

Your Excellency's letter and your new gift [sic] have renewed the feelings of gratitude for your earlier favors and the appreciation and friendship professed for me by your esteemed person, whose life I ask Our Lord [to] keep for a great many and contented years.

Madrid, 24 May 1787.

4

Spanish, French, and Latin Transcriptions

Franklin y el Príncipe

🏵 Document 1
Legajo 7016-5, Estado, AGS
Francisco Escarano al príncipe de Masserano, Londres,
13 de enero de 1774.
[Carta manuscrita, 4 págs.]
Original en español

Excelentísimo señor

Señor:

Respondida desde El Pardo a 7 de febrero de 1774[1]
    La comisión del pianoforte que vuestra excelencia se sirvió darme en su última carta no pudo llegar más a tiempo, porque estaba casi pronto a hacerse a la vela el navío español San Bernardo, capitán Antonio de Revilla. Creo que partirá mañana, y con él envío a Don Luis de Ventades un pianoforte de monsieur Polhman, alemán, de quien tiene uno mi señora la duquesa de Villahermosa, y de quien se servía el embajador de Francia. No sin gran trabajo pude persuadirle a que me cediese uno que tenía hecho para un caballero. Cuesta 16 guineas. El que ha enviado Don Miguel de Ventades para la marquesa de la Torrecilla ha costado 16 y nueve chelines, y creo que no sea tan bueno.

El de la duquesa de Villahermosa costó veinte, porque tenía algún requisito más del que envío a vuestra excelencia.

Ojalá hubiese podido yo desempeñar tan prontamente el otro encargo de la armónica que desea el señor infante Don Gabriel.

Luego que recibí la orden de vuestra excelencia fui a ver a mademoiselle Davis, que es la mujer a quien vuestra excelencia vio algunas veces tocar este instrumento, y habiéndole dicho deseaba tener uno semejante para una hermana mía, me respondió que no tenía sino dos: el uno aquí, que le servía, y el otro que le había dejado en Florencia, a donde contaba volver en breve. Me añadió que su padre, que era el inventor, acababa de morir, y que no encontraría ciertamente en Inglaterra quien me hiciese uno igual. Hícele mil promesas porque me cediese el que tenía en Londres, y no hubo forma de convenir en ello.

Oí que el famoso doctor Franklin, a quien vuestra excelencia conoce, tenía uno. Fui a verle y le manifesté mis deseos de que me le cediese. Este filósofo, que es el mejor hombre del mundo, me confesó tener dos instrumentos de los que yo quería: el uno en América, para donde va a partir en breve, y el otro en Londres. Me dijo asimismo que gustoso me renunciaría el que tenía en su poder si no tuviese cuatro o cinco vasos rotos, y si fuese perfecto. Que el componerle era cosa muy difícil, y que así, lo único que podía hacer era sugerirme un hombre que en otro tiempo solía trabajar tales instrumentos, pero que me prevenía me pediría más de cincuenta libras esterlinas en caso de determinarse a hacerle. Le di mil gracias por su consejo, y al despedirme le saqué casi la palabra de que, si el referido hombre no consentía en hacerme la armónica, me cedería la suya por lo que le había costado. No habiéndome sido posible ayer encontrar en casa al artista indicado, y siendo hoy día muy ocupado para mí, no podré irle a buscar sino mañana, por lo que me reservo al correo que viene el dar a vuestra excelencia cuenta de las resultas de mis diligencias. Nada me quedará que hacer por obedecer al señor. Infante, y me lisonjeo tener la dicha de ejecutarlo.

En cuanto a milord North, no tengo qué decir a vuestra excelencia. No le he vuelto a ver desde que me dijo en Palacio que enviaría a buscar al secretario de la Aduana, señor Stanley, y consultaría con él lo que podría hacerse en favor de vuestra excelencia.

Ayer se abrió el Parlamento, en donde este soberano pronunció la arenga de que incluyo a vuestra excelencia una traducción en francés.

Se ha quemado la casa de campo de Esteban Fox, hijo primogénito de milord Holland. Se prendió fuego por la noche y todos tuvieron que salir en camisa.

No se me ocurre otra cosa que comunicar a vuestra excelencia, de quien estoy deseando con ansia noticias para saber si se ha restablecido de su último ataque de gota.

Me ofrezco con el más profundo respeto a la obediencia de vuestra excelencia, y ruego a Dios le guarde muchos años. Como deseo. Londres, a 13 de enero de 1774.

Excelentísimo señor
A los pies de vuestra excelencia su más humilde y rendido súbdito.
Francisco Escarano

Document 2

Legajo 7016-7, Estado, AGS
Francisco Escarano al Príncipe de Masserano, Londres,
1 de febrero de 1774
[Carta manuscrita, 5 págs.]
Original en español

Excelentísimo señor

Señor:

Respondida desde Madrid, a 24 de febrero de 1774[2]
    Continuando en dar cuenta a vuestra excelencia de las resultas de mis diligencias para lograr la armónica que el señor infante Don Gabriel desea, diré a vuestra excelencia que, habiendo pasado a casa del obrero que me indicó el famoso doctor Franklin, me mostró con mucha dificultad el instrumento que tenía como una cosa muy rara, y preguntando si quería vendérmele para una hermana mía, me respondió que no se desharía de él por ningún dinero. Fueron inútiles todos mis ruegos para persuadirle a cedérmelo, y lo fueron también para reducirle a que me hiciese otro semejante, insistiendo siempre en decirme que ni por cien guineas le emprendería. Sabiendo que es casi imposible vencer la obstinación de un inglés, fui a contar lo que me había pasado a señor Franklin, quien después de tal cual resistencia, me ofreció darme su armónica por lo que le había costado, haciéndola componer antes. Como a los hombres de bien no debe hacérseles misterio, le confesé que se traba de complacer al señor infante, lo que le ha empeñado más a darme bien compuesto su instrumento, lo que no podrá ser antes de un mes. No sé a punto fijo lo que costará. Me inclino a creer que no llegará a veinticinco libras esterlinas o cuarenta doblones. Me tendré por sumamente dichoso cuando haya logrado desempeñar esta comisión a gusto de su alteza, y según lo exige mi deber, emplearé todo el celo y toda la actividad posible.
    He recibido con el debido aprecio la carta de vuestra excelencia de 27 de diciembre, que me consuela con la buena noticia de que se

hallaba muy mejorado de su último ataque de gota. Lo que ha celebrado mucho este soberano, quien continuamente se informa por menor de la salud de vuestra excelencia.

Don Miguel de Ventades queda en enviar a vuestra excelencia una explicación de cómo se han de poner los tornillos a las cerraduras que le ha remitido. Y queda asimismo en comprar la péndula con las circunstancias que vuestra excelencia se ha servido explicarme.

Don Josef Constant, que se pone a los pies de vuestra excelencia, dice que no tiene inconveniente en destinar un apoderado en Barcelona para cobrar el sueldo de su gobierno, si vuestra excelencia encuentra dificultad en la Secretaría de Guerra de que se le pague en Londres. Espera que vuestra excelencia disimule éste su recurso.

Es cierto que el señor duque de Gloucester ha estado algunos días incógnito en París, y me parece haberlo escrito a vuestra excelencia. Este monarca, que no tuvo el menor indicio de que su hermano quería hacer esta escapada, no la ha tomado a mal. Si no fuera por el duque de Cumberland, ya se hubiera reconciliado con el señor duque de Gloucester, a quien profesa verdadero cariño.

Me alegro que el señor conde de Fuentes haya ido a Aragón, porque el viaje le habrá servido para desechar en parte su tristeza por la desgracia pasada. suplico a vuestra excelencia se sirva ponerme a los pies de mi señora la duquesa de Villahermosa, y a la obediencia del señor marqués de Mora, como también a las del señor duque.

Aún estamos en el mismo estado con milord North. Antes de ayer quise hablarle en Palacio, lo conoció y se fue a buscar a milord Mansfield, que estaba en un rincón de la antecámara del rey.

El Caballero Porter hace un mes que está con la gota, y no se le ve.

Mylord Rochford no nos recibirá hasta el jueves, y entonces le instaré para que persuada a milord North sacarme de la incertidumbre en que estamos. No dude vuestra excelencia que dejaremos de lograr algo, pero querer decir a qué se reducirá sería exponernos a errarlo.

Sobre la casa de milord Harcourt nada he hecho, porque aguardo que vuestra excelencia me conteste a la carta en que le hice una descripción de ella. Me lisonjeo que esta contestación me llegará de hoy en ocho días, y entonces procederemos al ajuste, en el que se procurará conseguir la mayor ventaja. Recelo que vuestra excelencia se estará deshaciendo porque no adelanto en ninguno de sus negocios, y que me echará la culpa, pero aseguro a vuestra excelencia que no depende de mí el que no se hayan concluido.

Puskin asegura que han tomado a Silistria y que le han puesto fuego, pero al mismo tiempo dice que todo el ejército ha vuelto a repasar el Danubio, lo que es una prueba evidente de que ha quedado destruido.

Aquel inglés Lloyd que fue abate y bibliotecario del duque de Montealegre en Venecia, escribiente en Madrid, alférez de artillería en Barcelona y medio ayuda de campo del Príncipe de Brunswick en Alemania, es hoy mayor general al servicio de la Zarina.[3] Estos ministros la desean porque conocen sus buenas prendas.

La hermosa My Lady, que vive muy bien con su marido, vendrá el mes de marzo a Londres si no pasa un cierto sujeto el Estrecho. Si le pasa se quedará la pobre en su casa de campo. Me ha enviado una carta para mi Señra la duquesa de Villahermosa, la que incluyo, en la que escribo por medio de vuestra excelencia a su marido.

He visto al capellán de milord Grantham, que me ha venido recomendado por Don Bernardo del Campo. Me parece un hombre muy instruido y muy amable. Me dice había visto a Vuestra Excelenci la víspera de su marcha, y que entonces quedaba casi restablecido de su último ataque de gota, lo que celebro con todo mi corazón.

Esta soberana no parece ya en público por estar muy próxima al parto. Su majestad británica me pregunta siempre por vuestra excelencia y se alegra infinito de estar seguro de su vuelta a esta Corte. Todo el cuerpo diplomático corresponde como debe a las memorias de vuestra excelencia, a quien suplico rendidamente se sirva conservarme su protección y honrarme con sus preceptos. Dios guarde a vuestra excelencia muchos años. Como deseo y he menester. Londres, a 1 de febrero de 1774.

>Excelentísimo señor
>A los pies de vuestra excelencia su más humilde y rendido súbdito Francisco Escarano.
>La armónica se está componiendo. Me la entregarán dentro de tres semanas.

Document 3
Legajo 7016-6, Estado, AGS
Francisco Escarano al Príncipe de Masserano, Londres,
18 de febrero de 1774
[Carta manuscrita, 7 págs.]
Original en español

Señor:

Respondida desde El Pardo, el 8 y 10 de marzo de 1774

    Antes de contestar a la carta con que vuestra excelencia se sirvió de honrarme el 24 del próximo pasado, le diré que habiendo ido ayer a ver al doctor Franklin, me prometió entregarme la semana que viene sin falta alguna la armónica enteramente compuesta, con lo que podemos contar pues es hombre de palabra. Le pedí me diese una explicación del modo de tocar este instrumento, a lo que me respondió que en sus obras traducidas e impresas en francés, se hallaba una carta suya al célebre padre Beccaria de Milán,[4] en que se especificaba todo lo que yo deseaba, pero que no obstante, si después de haber examinado tal carta viese que no estaba muy clara, me formaría una clarísima instrucción y me la entregaría. vuestra excelencia ve que el doctor Franklin no podía haber procedido con más garbo y que debemos estarle reconocidos.

    Don Miguel de Ventades me ha dicho que antes de un mes saldrá un navío para Bilbao, y que puede ser vaya antes otro a San Sebastián. Aprovecharé del primero de los dos para enviar dicho instrumento. Aseguro a vuestra excelencia que me estoy deshaciendo por no serme posible servir al señor infante Don Gabriel con aquella prontitud que quisiera. Veo que se pasarán, por mi desgracia, tal vez dos meses antes que su alteza tenga ahí la armónica, pero este considerable retardo no depende de mí.

    Si la vajilla china y damascos que vuestra excelencia piensa enviar por Bilbao llegan antes de vuestra excelencia, iré a hablar a milord North y haré cuanto esté de mi parte para que dejen entrar el todo sin pagar derechos.

    No pongo la menor duda en que después de tantas buenas palabras hagan algo. Era menester que estos señores no tuviesen vergüenza para volverse atrás de lo prometido. No digo que me hayan especificado el grado a que llegarán sus condescendencias, pero me han repetido una y muchas veces que tendrán todas las que les sean posibles en consideración a la estima que hacen y han hecho siempre de vuestra excelencia.

Conforme vuestra excelencia me lo previene, se irán pagando los dos coches para que vuestra excelencia no tenga que pensar en esa deuda a su llegada.

[Josef] Constant ha recibido ya de [Miguel] Ventades su sueldo de gobernador. Se pone a los pies de vuestra excelencia y me encarga manifestarle su humilde reconocimiento.

El rey ha pagado ya el alquiler de la casa en que habito hasta último de julio, y así tendrá vuestra excelencia tiempo para buscar otra en que alojarse, si no le cede la suya milord Harcourt, cuyo agente no ha recibido aún ninguna respuesta a las proposiciones que le hice.

Cuando me lleguen las cuatro Guías de Forasteros[5] que vuestra excelencia tenía ánimo de entregar al conde de Priego, entregaré dos a milord Bristol para que dé una a este Soberano y se quede con la otra. Daré la tercera a milord Rochford y guardaré la cuarta para mí, por la que doy a vuestra excelencia rendidas gracias.

El domingo manifesté a su majestad británica el gusto que tenía vuestra excelencia en volver a hacerle su Corte, y además le dije que habiéndole obedecido en preguntar a vuestra excelencia si el señor marqués sería exento antes de que vuestra excelencia saliese de ahí, me respondía que el rey se había propuesto de no adelantar a ninguno que no hubiese hecho algún mérito personal en su servicio. Sirvióse su majestad británica decirme que eso era muy justo, pero que tal vez habría alguna gracia especial.

El conde de Searnafis me encarga decir a vuestra excelencia que sentirá infinito no estar aquí a su venida porque habiendo retardado ya su marcha cuatro meses más de lo que creía, no sabe aún si podrá prolongar su detención por algún tiempo. No sabemos si el asunto que ha dado lugar a las amenazas del caballero Linch se ha compuesto.

El conde de Pignatelli, el de Haslang, Sarnier y todos los del Cuerpo Diplomático me hablan siempre de los deseos de volver a ver vuestra excelencia, y a todos correspondo con las regulares expresiones.

Don Bernardino Delgado me ha escrito que suplique a vuestra excelencia le deje ahí bien recomendado al señor marqués de Grimaldi, que puede facilitarle alguna cosa buena, y yo lo ejecuto por complacerle, pidiendo a vuestra excelencia al mismo tiempo mil perdones por la libertad que me tomo confiando que su bondad me la disimulará.

Ha salido un folleto intitulado *La repartición de Polonia*. Es la más terrible sátira que pueda escribirse contra el rey de Prusia, la emperatriz reina y la zarina. su autor es, según creo, monsieur Lind, escocés, que vuestra excelencia vio aquí como ayo[6] del principillo Poniatowski.[7] La enviaré por una ocasión que se me presentará pasado mañana a Don Bernardo del Campo, y si estuviese en francés la enviaría también a vuestra excelencia. Todos la admiran por la gracia y espíritu con que está escrita. El mismo Lind es el autor de cuatro cartas sobre la Polonia que han hecho mucho ruido. En dicho folleto hay un diálogo entre el rey de Prusia y un judío Ephraim, su consejero y ministro de Estado, en que el rey le dice estas palabras:

"Ya te he dicho, Ephraim, que así lo quiero. He dado orden para que me envíen de Holanda cuatrocientos mil ducados. Los harás derretir y acuñar de nuevo, pero con tal liga que podamos ganar 25 sueldos[8] en cada uno. Escribe al conde de Maltzan y dile (si acaso sus estratagemas en los fondos no le ocupan demasiado) que nos procure algunas guineas, de que haremos el mismo uso. Cuando sepa lo que queremos hacer aumentará su celo en el desempeño de esta comisión. He tenido últimamente una prueba de los talentos de este conde, cuando empaquetó todos sus muebles e hizo el papel de un ministro a quien llama su Corte para que su conducta influyese en los fondos, y poder pescar en el agua turbia del Change-Alley[9] etc etc"

En otro paraje hay lo que se sigue.

El rey de Prusia hablando con la emperatriz:

"La prescripción o larga posesión no prueba nada contra una pretensión rancia, con tal que podamos sostenerla. Ni ningún derecho antiguo puede ser borrado por ningún Tratado, con tal que podamos violar el Tratado con impunidad".

Emperatriz reina:

"¿No es esto llevar las cosas demasiado lejos? Según ese modo de razonar, yo puedo volver a tomar Silesia siempre que guste, no obstante los Tratados que subsisten entre nosotros".

Rey de Prusia:

"No señora, no siempre que vuestra merced guste, sino siempre que vuestra merced pueda. Lo confieso, pero yo tendré cuidado de impedir que vuestra merced se tiente de hacer uso de mis máximas etc etc."

A la zarina es a quien tira más, y con razón.

Pasando ahora a otro asunto, diré a vuestra excelencia que el conde de Guines ha enviado aquí un sujeto de su confianza para tomar varias declaraciones que cree puedan serle favorables, y habiendo acudido a Garnier, le ha respondido que le permita no mezclarse en este asunto.

Estoy aturdido de que se porte con tanta ingratitud hacia su jefe, pero ha mucho tiempo que sabía su mal modo de pensar. suplico a vuestra excelencia reservar en sí estas especies.

El portero ha tenido la desgracia un mes ha de maltratarse muchísimo una mano con una vidriera que le cayó encima. Ha estado todo este tiempo en poder de un cirujano, que le ha pedido por la cura cuatro guineas. Ha acudido a mí para que se le paguen, y yo me he negado a ello. Piensa escribir a vuestra excelencia y le he dicho haga lo que quiera. Si vuestra excelencia tiene por conveniente hacerle la caridad de darle la mitad, esto es dos guineas, o lo que fuere de su agrado, se servirá decirme su voluntad, o dejar este punto para cuando esté aquí.

No hay nada de nuevo que merezca escribirse a vuestra excelencia, y más estando ahí en proporción de ver lo poco que digo de oficio. Por este motivo ceso de importunarle, pero no de suplicarle rendidamente me continúe su protección y sus preceptos. Dios guarde a vuestra excelencia muchos años como deseo y he menester. Londres, a 18 de febrero de 1774.

La adjunta es de la hermosa milady para su amiga mi señora la duquesa de Villahermosa, a cuyos pies pido a vuestra excelencia me ponga.

Excelentísimo señor
A los pies de vuestra excelencia su más humilde y rendido súbdito
Francisco Escarano

Document 4
Legajo 7016-9, Estado, AGS
Francisco Escarano al Príncipe de Masserano, Londres,
11 de marzo de 1774
[Carta manuscrita, 3 págs.]
Original en español

Excelentísimo señor

Señor:
Respondida desde Madrid, a 14 de abril de 1774

Ayer me envió el doctor Franklin la armónica acompañada de sus obras traducidas en francés, pidiéndome las remita al señor infante Don Gabriel, y suplique humildemente a su Alteza le haga la honra de recibirlas; con lo que podrá ver en la página 209 del segundo tomo el modo de tocar este instrumento. Con un navío que partirá en breves días para Bilbao le remitiré a Don Luis de Ventades, encargándole cuide mucho de su dirección y de la de los dos libros, que pondré dentro de un encerado[10] para que no se mojen o maltraten.

He dado al doctor Franklin las gracias, diciéndole que no dudaba que su Alteza leería con mucho gusto sus obras, y le he pagado el coste del instrumento y su compostura, cuyo gasto, con el del embarco y otras menudencias, subirá a unas veinte libras esterlinas con poca diferencia. La semana que viene enviaré a vuestra excelencia la cuenta y el conocimiento del capitán del navío, que quisiera estuviese ya en España. Crea vuestra excelencia que la dilación no ha dependido de mí, y que me he estado consumiendo por no haber podido desempeñar antes esta comisión.

Se empieza a tratar en el Parlamento el arduo asunto de las colonias de América, como vuestra excelencia podrá verlo en la carta que escribo al Jefe. El empleo de Charles Fox se ha dado a milord Beauchamp, hijo de milord Hardfort. El caballero Meredith ha sido hecho contralor del rey[11] en lugar de milord Pelham, que ha sido nombrado primer juez de los Bosques Reales, que es lo que aquí llaman un *sinecura*,[12] y nosotros beneficio simple, que tenía el duque de Leeds, a quien se ha dado una pensión que naturalmente pasará después de su muerte a su hijo, el marqués de Carmarthen.

Milord Rochford me dijo ayer que si vuestra excelencia tomaba la casa de Milord Harcourt, le haría muchas visitas. La mayor parte de esta nobleza decía que vuestra excelencia vaya a habitarla, pero vuestra excelencia sabe lo que más le conviene.

Hemos tenido esta semana un perverso tiempo, y no es extraño que hoy no haya llegado el correo.

Estoy mejor de mi fluxión a los ojos,[13] pero aún no libre enteramente.

Me imagino que esta carta, y la que tendré el honor de escribirle el correo próximo, encontrarán a vuestra excelencia aún en Madrid, y aguardaré después sus órdenes en cuanto al modo de dirigírselas.

Sé que vuestra excelencia ha bailado en casa del jefe, lo que me causa suma satisfacción porque es una prueba de su salud, en que me interesaré toda mi vida.

suplico a vuestra excelencia me honre con sus preceptos, y que esté siempre persuadido de mi gratitud. Dios guarde a vuestra excelencia muchos años como deseo. Londres, a 11 de marzo de 1774.

Excelentísimo señor
A los pies de vuestra excelencia su más humilde y rendido súbdito Francisco Escarano.

Document 5
Legajo 7016-10, Estado, AGS
Francisco Escarano al Príncipe de Masserano, Londres,
18 de marzo de 1774
[Carta manuscrita, 6 págs.]
Original en español

Señor:

Respondida desde Madrid a 14 de abril de 1774
 El navío Santo Domingo, y la Buenaventura del capitán Cotarro es el que lleva la armónica, cuyo coste importa veinte libras esterlinas según verá vuestra excelencia en la adjunta cuenta. Don Luis de Ventades pagará el porte hasta Bilbao, y cuidará de remitirla a Madrid con el mayor cuidado, según se lo prevengo. Le digo que espere las órdenes de vuestra excelencia o las del señor Marqués de Grimaldi, y que haga cuanto esté de su parte para que este instrumento llegue a la corte lo más presto que sea posible.
 Tres días ha me envió milord Rochford un paquete que había recibido para mí de París, y en él hallé una carta de vuestra excelencia con cuatro guías de forasteros. Inmediatamente llevé a milord Bristol dos para que pusiese en manos de su majestad británica la que venía en el estuche y se quedase con la otra, lo que ejecutó. Me ha pedido dar mil gracias a vuestra excelencia por su memoria y pasado mañana domingo me hablará tal vez este soberano sobre la que debe a vuestra excelencia. Milord Rochford ha agradecido también el regalo de vuestra excelencia como una prueba de su amistad, y yo le repito mis humildes agradecimientos por el que me ha tocado.
 He recibido la carta con que vuestra excelencia se ha dignado honrarme el 24 de febrero, por la que veo con sumo dolor la grave enfermedad del señor Marqués de Mora. No puedo ponderar a vuestra excelencia la aflicción que me causa el considerar la que tendrá su pobre padre. Espero que Dios le ha de consolar con la salud de un hijo, a quien tiene tantos motivos para querer en extremo. suplico a vuestra excelencia me ponga a la obediencia de uno y otro y a los pies de mi señora la duquesa de Villahermosa, a quien contemplo afligidísima.

vuestra excelencia sabe cuantas obligaciones debo a toda esta respetable familia, y así comprenderá el interés que tengo en todas sus cosas.

   Costant[14] ha cobrado ya aquí su sueldo de gobernador, con lo que no tiene vuestra excelencia que incomodarse en dar ningún paso.
Han llegado ya a Don Miguel de Ventades 130 botellas de agua de Celse, y tiene aviso del vino del Marqués de Vanmark, todo lo que vaya llegando se recogerá y cuidará hasta que vuestra excelencia llegue.

   Los coches están prontos. He hablado ayer con Wright, y según se me ha explicado no tiene, ni tendrá la menor pretensión por el interés del dinero que no se le ha pagado, ni por el alquiler de la cochera. Pasado mañana se le entregarán doscientas libras esterlinas a cuenta. Las ciento son de los ahorros de enero, y febrero, y las restantes son las que yo había de cobrar el último día de marzo. Costant con lo que ha ido ahorrando de las 50 libras que le doy cada mes tiene bastante para el gasto de abril: Cuando vuestra excelencia venga verá las cuentas desde 1 de enero de este año, y si gusta se las enviaré a París. He procurado que vaya todo con la mayor exactitud, y en ello no he hecho sino lo que es de mi obligación.

   En punto a casa no me ocurre que decir: He enviado a vuestra excelencia las listas de los muebles que son necesarios para la de Harcourt, y para la del general Clarc; le he expuesto las condiciones de las dos; con que así no me queda que hacer sino esperar la resolución de vuestra excelencia. Yo bien quisiera que vuestra excelencia no tomase ninguna hasta ver por sus propios ojos lo que más le conviene.

   Por lo que toca a entradas también he escrito a vuestra excelencia lo que me había pasado últimamente con milord North: De ello deduzco que nos facilitará algo, sino todo lo que deseamos. Antes que me olvide diré a vuestra excelencia que su majestad británica se sirvió decirme la semana pasada que esperaba que el rey al despedirse le daría la Patente de exempto para el señor Marqués. *Croyez- moi, ce sera le prevent du depart*,[15] fueron sus formales palabras. Yo me alegraría que su majestad adivinase.

   Del nuevo mayor general ruso no he vuelto a hablar a vuestra excelencia porque no me ha ocurrido añadir a lo expuesto. Se halla aún aquí, y siempre que va a Palacio le acoge con mucha benignidad este soberano: tiene ánimo de pasar al ejército del Danubio, si no se hace la paz este invierno. Del conde de Guines nada se sabe de fijo, pero todos creen que no volverá a esta Embajada. su pleito no ha empezado aún y será cosa muy larga. Siento en el alma ver que tenga por enemigos, o a lo menos por indiferentes aquellas personas, a quienes ha hecho bien, y a quienes ha tratado con tanta distinción. vuestra excelencia me comprende sin que tenga que explicarme más.

Si viene el conde de Fernán Nuñez le obsequiaré como es de razón. Es un joven de muchísimo mérito. Magallón también me hace entrever esperanzas de venir a Inglaterra pero aún no lo creo.

Ha llegado el Marqués de Cordón. Parece excelente hombre y que gustará en este país por su naturalidad, y franqueza. Se presenta en la Corte con una peluca al modo de la de Foresta,[16] aunque mejor peinada, y con sus vueltas de simple batista. El conde de Searnafis se dispone a partir a últimos de este mes.

Ya se empiezan a tomar resoluciones en el Parlamento en cuanto a las colonias de América. La Cámara de los Comunes ha consentido en la proposición de milord North, de que se saque la aduana de Boston, se transplante a otro paraje, se bloquee el puerto, y se le impida todo comercio de importación y exportación hasta que vengan a su deber, y empiecen por indemnizar a la Compañía de Indias de todo el prejuicio que le han causado.

No hay otra cosa de nuevo que merezca la atención de vuestra excelencia. Me temo que esta carta no le encuentre ya en Madrid, pero naturalmente habrá dado vuestra excelencia disposición para que se la remitan a Bayona. Deseo a vuestra excelencia un felicísimo viaje y le aseguro que anhelo con ansia volverme a poner a sus pies. Entretanto que logro esta satisfacción suplico a vuestra excelencia me dé la de obedecerle y obsequiarle. Dios guarde a vuestra excelencia muchos años como ha menester. Londres a 18 de marzo de 1774.

Me han dicho que la hermosa senñorita ha venido a Londres, pero no la he visto aún.

[nota al costado izquierdo]

Excelentísimo señor
A los pies de vuestra excelencia su más humilde y rendido súbdito.
Francisco Escarano

[cuenta adjunta]

Instrumento de vidrios llamado armónica

Libras esterlinas	Chelines
Por el coste de la armónica	17 17
Por el cajón y embalaje	01 05
Gastos de transporte al navío, y de aduana	<u>00 18</u>
	20 00

Importa el todo veinte libras esterlinas

[nota de recibo de pago firmada por Masserano]
    He recibido esta suma del señor infante Don Gabriel para quien es el instrumento nombrado la armónica, en Madrid a 11 de abril de 1774.

    Masserano

[nota adicional al final de la carta]

Señor

No sé si convendría que el señor infante Don Gabriel correspondiese al regalo de los libros del doctor Franklin con el suyo. Perdone vuestra excelencia este sugerimiento.

⌘ Document 6
Legajo 501, Archivo del Infante Don Gabriel, AGP
El príncipe de Masserano al duque de Béjar,
Madrid, 6 de abril de 1774
[Nota preliminar, 1 pág.]
Original en español

Serenísimo infante Don Gabriel
Carta del príncipe de Masserano y cuenta del coste, embalaje y derechos de aduana del instrumento llamado armónica que remite para su alteza el secretario de Embajada en Londres.

Se libró su importe a Hermenegildo Vázquez para entregarle a su excelencia en 7 de dicho, en extraordinario.

[Carta manuscrita con nota resumen al inicio, 2 págs.]
Excelentísimo señor.
Querido amigo y muy señor mío.

Acabando de recibir aviso de Londres del secretario de embajada Don Francisco Escarano, de haber remitido para el señor infante Don Gabriel la armónica que me mandó su alteza le hiciese venir, y remitídome la adjunta cuenta de su costo, la paso a sus manos a fin de que como sea de su agrado, bien remitiéndoselo en derechura o mandándomelo entregar para dirigírselo, se sirvan providenciar su importe de las 20 libras esterlinas que indica. Y con este motivo te renuevo las veras de mi amistad y afecto, deseando siempre servirte y que Dios te guarde muchos años, que puede. Madrid, 6 de abril de 1774.

    Excelentísimo señor
    Te besa las manos tu amigo y seguro servidor
    El príncipe de Masserano

[anexo, 1 pág.]

Instrumento de vidrios llamado armónica.

	Libras esterlinas	Chelines
Por el coste de la armónica	17	17
Por el cajón y embalaje	1	5
Gastos de transportar al navío y de Aduana	0	18
	20	00

Importa el todo veinte libras esterlinas

🏵 Document 7
Legajo 7016-11, Estado, AGS
Francisco Escarano al príncipe de Masserano,
Londres, 10 de abril de 1774
[Carta manuscrita, 4 págs.]
Original en español

Excelentísimo señor

Respondida desde París el 18 de mayo de 1774

Señor:
    Aunque me hallo con una fluxión a los ojos bastante fuerte no dejo de contestar hoy viernes santo a la carta que vuestra excelencia se sirvió empezar a escribirme el 7 y concluyó el 10 del pasado. La funesta noticia de la muerte de nuestro infante me ha penetrado de dolor: Me quedé atónito al leer la de oficio en que se me comunicaba esta desgracia. Ha sido una pérdida para toda la nación y sólo puede templar nuestro dolor la esperanza de que la princesa nuestra señora la repare dándonos otros Infantes, como se lo pido a Dios.
    El jefe me ha escrito mandándome dar las gracias a milord Rochford por la buena noticia del abandono de la Gran Malvina y al cumplir con esta orden me pareció conveniente entregar a dicho ministro traducción de la carta del señor Marqués, en la que se hacen los debidos elogios de este secretario de Estado quien *a été enchanté de la manière don't monsieur le marquis s'explique par rapport à lui*.[17]
    Doy parte hoy de lo que me ha dicho el expresado Lord que se ha ido a pasar las Pascuas en el campo, como también mister sufolk [*sic*].
    No ha pasado aún el navío que lleva la armónica. Ya conoce vuestra excelencia las cosas de ventadas:[18] a quince días que me dijo iba a hacerse a la vela. Me estoy consumiendo porque conozco que el señor infante estará esperando con ansia ver el dicho instrumento. suplico a vuestra excelencia (si acaso esta mía le encuentra en Madrid) ponerme a los pies de su Alteza, y rendirle humildes gracias por el libro que se ha dignado regalarme, el que guardaré toda mi vida como el mayor Tesoro. No dudo que el doctor Franklin apreciará tan magnífico regalo: así él como yo debemos estar muy reconocidos a vuestra excelencia que es quien nos lo ha facilitado.

Me imagino que en la primera carta que vuestra excelencia me escribe me contestará a la que tuve el honor de dirigirle dándole parte de las condiciones de mister Harcourt. Aunque vuestra excelencia se decida a tomarla procuraré no concluir nada hasta que se halle en París, y si puede ser hasta que llegue vuestra excelencia a Londres, pues así podrá ver lo que más le conviene.

Las proposiciones hechas a vuestra excelencia por el conde de Guines me parecen razonables: Por este motivo también iré llevando de día en día al agente de milord Harcourt.

Siento que el embajador de Francia ponga a vuestra excelencia en el embarazo de dar declaraciones: yo no sé a qué fin todo esto cuando está tan probada su inocencia. Malditos fondos que tanto han dado que sentir. No puede vuestra excelencia aborrecerlos más que yo. Por mi fortuna en el tiempo que he estado encargado de los negocios no se han ofrecido asuntos que tratar, y así me he librado de las calumnias que podrían habérseme suscitado. Estoy bien seguro que cualquier secretario particular que vuestra excelencia traiga vendrá persuadido de que no se le ha de permitir tratar directa, ni indirectamente con ningún comerciante. Cada vez conozco que son gente abominable y que un hombre de honor debe huir.

Dudo mucho que los coches puedan estar enteramente pagados para cuando vuestra excelencia llegue, si viene como lo deseo, a fin de mayo. Se han dado ya 200 libras, y nos faltan que entregar aún 150, poco más, o menos. Cuanto se podrá ahorrar en abril, y mayo se reducirá a unas 120. Crea vuestra excelencia que el sistema económico de esta su casa es uno de los puntos de que más he cuidado.

Si vuestra excelencia está aún en Madrid al recibo de esta mía verá lo que escribe de oficio, y así es inútil que le refiera lo muy poco que por acá ocurre; y si está en camino esta carta le llegará tan atrasada que no valdrá la pena de leerse. Además mis ojos me hacen tanto mal, que no puedo continuar.

suplico a vuestra excelencia me conserve siempre bajo su amparo, y me honre con sus preceptos. Dios guarde a vuestra excelencia muchos años como deseo y es menester. Londres a 10 de abril de 1774.

El conde de Haslang que se pone a la obediencia de vuestra excelencia me ha encargado suplicarle traerle un vestido de París, que debía traerle el conde de Guines. Dice que a vuestra excelencia no le harán ninguna dificultad en cuanto a vestidos y yo le he respondido que le harán muchas, aunque no lo creo.

A los pies de vuestra excelencia su más humilde y rendido súbdito.
Francisco de Escarano

Document 8
Legajo 6989-33, Estado, AGS
Francisco Escarano al Marqués de Grimaldi, Londres,
21 de marzo de 1775
[Carta manuscrita, 3 págs.]
Original en español

Señor:
 Hoy debe leerse por la tercera vez en la Cámara de los Pares el Bill[19] con que se prohibe a la provincia de la Nueva Inglaterra la pesca de Terranova, sobre cuyo asunto hubo el 16 del corriente los debates del que dí cuenta a vuestra excelencia en una de mis cartas del correo pasado. Habiendo podido después tener un extracto de la elocuente oración pronunciada aquel día por el Lord Campden en favor de los Americanos le remito a vuestra excelencia traducido en francés.
 El célebre doctor Franklin, natural de Filadelfia, ha partido para su país antes de ayer, y como se haya muy quejoso del Ministerio por haberle quitado un empleo de gran lucro que tenía con aquella provincia, se recela que conmueva aquellos ánimos, y los persuada a continuar en el espíritu de resistencia que han mostrado hasta ahora. Los que conocen a fondo las colonias inglesas de América temen vaya aumentando el fuego que allí se ha encendido, y que no pueda apagarle el Ministerio cuando quiera. El caballero Blaquier, secretario del virreynato de Irlanda, que se haya aquí con licencia, decía pocos días ha a un amigo suyo que era gran fortuna de la Inglaterra el que la España no pensase sino en la guerra de los marroquíes. No nombraría el sujeto si esta carta no fuese por mano de un oficial francés, que me ha prometido ponerla en las de mi correspondiente de Calais.
 Con la posta de Holanda que llegó ayer se ha esparcido la noticia de que una fragata de guerra inglesa había visitado a la desembocadura del Texel un bastimento mercantil Holandés destinado a América; que no había encontrado a su bordo armas, ni municiones de guerra, y sí sólo varias cartas, y papeles para Filadelfia, los que había remitido inmediatamente a este almirantazgo el capitán de dicha fragata.
 Es verosímil que la República se queje, si el hecho es cierto, y también lo es que no se le dará ninguna satisfacción. Esta Compañía de

Indias ha perdido en las costas de Africa el Navío el Middleton, que volvía interesado en ochenta mil libras esterlinas.

Ha muerto la hija menor del señor duque de Gloucester: dicen que este príncipe quería se hubiese enterrado en la bóveda que esta familia real tiene en la abadía de Westminster, y que no habiendo consentido en ello su majestad británica se enterrase en la catedral de Windsor.

Ha muerto también en Bath de un accidente de paralisia milord Brystol, el mismo que estuvo de Embajador en esta Corte: le hereda su hermano el Jefe de Escuadra Harvey. Ha llegado de París con licencia milord Ormond. Se cree venga a casarse con una hija de milord Harrington.

> Dios guarde a vuestra excelencia muchos años. Londres a 21 de Marzo de 1775.
> Excelentísimo señor
> Beso la mano de vuestra excelencia su más humilde y rendido súbdito
> Francisco Escarano

Document 9
Legajo 7016-53, AGS
Francisco Escarano al Marqués de Grimaldi, Londres, 31 de marzo de 1775 [1779], no. 469[20]
[Copia de la carta original, manuscrita, 1 pág.]
Original en español
Copia de carta del señor Don Francisco de Escarano al excelentísimo señor Marqués de Grimaldi, con fecha de 31 de marzo de 1775

Excelentísimo señor

Señor:
No ha llegado de Gibraltar, como ha corrido por muy cierta la noticia y como avisé a vuestra excelencia en mi carta de ayer, ninguna fragata. Quien ha venido es señor Stott, capitán de la llamada la *Allarme*, el que dejando su embarcación en Tolon y haciendo la mayor diligencia, se ha puesto en pocos días en Londres. Se me ha dicho por seguro y en gran secreto que viene desde Argel, cuyo Dey[21] le ha dado carta blanca para hacer un tratado de paz con esta Corte. Milord Rochford está lleno de gozo, y se prepara a sacar las mayores ventajas de las buenas disposiciones que muestra aquella regencia. Muy en breve volverá a partir el mencionado Stott con el tratado, y en recompensa se le nombrará cónsul general en aquel puerto con cinco libras esterlinas de sueldo al día, además del de capitán de fragata cuyo mando conserva.

En una ocasión como la actual, en que teme el Ministerio inglés, aunque diga lo contrario, que aprovechemos de sus críticas circunstancias para hacerle la guerra, o a lo menos para fomentar el fuego de las colonias de América, me ocurre el recelo, tal vez mal fundado, de que sea un punto de las instrucciones secretas de Sr. Stott el procurar persuadir a los argelinos emprender el sitio de Orán para darnos en qué entretenernos. El conde de Maltzan, con mucho misterio, me ha confiado haber recibido una carta de Holanda en que le dicen haber sido la Inglaterra quien ha excitado al rey de Marruecos a declararnos la guerra. Nunca me han merecido gran crédito las noticias de este ministro de Prusia, y la referida mucho menos, porque estoy persuadido que así él como los de Rusia y Dinamarca quisieran vernos romper con esta Corte.

Creyendo que conviene que llegue a manos de vuestra excelencia cuanto antes esta carta, que va por conducto seguro hasta Calais, envío copia al señor conde de Aranda, pidiéndole se la remita si le ofrece despachar algún extraordinario.

Dios guarde etc. A la vuelta.[22]

◼ Document 10
Legajo 6989-39, Estado, AGS
Francisco Escarano al Marqués de Grimaldi, Londres,
31 de marzo de 1775[23]
[Carta manuscrita, 3 págs.]
Original en español

Señor:
    En la conferencia que ayer tuve con milord Suffolk empezó por decirme que estaba admirado de la heroica Resistencia de Melilla, añadiéndome que según parecía por los grandes preparativos que se hacían en los puertos de España se hallaba el rey nuestro señor resuelto a concluir con un golpe vigoroso esta guerra, lo que no podían dejar de aprobar. Le respondí que vuestra excelencia no me había escrito cosa alguna en este asunto, pero que no extrañaría el que su majestad quisiese escarmentar la audacia del rey de marruecos, que sin considerar las grandes ventajas que le resultaban de su paz con nosotros había osado romperla.
    A esto se siguió el preguntarle si las noticias que les habían llegado de América eran tan buenas como yo deseaba; contestome diciendo que era favorable, y que les hacían concebir fundadas esperanzas de que las colonias se rindiesen a la razón. Manifestando darle crédito le dije que según eso suspenderían quizás el envío de tropas, y navíos; a lo que me replicó que no se suspendería, pues era menester hacer ver a los americanos que había modo de traerlos a su deber con la fuerza, y que sin embargo de saberse que el partido del gobierno hacía grandes progresos en aquellas provincias pasaría algún tiempo antes de restablecer en ellas una perfecta tranquilidad.
    El encargado de los negocios de Francia me ha dicho que hablándole milord Suffolk de nuestros preparativos marítimos había alabado mucho la determinación del rey caracterizándola de sabia, y prudente. Creo que en este caso no tiene este Ministerio otro partido que tomar, pues sería temeridad el pedirnos explicaciones en cuanto a nuestros armamentos cuando nosotros no se las pedimos por los que disponen para América. Además de esto me imagino no les pesa vernos empeñados en gastos, y ocupados con los marroquíes.

Casi todos los ministros extranjeros se han quedado admirados de oír decir a milord Suffolk que habían recibido favorables avisos de Boston, cuando es constante haber sido malísimos y tales cuales he comunicado a vuestra excelencia en mi carta número 468 que envié ayer por ocasión segura a Calais. Hasta aquí hemos hallado muy sincero a este Secretario de Estado, pero debe tener en el día motivo para publicar que los negocios de América van bien siendo justamente lo contrario.

Ayer pasó su majestad británica al Parlamento para aprobar el Bill[24] de la prohibición de la pesca de Terranova a los habitantes de la Nueva Inglaterra. Luego que se imprima procuraré enviarle a vuestra excelencia para que vea los términos en que está concebido.

Los que conocen bien aquel país son de dictamen que no puede producir buen efecto: acabarán de inflamarse aquellos ánimos, y vendrán a un golpe de desesperación. El Ministerio ha visto partir de aquí con sumo sentimiento al célebre doctor Franklin. Resentido como estaba contra este gobierno por haberle quitado un empleo de gran lucro que tenía en Filadelfia,[25] es verosímil haga mucho mal en aquella Provincia, en donde le miran como el padre de la patria. Repito a vuestra excelencia que no se prevee puedan componerse las diferencias de las colonias sin la caída de los actuales ministros; y los más de ellos lo creen así. Si este Soberano hace ver a los colonos que por complacerlos ha mudado de ministros puede ser se reduzcan a la obediencia, pactando antes la confirmación de sus privilegios: En todos casos me parece vendrán a ganar los Americanos.

Dios guarde a vuestra excelencia muchos años como deseo. Londres a 31 de marzo de 1775.

Excelentísimo señor
Beso la mano de vuestra excelencia su más humilde y rendido súbdito
Francisco Escarano

Document 11
Legajo 738, Archivo del Infante de Don Gabriel, AGP
Benjamín Franklin a su Excelencia Don Gabriel de Borbón y Sajonia,
Filadelfia, 12 de diciembre de 1775
[Carta principal, 3 págs.]
Original en inglés

◈   Document 12
Legajo 6990-15, Estado, AGS
El Príncipe de Masserano al Marqués de Grimaldi, Londres, 27 de junio de 1775, no. 25
[Carta manuscrita, 5 págs.]
Original en español

Excelentísimo señor

Muy señor mío:
   Continúan en venir muy malas noticias de América. Las cartas de Boston confirman haber bloqueado los rebeldes aquella capital. Que de resultas de una asamblea que habían tenido sus vecinos, habían expuesto al general Gage que, después de las crueldades cometidas por sus tropas, no podían reconocerle por gobernador ni obedecerle en nada. Que habiéndole pedido permiso para retirarse de la ciudad, les había respondido se lo concedería con tal que saliesen sin armas, condición que no habían admitido. Que la guarnición carecía de todo género de provisiones frescas, no manteniéndose de mucho tiempo a esta parte sino de carne salada. Y que se hallaba en la mayor consternación.
   Dicen haberse aumentado ésta con una desgracia sucedida el 10 del próximo pasado.[26] Estando algunos soldados recibiendo en uno de aquellos cuarteles una porción de cartuchos, se pegó fuego casualmente a uno de ellos y, comunicándose a los demás, se quemó no sólo la pieza en que estaban sino también varios almacenes allí inmediatos, pertenecientes a diferentes particulares. Pérdida que unos hacen subir a veinte mil libras esterlinas, y otros al doble.
   Por las cartas de Cambridge en la Nueva Inglaterra, con data de 18 de mayo, se sabe que los rebeldes se habían hecho dueños sin perder un hombre de Ticonderoga, fortaleza de grande importancia en aquella provincia. Refieren el hecho de este modo: doscientos y cuarenta milicianos, mandados por los coroneles Allen y Easton, se dirigieron al lago cerca de Ticonderoga y, atravesándole unos ochenta, llegaron al fuerte al amanecer. La centinela avanzada disparó, pero los milicianos se aseguraron de él inmediatamente y, pasando por el camino cubierto, penetraron hasta la parada en donde encontraron la guarnición durmiendo en sus camas. Formaron un cuadro y encerraron en él a los

soldados después de una ligera escaramuza. Al acudir el oficial que mandaba en el fuerte, le intimó el coronel Easton <u>en nombre de América</u>[27] [a] rendirle. El oficial hubo de ceder a la fuerza y dar orden a su gente que entregase las armas. Los rebeldes hicieron prisioneros a todos y tomaron posesión de aquella considerable fortaleza, en que hallaron más de cien cañones de diferentes calibres, algunos morteros y no pequeña cantidad de pólvora y otras municiones. Después de esto, dos destacamentos de los rebeldes fueron a ampararse [en] dos castillos llamados Crownpoint y Skenesborough. En el primero hallaron muchos cañones, y en el segundo unas cuantas piezas de artillería pequeñas. En este último hicieron prisionero al sargento mayor Skene y a toda su familia.

Hay también cartas de Filadelfia que dicen haber llegado allí el famoso doctor Franklin, a quien habían recibido casi en una especie de triunfo, y que le habían dado un empleo de igual valor al que le quitó este gobierno. Añaden que aquel Congreso General quería hacer un manifiesto implorando la protección de las potencias extranjeras, lo que si fuese cierto, indicaría la ninguna disposición que tienen aquellos pueblos a reconciliarse con el gobierno de la Gran Bretaña.

En confirmación de la noticia que di a vuestra excelencia la semana pasada, de que se pensaba enviar algunas fragatas a América como más propias para acercarse a las costas y cortar el comercio a aquellas colonias, le diré hoy haberse mandado armar cuatro, que son *el Milford, el Acteon, el Solebay y el Lizard*.[28] Sin duda marcharán a Boston apenas estén prontas.

Se ha dado también orden de armar otra fragata, la Aretusa, que irá al Mediterráneo.

Ha salido ya de Portsmouth para los mares de Vizcaya la escuadra de evoluciones mandada por el caballero Parker.

La ciudad de Londres ha determinado presentar a este Soberano una segunda representación en favor de la causa de los americanos. Mañana irán los *sheriffs* a Palacio para saber qué día querrá recibir su majestad británica al Lord Corregidor, que es quien, acompañado de los demás magistrados, ha de ponerla en sus manos. No tendrá respuesta más favorable que la primera.

No he visto a Milord Rochford estos días por estar en el campo, y así no tengo otras noticias que comunicar a vuestra excelencia, cuya vida guarde Dios muchos años como deseo.

Londres, a 27 de junio de 1775.
Excelentísimo señor
Beso las manos de vuestra excelencia
su mayor servidor
El príncipe de Masserano.

Document 13
Legajo 6991-26, Estado, AGS
El Príncipe de Masserano al Marqués de Grimaldi, Londres, 19 de septiembre de 1775, no. 88
[Carta manuscrita, 2 págs.]
Original en español

                    Excelentísimo señor

Muy señor mío:
    Las ciudades de Leicester y de Liverpool, siguiendo el ejemplo de la de Manchester, han presentado a su majestad británica por medio del Lord Darmouth unas arengas muy rendidas, suplicándole hacer respetar su autoridad real en las colonias de América, y ofreciéndose a contribuir a este fin con cuantos medios estén de su parte.
    El Congreso General de Filadelfia ha nombrado al célebre doctor Franklin por Jefe de los Correos de toda la América. Este sujeto había sido Director de los de Pensilvania y otras provincias inmediatas, pero el Ministerio le quitó el empleo el año pasado reconociendo sostenía la causa de los americanos con demasiado celo. El mismo Congreso ha resuelto juntar un millón de pesos para continuar los gastos de la guerra, y no se duda que los encuentre.
    Ha llegado la mujer del general Gage, que según dicen salió de Boston el 20 del próximo pasado. Por algunos que han venido acompañándola se sabe que los dos ejércitos continuaban entonces en la inacción, y que el de los rebeldes, infinitamente superior al de las tropas reales, estaba sobre la defensiva y en disposición de resistir con ventaja a cualquier ataque.
    No se me ofrece otra cosa que comunicar a vuestra excelencia, cuya vida guarde Dios muchos años como deseo. Londres, a 19 de septiembre de 1775.

    Excelentísimo señor
    Beso las manos de vuestra excelencia
    su mayor servidor
    El príncipe de Masserano

Franklin el Diplomático

🔅 Document 14
Legajo 4003, AGS
El conde de Aranda al Marqués de Grimaldi, París, 28 de junio de 1776, no. 753[29]
[Carta manuscrita, 5 págs.]
Original en español

Excelentísimo señor

Muy señor mío:
    El día antes de venir a esta capital, recibí en Marly una carta de que incluyo copia a vuestra excelencia firmada Barbeu Du Bourg,[30] y respondí de palabra al portador su criado que, si su amo quisiese hablarme, me hallaría en París, a donde yo me transfería por cuatro días.
    Con efecto vino ayer a verme, y explicó ser apoderado de las colonias Inglesas de América y corresponsal del doctor Franklin, uno de los miembros principales del Congreso General de Filadelfia, que habiendo dado con este Ministerio diferentes pasos para conseguir algunos socorros, y obtenido facilidades para la compra y remesas de diferentes efectos que iba enviando, venía a implorar de la España iguales facilidades, dirigiéndose a mí con la proporción de hallarnos ambos en esta Corte.
    Respondile que yo no podía entrar en sus miras porque mis facultades se reducían a los negocios particulares de España con Francia, y no las tenía para injerirme[31] en otros extraños, sobre todo, siendo contrarios a una Potencia con quien el rey mi amo estaba en una paz conocida. Cuya reflexión me parecía le persuadiría el justo motivo porque yo me abstenía de entrar con él a recibir sus proposiciones.
    No obstante esto, como conversación privada y a título de saber por curiosidad el estado presente de las colonias, sus fuerzas, disposición de ánimos e ideas que hubiesen formado de sostener su separación, entré con él en discurso, y me dijo que en general todas las 13 colonias pensaban uniformemente en sacudir el yugo de los ingleses, y sólo

habían variado algunas en resistir que desde luego se hiciese la declaración formal de su pretendida independencia, resistiéndose todas en cuerpo para conseguirla, pero difiriendo su publicación hasta que las cosas estuviesen más seguras. Pero que, en fin, ya habían promulgado el comercio abierto con todas las naciones del mundo, menos con los vasallos de la Corona Británica.

Que era increíble las fuerzas marítimas que iban disponiendo las colonias, por la gran proporción que tenían a causa de ser sus habitantes tan dados a la navegación y haber sido ésta su fuerte, por medio del comercio, para el engrandecimiento que habían adquirido. Y que aunque los ingleses les habían hecho muchas presas, aún excedían sus pérdidas, siendo más en número y de mayor consecuencia las que los insurgentes habían conseguido.

Que había obtenido de esta Corte sacar de sus almacenes 15 mil fusiles, a título de comprarlos del asentista de ellos, quien los reemplazaría, y hallarse ya 6 mil de ellos embarcados en Nantes para hacer viaje al primer viento.

Que su pretensión en el día se dirigía a la extracción de 300 piezas de cañón de diferentes calibres, y de bronce, que no se le dificultaban aquí escoger de 1.200 que había en diferentes parajes, ya servidas. Pero que el embarazo consistía en tener todas ellas las armas de Francia, las cuales, bien que se podían limar, causarían aquí una notoriedad difícil de ocultar. Por lo que [se] le había ocurrido si, pretextándose comprarlas la España, y con este motivo borrarles las armas de Francia, se podrían después transportar quedando desconocido el origen de su extracción, tanto en el uso de dicha artillería llegando felizmente a su destino, cuanto en caso de ser interceptada por los ingleses en su avío. Que él discurría me hubiera ya hablado este Ministerio para ello, y por tanto venía a interesarme también de parte de sus principales para condescender en este medio, que les facilitaba unas armas de que tenían necesidad.

Díjele que el Ministerio de esta Corte nada me había tocado de lo que refería, y que no sabría sino repetirle que mis facultades no se extendían a más que a los negocios de mi embajada.

Volvió a preguntarme que, hablándome este Ministerio, si accedería a la proposición. Volví a decirle que en ningún asunto podía yo tomarme facultades que no tuviese. Que si el Ministerio se me explicaba, vería en qué términos lo hacía y en los que yo debiese contestarle.

Con esto terminó nuestra conversación, y quedamos como conocimiento indiferente en que me vendría a ver algunas veces.

Lo comunico a vuestra excelencia para que se sirva ponerlo en noticia de su majestad, y ruego a Dios guarde a vuestra excelencia muchos años. París, 28 de junio de 1776.

Excelentísimo señor
Beso la mano de vuestra excelencia
su seguro servidor
El conde de Aranda

Document 15
Legajo 4605, Estado, AGS
El conde de Aranda al Marqués de Grimaldi, París, 14 de diciembre de 1776, no. 83
[Fragmento de carta manuscrita, 5 págs.]
Original en español

[DuBourg] mudó conversación para darme la noticia que acababa de recibir de Nantes, de haber desembarcado el famoso doctor Franklin, miembro del Congreso americano, el cual entró en dicho puerto en una fragata bien armada y con dos presas inglesas que había hecho en su ruta. Que pensaba luego trasladarse a París, trayendo consigo tres hijos para ponerlos en educación. Que decía hallarse los americanos en mejor estado del que acá los pintaban, y haber resuelto ya para la campaña próxima el juntar hasta más de 80 regimientos de 800 hombres cada uno. Que a su partida, un cuerpo de las tropas de la Carolina se había dirigido a ocupar las Floridas. Que no había que pensar en acomodamiento. Que aunque hasta entonces no había sido grande la deserción de las tropas inglesas, había empezado ya, y los hessesses estaban contentos entre los insurgentes. Que estos habían hecho un golpe de mano sobre la isla de Staten y habían causado bastante daño a los restos ingleses que allí había.

Dije al señor conde Devergennes[32] que el nombre de Franklin alarmaría a los ingleses, y que era natural viniese con plenos poderes del Congreso ya independiente para alguna proposición. Respondiome que era menester aguardar su llegada.

Preguntele también si habían salido las embarcaciones cargadas de socorros para los americanos, a que me contestó creyendo que ya se habían hecho a la vela, pero que no lo sabía de positivo. Dije a su excelencia: y bien, si los ingleses las interceptasen por la publicidad de su destino ¿qué haría esta Corte? Me dijo que reclamarlas como yentes a Santo Domingo.[33] Le repliqué ¿pero si la publicidad acredita que no, y con ella pretextasen los ingleses su retención? Y se salió con que esperaba no sucediese.

Vi también al señor conde de Maurepas, a quien expresé lo relativo al oficio de vuestra excelencia, tocante a las compensaciones de ganancias por descalabros y de rescate de Mahón y Gibraltar. No me pareció en ánimo de entrar en discursos, pues de sí mismo se desvió preguntándome si había oído que la Inglaterra negociase con la Rusia tropas para Portugal. Respondile que no, pero sí que los hannoverianos se disponían para ello. Díjome ¿qué me parecía de ambas especies? Respondile que de los rusos aún lo dudaría, porque la Zarina se miraría mucho en chocar con las potencias borbonas, y que de los rusos no se me daría tanto porque, aunque tropa superior de muchos grados a los hannoverianos, no podría contarse con ella hasta pasados los hielos del Báltico, que iban largos, que su navegación era dilatada y que en tal caso habría el recurso de interceptarlos con fuerzas navales. Que respecto a los hannoverianos, era público que subían la composición de sus tropas, entre aumento a los cuerpos viejos y nueva formación de otros, hasta treinta mil hombres, inclusos los de guarnición en Gibraltar y Mahón. Que su paso a Inglaterra era fácil, y de ésta a Portugal también corto y en pabellón inglés, con el cual nunca podían embarcarse los rusos, porque apenas tienen los ingleses el bastante para su empeño de América.

> Dios guarde a vuestra excelencia muchos años. París, 14 de diciembre de 1776.
> Excelentísimo señor
> Beso la mano de vuestra excelencia
> su seguro servidor
> El conde de Aranda

🌀 Document 16
Legajo 6995-77, Estado, AGS
El Príncipe de Masserano al Marqués de Grimaldi, Londres, 17 de diciembre de 1776
[Carta manuscrita, 3 págs.; original en español]
[Nota manuscrita adjunta, 1 pág.; original en francés]

Excelentísimo señor

Muy señor mío:
Con el fin de sembrar cizaña ha publicado estos días el partido de oposición que el famoso doctor Franklin dejando el Congreso de Filadelfia ha ido a París, por conocer que al cabo las tropas reales triunfarán de los Americanos, a quienes faltan fuerzas para oponerse a ellas. Como las respuestas de los diputados de dicho Congreso al general Howe denotan su ninguna intención de aceptar la paz que se le propuso dudo mucho sea cierta la noticia de la ida a Francia del referido sujeto.

Se sabe que el Emperador debe haber emprendido el 8 del corriente su viaje a París por el Austria, y Munick [sic]; que estará en aquella capital a principios de febrero; que tomará el título de conde de Lickestein; que no quiere fiestas, ni visitas; y que le acompañarán solamente su caballerizo mayor, y un general favorito suyo. Ha escrito a este su ministro conde de Belgioioso, diciéndole que ha mucho tiempo que no le ve, y que puede hallarse a primeros de febrero en París para pasar dos o tres semanas juntos, teniendo ánimo de hallarse de vuelta en Viena sin pasar por Flandes antes de que concluya el mes de marzo.

A esta noticia se añaden las de que ha mandado tener prontas en sus Estados a primeros de abril treinta mil reclutas; y de que el rey de Prusia ha dado igualmente orden para que hacia aquel tiempo se hallen sus tropas en disposición de marchar. Como ese último soberano no suele dar tanto lugar a su ejército para ponerse en movimiento, teniéndole acostumbrado a marchar al toque de la generala no doy mucho crédito a estas voces, que si fuesen ciertas las sabrá el rey en derechura por los conductos regulares. Para acreditarlas aquí se fundan en el grande armamento que prepara la Inglaterra, y que causa con razón recelos a todos, sin embargo de las protestas que hacen los príncipes de Europa de desear unánimemente la paz. Pudiendo a pesar de ellas sobrevenir la guerra cuando menos lo pensemos conviene estar prevenidos para cualquier evento; y para ello hay también el justo motivo de recuperar el rey lo que contra toda buena fe han usurpado los Portugueses en un tiempo en que la Corte de Lisboa le estaba asegurando de sus deseos de conservar la mejor armonía.

Estos ministros aprovechando de las vacaciones del Parlamento y de lo suave de la estación han ido a pasar algunos días en sus casas de campo.

Tenía escrito hasta aquí cuando se me ha dicho por muy seguro que antes de ayer llegó un Extraordinario despachado por milord Stormont con el aviso de haber desembarcado en Nantes el doctor Franklin, y otro miembro del Congreso de Filadelfia, y que se les aguardaba en París.

El embajador de Francia despacha esta noche un correo a su corte, y yo aprovecho de él para enviar esta carta a mi correspondiente de Calais, en la que no tengo más que decir a vuestra excelencia sino que se aumentan los motivos que le he dicho tener para creer que hay alguna discordia entre los que componen este Ministerio por lo que no extrañaré haya alguna mudanza.

    Dios guarde a vuestra excelencia muchos años como deseo.
    Londres a 17 de diciembre de 1776.
    Excelentísimo señor
    Beso las manos de vuestra excelencia
    su Mayor Servidor
    El Príncipe de Masserano

[Nota adjunta en francés]

Londres, le 17 Décembre 1776

Le 12 de ce mois les Communes ne s'occupèrent que d'affaires de nulle importance; et le 14 les deux Chambres ne s'assemblèrent que pour se rendre au service Divin à l'occasion d'un jeûne observé pour le rétablissement du bon ordre en Amérique. Après quoi, les Pairs s'ajournèrent au 23 de Janvier prochain et les Communes au 21 du dit mois.

Document 17
Legajo 6995-80, Estado, AGS
Príncipe de Masserano al Marqués de Grimaldi, Londres, 20 de diciembre de 1776
[Carta manuscrita, 3 págs.]
Original en español

Excelentísimo señor

Muy señor mío:
Doy a vuestra excelencia las mayores gracias por el importante aviso que se sirve comunicarme en carta de 2 de este mes de haberse transferido en robusta salud del sitio de San Lorenzo el Real a su Palacio de Madrid el rey, príncipes nuestros, señora infanta, y demás personas de su real familia.

Nada he sabido del Canadá después de las noticias que he avisado a vuestra excelencia haber esparcido aquí a su llegada de Quebec el general Bourgoyne, con quien habiendo hablado me he confirmado en que viene sin más licencia que la del general Carleton, y que no está bien con él, tachándole de lentitud en la expedición al Lago Champlain, que es a lo que se ha reducido toda la campaña. Me ha dicho que los rebeldes se mantienen bien atrincherados en Ticonderago [sic];[34] que es imposible ir por tierra a atacar aquella Plaza no habiendo más camino que un bosque impenetrable para la artillería, y que sólo por agua se puede arrimar a ella hacienda un desembarco de tropa, pero que los hielos impiden desde principios de noviembre tal operación. Hay quien dice que este general ha venido con ánimo de proponer un nuevo plan para la campaña próxima, pero dudo se le admita, pues no ha sido bien recibido de este monarca.

Hace mucho ruido aquí y ha causado baja en los fondos la llegada a Francia del famoso doctor Francklin [sic]: muchos objetos se atribuyen a este primer móvil del congreso de Filadelfia. El primero es tratar de las ventajas de los americanos con la Francia; el segundo el de querer tratar con la Inglaterra desde paraje seguro para su persona; y el tercero el separarse del congreso por haber entre los magnates que le componen grandes discordias. Ha tomado el pretexto de traer a sus hijos para educarlos en Francia. El tiempo aclarará la verdad.

Ha llegado de Lisboa el Caballero Horta que va por Ministro a Holanda. Es un joven de 22 años que sale de sus estudios: partió de aquella Corte con el Paquebote el primero de este mes: Dice que el rey su amo quedaba algo mejor, y que pronunciaba con dificultad algunas palabras: Añade que cuando no se le entendía escribía con lápiz lo que quería, y que de este modo mandó se obedeciese en todo a su ministro. Me imagino que el marqués de Pombal le habrá guiado la mano para ello.

Estos ministros muestran esperar que si falta aquel monarca se compondrán nuestras disputas con aquella Corte.

Para convalecer según dice de su último ataque de gota se ha ido el señor Suffolk a su casa de campo, y por eso no tuvo ayer conferencia con los ministros Extranjeros.

Concluyo diciendo a vuestra excelencia haber puesto en clara su carta en números de 30 de noviembre sobre cuyo contenido no tengo que responder.

Dios guarde a vuestra excelencia muchos años como deseo. Londres a 20 de diciembre de 1776.

P. S. Ha llegado milord Dunmore, Gobernador de la Virginia.

> Excelentísimo señor
> Beso las manos de vuestra excelencia
> Su mejor servidor
> El príncipe de Masserano

Document 18
Legajo 4609-5, Estado, AGS
El conde de Aranda al Marqués de Grimaldi, Paris,
4 de enero de 1777
[Nota de presentación manuscrita, 1 pág.; carta manuscrita, 3 págs.]
Original en español

[1-Nota de presentación]
París 4 de enero de 1777
El conde de Aranda
(Por extraordinario francés)

Ofrece un correo suyo dentro de pocos días y entretanto remite dos memorias que le ha entregado aquel Ministerio una sobre proyecto de un tratado con las colonias inglesas presentado por ellas y otra de reflexión acerca de una situación actual con la Inglaterra y de las medidas que conviene tomar prontamente así por la España como por la Francia.

[2-Carta]

Excelentísimo señor

Muy señor Mío:
    Esta Corte despacha a su Embajador el Marqués de Ossun el correo de cuya ocasión aprovecho; remitiéndole los dos papeles de que son copia los adjuntos que me ha comunicado el señor conde Devergennes.
    El uno es la proposición que ha entregado el doctor Franklin para un tratado de amistad y comercio de las colonias con la Francia. El otro es una memoria formada por el señor conde Devergennes, y aprobada por el rey cristianísimo para comunicarla a su tío el rey católico sobre el estado presente de apariencia de un posible rompimiento con la Inglaterra.
    Con el correo Lintillac y fecha de 14 de diciembre avisé a vuestra excelencia el arribo del doctor Franklin a estos Reinos: y hasta el 21 del mismo mes dicen que no llegó a París. El 28 tuvo su audiencia del señor conde Devergennes por la mañana, porque según me dijo dicho señor conde había creído que como nadie dudaría que Franklin habría

sido oído de este Ministerio, había encontrado por menos reparable el no hacer misterio, y en ella entregó a su excelencia el escrito, o idea del tratado de amistad, y comercio, como si fuese su única comisión.

El 22 por la noche estuvo a verme mister Franklin con sus compañeros Dean, y Lee, diciéndome que habían estado en Versailles, que el señor conde Devergennes les había asegurado de la estrecha unión que reinaba entre las Cortes de Madrid y París; que podrían explicarse con el embajador de España; que en consecuencia empezaba por dar las gracias del buen tratamiento que había experimentado el pabellón de las colonias en los dominios del rey católico: que me pasaría otra proposición conforme a la presentada a la Francia respectivamente a la España para dirigirla a mi Corte; pero hasta este día no ha vuelto a parecer.

Como ha de partir el correo Villa dentro de pocos días con los encargos que me tiene hechos vuestra excelencia, me remito a su despacho, pues tampoco tenía tiempo para aprovechar de este; y mientras llegue Villa podrá vuestra excelencia enterarse de los escritos que acompañan, y de lo que el embajador expusiera a vuestra excelencia.

>Dios guarde a vuestra excelencia muchos años. París 4 de enero de 1777.
>Excelentísimo señor
>Beso la mano de vuestra excelencia
>su seguro servidor
>El conde de Aranda

Document 19
Legajo 3884, Estado, AHN
El conde de Aranda, embajador en París, al marqués de Grimaldi, París,
13 de enero de 1777, no. 938 and no. 4[35]
[Carta manuscrita con nota resumen al inicio, 33 págs.]
Original en español

El conde de Aranda:
(por extraordinario)
    Su conversación con aquellos ministros relativas[36] a los asuntos de las colonias Inglesas y a sus Comisarios residentes en París, e ideas que allí se tenían sobre un próximo inevitable rompimiento.

Excelentísimo señor

Muy señor mío:
    Con el extraordinario de 14 del pasado, y al n° 911, dije a vuestra excelencia el arribo del doctor Franklin a este Reino, y lo que sobre él habíamos hablado el señor conde de Vergennes y yo. Corrió entonces que inmediatamente se transfería a París, y también se dijo si por alguna prevención de este Ministerio se detendría sin llegar a la Corte, explicándose antes reservadamente por escrito o persona interpuesta sobre la idea de su viaje.
    El martes 17 pregunté al señor conde de Vergennes en qué estábamos de la venida de Franklin, y me contestó en unos términos que me parecieron ambiguos.
    El *Amphitrite*, que es la embarcación principal que lleva el socorro de oficiales y efectos a los americanos, había salido del Havre el 14, y el 16 a la noche llegó al mismo puerto correo de este Ministerio al comisario ordenador de Marina, monsieur Mistras, con orden para que, si no hubiese partido dicho bastimento, se detuviese, y habiéndolo ejecutado, despachase otro de alcance con la orden de que volviese a entrar.
    El dicho comisario juntó en el instante los pilotos más acreditados, y unánimes le respondieron sería infructuoso después de tres días, pues ya había ganado la mar abierta y tampoco sería posible alcanzarlo en el curso de su viaje, porque antes de prevenir un buque a propósito para

ello, y vituallarlo, pasarían bastantes días. Lo que supe exactamente el 19, y me pareció sería del caso explorar un poco esta novedad en su raíz.

Pasé el viernes 20 a Versailles y solté la especie al señor Devergennes, quien me la confesó, pero con unas excusas del paso practicado, y no conseguido, que no me dejaron duda de la timidez que reinaba, y de que no era totalmente liso y llano el modo con que se me comunicaban los asuntos pendientes con los insurgentes.

Volví a preguntar a su excelencia por Franklin y, respondiéndome que no sabía cuándo llegaría, le dije haberme[37] ocurrido si se le habría prevenido el no presentarse en París y manifestar secretamente el objeto de su venida, para disimular mejor en el público el motivo de su misión. Pero volvió a decirme que lo aguardaba, en un tono también embarazado. Y a título de dictamen mío, le expuse que siendo notorio su arribo a Quiberon, cerca de Nantes, desde el día 6, me parecía que habían pasado demasiados días para estarse aún sin tener luces de una cosa tan importante. A lo que me respondió que tenía razón, y que le aseguraban no tardaría Franklin en llegar a París.

El 21 recibí las cartas de vuestra excelencia por el ordinario,[38] y entre ellas la que trataba de la regencia de la reina de Portugal, con la respuesta del rey nuestro señor, y la otra del puño de vuestra excelencia sobre la idea de socorrer la España en derechura a los americanos, la cual se me comunicaría. Y pasé el 22 a Versailles con motivo de participar la primera y hacer uso de la segunda, según explorase el campo, porque tenía formado el concepto de que se me hablaba con reserva de Franklin, y de que convenía a la España, aún más que a la Francia,[39] el no perder de vista el negocio de los insurgentes. Fui muy temprano, porque, como domingo, habría infinitas otras gentes que pudiesen interrumpir, y empecé por el oficio de vuestra excelencia tocante a la Regencia de la reina fidelísima.

Después de haberlo evacuado con sumo espacio, caí en el particular de Franklin, a que me dijo el señor de Vergennes no lo había visto aún, y repitiéndole yo que se perdía tiempo en saber positivamente si su venida era por nada más que ausentarse de aquellos disturbios, o con comisión, me contestó en términos de que ya lo haría, pero sin poder encubrir bien su embarazo. Entonces me determiné a decirle que yo no podía dispensarme, como embajador, de solicitar de su excelencia que uno u otro se había de poner en claro, y que la España tenía derecho a saber positivamente cuanto hubiese sobre la venida de Franklin, pues a solicitud de esta Corte había entrado en la idea de socorrer a los insurgentes, había contribuido con un millón de libras tornesas, y aún la Francia había vuelto a proponer que se las ayudase en la respuesta que me había dado por escrito en Fontainebleau a principios de noviembre. Que mi Corte, sin duda por estos estímulos de la Francia, y por obrar con ella de concierto, estaba pensando cómo socorrer las colonias por diferentes términos, que así se me decía en las cartas recibidas el día anterior. Y que, por fin, tanto por lo ya practicado como por lo que se pensaba hacer, no había de ignorar el rey católico nada de lo que llegase a noticia de la Francia, ni debían retardársele las noticias convenientes para el acierto de sus resoluciones.

Estrechado así el señor de Vergennes, me dijo que Franklin había llegado a París el día antes, sábado. Que el viernes por la tarde había entrado en Versailles donde lo aguardaba monsieur Dean, el apoderado antiguo de las colonias. Que no había querido verlos, sí sólo prevenirles que se transfiriesen a París, y se acordaría el disimulo con que pudiese entenderlos. Que no lo retardaría y me comunicaría sus resultas. Con lo que corté la conversación, esmerándome en confianzas de la amistad de ambas Cortes, etc.

Vuelto a París, tuve noticias el lunes 23 que podían persuadirme haber llegado Franklin a París algunos días antes, como de haber guardado el incógnito con sumo recato, y eran bastante probables. Lo que con las sospechas que yo me tenía, no dejó de aumentármelas.

El martes 24 puse de nuevo en la conversación a monsieur de Vergennes, y no diciéndome otra cosa que repetirme el paso de Franklin por Versailles la tarde del viernes, y su estancia por la noche, como acusando yo a Franklin de que hubiese estado en París días antes escondido, y que su ida a Versailles el viernes hubiese sido de intento desde esta capital y no de paso de viaje, le dije haber llegado a mi noticia que Franklin, días antes del que su Excelencia me había expresado haber transitado por Versailles, hubiese estado muy incógnito en París. No convino en esto, asegurándome no podía ser, y que monsieur Dean había venido a su encuentro en Versailles, y de esto podía estar seguro.

Renové al señor de Vergennes la urgencia de saber los fines de Franklin, haciéndole observar que como cualesquiera que fuesen, si aquí no se perdía tiempo por ocho días de diferencia, se atrasaría mucho su examen mediando la distancia de Madrid adonde debían comunicarse. Era digna de atención esta circunstancia para salir cuanto antes de dudas.

Entonces me dijo que había prevenido a monsieur Dean por medio del primer comisario[40] de Estado, monsieur Gerard, que ni él ni Franklin hablasen con persona alguna del objeto de la venida de éste, reservándose mucho del médico monsieur DuBourg y de Beaumarchais, que hasta ahora habían sido confidentes de monsieur Dean. Que pusiesen por escrito la comisión de Franklin con las proposiciones que hubiese de exponer, y entonces me comunicaría su contenido. Que como era obra que exigía mucho cuidado, era regular tardasen en su extensión. Repliquéle a esto que me perdonase si yo no concebía tan regular la demora, pues un hombre consumado como Franklin, que traería sus instrucciones bien distinguidas para las primeras proposiciones, y para alterarlas según el aspecto de la negociación, que había venido embarcado por tan largo viaje sin distracciones que lo ocupasen, y hacía ya medio mes que estaba en Francia, no necesitaba de muchas horas para arreglar su demanda ni era regular perdiese tiempo, siempre que su Excelencia le diese facilidades para producirse.

Así se cortó este punto en dicho día, y yo quedé muy en dudas de si hubiese mediado ya algún examen secreto, o desease más presto esta Corte eludir las explicaciones de las colonias.

Manifestándome confianza, me dijo que había empezado un trabajo sobre tomar ya determinadamente un partido con la Inglaterra, siendo indispensable el rompimiento según las cosas se iban poniendo y la Inglaterra se armaba. El cual me quería mostrar, bien que aún estaba sin acabar. Leyome lo que tenía hecho, y nos remitimos a verlo fenecido que fuese.

En lugar de volver a Versailles entre semana, y para tener alguna prenda del señor conde de Vergennes sobre las explicaciones de Franklin, como también sobre el escrito suyo empezado que me había leído, preferí escribirle un papel el sábado 28 en los términos del incluso "A,"[41] y con efecto conseguí mi intento en ambos puntos, según su respuesta "B" del propio día.

Díceme que aquella misma mañana había tenido la visita de Franklin, y haberse explicado sólo y someramente sobre Comercio, remitiéndose a la memoria que presentaba y necesitaría de algunos días para traducirse etc. Respecto al trabajo que me había confiado, dice que lo había concluido y pasado a la vista del rey cristianísimo, mereciendo su aprobación. Que se me comunicaría, y a mi Corte, pensando despachar un correo en primeros del año a su Embajador para saber el dictamen y correcciones del rey católico, a quien igualmente instruiría de lo ocurrido en aquel mismo día con Franklin.

En la noche del mismo sábado tuve el papel adjunto "C"[42] de Franklin, pidiéndome hora para verme, y como en aquel momento aún no había recibido la contestación del señor de Vergennes, dije al portador que yo respondería.

Habiéndome llegado un rato después, y viendo en ella que ya se le había presentado Franklin, y lo demás que contiene, avisé por recado en el día siguiente, domingo, a Franklin que lo recibiría a las siete de la noche. Y con efecto vino con sus dos compañeros Dean y Lee, los que hice entrar en mi habitación interior sin que el resto de la familia se percibiese.

Franklin habla muy poco francés, Dean mucho menos, y nada Lee, con lo que mediaron sus trabajos[43] para entendernos, pero en fin lo conseguimos. Díjome Franklin su ida a Versailles en el día anterior, que había presentado al señor conde de Vergennes una Memoria sobre buena correspondencia y comercio. Que su excelencia le había manifestado la unión de las Cortes de Madrid y París y que podía explicarse conmigo con toda seguridad. Que en esa inteligencia venía, empezando por dar gracias a mi Corte del asilo que había experimentado en sus puertos el pabellón[44] de las colonias Unidas de América. Que me entregaría una copia del escrito presentado al señor de Vergennes y me pedía lo trasladase a mi Corte, a que le respondí que así lo haría cuando me lo pasase.

Parecióme conveniente explorarlo un poco. Le pregunté si traía plenos poderes del Congreso para un todo. Me respondió que sí.

Si la memoria que había presentado la traía hecha, o la había trabajado desde su arribo, me dijo que era arreglada por el mismo Congreso.

Expliquele que me admiraba no comprendiese otra cosa que la buena correspondencia, cuando en los aprietos en que se hallaban, cualquiera juzgaría que su venida se dirigía más presto a buscar auxilios y solicitarlos con otras proposiciones gratas a las Cortes que buscaban, que no a entrar tratando de buenas correspondencias cuando aún no eran dueños pacíficos de su libertad. Me respondió que aún tenía que exponer en otra memoria, y que estaba sacando una copia de la presentada para dirigirla al Ministerio de España por mi conducto.

Preguntele sobre el estado actual de las colonias respecto a sus fuerzas y a su animosidad contra los ingleses. Me respondió que a fuerzas no tenían que temer, y que por el encono general tampoco que recelar en sostener el empeño. Que deseaba saber de mí si en los puertos de España se permitiría a sus corsarios, no sólo el abrigo y refresco que necesitasen, sino también el entrar con sus presas y venderlas.

Le dije que en la primera parte habría visto que su pabellón había entrado en nuestros puertos, y aún sido protegido, no obstante las diligencias contrarias de la Inglaterra. Que en la segunda de presas no le podía satisfacer, ya porque ignoraba cómo pensaría mi Corte, ya porque sobre semejantes casos había también sus reglas recibidas, de que no estaba instruido porque pendían de tratados particulares entre las Potencias.

Hice todo lo posible por descubrir si antes de haber presentado la memoria había tenido explicaciones preparatorias con este Ministerio o algún comisionado suyo, pero ya con la dificultad del lenguaje, ya con alguna reserva que observé, no lo pude sacar en limpio.

Pregunteéle si venía autorizado con poderes abiertos del Congreso para todo lo que pudiese tratarse. Me respondió que traía sus instrucciones, y sus poderes eran amplios.

El martes, último día del año, pasé a Versailles por la tarde con ánimo de aprovechar en su noche un rato con el señor conde de Vergennes. Así lo conseguí en parte, bien que fuimos interrumpidos, y me dijo tener aprobado por su majestad el papel que había concluido.

Leyome con efecto el señor conde de Vergennes el que había presentado al rey, y observé que era el mismo que me había confiado hasta donde estaba hecho. Me dijo que el sábado 3 de enero lo despacharía a Madrid con correo, y al mismo tiempo la copia de la proposición de Franklin para un Tratado de amistad y comercio, que ya tenía traducida. Que también me comunicaría un traslado[45] de ambas piezas, para que yo pudiese escribir con conocimiento de ellas si quería aprovechar de su correo. Manifestéle que sí, le di las gracias por la oferta, y sólo le dije entonces que me admiraba se redujese la pretensión del Congreso americano, según me decía, a querer desde luego un tratado de amistad y comercio, cuando aún no estaba independiente y afirmado en su dominio. Y que siendo notorios sus ahogos, no empezase por reclamar la protección y auxilios de las Coronas con quienes quería la amistad, haciéndolas a más algunas ofertas ventajosas.

Respecto al contenido de su memoria, dije al señor conde de Vergennes que no observaba en ella se propusiese un partido que tomar, sino quedarse sustancialmente en preparativos y amenazas, aguardando a ser insultados para resolver lo que se podía hacer. Que de las tropas de tierra que disponía, hallaba las de Francia bien destinadas, pero no las de España en Ferrol y Cádiz. No en el Ferrol, como amenazando la Irlanda, porque si se acordaba su excelencia de conversaciones nuestras antiguas, ni su excelencia ni lo demás del Ministerio habían creído que se hubiese de practicar semejante intento en ningún caso contra Irlanda, sino fomentar la indisposición de sus naturales, ayudarlos en otras formas y distraerles por otros lados las fuerzas de la Inglaterra. Que a más de eso, aun tomándolo como amenaza, sería infructuosa pues la conocerían los ingleses porque no la verían acompañada con las apariencias de realidad, las cuales exigirían un apronto de multitud enorme de bastimentos de transporte, trenes de artillería,[46] municiones de guerra y boca, con todos los ruidos propios para comprobar ser una empresa decidida y exequible[47] al primer momento. De modo que hacer la España gastos semejantes en balde, y por sólo figurar, cuando estaba empeñada en otros tan costosos, sería un dinero malogrado, y lo peor de todo sin dar cuidado a los ingleses lo respectivo a fuerzas de tierra porque, de todos modos, contra las marítimas del Ferrol destinarían las convenientes a observarlas y contrarrestarlas, siendo mucho mejor para ellos si las nuestras hubiesen de salir con un convoy de tanta magnitud, porque el cubrirlo embarazaría más los buques de guerra de su escolta. Y solas las fuerzas marítimas en estado de salir y combatir les causarían mucha más sujeción.

Que aun cuando pudiesen tragar los ingleses la expedición de Irlanda, no tendría otras resultas que hacerles tomar más tropas extranjeras para guarnecer aquella isla, y en este caso, aquella disposición que pudiese haber en sus naturales para moverse, en lugar de fomentarse, estando desguarnecidos se acobardaría. Que los ingleses se alegrarían de semejante inutilidad de tropas abocadas al Ferrol como embarco, porque desde luego las juzgarían como pérdidas para cualquiera otro objeto, respecto a que 20 mil hombres por allí nada espantarían tampoco a Portugal, pues aquella entrada no es temible para tan poca gente, no yendo por otro lado fuerzas superiores.

No en Cádiz para dar miedo a Gibraltar, porque sabían bien los ingleses que dicha plaza no es atacable por tierra, y vivirían tranquilos de semejante idea. Ni como llamada interesante hacia Portugal, pues la entrada de los Algarves tampoco les daría cuidado. Que para acudir extraordinariamente a algunos puntos de América desde Andalucía y Galicia, siempre había en ambas provincias tropas de que echar mano.

Que el hacer la Francia disposición en sus costas para desembarco en Inglaterra variaba mucho de circunstancias, porque esta operación, en cualquiera rompimiento estaba indicada por naturaleza, sabiendo bien los ingleses que es inevitable en queriéndola practicar, que es un golpe mortal que salta a los ojos y que no admite chanzas, siempre que la Francia jugase su resto y usase de su actividad y posibilidades. De tal modo que sola ella bien aparentada haría más que todo, pues sus tropas de América, en lugar de aumentarlas, habían de minorarse para volver a cubrir la casa propia, so pena de dejarla indefensa si no lo hacían. Y de este hecho ya resultaba a las colonias cuanto podían desear para debilitar a su enemigo y tomar ellas aliento. El mismo amago de tierra obligaría a la Inglaterra a una fuerte escuadra más para el solo canal[48] e impedir el pasaje, que por la Francia nunca se debía hacer con buques de guerra. Y por consecuencia, obligar a la Inglaterra a tener navíos a la mar con batallones a la costa, era un hallazgo.

Con el señor conde de Maurepas tuve sustancialmente los mismos discursos. Pareciome que, aunque al parecer indecisa la explicación que ha hecho esta Corte por su correo último, hay en lo interior mucha disposición de que el rey católico podría aprovechar, pues comprendo que combaten el conocimiento de lo que se debiera practicar por una potencia como la Francia, y la cortedad de su actual espíritu sostenida de la esperanza de privadas conveniencias.

Esta idea ha dominado hasta aquí en parte del Ministerio, figurándose que la Francia va a ganar infinitamente con la sola independencia de las colonias. Porque se prometía que, encaminadas al tráfico de la Francia, vendrán a ellas por todos los artículos de que abunda y ellas carecen, trayendo los que faltan a este país. El pabellón francés haría lo mismo en derechura. sus islas, como intermedias y más a mano, serían el emporio del Comercio, y por consecuencia florecerían éstas y la Francia misma, creyendo que la Inglaterra insensiblemente debe descaecer, consumada la separación de sus colonias y disminuido el comercio que practicaba con ellas, quedándole el sobrehueso[49] de la deuda nacional, y la escasez de caudales por las expensas de esta guerra.

El que la Inglaterra, aún verificado este caso por el pronto, se restableciese después lo bastante para aguardar la suya, y en una ocasión que la Francia tarde o temprano se halle embarazada con alguna guerra en el continente y se le eche encima entonces, se ha mirado con indiferencia hasta aquí, porque se contaba con disfrutar en tal caso de la España como fina auxiliar, y en el concepto de que guardando ésta las espaldas, bastarían las dos potencias juntas a parar y conllevar el expresado riesgo. Pero ya se va conociendo que lo verdadero sería aniquilar la Inglaterra para siempre, porque sería asegurarse de los peligros venideros y afianzar la misma idea que he dicho. Sobre todo, cuando en siglos no se presentará ocasión semejante a la presente para reducir la Inglaterra por los ahogos en que se ha metido.

Quien creyera que la Francia llegaría a poner la cláusula *"C'est par lassitude et par l'epuissement, qu'il faut aspirere â les vaincre, plutôt que par des combats, ou ils auroient sur nous l'avantage que donnent la Science, et l'experience;"*[50] y con todo que parece que el principio de ella promete en la memoria un plano de *"lassitude et d'epuissement,"*[51] que sentemos sería prudente y bueno. En lugar de disponerlo por esos mismos medios, pero actoras la España y la Francia, viene a parar sustancialmente en que depende de la voluntad de la Inglaterra según ella rompiese, o no. Si ella no tiene gana de aumentarse cuidados hasta que encuentre su momento conveniente, no tiene que temer de los preparativos, y se habrán gastado en ellos sumas inmensas que quedarán inutilizadas, y a más una ocasión única perdida. Y cuando llegue a explicarse con su *science et experience,*[52] puede tomarse poco cuidado.

Si se coteja esta memoria con las de septiembre y noviembre, respecto a los recelos de una revolución entre las potencias del continente, se verá que en la primera no se creían, en la segunda se daban infalibles, y en esta tercera como si se ignorase que hay Austria y Prusia, mencionando sólo la Rusia, Dinamarca y Holanda, y aun exponiendo consideraciones para asegurarse de ellas.

Tiene vergüenza esta Corte de comparecer como indolente al mismo tiempo que busca prepararse para cuando se la echen encima. Procura disuadir a la España de la frialdad que le acusaría, e igualmente no comunicársela para tenerla en estado de valerse de ella a sus fines y urgencias. Por eso vemos la inconexión de sus proposiciones anteriores con las posteriores, la confusión con que presenta sus ideas. No quiere ni querrá pérdidas de la España, porque éstas se refundirían en beneficio de otros enemigos suyos, y la debilitarían para ser buena auxiliar de la Francia. Pero tampoco quiere ni querrá que la España adelante un dedo, por que no se le suba a mayores ni se le resista a sus órdenes, y al usufructo que de ella tira tan considerablemente. Descubre que los tiempos iluminan, los parentescos se alejan, los desengaños se multiplican, el interés de cada Monarquía es su primera obligación y que la España discurrirá como cualquiera otra. El tenerle, pues, el pie encima, es el preservativo de todo y la máxima de la Francia, y esta verdad ruego al rey, como fiel vasallo suyo, que la tenga presente para los partidos que hubiere de tomar.

No hablemos de Portugal, en que su majestad ha visto lo que ha pasado. Reduzcámonos a la Inglaterra, de quien se puede rescatar Gibraltar o Mahón, abatiendo al propio tiempo su poder para lo sucesivo. Esta es causa común con la Francia, separada de sus miras sobre la España. Y del día pende el que ésta tenga voz activa o pasiva. Si se aguarda a que la Francia sea insultada, saldrá la España pasivamente en su socorro. Si ambas potencias, aprovechando del embarazo de la Inglaterra, se ponen de veras a emprenderla como actoras, igualmente tendrá la España derecho suyo independiente para sacar su partido sin sombras de la Francia. Y esto pende de impelerla a que lo mismo que ha de ser en otro tiempo, lo ejecute desde luego[53] y no aguarde a que la provoquen. Una vez explicada la Francia, no dudo que hará todas sus habilidades, y estas son las que necesita la España contra la Inglaterra. A más que el hacerse dueños de las acciones, o depender de las llamadas de su contrario, muda enteramente la suerte de las armas. La Inglaterra, sin batallas navales por la ciencia y experiencia que le atribuye la Corte de París, puede llegar a la agonía de su enfermedad, y entonces verse precisada a rescatar su salud, aunque desjarretada[54] a sangrías o separación de miembros, por no gangrenarse del todo.

La España tiene una inmensidad de objetos que guardar en América, y no los puede cubrir ahora de presente ni en lo venidero. No debe dudarse de que la Inglaterra ha de ir a buscarla en todos tiempos por aquellas partes, y con muchos puntos de elección se dirigirá a los más descubiertos. Conque ¿cuál sería el remedio radical para evitar estos riesgos, sino el de reducir la Inglaterra a que nunca volviese a levantar?

Si el enredo presente en que dicha potencia se halla, es propia ocasión para acabar de abatirla; si con el tiempo puede presentarse otro momento en que aún estuviese más embarazada; si la España entonces estaría más libre y en mejor estado que ahora; si la Francia también podría entrar en el empeño con más o menos libertad, con más o menos motivos de resentimiento y de interés, con mejor o peor estado de sus fuerzas marítimas, cuando actualmente se ha puesto ya como no había estado; y cuánto basta y sobra para el intento, unidas las soberanías de Borbón, son reflexiones que merecen profundizarse para responder a la explicación pendiente de esta Corte, y tomar el partido que pudiese convenir.

Por el enlace histórico de las cosas que contiene este oficio, he inserto en él la primera abertura[55] del doctor Franklin, y respecto a que los pasos posteriores forman ya un punto que merece separación, me remito al oficio que sigue a éste, en el cual proseguiré lo concerniente a la comisión y proposiciones de los apoderados de las colonias Inglesas de América.

París, 13 de enero de 1777.

Dios guarde a vuestra excelencia muchos años.
Excelentísimo señor
Beso la mano de vuestra excelencia
su seguro servidor
El conde de Aranda

[Anexo A, una página]
El conde de Aranda al conde de Vergennes, París,
28 de diciembre de 1776.
Original en francés

A Paris ce 28 Décembre 1776
    Les lettres de ma Cour d'aujourd'hui ne me portent rien. Monsieur le Comte qui exige vous incommoder, je ne sais pas si vous avez encore quelque chose à me dire touchant monsieur Franklin, car dans ce cas-là je me transporterai demain à Versailles, et à vos ordres. Autrement je comptais me présenter à Votre Excellence le mardi au soir, veille du jour du nouvel an, puisque les Ambassadeurs remettent le mardi ou mercredi pour faire leur cour a Sa Majesté et profiter ce soir- là de quelque moment d'entretien avec vous sur l'article dont vous me fîtes le plaisir de me confier la lecture de votre sage prévoyance. Dans les premiers jours du mois prochain je devrais expédier mon courrier à Madrid, et il serait important à ma Cour d'être instruite des idées des Insurgents dont monsieur Franklin doit être chargé. J'espère que vous

jugerez de même, et que vous voudrez bien me donner des
éclaircissements sur cette matière.

J'ai l'honneur d'être avec le plus parfait attachement monsieur=/>
De Votre Excellence le très humble et très obéissant serviteur=Le Comte
d'Aranda= Son Excellence monsieur le Comte de Vergennes.

[Anexo B, dos páginas]
El conde de Vergennes al conde de Aranda, embajador de España en
Francia, Versailles, 28 de diciembre de 1776.
Original en francés

À Versailles ce Samedi 28 Décembre 1776
    Comme je comptais, monsieur le Comte, d'avoir l'honneur de vous
voir demain, je ne vous ai pas écrit aujourd'hui pour vous informer que
j'ai eu ce matin la visite du Docteur F ...[56] et de ses collègues. Elle n'a
été ni longue ni bien intéressante, il ne m'a parlé que de Commerce,
encore sommairement, s'en rapportant à un projet qu'il m'a remis, et qui
demandera quelques jours pour le traduire. Il a évité de s'en rapporter à
sa mémoire pour me donner des notions exactes de l'état des affaires de
son pays, et de la disposition des esprits, c'est par écrit qu'il veut m'en
donner la notice. Le personnage semble intelligent, mais très
circonspect, cela ne m'étonne pas. Il m'a promis de ne se laisser
pénétrer par qui que ce soit, Votre Excellence seule exceptée s'il a
occasion de la rencontrer. Il est prévenu que l'identité la plus parfaite
des vues et d'intérêts existe entre nos Cours. Les choses dans cet état,
Votre Excellence sera à temps de ne venir ici que mardi, demain je
n'avais rien de plus essentiel à lui dire que ce que je lui écris dans le
moment. L'ouvrage dont Votre Excellence a vu le commencement est
achevé, il a passé sous les yeux du Roi qui l'a approuvé et m'a autorisé
à le communiquer à Votre Excellence et à sa Cour. Je compte dans les
premiers jours de l'année l'expédier par un courrier à notre
Ambassadeur pour avoir l'avis et les corrections de Sa Majesté
Catholique. J'y joindrai le détail de ma conférence de ce matin, et la
copie du projet dont le contenu ne m'est pas encore connu.

    J'ai l'honneur d'être etc = de Vergennes.

[Anexo C, una página][57]
Franklin, Dean y Lee, al conde de Aranda, París,

28 de diciembre de 1776
[Nota manuscrita, original en español, traducido del inglés en la época. 1 pag.][58]

Señor:
    Nosotros deseamos de informar a vuestra excelencia que somos dirigidos o enviados por las provincias unidas de América para cultivar la amistad de las Cortes de España y Francia. A este propósito, como también para hacerle presente nuestro respeto personal, nos proponemos de ir a ver a vuestra excelencia mañana o cualquiera otro día que sea más conveniente, y a cualquiera hora que vuestra excelencia guste señalarnos.

    Tenemos la honra de ser
    Los más obedientes y humildes servidores
    de vuestra excelencia = B.Francklin [sic] = Silas Deans [sic] = Arthur Lee
    Plenipotenciarios del Congreso de las Provincias Unidas de América Septentrional

Document 20
Legajo 388, Estado, AHN
El conde de Aranda al Marqués de Grimaldi, París, 13 de enero de 1777, no 939, no. 6,
[Carta manuscrita, 38 págs.]
Original en español

Excelentísimo señor

Muy señor mío:
    A consecuencia del oficio antecedente, diré a vuestra excelencia que, viendo no se me explicaba el doctor Franklin no obstante su promesa, le hice entender que desearía hablarle, y efectivamente vino acompañado de Arthur Lee la noche del sábado 4 del corriente.
    Por la dificultad de entendernos me pareció que sería muy del caso valerme del conde de Lacy, ministro plenipotenciario del rey en la Corte de Petersbourg y alojado en mi casa, quien posee la lengua inglesa, para que aclarase a Franklin y Lee la inteligencia de los puntos que se tocasen si no los concebían bien, y a mí igualmente por la explicación de ellos.
    Pregunté al doctor Franklin cuándo entregaría el papel de proposición para la España, respecto a que había proporción de dirigirlo. Respondió que lo tenía ya formado, faltando sólo el confrontar su copia, y haberse retardado por haber estado algo indispuesto monsieur Dean.
    Si dicho papel contenía alguna cosa diferente del entregado a la Francia. Respondió que no, y ser idéntico, como también conforme a las órdenes que tenía del Congreso.
    Si no había alguna diferencia, precisamente atendiendo a que la posición de los dominios de España y sus nombres siempre exigían un contexto, que había de variar del de la Francia. Respondió que estaba autorizado del Congreso para tratar con cada una de las dos Cortes según sus intereses, y con plenos poderes para cuanto ocurriese.
    Cómo es que sin hallarse aún asegurados de su independencia, y sin estar tampoco reconocidos aún por estas potencias, venían proponiendo tratados cuando todo el mundo creía que la venida del doctor Franklin se dirigía más presto a solicitar auxilios que los ayudasen hasta conseguir su separación. Respondió que por medio de

semejante tratado verían la potencia que quisiese ser su amiga de veras, y que hasta haberse asegurado de esta calidad, no habían creído conveniente entrar en el punto de necesidad, tanto más que su situación aún no era tal que necesitase inmediatamente auxilios directos.

Si era cierto que habían recibido ya socorros de este reino. Si había partido el *Amphitrite*, y si otros dos bastimentos que debían seguirle, lo hacían o se suspendían. Respondió que de esta potencia no habían recibido socorros algunos. Que por medio de una compañía se les habían provisto diferentes géneros, armas y municiones. Que también se habían recibido oficiales a su servicio, y que en todo esto no había hecho la Francia otra cosa sino el no oponerse y dejar libertad de practicarlo. Que el *Amphitrite* había salido, y creía haberse suspendido la salida de los otros dos buques.

Cuáles serían los auxilios que más les urgían en la actualidad. Respondió que cañones de bronce y buques de guerra, respecto a que los bastimentos que tenían hasta ahora eran inferiores en fuerza a los ingleses. Y bien que eran muchos sus armadores y habían hecho cantidad de presas hasta el importe de millón y medio de libras esterlinas, según cómputo hecho en el mismo Londres, como no podían presentarse a las naves de guerra inglesas, siempre era una inferioridad que necesitaban reparar. Tanto más que los ingleses, con sus muchas naves de guerra y las de transporte cubiertas de ellas, estaban en estado de llevar sus tropas y víveres a cualquiera parte de aquel continente.

Por qué no hacía de una vez para la Corte de Madrid todas las explicaciones que tuviese que hacerle, respecto a que por la distancia no había la proporción de manifestarlas de un día a otro, como se podía practicar en Versailles, sabiendo desde luego también sus respuestas. Respondió que en esta consideración entregaría otro papel que contendría cuanto se le había indicado. Que si convenía que uno de sus compañeros diputados pasase a Madrid, lo haría desde luego. A esto le dije que el hacerlo o no, era libre en ellos, pero que no se adelantaría tanto porque entre sí tendrían que entenderse por los correos ordinarios, y la Corte de Madrid, en cualquiera proposición que recibiese, querría consultarla con la de París, siendo mejor hacer aquí las explicaciones porque ya se comunicarían a Madrid con el dictamen de esta Corte. Y le repetí que, si lo querían, que se propondría a Madrid. Hicieron ambos con este motivo muchas demostraciones de respeto hacia el rey católico, y que su principal fin era el de convencer que de su parte anhelaban su protección.

Si hacían algún comercio con los dominios españoles de América. Respondieron que antes, estando bajo la dominación británica, hacían alguno por la parte de la Jamaica, pero que en estos tiempos no lo practicaban.

Si tenían muchos oficiales extranjeros. Respondió que el mayor número era de franceses, algunos alemanes, y un polaco. Que al principio habían pasado algunos desde Santo Domingo, y otros transferídose desde los puertos de Francia, habiendo tenido el pensamiento de levantar tres regimientos en el Canadá, pero inutilizádose por haberlo ocupado los ingleses. Que mantenían dichos oficiales asalariados, bien que sin emplearlos.

Si no entraría la mala inteligencia en los miembros del Congreso. Respondió muy sucintamente que no.

Para abrirles un poco el ánimo y que no extrañasen las cuestiones que se les había hecho, les dije que se dirigían a tomar una luz del estado en que se hallaban, y que recíprocamente podían preguntar lo que les pareciese, pues en lo que yo pudiese corresponderles se les diría con franqueza, como también si no me hallase en estado de contestarles.

Entonces me preguntaron si tenía probabilidad que la Rusia acordase un cuerpo de tropas a la Inglaterra contra los americanos, en tono de hacerles mucha impresión este recelo. Y les dije que las noticias públicas de Gaceta habían hablado de ello, pero que nada más se sabía.

Expusieron que el Congreso había enviado a Cádiz seis cargamentos de su cuenta, dirigidos a la Casa inglesa de Buick y Compañía, la cual se resistía a sus pagos, siendo este caudal urgente porque el Congreso lo había destinado para hacer en Francia las compras que necesitaba. Y preguntaron qué medio habría de conseguir de dicha Casa tan justa satisfacción, respecto a que se negaba a toda contestación sobre este asunto.

Les dije si sería acaso una especie de represalia como Casa inglesa, por descubiertos que otros negociantes de las Islas Británicas tendrían con los americanos. Y a esto respondieron que no podía ser, pues la correspondencia de los particulares nunca se había cortado, antes bien vigilado el Congreso en que se mantuviese con toda exactitud, de tal modo que en su propio bastimento[59] habían venido varias letras de cambio para el comercio de Londres. Se les explicó, pues, que el modo de solicitar el cobro de la Casa de Buick sería el presentarse un particular con los conocimientos de su deuda y poderes necesarios, pidiendo ante el tribunal que correspondiese el pago de lo que se les debiese. Y que en este caso se podría buscar un apoyo de la autoridad para que se les administrase justicia sin demora.

El martes 7, en la conferencia ordinaria de embajadores, me preguntó el señor de Vergennes si me había entregado Franklin sus papeles. Le respondí que aún no, bien que habiéndolo visto la noche del 4, me había ofrecido lo haría en breve. Diciendo a su excelencia la sustancia de los discursos que habíamos tenido, le parecieron muy propios. Quedamos en que apenas me los pasasen, si estaban en inglés se encargaría su excelencia de hacérmelos traducir, en lo que convine muy gustoso, pues de todos modos yo se los había de comunicar.

El miércoles 8 por la noche recibí los papeles del doctor Franklin, que él mismo me trajo acompañado de Lee, y en la propia los remití al señor conde de Vergennes, quien los recibió en la mañana del jueves para su traducción. Y estos se reducen al acto de confederación y a la memoria concerniente a su estado actual, que van inclusos.

El viernes 10 pasé a Versailles. Me dijo su excelencia que se estaba haciendo la versión,[60] y me dio copia de la proposición posterior de Franklin, pidiendo a la Francia que se les facilitasen buques de guerra a su coste, como verá vuestra excelencia por la del n° 1, y por la del n° 2 la respuesta de su majestad cristianísima, ofreciéndoles otros socorros secretos.

Me dijo de Vergennes que esta respuesta se les haría leer a Franklin, Dean y Lee por su primer commis monsieur Gérard, dejándoles tomar una sustancia de ella para que nunca resultase documento demostrable. Que el rey había concedido dos millones de libras tornesas, con los cuales podrían hacer el giro de seis en las compras necesarias mediante las reglas de comercio y los muchos negociantes que tomarían parte en proveer a los americanos de lo que necesitasen. También me dijo que el *Amphitrite*, que había arribado a los puertos de Francia por malos tiempos, habiendo padecido en ellos, volvería a partir, y que los otros dos bastimentos suspendidos en el Havre se harían igualmente a la vela, bien que se tomaban disposiciones para que todo se ejecutase con más disimulo que hasta aquí.

Proponen los americanos solamente la buena amistad y comercio recíproco, pero si es suficiente para la Francia, no sería adaptable a la España sin limitar que se entienda sólo y estrechamente con su Reino en Europa. Porque si la concesión se extendiese también a sus dominios de América, quedaría perdido el Comercio nacional. De esta reflexión bien es creíble que las Provincias Unidas Americanas se hiciesen cargo, contentándose con reducir su correspondencia y tráfico a la España europea, y si reconviniesen con solicitar su acceso a nuestras islas como lo tendrían en las de Francia, se les podría oponer que las nuestras ligan con aquel continente, de cuyas reglas son inseparables, cuando los franceses nada tienen en él y sus islas se consideran totalmente unidas a estos Reinos, aunque situadas en aquellas partes.

Claman también por otros particulares que les serían conducentes para afianzar el buen éxito de su resistencia, y la Francia se presta por los términos que considera posibles, como uno y otro resulta de los papeles anexos.

Pero dejaré aparte todos estos accidentes auxiliares de las colonias para su independencia, y voy a exponer al rey el aspecto presente de su Monarquía y el de sus intereses sucesivos.

Cuatro potencias europeas dominaban el continente de América: la española en lo que posee, la Francia en el Canadá que perdió, la inglesa en las colonias septentrionales que se le han separado, y el Portugal en su Brasil, que lo ha duplicado insensiblemente con usurpaciones a la España.

Mientras durase esta división, las miras de la España se debían dirigir a la conservación de lo suyo, procurando el equilibrio de los otros competidores, y aun valiéndose indiferentemente de cada uno de ellos para contener al que se le desmandase. Pero ya muda el sistema, ya son indispensables otras reflexiones políticas.

La España va a quedar mano a mano con otra Potencia sola en todo lo que es tierra firme de la América Septentrional. ¿Y qué potencia? Una estable y territorial que ya ha invocado el nombre patricio de América con dos millones y medio de habitantes descendientes de europeos, que según las reglas que toman para su propagación, duplicará sus vivientes cada 25 o 30 años, y en 50 o 60 puede llegar a ocho o diez millones de ellos, mayormente que de Europa misma continuará la emigración por el atractivo que ofrecerán las leyes de aquel nuevo dominio.

Para la conservación de sus propias posesiones de América, a fin de distraerlas del ejemplo de las colonias Inglesas desahuciadas de su apoyo, y a fin de impedir a estas el socorrerlos, importa a la España el asegurarse de aquel nuevo dominio por medio de un tratado solemne, y cogiéndolo en el momento de sus urgencias con el mérito de sacarlo de ellas.

Si antes del levantamiento de las colonias hubiese sido de la elección de la España el que sucediese o no, habría habido sin duda poderosas razones para dudarlo, porque en fin es cuestionable la diferencia de tener por vecino un Estado consistente en propiedad, o que sólo fuesen provincias de una Corona distante. Un Estado que si aumentaba como colonia lo haría con mayor lentitud, y desprendido del vasallaje y entregado a su progreso va a multiplicar rápidamente los medios de su auge.

Pero de nada sirven estas consideraciones para el día, ni tampoco es tan grande la diferencia del teatro para la España, porque habiendo quedado sola la Inglaterra en la América Septentrional, y uniendo sus posibilidades de Europa con las que iba preparando en América, si bien se reflexiona, tal vez se deduciría que menos contrarrestos pudiera presentar la España en aquellos parajes de los que ahora puede proporcionar si se resolviese a consumar un plano reflexionado, atando bien todos los cabos que ofrece la presente ocasión.

Ya, pues que no tiene otro recurso el evitar la insurrección, sino el deseo de que la Inglaterra consiguiese su abatimiento triunfando completamente de sus rebeldes, y que el remedio sería peor que la enfermedad, pues la Corona británica quedaría indomable y para siempre jamás mucho más temible que nunca a la España, véase si en este contraste de circunstancias cupiera un medio menos nocivo que precaviese los dominios de la España en la América, y pusiese de mejor semblante su consistencia en Europa.

Parece que aún la necesidad exige ya el asegurar con la nueva Potencia de América el reconocimiento de las antiguas propias posesiones, el unirse para una garantía recíproca, y el formar por un tratado solemne las reglas de buena correspondencia para lo sucesivo. Y si esto se difiriese a cuanto hubiese salido de sus aprietos, ni su voluntad estaría tan bien dispuesta, ni sus urgencias servirían de apoyo para sacar mejor partido.

Si alguno ha de conseguirse ventajoso, no ha de ser por los medios ocultos de auxilios secretos e insuficientes, porque ni sirven de gran mérito ni ponen en el caso de atraer la otra parte a una convención seria y formal. El tiempo se pasaría en buenas razones y nada se habría asegurado de importante.

El entrar desde luego a un declarado apoyo para el logro de la independencia, cuando su suerte vacila aún y está a la vista de los enormes esfuerzos que la Inglaterra hará [para] evitarla, sería el medio de pactar lo que se quisiese con las colonias. Esta verdad es innegable, y sólo resta que discutir si el romper con la Inglaterra sería o no un desacierto, y si las consecuencias podrían volverse en mal creyendo adquirir un bien.

Para romper la primera consideración, debe ser la de calcular la resistencia del enemigo y las fuerzas propias y aliadas que se le podrían oponer.

La Inglaterra en el día está reducida a un tercio de sus naturales antiguas fuerzas, por un cálculo innegable.

Las colonias daban a su marina de Guerra el tercio de sus tripulaciones. Yo he oído al doctor Franklin que ascendían de 25 a 30 mil hombres los marineros americanos que en las precedentes guerras servían en las escuadras británicas. Desde la sublevación ya no subsiste este tercio, conque desde luego lo tiene de menos la Inglaterra y ha quedado con solos los otros dos.

El tercio distraído, habiendo tomado las armas, tiene empleado contra sí uno de los dos remanentes a lo menos, conque resulta un solo tercio que conceder a la Inglaterra en estado de disponer a su arbitrio.

Se sabe que para armar los 45 navíos y número de fragatas que quiere tener en estado, no alcanzan las mayores violencias de la leva ni los buenos enganchamientos que ha ofrecido. A más fuerte razón no cabe que alcanzase a tripular 60 navíos y fragatas correspondientes que se le quisieren acordar, por no incurrir en la reconvención de que se le minoran a la Inglaterra sus fuerzas estudiosamente, por apoyar la idea sobre un supuesto voluntario.

Si a esta reducción se añade lo demás que padece en sus intereses, desguarneciendo el comercio marítimo para completar su armamento; el descaecimiento de sus artes y fábricas por la interrupción con las colonias; los impuestos y gravámenes exigidos para atender a los indispensables gastos corrientes; el incremento de su deuda nacional y, en fin, el ahogo en que casa día se sofoca más, destruyendo el interior y exterior de sus Reinos, se habrá de convenir que real y físicamente se halla la Inglaterra en la actualidad al punto que se ha supuesto.

Las fuerzas propias y aliadas que se le podrían oponer, consisten en 80 navíos de línea y fragatas a proporción, según las explicaciones de las Cortes de Madrid y París, conque véase desde luego la superioridad considerable que resulta, siendo constante que estas fuerzas son efectivas, y las que se conceden a la Inglaterra tienen mucho de gracia e imaginario.

Por ella se vería comprometida la Inglaterra en el momento de peor disposición que haya tenido desde que se abrogó el predominio marítimo, pues la sufriría pasivamente con menos fuerzas y con enemigos que nunca encontró en mejor estado.

La España no puede olvidar un Gibraltar, un Mahón, y su pérdida sería para la Inglaterra uno de los mayores golpes, y un sacrificio inexcusable por el derecho con que se les pediría. Y porque el restituir una usurpación los salvaría de su mayor ruina. La Francia tomaría igual parte que la España en procurar este desmembramiento de la Inglaterra, y tanto cuanto resiste otras ideas de la España sobre Portugal, sería su parcial respecto al reintegro de dichos puertos.

La Francia no puede menos de conocer que tanto le conviene ahora romper con los ingleses como a la España, porque la Corona británica es su mayor enemigo natural. Porque si no lo abate, lo tendrá encima siempre que su comercio florezca o quiera restablecer su marina, y siempre que por las indispensables circunstancias de la Francia se halle empeñada con otras potencias del continente, aprovechando entonces la Inglaterra de la ocasión para atropellarla. La afrentosa sujeción de Dunkerke tampoco se redime sino en ocasión semejante. De modo que la Francia debiera temer en todo tiempo a la Inglaterra, si no rematase ahora el cortarle las alas para siempre.

El tratado propuesto por los americanos, que esta Corte remitió por su correo últimamente, está concebido con mucho arte y tiene sus observaciones que hacer.

Proponen amistad y comercio como si fuese ya una potencia consolidada. Al artículo 7 sólo ofrecen a la Francia, en caso de guerra con la Inglaterra, el no asistir a ésta de hombres, dinero, navíos etc, y al 8° exigen la renuncia de cuantas posesiones pudiese pretender por sus derechos antiguos, según se expresan en él, conviniendo en la pesca de Terranova.[61]

En este mismo mezclan a la Florida, que sólo puede tocar a la España. Y está firmado su original por Hancock, el presidente del Congreso, de modo que sus emisarios no han hecho más que comunicar el traslado[62] de su original.

Observará vuestra excelencia que no remito la separada proposición para España, bien que me la ofreció Franklin. Pero no me la ha traído aún, y en su visita del 8, cuando entregó los otros papeles, me indicó si podría dispensarlo, respecto a tener ya un tanto[63] por esta Corte y hallarse ellos agobiados sin personas de quien fiarse, y monsieur

Dean con tercianas,[64] como en efecto las tiene, pues por un conocido suyo le envié de la buena quina con que me hallo.

Estoy instruido, por conducto que me parece confidente de ellos, de quien no se guardan escrupulosamente, de que no quiso el Congreso entrar pidiendo con humillación ni manifestar extremas necesidades, por no recibir una ley dura que temió se les impondría, y se ve que en la memoria última pidiendo navíos, también ofrecen su satisfacción,[65] y nada quieren de balde.

Pues todo esto pende de una misma operación, que sería la de declarar la guerra a la Inglaterra abiertamente, ofreciendo a las colonias el ejecutarlo si mediante un tratado favorable se prestasen a merecerlo. Ellas sin duda lo aceptarían por abreviar su establecimiento, por aliviarse de sus trabajos, por no arriesgar su suerte. Y se obligarían a continuar en apoyo de sus aliados hasta que por todos se conviniese en una paz general.

Esta guerra declarada no necesita de la mayor actividad ni de aventurar acciones, pues su conducta, como se dirá, causaría el total efecto que se desea.

Desde luego, el plano que ha propuesto la Francia como precaución para en caso de ser insultada sería cuanto se necesita, con leves variaciones en su reparto con la sola circunstancia de verificar la declaración de la guerra.

Por ella se verían los ingleses en el caso de disminuir sus esfuerzos contra los insurgentes, y estos en el de resistirles y aniquilarlos.

Por ella quedaría el comercio de las Islas Británicas totalmente destruido, pues no podrían continuar el que les ha quedado, y ésta sería una batalla decisiva para batir las posibilidades, sin que precediesen combates aventurados.

Por ella se aumentarían los gastos que desustancian[66] a la Inglaterra.

Por ella tendrían sus flotas que consumirse si salían a la mar, quedándose las de España y Francia en sus puertos aguardando las ocasiones.

Por ella se dividirían en diferentes objetos y escuadras, no pudiendo ser tan numerosas las que proveyesen 60 navíos cubriendo varios destinos, como las que podrían componer 80 con la elección de ir a caer en mayor fuerza sobre aquellas, dirigiéndose a las que pareciesen más atacables.

Por ella el corso de España, Francia y Americanos sería superior con extremo al que pudiesen dar de sí las Islas Británicas, con la suma ventaja de sus posiciones para salir y refugiarse los armadores.

Por ella se había de encender en la misma Inglaterra una disensión civil que enervase sus esfuerzos, y que obligase su Ministerio a rescatar su total ruina con el sacrificio de algunas pérdidas, aunque le fuesen sensibles.

En este aspecto, las consecuencias humanamente no deben volverse en mal, sino en bien.

Una de las grandes precauciones de la España, parece que sería la de precaver el no quedarse con dos enemigos naturales en estado ambos de perturbarla. Y lo serían sin duda las colonias de América, no habiendo asegurado desde luego su buena correspondencia, y la Inglaterra en restableciéndose de su empresa de América, aunque disminuida de un tercio.

Si la España obtuviese el destruir la Inglaterra para que no levantase más la cabeza, conseguiría el tener de menos uno de los dos enemigos; y tanto habría ganado para en adelante y sus intereses de Europa, quedándose mano a mano con el de América, si se resolviese.

Los actos de unión manifiestan bien las miras con que se han resuelto a formar un Estado libre, y que su objeto es radicarlo para florecer en cultivo, artes y comercio. Que su sistema es pacífico y consiguiente al modo de pensar de sus autores, que los más son cuáqueros[67] de religión. Esta observación es importante para deducir que cualquiera medio que les abrevie su tranquilidad y el poner mano a la obra de su sistema, será bien recibido de las colonias, y por él se prestarán a cuanto les sea arbitrable.

De aquí nace también que la España debería fijar sus límites para evitar cuestiones en lo sucesivo. Y porque como no los tenía arreglados con los ingleses tierra adentro y a la espalda de las colonias, si no se precaviese esto, con lo que ellas irán aumentando de población y extendiéndose a voluntad, se podrán internar hacia nuestras posesiones por la espalda de la Luisiana.

Hay que tener presente que el río San Lorenzo por el Canadá sube hasta el lago Ontario, y éste comunica con el lago Erie u Oswego. Que cerca de éste nace el río Ohio, que cae en el Mississippi y por él baja a la Nueva Orleans. Que el lago Erie comunica también con el lago Hurón, y éste con los otros llamados superior y Michigan, más allá de los cuales viene corriendo el Mississippi.

No entro en determinar cuáles límites convendrían, pues me reduzco a exponer que unos u otros son importantes. Que la constitución de aquel país tan cruzado de ríos y lagos será muy apreciable a un pueblo que aumentará a pérdida de vista[68] por la libertad y buen tratamiento de sus leyes, como por el cultivo, artes y comercio en que fundará su felicidad. Y deduciré que el conseguir de dichas Provincias Unidas un tratado favorable, dependerá de sacarlas a cara descubierta de su aprieto, y de valerse de esta ocasión para convenir con ellas.

Por el rompimiento con Inglaterra en el tratado formal con las colonias, a más de lo dicho se conseguiría la reintegración de la Florida, cuya adquisición hizo la Inglaterra en la última paz, ya por el derecho que la España tiene a ella para en todo tiempo, y no la disputarían ahora las colonias, pero sí después como conquista sobre otro, ya porque dicha provincia aún no forme una de las de confederaciones, ya porque es importantísimo que aquel nuevo dominio no cargue con aquella posición, que es la que forma precisamente el Canal de Bahama, y llega hasta el río Mississippi y a las puertas de la Nueva Orleans con el célebre puerto de Panzacola en lo interior del Seno Mexicano. Ciertamente la España no necesita de extensiones, pues las que tiene la gravan más que la utilizan, pero en el caso presente sería nocivo el perder la ocasión de volver a sí el uso del canal de Bahama por ambas costas, y el dejar introducir en el Seno Mexicano aquella potencia estable.

También pudiera la España sacar partido en la pesca de Terranova y asegurar algún pedazo de su costa para su peculiar uso.

Si la Francia quisiese volver a la posesión del Canadá, lo conseguiría actualmente sin réplica de las colonias por el mero hecho de su alianza y rompimiento con Inglaterra. Y fuera lo que conviniera a la España, porque las colonias Unidas de América quedarían sujetas por los dos lados, y habría un contrarresto recíproco entre España y Francia siempre que ellas se desmandasen. A más que en tal caso de reponerle la Francia en sus antiguos dominios, sería también más natural y sólida la garantía mutua de las dos potencias con la nueva.

Esta idea bien la ha tenido la Francia, y aún la de formar del mismo Canadá otra república, según participé a vuestra excelencia en mi nº 853 de 10 de octubre. Si ahora se distrae de ella, será por la nueva que ha formado de que su comercio, sin otras atendencias, es la mayor ventaja que le puede resultar de la separación de las colonias. Pero sea como fuere, la Florida siempre convendría rescatarla.

De una cosa se habían de persuadir la España y Francia, y es de que los ingleses no volverán a sus Islas vencedores o batidos de los americanos, sin aprovechar sobre su camino de las fuerzas y armamento que tienen en aquellos mares. He dicho sobre ello a vuestra excelencia repetidas veces en mis anteriores los recelos casi evidentes con que debemos aguardarlo, y así excuso su repetición.

En América, los motivos expresados para con las colonias. En Europa, un Gibraltar y Mahón. Unos Tratados de Comercio existentes gravosos al de la España, y la utilidad que habría en formarlos de nuevo con otra equidad. Un reducir la Inglaterra, cuando está más ahogada que nunca, a que jamás levantase cabeza. Un buen estado de Marina en que se hallan las dos Coronas borbonas. Un método de rompimiento que sin acciones aventuradas darían el fruto deseable de la guerra con la Corona británica en esta ocasión, son las razones con que resumo el exponer a su majestad que este punto merecería su alta reflexión, y oír con un maduro examen el sentir de sus sabios ministros, para la más acrisolada resolución.

De la memoria de la Francia diré también que juzgo que, aunque indecisa, quisiera ella misma que el rey católico la impeliese, y puedo opinar así según he percibido en parte del Ministerio que lo desea.

Creo firmemente que como no se trata de Portugal, que ha sido siempre la piedra de toque, y sólo de la Inglaterra, cuyo abatimiento importa tanto a la Francia, procederá ésta con vigor y buena fe en declarándose. Y creo que todo pende de la resolución del rey Nuestro señor, y de los términos con que se dirigiese esta obra.

Dios guarde a vuestra excelencia muchos años. París, 13 de enero de 1777.
Excelentísimo señor
Beso la mano de vuestra excelencia
su seguro servidor
El conde de Aranda

Document 21
Legajo 4609-47/48, Estado, AGS
Al conde de Aranda, El Pardo 4 de febrero de 1777
[Carta de presentación manuscrita, 1 pág.; carta manuscrita, 4 págs.]
Original en español

[1-Carta de presentación]
El Pardo 4 de febrero de 1777
Por extraordinario con número 2

Respondiendo a varias especies sueltas de sus despachos por no deberse decir en la carta del número anterior la cual es ostensible.

[2-Carta]

Excelentísimo señor:
 Como la carta del número precedente se reduce a manifestar el modo de pensar del rey con respecto a los dos asuntos esenciales del día y dirigida a que vuestra excelencia pueda entregar copia de ella a este Ministerio no ha correspondido que toque yo algunas especies particulares de sus despachos anteriores.
 En la carta número 938 refería vuestra excelencia extensamente todos los [ilegible] que habían ocurrido desde que se supo la llegada a Francia del doctor Franklin hasta el [ilegible] de tener efecto varias conferencias con él y sus asociados; pero se inclinaba a creer que por parte del señor conde de Vergennes se había procedido con alguna especie de misterio no contando a vuestra excelencia todos los pasajes según iban sucediendo. No cabe realmente poner en duda los hechos que vuestra excelencia mismo con su perspicacia haya podido observar; pero no descubriéndose por otro lado un verdadero interés en usar con vuestra excelencia de aquella especie de extrañeza (porque en el día no puede tener la Francia con las colonias distintas miras que la España) parece más natural atribuirla a otra causa inocente o a que ese Ministro de Estado excusaba hablar del asunto hasta poderlo hacer con mayor instrucción de las ideas de los diputados.
 En la misma carta se explaya vuestra excelencia sobre las preguntas que hizo a Franklin con designio de sondear todas sus ideas y

hasta qué punto alcanzaban sus facultades. Esta advertencia de vuestra excelencia es propia de su penetración y como tal la ha estimado el rey.

Añade vuestra excelencia muchas reflexiones para persuadir que en el día se hallaba ese Ministerio muy inclinado a abrazar desde luego el rompimiento si de acá se le daba algún impulso. Pero en este particular aunque en sus discursos familiares y diarios con vuestra excelencia habrá tal vez soltado especies de donde se colija aquella máxima es menester observar que en todos los escritos que nos presenta y en sus frecuentes despachos al marqués de Ossun no lo manifiesta: y de todos modos las razones en que hasta ahora ha fundado el rey su determinación son sólidas y ponderosas que la misma Francia las reconoce por tales y se ha inclinado por sí al propio sistema de esperar algún tiempo más hasta ver el rumbo que toman los negocios de los americanos en la primavera próxima.

No me es posible entrar en por menor sobre las demás combinaciones y discursos que forma vuestra excelencia en la carta ya citada y otras sucesivas, ni lo juzgo necesario habiendo evacuado la parte principal que ha sido leerlas a su majestad para que no ignore hasta donde llega su celo y su lealtad; pero repetiré que lo ha estimado mucho.

Dios guarde a vuestra excelencia.

Document 22
Legajo 3884, Estado, AHN
Benjamín Franklin, Silas Deane, y Arthur Lee a su Excelencia el conde de Vergennes, París, marzo de 1777, no. 35
[Anexo al Document no. 6 anterior, 4 páginas]
Original en inglés

Document 23
Legajo 3884, Estado, AHN
Benjamín Franklin al conde de Aranda, París, 7 de abril de 1777, no. 23
[Carta principal, 3 páginas]
John Hancock, Comisión Parlamentaria, 2 de enero 1777, (no. 21)[69]
[1 página (sobredimensionada)] en folio 1, expediente 3.
Original en inglés

Document 24
Legajo 3884, folio 20, Estado, AHN
El conde de Aranda al conde de Floridablanca, París, 13 de abril de 1777, no. 1011 and no. 20[70]
[Carta manuscrita, 12 págs.]
Original en español

Excelentísimo señor

Muy señor mío:
    El jueves 3 del corriente por la tarde llegó a esta Corte Sr. Arthur Lee, inmediatamente me avisó su arribo por un papel pidiéndome le recibiese en compañía de sus asociados. Respondí de palabra, dándoles hora para el sábado 5 anochecido, por si acaso las cartas del ordinario que recibiría el mismo día a las dos o tres de la tarde, me decían algo relativo a dicho Lee, y cuando no, limitarme a oír dándome por desprevenido para contestarle.
    Con efecto me llegaron en dicha hora tres cartas de vuestra excelencia de 24 del pasado, y entre ellas el n° 2 expresivo de cuanto había ocurrido con Sr. Arthur Lee, de su entrevista con el señor duque de Grimaldi, de las resultas de ella y de las intenciones del rey para mi gobierno.
    Vinieron los tres Diputados de las colonias Americanas, Franklin, Dean y Lee, a la hora indicada, y pasadas las cortesías acostumbradas les pregunté qué traían que exponerme.
    Empezó Lee preguntándome si tenía yo en mi poder algunas letras de cambio giradas para Holanda en favor de ellos, y le respondí que no, y en qué se fundaba para haber concebido que estuviesen en mi poder. Díjome que habiéndose puesto en camino para Madrid llegó a Burgos, en donde lo encontró el señor duque de Grimaldi, quien le persuadió no pasase adelante sino que le descubriese todas sus solicitudes, sobre las cuales tratarían ambos, su excelencia daría cuenta al rey, y se recibiría la resolución de su majestad a ellas, por convenir así para que las buenas intenciones con que el rey católico se hallaba en favor de las colonias se pudiesen facilitar sin que se interpusiesen obstáculos, que naturalmente resaltarían llegándose a penetrar el arribo a Madrid de un diputado americano. Que aunque su ánimo había sido llegar a la Corte,

concibiendo que su existencia en ella con todo incógnito sería de
conveniencia mutua para España y Provincias Unidas, a fin de no perder
tiempo en cualesquiera especies que recíprocamente se suscitasen, había
cedido a la eficacia del señor duque de Grimaldi, respecto a que se le
declaraba autorizado por el rey para aquella entrevista, y le había
expuesto las urgencias actuales de los insurgentes, su ánimo resuelto de
no prestarse por ningún partido a la reconciliación con la Corona
británica, los esfuerzos de ésta para subyugarlos con la probabilidad de
que sus armas de tierra no lo consiguiesen, pero sí que fuesen más
poderosas por mar, cortando el arribo de los socorros y el comercio que
hasta aquí habían sostenido con alguna posibilidad para proveerse con el
mismo a sus necesidades. Que los ingleses tenían hasta 86 buques de
guerra desde 50 cañones abajo, y algunos se iban aumentando a la
desfilada de 50 a 74. Que las colonias no tenían por ahora más que
pequeños armadores, y carecían de buques mayores con que poder
contrarrestar a los británicos. Que aunque iban construyendo fragatas, y
respecto a obreros, maderas y hierros no carecían, les faltaban artillería,
velamen, cordaje y algunas otras cosas, que como antes las sacaban de
Inglaterra en trueque de los efectos de su continente, no las habían
radicado aún en él. Que la misma interrupción de su tráfico y
considerables expensas para formar un ejército, agotaban los caudales de
los americanos. Que el empeño de la Inglaterra, tan enardecido como
estaba, haría tales esfuerzos que pondrían las colonias en grande riesgo
de someterlas. Que si lo conseguían las destinarían a no dejarles tomar
otro incremento que el que bastase para valerse de ellas mismas en
aquella parte del mundo contra la España, así para irles cortando el
vuelo, como por la proporción que en ello había, según anteriormente
siempre había sucedido, pues las fuerzas de la Inglaterra contra la
España no habían salido de Europa en su totalidad, sino en una ínfima
parte. Que las colonias quedarían tan agradecidas al rey católico de
haber concurrido a su independencia, que podría contar su majestad con
ellas para cuanto la Inglaterra pudiese intentar contra sus dominios.
Díjome muchas otras razones que había alegado, y no pude retener con
bastante exactitud para referirlas.

 Supúsome Sr. Lee que el señor duque de Grimaldi despachó un
correo desde Burgos, que lo hizo retroceder a Vitoria para aguardar allí
la respuesta de la Corte, que llegó ésta y se la comunicó el mismo señor
duque de Grimaldi, reducida a repetirle las consideraciones que le había
objetado en Burgos, y ser las que no permitían a la España entrar desde

luego en el total de las miras y deseos de las colonias, pero que deseando igualmente que[71] ellas su independencia, había tomado algunas medidas para socorrerlas de efectos útiles a la continuación de su guerra, no sólo desde los puertos de Europa, sino también de los de América, particularmente por la Luisiana, con cuyo gobernador ya se había explicado el general Lee en el año pasado cuando mandaba las tropas de aquellas provincias inmediatas. Que el rey acordaba desde luego un subsidio en dinero (pero no me expresó Lee la cantidad) que recibiría por medio de cambiales[72] para Holanda, pues se les darían como de negociantes sin que la España sonase en ello, debiendo el dicho Arthur Lee restituirse inmediatamente a París, en donde con sus compañeros podría valerse del embajador de su majestad y del Ministerio del rey cristianísimo, con cuyo conocimiento había de obrar siempre la España en un todo. Que a consecuencia de dicha oferta, deseaba saber las órdenes que yo tuviese para hacer efectivas las letras prometidas.

Como vuestra excelencia en su citado oficio no me dice si vendrían o no por mi mano dichas cambiales, ni la cantidad acordada, me pareció mejor desentenderme por el pronto de estar noticioso de lo ocurrido, y me reduje a lo que también me indica vuestra excelencia de suponer por mis noticias particulares la buena disposición del rey. Así pues, le respondí que todo cuanto el señor Grimaldi le hubiese ofrecido, podía estar seguro que se le cumpliría, porque a más de que en ello habría obrado según la positiva voluntad de la Corte, yo tenía entendido por mis correspondencias privadas que su majestad pensaba con inclinación a las colonias, y sabía por experiencia que su real palabra era firme y constante y una prenda que valía por el más solemne documento. Que se tranquilizase y creyese que en el día y hora menos pensada se hallaría con las letras para hacer uso de ellas en la forma que se le hubieren prometido.

Concluido este discurso con Arthur Lee, salió el doctor Franklin con que acababa de recibir del Congreso una orden para pasar él mismo a España, y la credencial formal que me presentaba con diferentes instrucciones para su comisión. En cuya virtud se hallaba en el caso de haber de obedecer a sus principales.

Expúsele que yo no podía menos de persuadirle que no lo practicase por ahora, pues subsistían las mismas causales que habían detenido en el camino a su compañero, y siendo tan reciente, disgustaría al rey católico una insistencia que no difería del paso dado por Lee sino en tener el Franklin credenciales más formales. Que se hiciese cargo de la cautela con que la España debía proceder mientras subsistiese en paz con la Inglaterra. Que reflexionase que la España se hallaba también empeñada en su América Meridional con un destino considerable de fuerzas, cuyo éxito necesitaba aclararse y no se dejaría percibir hasta de aquí a algunos meses. Que para todo se había de poner primero la España en estado, y era bien público que lo practicaba para cuanto pudiere ocurrir. Que todas las cosas exigían el aguardar un momento favorable, que debían suponer examinaría bien el rey católico. Que se prestasen a disfrutar de las gracias que habían conseguido, y diesen tiempo al tiempo. Que cuanto tuviese que proponer de parte del Congreso lo podía ejecutar por escrito, que éste pasaría a mi Corte y bastaría a ambas partes el haberse entendido. Sobre lo cual yo no podía pensar diferentemente de lo que le aconsejaba, ni concurrir en forma alguna a su viaje.

    Allanóse el doctor Franklin, mediante que me pasaría por escrito una memoria que contuviese las especies que se le mandaban proponer. Y devolviéndole yo la credencial que había puesto en mis manos, por parecerme original, insistió en que la retuviese para enviarla con su memoria, respecto a que él la tenía duplicada y quería hacerla ver en debida forma. Como verá vuestra excelencia por una y otra pieza que le incluyo, habiéndome pasado la segunda el martes 8 por la noche en pliego cerrado, por haberles yo prevenido que sería lo más prudente el que no frecuentasen mi casa aunque fuese en horas oscuras, sino que por escrito me manifestasen sus deseos en inteligencia de que yo no podía contestarles en la misma forma, pues cuando tuviese que prevenirlos de algo, los citaría por un recado.

    He comunicado al señor conde de Vergennes todo lo referido, y aún le pedí me hiciese traducir la credencial y la memoria, respecto a no hallarme con persona de confianza a quien cometérselo. Y por eso puedo pasar a vuestra excelencia las originales en inglés y sus traducciones en francés.

    Observo en la proposición de las colonias que los partidos que ofrecen son de ninguna consideración para recompensa de lo que piden se hiciese por ellas, y que Franklin pone de suyo que la proposición es susceptible de las modificaciones que fueren convenientes.

    Para que el rey tenga una luz del movimiento que el comercio francés se da para con los americanos, dirijo a vuestra excelencia el plano que ha formado una Compañía de negociantes entre sí, como[73] la cual, y sin la cual, es inexplicable el tráfico que se hace de estos puertos.

>Dios guarde a vuestra excelencia muchos años. París, 13 de abril de 1777.
>Excelentísimo señor
>Beso la mano de vuestra excelencia
>su seguro servidor
>El conde de Aranda.

Document 25
Legajo 1452-47, Estado, AGS
Informe de Lord Stormont al gobierno de Francia. Enviado por el Príncipe de Masserano al conde de Floridablanca, Londres, 22 de abril de 1777
[Manuscrito en español, 2 págs.]
Original en inglés

Document 26
Legajo 2596, Santo Domingo, AGI
Comisionados por el Congreso de las Provincias Unidas de Norteamérica a Bernardo de Gálvez, Filadelfia, 12 de junio de 1777, no. 168
[Cartas manuscritas, 3 págs.]
Original en español[74]

Filadelfia y junio 12 de 1777

Señor:

    Estamos informados por medio de Don Olivero Polock de la disposición tan favorable que se ha dignado manifestar para en lo adelante a el interés y causa de los vasallos en los Estados Unidos libres e independientes de América, en cada una de las ocasiones que se le han presentado después que su Excelencia ascendió a el gobierno del Nueva Orleans y Luisiana, y nos asegura particularmente [el] señor Polock cómo está inclinado a dar toda la protección que puede para animarnos a que dirijamos aquellos navíos o embarcaciones con que quisiéramos comerciar a el Missisipi.

    Como nosotros abajo nominados, miembros del Congreso, estamos asignados y cometidos con la superintendencia y manejo del comercio público de estos Estados, juzgamos ser nuestra incumbencia corresponderle muy agradecidos por aquella amistosa parte que se ha tomado, y le rogamos por la continuación de igual.

    Los poderosos, en el arreglo de estos Estados, están dispuestos igualmente a promover una amistosa comunicación y mutua correspondencia de acciones agradables entre los vasallos de su majestad muy católica y los propios suyos. El Congreso ha enviado un comisionado a la Corte de Madrid con sus poderes para entrar en un tratado de comercio y amistad, y tenemos toda razón para creer aquella Corte muy dispuesta a asistirnos con su amistad. Es evidente que de nuestro comisionado hemos tenido ya avisos de que fue encontrado en un paraje llamado Gastos[75] hacia Madrid, por una persona de consecuencia quien le dio seguridad que serían socorridos, así de frazadas y vestuario, como de efectos militares, los que se ordenarían de La Habana a la Nueva Orleans, y depositarse allí para nuestro uso, donde debían demorarse hasta que enviásemos por ellos. Y sin embargo hemos aguardado hasta oír más sobre el particular antes de tomar alguna disposición en procurar estos suplementos, pero si algunos semejantes arribaren en el ínterin, no dudamos que su excelencia nos notifique de ello.

Es muy probable que sea agradable el saber de nuestra presente situación, el tiempo no nos permitirá dársela por menor, pero en pocas palabras se puede contar que el general Howe subsiste con el grueso de su ejército en Brunswick de Nueva Jersey, dentro de los trabajos fuertes que levantó el invierno pasado, cuando el general Washington lo hizo retirar atrás de Trenton y Princetown, ha estado colectando allí sus fuerzas por largo tiempo, y haciendo preparativos para abrir la campaña. Nosotros no hemos estado ociosos de nuestra parte, y así todo lo que esperamos es que Sr. Howe marche de un instante a otro y que dirija su objeto hacia esta ciudad. Ya el general Washington se ha apostado en un paraje muy fuerte de este territorio detrás de Mr Howe y muy cerca de él, preparado para defender y ofender según la causa de la guerra lo requiera. Los ejércitos son casi iguales en número, pero ellos tienen la ventaja de ser mejor disciplinados y en armas y vestuario. Los nuestros son más activos y mejores apuntadores, y pelean por mejor causa, y asimismo serán sostenidos por la milicia del país si fuere urgente, una milicia que ha participado ya de la gloria de derrotar a un enemigo tan formidable.

Nuestro ejército en Ticonderoga bajo el general Gates, está igualmente preparado para el recibimiento del general, el señor Guy Carleton y el general Burgoyne. En suma, estamos medianamente preparados, pero nuestros soldados como nuevos, esperamos a el abrirse la campaña, probable tememos se vuelvan contra nosotros, aunque no tenemos duda de concluir con mucho honor y ventajas de América, y que al fin estableceremos firmemente nuestra libertad y la independencia que ningún poder humano será capaz nunca de privarnos de ellas. Tenemos el honor de remitirle algunas gacetas, las que repetiremos con nuestra correspondencia en las ocasiones que se presenten. Somos de su excelencia los más obedientes y muy rendidos servidores.

Cometidos para el comercio por el Congreso.

Document 27
Legajo 4611, AGS
El conde de Aranda al conde de Floridablanca, París, 22 de junio de 1777, no. 1055
[Carta manuscrita, 9 págs.]
Original en español

Excelentísimo señor

Muy señor mío:
 El miércoles 18 a media tarde llegó el correo Uribarri con la expedición de vuestra excelencia de 11 del corriente, consistente en dos solos números, el 1º ostensorio y el 2º reservado, ambos sobre la suspensión de armas que el rey acababa de convenir con la Corte de Lisboa para la América Meridional.
 Remití inmediatamente al señor conde de Vergennes el pliego de vuestra excelencia y el de ese embajador, como también al Lord Stormont el del Lord Grantham, y al Embajador de Portugal el de su hermano.
 Pasé en la mañana inmediata a Versailles, hice leer al señor de Vergennes el nº 1 para su completa instrucción de los términos en que estaba concebido. Y como el 2º reservado me daba cuantas luces convenían para dirigir mis explicaciones, las hice arreglado a él, disimulando la buena inteligencia que reservadamente se ha entablado entre el rey y reina fidelísima, su sobrina.
 Curioso el señor de Vergennes de profundizar cómo habría sido tan pronta y pacífica desistencia[76] del rey católico, le dije ser la cosa más sencilla del mundo, porque su majestad, satisfecho de su decoro resarcido con el buen efecto de sus armas, y habiendo ocurrido en el intermedio el fallecimiento del rey fidelísimo y separación del marqués de Pombal, quienes habían ofendido sus respetos, había tenido inmediatamente aperturas de las reinas fidelísimas, su hermana y sobrina, deseando reparar los agravios cometidos con desaprobación de ellos. Que el rey católico, usando de su natural generosidad, y no habiendo jamás querido morder a Portugal de lo que fuese suyo legítimamente, comprendido de la buena fe de las dos princesas, había dado muestras de su moderación contribuyendo a sus consuelos. Que

este era un hecho noble y connatural con el carácter del rey, y esta era la causa de tan pronta apariencia de composición. A la que sin duda se prestaría el rey mi amo con más facilidad y desestimiento de sus pretensiones, que si subsistiesen el rey difunto y el ministro retirado.

Pasé después a la Corte del rey cristianísimo, quien me dijo <u>parece que las cosas se componen,</u>[77] y le respondí que como el rey mi amo se hallaba con dos señoras respetables y de su propia sangre, que ya le habían manifestado sus deseos de reconciliación, había sin duda querido manifestarlas su noble modo de pensar.

Más tarde fui a ver al señor conde de Maurepas, a quien hallé con los señores de Vergennes y Sartine. Tuve el mismo discurso, y como Maurepas por lo más gusta de estilo chancero, lo seguimos con la galantería española, de modo que si no han sido muy reservados estos ministros en no manifestarme sus sospechas, por la apariencia creería yo que no recelan tanta buena interior inteligencia como me indica vuestra excelencia haberse establecido.

Causóme novedad el ver allí a monsieur de Sartine, porque el día antes me había dicho en París que no volvería a Versailles hasta el viernes a comer, y aún me había propuesto de hacerle compañía si yo iba aquel día a Versailles, como en efecto se lo prometí porque pensaba ir.

Me ocurrió[78] si con motivo de haber recibido la noticia de la suspensión de armas en la tarde anterior, lo habría citado el señor de Maurepas como a de Vergennes, para conferir sobre las resultas. Lo que observé mientras estuvimos juntos los cuatro, es que los tres conministros[79] conformes[80] me dijeron que la reconciliación de España con Portugal sería muy sensible a los ingleses, porque no sólo quedarían expeditas las fuerzas españolas dedicadas antes contra Portugal, sino que les faltaría éste para valerse de él como instrumento de diversión. Pregunteles si tenían satisfacción en el paso dado, por la resulta que suponían. Me dijeron que sí, pero si yo creía que pasaría en sola neutralidad de Portugal. Respondiles que ésta sola sería siempre una ventaja, que el exigir volverlo en enemigo de la Inglaterra sería difícil, que para esto hubiera sido necesario que Cevallos, después de haber recuperado todas las pretensiones del rey, se entrase en las propiedades de Portugal y las pusiese bajo las armas del rey católico, para con este motivo dar la ley a Portugal como condición de restituírselas, el aliarse con las Cortes de Borbón. Y si ellos mismos hubiesen visto estos progresos, habrían dicho a la España que iba a resolver el mundo entero, a causar una guerra general cuando no tenían gana de ningún ruido.[81]

Como el nº 2 reservado me manifiesta lo conveniente que será disuadir de la estrecha inteligencia que se ha entablado entre Madrid y Lisboa para evitar que se injieran los extraños, me pareció que sería bueno aparentar que, aunque las cosas se componen buenamente, no llega a tanto la intimidad de ellas que se puedan emprender proyectos de difícil consecución, cuando otro no fuese que para distraer este Ministerio de hostigar al español con semejantes especies. Tanto más creíble en mí este modo de pensar de resultas del partido tomado por el rey de prestarse desde luego a la suspensión de hostilidades, cuanto yo me había manifestado anteriormente con este Ministerio como parcial de la segregación de Portugal de la Inglaterra.

Yo pensaba despachar a vuestra excelencia el 19, teniendo prevenido el oficio que sigue a éste. Y bien que algunas de sus especies puedan llegar tarde según el estado de las cosas, habiendo otras que enterarán a vuestra excelencia del modo de pensar de este Ministerio en aquellos días, y ligando cuanto contiene con el curso actual, lo paso a vuestra excelencia tal lo tenía ya extendido.

Observo palabras sueltas en estos ministros que me persuaden hallarse persuadidos de que la guerra con la Inglaterra es inevitable. Aun cuando estábamos juntos el jueves 19, se les fueron algunas.

Para sondear yo mejor el interior del señor de Vergennes en aquella misma mañana y nuestra primera entrevista, le pregunté si había visto un papel formado por Franklin nuevamente. Me respondió que no, y se alegraría verlo si yo lo tenía. Se lo mostré, porque justamente lo había conseguido el día antes. Lo leyó con atención y me pidió una copia. Le pedí lo volviese a leer hasta hacerse bien cargo, respecto que al confiármelo una persona curiosa, había exigido de mí la palabra de no dar copia de él a ninguno, y se lo había ofrecido. Que sería natural que estando formado directamente para la Francia, le llegase por uno u otro conducto. Me preguntó si algún parcial del duque de Choiseul me lo había dado, pues ese partido hacía mucho ruido con las solicitudes de las colonias para apoyarlas. Respondile con verdad, ser un extranjero quien me lo había franqueado. Tanteé qué le parecía, y lo vi confuso. Por lo propio me abstuve de entrar en discursos, diciéndole sólo que aquellas mismas razones, bien se acordaría que las habíamos hablado diferentes veces, y aún de un año atrás. Como yo estoy identificado con mi Corte, no falto a mi palabra en dirigir a vuestra excelencia un tanto del dicho escrito.

El 18 por la mañana, cuando vi a Sartine en París, me dijo que disponía el enviar hacia Santo Domingo y Martinica cinco fragatas que, con otras tantas que existían en aquellos mares llegarían hasta diez, y que al septiembre pasarían tropas a Santo Domingo y algunos navíos de línea. Respondile que si partían de aquí al septiembre, no llegarían hasta fin de octubre o entrado noviembre, y que si llegaban tarde de qué servirían. No contestó, pero me dijo que a fin de este año podría contar el rey cristianísimo con 50 buques de línea y fragatas a proporción, y que ahora mismo en estado de navegar tenía 43 navíos. Le dije, como chanceando,[82] parece que andan vuestras mercedes recelosos ahora más que antes. Y me respondió que había mucho que temer, y que los ingleses se desataban sin guardar respetos. Yo concluí con que tuviese presente que la Francia había hecho bastante para dar motivos de quejas a los ingleses con los socorros públicos dados a los insurgentes, y muy poco para sacar a estos de aprietos y asegurarlos.

Dios guarde a vuestra excelencia muchos años. París, 22 de junio de 1777.
Excelentísimo señor
Beso las manos de vuestra excelencia
su seguro servidor
El conde de Aranda.

Anexo, Informe de Benjamin Franklin, Junio de 1777.
[Manuscrito, 7 págs.]
Original en francés

Papel del Dr Franklin en junio de 1777[83]
Il parait que la résolution actuelle de la Cour de France (et bien de gens pensent que c'est une résolution sage) est d'éviter, du moins d'ici à quelques temps, de prendre aucune part dans la contestation présente entre la Grande Bretagne et les Etats Unis de l'Amérique Septentrionale, présumant que la Puissance Angloise s'épuisera elle-même au point d'offrir à la France dans quelque temps une conjoncture plus favorable pour commencer avantageusement la guerre. Cependant cette politique est trop subtile, trop précaire, et trop désavantageuse pour être encore longtemps celle d'un Gouvernement sage. Elle est fondée sur deux suppositions dont chacune est non seulement incertaine, mais encore peu vraisemblable.

La première est que la Grande Bretagne deviendra bientôt dans le fait beaucoup plus faible, et moins en état de résister aux entreprises d'une Puissance Européenne, qu'elle ne l'est à présent, et c'est ce qui n'est moins que probable. Sans doute l'Angleterre augmentera sa dette publique, mais cette augmentation ne la rendra pas moins formidable. Aussi longtemps qu'elle jouira de la paix en Europe, elle ne sentira point immédiatement l'affaiblissement résultant de sa dette nationale, parce qu'elle pourra toujours emprunter autant d'argent qu'elle le jugera à propos. Elle ne cessera de grossir journellement le nombre de ses troupes, de ses vaisseaux de guerre. En les employant contre les États Unis d'Amérique, elle augmentera considérablement le courage, la discipline, et l'expérience de ce qui compose ses forces de terre et de mer, tandis que celles de France entretenues à presque aussi grands frais languiront dans l'inexpérience, et l'oisiveté. La Grande Bretagne, quoique plus chargée des dettes aujourd'hui que l'été dernier, est cependant plus en état à présent qu'elle ne l'était alors de faire la guerre, de la même manière que dans la guerre précédente, quoique sa dette se fut accrue de près de 80 millions sterlings, elle était plus formidable à la fin de la guerre qu'au commencement.

La seconde supposition est que la présente guerre entre la Grande Bretagne et les États Unis doit certainement durer un temps considérable sans que la France s'en mêle, supposition encore moins probable que la première. Le Gouvernement Britannique a tout à perdre et rien à espérer en continuant cette guerre par de là, la campagne actuelle. Il se propose donc sagement de faire ses plus grands et ses derniers efforts pour recouvrer la souveraineté de l'Amérique. Les Ministres espèrent que les hasards de la guerre leurs procureront quelques succès qui, joints aux besoins et aux souffrances de celles-ci, pourront engager celles-ci à rentrer avec plus ou moins de restriction sous la dépendance de la Grande Bretagne. Ils sentent que si le cours de cette campagne ne peut rien produire de décisif pour la réduction de l'Amérique, il n'y a rien à attendre de tous les efforts ultérieurs, qu'une plus longue continuation d'hostilités ne peut qu'augmenter et prolonger les risques d'une guerre en Europe. En conséquence, leur projet est, après avoir tenté le sort de cette campagne, de mettre quel qu'en soit vissé, fin à la guerre aux meilleures conditions qu'ils pourront obtenir, et s'il est absolument impraticable de réduire les Américains â l'état de sujets, de reconnaitre immédiatement leur amitié et la jouissance de leur commerce.

Cette détermination fixe et sérieuse du Ministère Britannique s'est pleinement manifesté par les derniers débats dans la chambre des Pairs à l'occasion de la proposition du Lord Cathan. On peut en être d'autant plus sûr que ce parti est le seul raisonnable. D'ailleurs cette certitude est encore confirmée par des informations particulières et authentiques.

La France ne peut donc prévenir la réconciliation prompte des Colonies avec la Grande Bretagne soit comme sujets, soit comme alliées, qu'en formant immédiatement avec elles des engagements tels, qu'en fermant la porte à toutes autres liaisons les Colonies y trouvent l'assurance des secours et du commerce dont elles ont besoin, et soient misses en état de repousser les attaques, et de rejeter les offres de la Grande Bretagne.

Il ne faut pas oublier que la première résistance des Colonies n'a pas eu pour objet l'indépendance, mais seulement le redressement des griefs, et que même encore à présent plusieurs de leurs habitants se contenteraient de demeurer sujets de la Couronne Britannique avec quelques restrictions. Le plus grand nombre d'entre eux, il est vrai se sont déclarés pour l'indépendance, mais ils se sont principalement portés à cette démarche dans la confiance que la France, connaissant et poursuivant ses plus importants intérêts, les appuieront bientôt ouvertement et d'une manière effective. Lorsqu'ils se trouveront trompés dans leur attente, lorsqu'ils verront que plusieurs États de l'Europe aident avec ardeur la Grande Bretagne à les subjuguer, qu'un autre État a publiquement interdit et proscrit le commerce avec eux, et que même les plus affectionnés se contentent de demeurer spectateurs oisifs de la querelle, et leurs refusent jusqu'à une reconnaissance verbale de l'indépendance qu'ils réclament, il est bien probable que désespérant d'être secourus au dehors, et pressés par le sentiment de leurs besoins et de leurs maux intérieurs, ils pourront penser à accepter les conditions que le Gouvernement Britannique sera disposé par son intérêt à leurs offrir.

Le Lord George Germaine a dernièrement déclaré dans la Chambre des Communs que ses espérances de terminer la guerre d'Amérique dans le cours de cette année étaient principalement fondés sur le découragement et le désespoir qui se répandaient parmi les Américains, lors qu'ils sauraient que la France ne leur donnera aucun secours. Les émissaires et les adhérents de la Grande Bretagne n'épargneront rien pour étendre et pour accroître ce désespoir et ce découragement. Déjà ils ont commencé à insinuer que la France, également ennemie des deux parties, fomente les contestations actuelles dans la seule vue de les faire servir mutuellement d'instruments à leur propre destruction et sans vouloir que les Colonies deviennent jamais indépendantes.

Si par ces artifices, ou par d'autres semblables, la Grande Bretagne parvient à détacher les Colonies de la France, et à se les unir à elle-même, ce dernier Royaume perdra sans retour l'occasion la plus favorable qui se soit jamais présentée à aucune nation d'accroitre sa propre richesse et sa puissance en humiliant et affaiblissant l'ennemi le plus formidable, le plus insolent et le plus invétéré. Cessation qu'aucune prudence humaine n'aurait pu amener, et que le patriote le plus celé pour la France pourrait à peine espérer de voir naitre dans ce siècle. Quod nemo divum promittere auderet, en tempus attulit ultro.[84]

Mais ce n'est pas seulement l'occasion de s'enrichir elle-même et d'humilier la Grande Bretagne, que perdra la France en continuant de rester dans l'inaction. Elle mettra encore dans le plus grand danger la sureté au moins de toutes ses possessions américaines. Le Ministère Britannique sait, ou croit savoir, que la France a déjà secrètement aidé les Américains dans leur résistance, et non seulement le Ministère, mais le Roi et la nation Britannique sont déjà animés contre les Français, que si la guerre avait été déclarée ouvertement. Dans la vérité, la France en a déjà trop fait si son intention n'est pas de faire davantage. Ne donnant point aux États Unis un secours vraiment efficace, il aurait mieux valu ne leur en donner aucun. La nation Anglaise, naturellement ennemie de la France, envisage et soupire après le rétablissement de la paix de l'Amérique à fin de pouvoir tourner ses armes contre ce Royaume et satisfaire à la fois par là sa vengeance et ses intérêts. Elle est bien déterminée à faire succéder immédiatement la guerre contre la France, à la réconciliation avec les Colonies.

Tel est maintenant le langage universel de la nation, et en particulier des chefs, ou ce qu'on appelle en Angleterre la minorité.[85]

Le sage, le paisible Lord Camden, lui-même il y a peu de jours a conclu un discours très long, et très applaudi dans la chambre des Pairs en souhaitant ardemment la paix avec l'Amérique et la guerre avec tout le reste du monde.[86] A la vérité, le Ministère a prudemment évité de s'expliquer ouvertement sus ces desseins. Mais quiconque réfléchira sur les considérations précédentes et sur le vif ressentiment dont on sait que le Roi de la Grande Bretagne est si excessivement susceptible, ne pourra douter qu'aussitôt que la paix sera faite avec l'Amérique, quelles qu'en puissent être les conditions, toutes les forces que la Grande

Bretagne a maintenant sur le continent de l'Amérique, ne soient sur le champ transportées aux Indes Occidentales et employées à conquérir les îles à sucre françaises pour indemniser l'Angleterre des pertes et des frais que lui aura couté la guerre présente, et pour la venger des encouragements et des secours qu'on impute à la France d'avoir donné en secret aux Colonies contre leur métropole. Certainement il ne reste pas au Ministère Britannique d'autre moyen de calmer les esprits irrités et de faire tolérer à la nation la perte de ses espérances trompées par l'événement de la guerre américaine. On lui avait promis que l'Amérique rendrait toutes les dépenses employées à la subjuguer; mais une telle promesse ne peut jamais être remplie, car l'Amérique fut-elle réduite au dernier degré de l'asservissement, jamais elle ne pourrait d'ici â long tems fournir aucun revenu à la Grande Bretagne. Dès lors le Gouvernement Anglais doit chercher à se dédommager d'un autre coté des dépenses de cette guerre, et en même temps à assoupir la haine et les ressentiments de la nation en employant contre les possessions américaines de la France ces mêmes troupes étrangères dont l'Angleterre ne peut se dispenser de rester chargée qu'après avoir averti longtemps d'avance leurs souverains respectifs.

Les esprits des deux nations, Française et Britannique, sont maintenant trop irrités et il naitra journellement trop des sujets de dispute pour que la guerre entre les deux Couronnes puisse être longtemps évitée. Il semble donc que l'intérêt évident de la France est de la commencer incessamment, avant que la Grande Bretagne ait le temps de se préparer et de se fortifier davantage elle-même, et pendant que les Colonies n'étant point encore subjuguées ont à la fois le pouvoir et la volonté de donner aux armes françaises l'assistance la plus efficace et la plus décisive.

Document 28
Legajo 4611, Estado, AGS
El conde de Aranda al conde de Floridablanca, París, 23 de junio de 1777, no. 1067 and no. 28
[Carta manuscrita, 3 págs.]
Original en español

Excelentísimo señor

Muy señor mío:

Ha venido hoy a mi casa el doctor Franklin para expresarme su reconocimiento por los socorros recibidos para las colonias americanas, no sólo en dinero sino también en efectos de guerra, y la vía de Bilbao.

Me ha insinuado con este motivo cuán importante sería para sus colonias el tener buques de línea, y que si la España y la Francia pudiesen cederles algunos, lograrían con ellos el ponerse sobre otro pie de resistencia, obligándose siempre a satisfacer aquello en que se estimaron. Le contesté que en este particular no podía decirle nada de positivo, porque aunque era considerable nuestra armada, siempre se necesitaba de buques excedentes para reemplazar los que fuesen quedando inservibles, respecto de los muchos objetos a que era preciso atender.

Me he valido de esta conversación con monsieur Franklin para preguntarle qué probabilidad podían tener las ventajas que se decía haber tenido los ingleses sobre los insurgentes, como también qué grado de asenso[87] daba él a las voces que se esparcían de que en el Congreso tenía la Inglaterra mejor disposición para atraerse los votos en favor de su causa. Me aseguró, en cuanto a las ventajas, que no eran ni con mucho tanto como las hacían sonar. Y en cuanto a lo otro, que no creía en manera alguna hubiese desunión en el Congreso, porque no había razón ni aún visos de persuadírselo, pues en este año se hallaban las colonias en mucha mejor situación que el pasado, bien provistas de armas y municiones. Y me añadió, en prueba de lo que me aseguraba, que posteriormente les había llegado a Boston una embarcación con doce mil fusiles, y alguna más a varios puertos con iguales efectos, en las cuales no comprendía el Amphitrite y otras, por no haber aún tenido noticia de ellas.

Lo participo a vuestra excelencia para que lo ponga en noticia del rey nuestro señor.
Dios guarde a vuestra excelencia muchos años.
París, 23 de junio de 1777
Excelentísimo señor
Beso la mano de vuestra excelencia
su seguro servidor
El conde de Aranda

☒ Document 29
Legajo 3884, Estado, AHN
Memoria presentada por Benjamín Franklin, Julio de 1777, no. 29
[Manuscrito, 7 págs.]
Original en francés

En julio de 1777= Del Dr Franklin[88]

Mémoire
    Dans un Mémoire précédent on a dit d'après l'autorité de la raison, d'après des nouvelles particulières très authentiques, et l'opinion générale des gens de tous les partis en Angleterre, que la guerre contre les États Unis finiront cette année, que si la Grande Bretagne manquait de les réduire sous sa domination, elle désespérerait de pouvoir jamais y parvenir, et qu'elle prendrait le parti de faire une alliance avec eux pour recouvrer autant qu'il serait possible leur amitié et leur commerce.
    Des fortes raisons et des avis sûrs nous portent pareillement à croire que lorsque la Grande Bretagne fera sa paix avec les États Unis, elle entrera aussitôt en guerre avec la France. C'est aujourd'hui le voeu du parti de l'opposition à Londres, et le Ministère lui-même ne tardera pas à juger que cette guerre est nécessaire à sa propre conservation. Le peuple d'Angleterre s'est laissé entrainer dans cette guerre américaine parce qu'on lui promettait que les Colonies seraient bientôt réduites et qu'on en tirerait un revenu considérable. La première partie de cette promesse s'est déjà évanouie, et il en sera de même de la dernière, car si les colonies ne sont pas subjuguées, on ne tirera d'elles aucun revenu, et si elles le sont, il est certain qu'elles se trouveront trop épuisées pour pouvoir de longtemps payer aucun subside.
    C'est ce que savent très bien les Ministres Anglais, mais toutes les fois qu'ils ont paru reconnaitre cette triste vérité et qu'ils ont voulu abandonner l'idée de retirer un revenu de l'Amérique, la Chambre des Communes et particulièrement les propriétaires des terres dans cette Chambre, ont pris l'alarme et ont fait craindre une révolte générale. Ainsi il éclatera beaucoup de mécontentement et d'animosité dans la nation Anglaise, lors qu'elle saura, à n'en pouvoir douter, qu'elle a été trompée par ses Ministres et qu'on ne doit attendre ni revenu ni aucun

autre bénéfice qui puisse dédommager du sang et de l'or prodigué si follement dans la guerre actuelle. Il est donc clair que pour détourner la vengeance publique de dessus leurs têtes, les Ministres actuels seront dans la nécessité de chercher à lui donner cours par d'autres voies, et d'attribuer leur mauvais succès à l'encouragement et aux secours secrets donnés par la France aux américains. C'est ce qui ne manqueront pas de publier et de faire sonner bien haut, tant pour excuser leurs propres fautes que pour faire tourner les ressentiments du peuple contre cette Puissance. L'intention où sont les Ministres Anglais de suivre ce plan de conduite s'est déjà manifesté par plusieurs procédés et publications. Cette animosité dont les Anglais s'enflamment si aisément contre la nation Française a déjà éclaté depuis peu en diverses occasions. Or, le soin qui prend le Gouvernement d'exciter cette animosité est une preuve bien plus certaine de ses dispositions à la guerre qu'aucune augmentation qu'ils puissent faire dans ses armements de mer, ou que les vingt nouveaux Régiments que l'on sait qu'on est prêt de lever dans la Grande Bretagne et l'Irlande.

En quelque temps que la Grande Bretagne se décide à commencer une nouvelle guerre, elle débutera infailliblement comme dans la dernière, c'est à dire par quelque hostilité soudaine et inattendue qui puisse assurer le succès définitif de la guerre et affaiblir son ennemi. Sa situation actuelle favoriserait merveilleusement une telle manière de procéder. Ses auxiliaires Allemands ne sont pas engagés pour être transportés en Amérique, mais ils y sont; ses forces de terre et de mer y sont déjà rassemblées et ils forment l'armée la plus formidable. Si elles échouent dans cette campagne, le Ministère Anglais hâtera-t-il sa propre chute et sa honte en les rappelant en Europe? N'aimera-t-il pas mieux donner des ordres à ses Plénipotentiaires pour faire la meilleure paix possible avec les États Unis et se servir de ses forces terribles pour tomber tout à coup sur les possessions américaines des Français ou des Espagnols? La plupart seraient conquises avant même qu'on eut appris ici le projet des Anglais. Cette conduite fournirait au Ministère Britannique le moyen de pourvoir à leur propre sureté, et les maintiendrait dans leurs places en même temps qu'elle satisferait l'avance et le ressentiment de la nation. Cet heureux début, et une guerre entreprise de cette manière empêcheront une baisse considérable dans le fonds Anglois et probablement fournirait à la Grande Bretagne pour la continuer avec vigueur tandis que la France, ayant reçu le premier échec, éprouverait les plus grandes difficultés à trouver de l'argent. Pour la commencer ainsi, le Ministère Anglais n'aurait besoin d'autre prétexte que la secrète assistance que la France est supposée avoir donné aux États Unis.

On se flatte en Angleterre que les finances de la France sont en trop mauvais ordre pour qu'elles puissent s'engager dans une guerre, mais quelque degré de vérité qu'il y ait dans cette assertion, on n'y voit aucune raison qui puisse retarder l'opération de causes déterminantes d'après lesquelles le Ministère Anglais doit commencer la guerre.
Au contraire, c'est ce qui l'encouragera plutôt à la faire. L'insensibilité de la France, son indolence, ne raccommoderont point ses finances, si réellement elles sont si dérangées, et elles n'empêcheront pas que les Anglais ne l'attaquent. Des embarras et des dangers réels veulent être prévenus avec promptitude et confiance. Obsta principiis[89] est une sage maxime. Ce n'est qu'en faisant promptement la guerre que la France pourra s'assurer pour l'avenir une paix permanente. Si l'on attaque actuellement la Grande Bretagne, tandis qu'une grande partie de ses forces est employée contre les États Unis, bientôt on la métrait hors d'état de troubler jamais les Puissances de l'Europe. Une simple déclaration de guerre de la France contre la Grande Bretagne dans la circonstance actuelle rendrait la perte de l'Amérique inévitable pour les Anglois aux yeux de tout l'univers, et les métrait par conséquent dans l'impossibilité de faire le moindre emprunt. La nécessité les forcerait donc à se soumettre sur le champ. La guerre serait donc non seulement très courte, mais très peur dispendieuse. Dans un moment où la Grande Bretagne est aussi occupée avec l'Amérique, la France n'aurait pas besoin d'autres efforts que ceux qu'elle est en état de faire actuellement par un usage vigoureux de ses forces de terre et de mer. Tout l'argent qui pourrait être nécessaire se trouverait aisément avant le commencement des hostilités, au lieu que si on laisse l'Angleterre faire d'abord sa paix avec l'Amérique pour ensuite attaquer la France, il faudra des sommes beaucoup plus considérables, et les emprunts deviendront impraticables.

La Grande Bretagne parait n'avoir aucun allié dont elle puisse espérer quelque secours considérable si on l'attaque actuellement. La Russie elle-même restera probablement dans l'inaction, d'autant plus qu'elle est trop éloignée pour faire aucun mal à la France et à l'Espagne, et d'ailleurs il est probable qu'elle aura assez d'affaires sur les bras chez elle. Une guerre avec l'Angleterre actuellement ne pourrait manquer d'être courte et heureuse, et il parait que c'est le seul moyen économique, sage et sûr pour prévenir l'effusion de sang et la perte immense d'argent qu'entrainerait une guerre longue et douteuse, lorsqu'une fois la Grande Bretagne aurait fait sa paix avec l'Amérique.

La querelle actuelle de l'Angleterre avec l'Amérique parait avoir été désignée par la providence pour l'élévation et la gloire de la France. Le ciel dans la disposition des affaires humaines a rarement offert à une nation une occasion aussi favorable de s'agrandir et d'humilier ses adversaires, et ce moment si beau ne se présentera pas une seconde fois. C'est à ceux qui vivent à cette époque que l'honneur en est offert, et s'ils ne savent pas s'en saisir, leur négligence ou leur aveuglement attireront sur leur mémoire les plaintes et les reproches de la postérité.

Si on objecte que la France n'a pas des justes motifs pour faire la guerre à l'Angleterre, les hommes, répondra-t-on, ont un tel fonds de raison qu'il ne leur en manque guère pour faire tout ce qui leur plait. Les nations sont toujours adroites à imaginer des prétextes spécieux pour les guerres, qu'elles veulent faire par des motifs d'intérêt ou par des raisons encore plus condamnables. Mais on ne s'y laisse plus tromper, et très peu de personnes prennent garde aux raisons qu'allèguent les Etats pour justifier leur conduite. On se donne encore moins la peine de chercher si elle est conforme aux strictes règles de la morale.

Si une guerre est entreprise d'après les principes d'une sage politique, et que ses opérations réussissent, elle est toujours applaudie comme juste et glorieuse. Les nations qui se sont alliés contre Louis XIV n'avaient jamais eu et ne prétendaient avoir aucun juste sujet de plainte contre lui. Elles publiaient seulement qu'elles redoutaient le trop grand accroissement de son pouvoir. Une pareille alarme justifierait une semblable Alliance pour séparer l'Amérique de la Grande Bretagne, et pour rendre libre un commerce dont elle voudrait avoir seule le monopole.

Mais après la manière inexcusable dont l'Angleterre a commencé la dernière guerre, manquera-t-elle jamais de bonnes raisons pour la renouveler? En s'emparant comme elle l'a fait contre tout droit et justice des vaisseaux et des matelots français, ce qui en grande partie a ruiné la marine de France, et en la mettant par la suite dans l'impossibilité de défendre ses possessions, elle a pour jamais investi la France non seulement du droit, mais de l'obligations de faire tous ses efforts pour les recouvrer aussitôt que l'occasion s'en présentera, et le moment est certainement arrivé.

Mais si l'on croyait qu'il ne fut pas convenable d'alléguer d'anciens griefs, il serait aisé de trouver des causes de rupture beaucoup plus récentes. L'arrogance des officiers de marine anglais et de leurs matelots s'est déjà manifesté en différents endroits par des actes de violence, qui au moyen des justes représailles de la part de la France seraient multipliés et aggravés par les Anglais au point d'autoriser de reste la France à la guerre.

Si malgré tout cela le Gouvernement de France aime mieux établir sa sureté sur les futurs contingents plutôt que de la rendre stable par une guerre courte et heureuse, ce qu'il aurait de mieux à faire dans cette circonstance ce serait d'engager quelques- unes des Puissances de l'Europe à reconnaitre l'indépendance des États Unis. Il y aurait peur être moyen de déterminer l'Empereur d'Allemagne, les Rois d'Espagne, des Deux Siciles, de suède et de Prusse, ainsi que le Grand- Duc de Toscane à faire cette démarche de concert avec la France. En supposant qu'il n'y eut qu'un certain nombre de ces États qui s'y prêtât, ils seraient encore en trop grand nombre pour que la Grande Bretagne peut leur déclarer la guerre à tous à la fois. Et si cette déclaration était faite de la même manière et en même temps par ces Puissances, leur offense serait tellement égale que la Grande Bretagne n'aurait point de prétexte pour s'en prendre à l'une plutôt qu'à l'autre. Une telle reconnaissance ranimerait le courage des États Unis, au point de leur faire rejeter toutes les propositions d'accommodement avec la Grande Bretagne. Toute l'Europe verrait par- là que cette Puissance a perdu pour toujours la totalité de son ancien commerce et de ses possessions en Amérique, et par conséquent qu'elle doit par la suite se trouver hors d'état de payer même l'intérêt de ses dettes publiques. Elle verrait son crédit ruiné, elle se trouverait dans l'impuissance, non seulement de commencer une guerre en Europe, mais de continuer celle qui subsiste en Amérique. Une telle déclaration n'exposerait donc à aucuns risques les Puissances qui y concourraient, mais au contraire elle contribuerait à leur sûreté; et comme elle ne couterait rien que des mots, les États -Unis ont certainement droit d'attendre un secours aussi léger de la part de ceux qui tireront de si grands avantages de leur séparation de la Grande Bretagne.

Mais si on prend un autre parti, et si on souffre que la Grande Bretagne soit le premier État qui reconnaisse l'indépendance des États Unis, il sera naturel qu'ils ne se croient que très faiblement obligés envers les autres Puissances, et qu'ils ne donnent de nouveau à la Grande Bretagne une plus grande part dans leur commerce et dans leur amitié qu'il ne sera de l'intérêt de la France et de l'Espagne, dont la prospérité et même la sureté pourront être compromises par cet arrangement.

Anexo
Pasquín[90] en el café de Lloyd fechado el 3 de julio de 1777.
[Copia manuscrita, 1 pág.]
Original en francés
Affiche au café de Lloyd daté 3 Juillet 1777.
N [91] (Ce café est celui ou tous les assureurs et capitaines des navires s'assemblent journellement)[92]

«Les négociants, propriétaires des navires et assureurs, remarquant que les français, contre la loi des Nations, permettent aux corsaires américains, non seulement d'amener les navires et cargaisons britanniques dans leurs ports d'Europe et d'Amérique, mais de les vendre quoiqu'il soit bien connu que nombre de ces corsaires appartienne taus français, et que l'équipage est composé de la même nation. Et comme la continuation de pareil précédé ne peut de moins que tendre à la ruine du Commerce et de l'intérêt de ce Royaume. Les propriétaires de pareils navires et cargaisons qui ont été pris, ou pourraient être pris et vendus, soit dans les ports de France ou d'Amérique, sont très particulièrement priés d'en donner les particularités au Lord Vicomte Weymouth, Secrétaire d'État pour le Département du sud, et aussi aux Seigneurs de l'Amirauté, a fin que le Gouvernement puisse être informé en détail et instruit de l'entendue et des conséquences alarmantes de ces déprédations.»

Document 30
Legajo 4611, Estado, AGS
El conde de Vergennes a Franklin y Deane, Versailles,
16 de julio de 1777
[Copia de carta, manuscrita, 5 págs.]
Original en francés

Copie de la lettre de monsieur le Comte de Vergennes à Messsieurs Franklin et Deane.

À Versailles le 16 Juillet 1777.

Vous ne devez pas avoir oublier, Messieurs, que dans le premier entretien que j'ai eu avec vous conjointement, je vous assurai que vous jouiriez en France pour vos personnes de toute la sûreté et de tous les agréments que nous y faisons éprouver aux étrangers, et pour votre navigations et cotre commerce de toutes les facilités qui seraient compatibles avec l'exacte observance de nos traités avec l'Angleterre qu'il était dans les principes du Roi de remplir religieusement. Pour prévenir toute équivoque sur l'espèce des bâtiments qui pourraient jouir des faveurs que nos accordons dans nos ports aux nations amies, je vous fîs lire l'article du traité qui nos interdis la faculté de permettre aux corsaires le libre accès dans nos ports si ce n'est pour des besoins pressants, ainsi que le départ et la vente de leurs prises. Vous avez promis, Messieurs, de vous y conformer.

À l a suite d'une explication aussi précise, nous ne pressâmes point la sortie du navire La Représaille qui avait conduit en France monsieur le Docteur Franklin, parce qu'on assurait qu'il était destiné à faire son retour en marchandise. Nous avions perdu ce bâtiment de vue et nous le croyons dans les parages de l'Amérique lorsque nous apprîmes avec surprise qu'il était entré à L'Orient après avoir fait diverses prises. L'ordre lui fut donnée immédiatement de partir dans les vingt- quatre heures et de faire passer ses prises aux seules Amirautés qui peuvent être autorisées pour en juger la validité.[93] Le capitaine Wiker excipa d'une voie d'eau. Visite faite par des experts, son allégation fut reconnue légitime et admise. On lui permit les réparations nécessaires et lui fut enjoint de reprendre la mer.

Après tant d'avertissements répétés et dont le motif vous avait été développé, nous ne devions pas nous attendre, Messieurs, que le dît Seigneur Wiker continuerait la course dan les mers d'Europe, et nous ne pouvons qu'être étrangement surpris que s'étant associé avec les corsaires le Lexington et le Dolphin pur infester les côtes d'Angleterre, ils soient venus ensuite tous trois prendre refuge dans nos ports.

Vous êtes trop éclairés, Messieurs, et trop pénétrés pur ne pas sentir combien ce procédé blesse la dignité du Roi mon maître en même temps qu'il offense la neutralité dont Sa Majesté fait profession. J'attends donc de votre équité que vous serez les premiers à condamner une conduite si opposée aux devoirs de l'hospitalité et de la bienséance. Le Roi ne peut la dissimuler, et c'est de son ordre exprès que je vous préviens, Messieurs, que les ordres ont été envoyées dans les ports où les dits corsaires ont pu aborder pour qu'ils y soient séquestrés et retenus jusqu'à ce qu'on puisse avoir des sûretés suffisantes qu'ils retourneront en droiture dans leur patrie sans s'exposer par de nouvelles hostilités à venir chercher asile dans nos ports.

Pour ce qui est des prises qu'ils peuvent avoir faites, s'ils en ont conduit dans nos ports, elles auront ordre d'en sortir immédiatement, et il en sera use de même envers tous capteurs ou capture de quelque nation qu'ils puissent être. Telles sont les obligations de nos traités conforme à nos ordonnances de Marine dont le Roi ne peut en aucune manière s'affranchir. Il ne pourra être que très à propos que vous faites connaitre cette disposition où vous le jugerez convenable, à fin que de nouveaux armateurs, attirés par l'exemple des abus que se sont permis ceux contre lesquels nous sommes obligés d'user de rigueur, ne s'exposent as aux mêmes embarras.

Ce que j'ai l'honneur de vous faire connaitre, Messieurs, des dispositions du Roi, ne change rien aux assurances que j'ai été autorisé à vous donner lors de votre arrivée, et que je le suis encore à vous renouveler pour la sûreté de votre résidence et de tous ceux de votre nation auxquels conviendra d'habiter parmi nous, ainsi que pour celle du commerce permis que l'on facilitera de notre part autant que nos lois et nos usages le permettent.

J'ai l'honneur d'être avec une parfaite considération.

🌸 Document 31
Legajo 3884, Estado, AHN
El conde de Aranda al conde de Floridablanca, París, 20 de julio de 1777, no. 1079 and no. 28
[Carta manuscrita, 20 págs.]
Original en español

                Excelentísimo señor

Muy señor mío:
  El martes 8 del corriente, día ordinario de audiencia de embajadores, parece que el de Inglaterra expuso al señor conde de Vergennes con la mayor actividad la queja del refugio que los corsarios americanos tenían en los puertos de Francia, siendo tan gravoso a la Inglaterra que aún la navegación de sus costas padecía en el tráfico regular de su mantenimiento, pues hasta las barcas de carbón se hallaban atacadas. Que en los puertos de Francia se vendían públicamente las presas, lo que era contra los Tratados mismos de ambas coronas para semejantes casos. Que esto, y muchas otras cosas, no correspondían a las explicaciones recíprocas de buena inteligencia que habían mediado desde que se hallaban en guerra con los insurgentes.
  Monsieur de Vergennes nada más me dijo entre semana, sino que el lord Stormond estaba muy agitado y que se explicaba con resentimiento aún en discursos familiares. Respondile que así llegaba también a mi noticia, y como no me dijo los que él sabía, tampoco yo quise contarle los que me referían.
  Estos eran, hablando con varios de sus más habituales conocimientos, que todo era una maniobra de esta Corte disimulada con el colorido de la libertad de comercio. Que bajo dicho título, en los puertos de Dunkerke, San Malo, Nantes, La Rochelle y Bordeaux, había un tráfico abierto con los americanos, hallándose cubiertos sus muelles de efectos de guerra que públicamente se embarcaban tanto en buques franceses que americanos, a título de ser géneros de venta permitida en este Reino. Que ya lo había representado con claridad, y no comprendía cómo se hallaba aún en París, pues de un día a otro se consideraba en el caso de partir.[94]

De tales expresiones del embajador de Inglaterra, unos deducían que iba ya sembrando motivos de queja para poner en uso el Ministerio británico las ideas formadas para en evacuando el objeto de las colonias bien o mal. Otros las graduaban de echadizas[95] para que la Corte de París se moderase, a lo menos en los esfuerzos que se le acusan de sostener a los rebeldes aunque bajo mano.

El martes 15 me habló de sí mismo el señor de Vergennes, leyéndome la respuesta que tenía preparada para el lord Stormond cuando entrase, y entonces me dijo la explicación activa que había hecho el martes anterior. Como yo la vi extendida a modo de oficio, a que sólo faltaba la firma, y me pareció que sería una prenda de mucha sujeción una vez soltada, le expuse mi observación, preguntándole si el lord Stormond [sic] le había presentado memoria, pues le contestaba por escrito. Me respondió que todo se había pasado de palabra, y aquel papel no era más que para leérselo, por estar en él atados los cabos sin riesgo de olvidar alguno ni de explicarlos en términos diferentes de lo que convenía. Que enviaría una copia a monsieur D'Ossun para que la comunicase a vuestra excelencia, y aprovecharía de mi correo extraordinario, de que justamente yo lo había prevenido por si tenía que valerse de él.

Como monsieur de Vergennes no hizo más que leerme rápidamente su apuntación, no se me quedaron las especies impresas con exactitud, sólo retengo que hay muchas ofertas de proveer al exceso de los corsarios y ventas de las presas, que al fin se producen también quejas de contrarresto sobre insultos que sufre el pabellón francés, las visitas de sus buques y detención de algunos con el pretexto de géneros que pasan a los insurgentes. El rebato del capitán americano en Cherbourg, sobre que la Francia se promete también satisfacción, y algunas frases pomposas de manifestar vigor, al propio tiempo que se reconoce la parte en que puedan tener justicia los recursos ingleses.

Hice ligeramente al señor conde de Vergennes la observación de que todo aquello sólo serviría para trampear el tiempo, porque los ánimos de los ingleses estaban ya tan acalorados sobre el refugio de los americanos en los puertos de Francia, que a cualquiera pequeña cosa que sucediese recibirían las antecedentes. Que los insurgentes estaban tan acostumbrados a los puertos de Francia, y los comerciantes de este Reino tan interesados con ellos por el inmenso lucro que les resultaba, que sería imposible el evitar ocasiones ni disimularlas tampoco. Que para cortar de raíz todos los lances que podían ocurrir por causa de los americanos, no habría otro medio que prohibirles el tráfico y reducirlos a las arribadas de proveerse de víveres o repararse.[96] Que si esto se hiciese, no sólo se privaría a los insurgentes de los medios de sostener su guerra, sino que produciría el declarárselos por enemigos con el tiempo, alegando ellos el haberlos abandonado a lo mejor, y después de haberlos dejado empeñar, confiados en que subsistirían el buen acogimiento y recursos de proveerse de lo necesario. Que en cualquier aspecto que mirase la posición actual de las cosas, ya estaban en una crisis que no podían parar en bien, y sería el dichoso el que previniese la acción del otro con un golpe de entidad. Que se acordase de mis instancias para cubrir sin pérdida de tiempo los puntos expuestos, preparándose a todo cuanto pudiese sobrevenir.

Me dijo monsieur de Vergennes que sin falta en este mes de septiembre partirían seis batallones veteranos en el pie de campaña, tres para Santo Domingo y los otros tres para la Martinica y Guadalupe, con 600 artilleros para distribuirlos en ellas, y 200 dragones para montarse en la primera. Que ya había en dichas islas otros seis batallones, y a más los cuerpos fijos, para los cuales se enviaban 4 mil reclutas a fin de ponerlos igualmente hasta el pie de guerra. De modo que en estando allá todo, se podía contar con once mil hombres.

Después de dicha conversación, corre por aquí la copia de un cartel o afiche que se dice puesto en Londres por orden del Ministerio británico en los lugares públicos, cuyo traslado incluyo a vuestra excelencia, quien verá que se dirige a tomar conocimiento de los agravios que suponen recibir de la Francia. Si fuese cierto, indica bastante. Y si supuesto por algún particular tomando el nombre del gobierno, se ve que tira a exaltar la nación y a imponer al mismo Ministerio, acusándolo de que sufre sin aplicar remedio, abriendo la puerta por este medio a que a un mismo tiempo concurra un sinfín de quejas que exciten con actividad al Gabinete y a la nación. Desde luego, de una u otra forma se ve venir que la Corte de Londres pedirá a la de París que subsane los perjuicios causados por el abrigo de los corsarios americanos, repetirá las ventas hechas en sus puertos, que son varias y considerables, y la Francia sin deshonor suyo no podrá prestarse a semejante solicitud. En el Tratado de Navegación y Comercio de Luis IV con la reina Ana el año de 1713, verá vuestra excelencia en qué apoyarán los ingleses su pretensión.

Yo estoy aturdido de haber observado que esta Corte conoce los riesgos a que está expuesta. Muchos de sus miembros han pensado con vigor, y en junto no corresponde la conducta, por haber predominado la esperanza y consideración de que los ingleses quedarían extenuados por lo mucho que padecen, y pensarían sólo en recuperarse.

Confieso que no soy parcial de esta opinión y embeleso, porque la Inglaterra, tan disgustada como está con la Francia, no se parará en caudales, a que toda la nación se prestará con igual gusto de contribuirlos contra su genial enemigo, que repugnancia ha tenido de invertirlos contra los que reputaba por sus hermanos y compatriotas. Añádase que el talento y coraje inglés no perderá la circunstancia real y verdadera de hallarse armado al fin de su guerra con las colonias, logre o no reducirlas. Y como ésta es la parte más esencial para los empeños, habremos de convenir en que si su carácter duro y enconado lo conoce así, pues es más claro que el día, y si se calienta de cascos[97] prometiéndose para lo venidero el conservar la prepotencia marítima sobre las demás naciones, no se detendrá en subsidios, cuando de ellos dependa el no inutilizar sus actuales fuerzas y probar el reparo de sus desgracias.

Otra de las razones que han entibiado también a esta Corte ha sido la consideración de que los ingleses e insurgentes se destruían entre sí mismos; que la Corona británica se debilitaba, y que para echársele encima sería mejor después de enervada.[98] No me apartaré de esta reflexión política, pero bien preguntaré si se sabe cuántos años durará el empeño para aguardar el último de ellos y coger la Inglaterra mientras aún esté enredada con su contrario, que es el grande negocio si hubiere de ocurrir un rompimiento, para llevarse de rasgo la abertura y desde el principio destruir radicalmente al enemigo, sin aguardar a quedarse mano a mano, en cuyo caso sería el bocado más duro.

La variedad de tonos con que oigo discurrir a estos ministros por semanas, por días y aún por horas, unas veces animados, otras templados, y otras confiados, no me permite formar juicio positivo de sus ideas. No obstante, he observado que desde nuestro armisticio con Portugal cuentan con que dicha potencia no tendrá parte con la Inglaterra en lo sucesivo, ni la España motivo de distraerse como antes, y por consecuencia quedará íntegra para lo que ocurriere. Que seguros de un tal enemigo menos, y comprendiendo que el año próximo quizá sería el último de hallarse empeñada la Inglaterra, ya se van explicando más conformes entre sí sobre que puede ser el momento conveniente para romper, empezado que hayan los ingleses la campaña ventura[99] contra los insurgentes, o aún antes de abrirla, mientras se hallen ocupados en sus preparativos y convoyes, cogiéndolos en el acto de sus envíos.

La razón principal que ha predominado en esta Corte desde el principio hasta ahora para excusar una guerra, ha sido el recelo de su duración y la falta de fondos para sostenerla si fuese larga. Concedo que sean razones prudentes y bien vistas, si el evitarla consistiese en su sola voluntad y sin riesgo de que la Inglaterra pensase diferentemente por ahora y para después. Pero aún con esta seguridad era preciso que la conducta de la Francia hubiese sido tan indiferente con los americanos que en ningún modo disgustase a los ingleses ni les diese pie para salir, en pudiendo con algún ajuste de cuentas y agravios que repetir. Era también necesario estar seguros de la estabilidad del presente Ministerio, a quien se hubiese hecho el agasajo de no embarazarlo más durante su empeño con los rebeldes, para salir de él con gloria. Y era indispensable ser una potencia que no tuviese en lo sucesivo motivos de altercación[100] con la británica por la constitución de ambas, dependiendo la buena armonía del espíritu tranquilo de ellas sin acasos ni intereses que se cruzasen para alterarla. Ni la conducta ha sido así, ni los objetos de ambas Coronas pueden dejar de producir mil disputas, sino en el caso que una de las dos quede tan inferior a la otra que no pueda suscitarlas por no poder sostenerlas. Conque la voluntad de poco sirve.

La duración insoportable por falta de fondos, que es una reflexión digna de tenerse en todos casos, si bien se examina en el día no tendría lugar, porque la ruina total de la Inglaterra pende de la primera campaña, si en ella se practica lo que está saltando a los ojos. De modo que el destroncarla se haría en la primera, y el acabarla de oprimir se lograría con sólo mantenerle el pie encima, para que en su extremo ahogo recibiese por misericordia la ley que se le quisiese dar.

Es de pura verdad que se le ha destacado a la Inglaterra el tercio de sus fuerzas antiguas con la separación de los insurgentes. Que contra ellos tiene empleado el otro tercio a lo menos, y que sólo le resta uno de que echar mano contra la poderosa Casa de Borbón, la cual, aún juntos sus tres tercios, tendría fuerzas para contrarrestarlos. Es innegable que se halla con un enemigo más en la actualidad, que sólo él la lleva a mal traer por tierra y por mar, y un compañero semejante jamás se lo podían aguardar la España y la Francia.

Si estas, con medianas fuerzas marítimas no más cayesen de golpe encima de las que tienen los ingleses esparcidas en la América

Septentrional, las barrerían como con una escoba, y las americanas entonces se vendrían a Europa a aumentar la confusión de la Inglaterra.

Si las fuerzas marítimas inglesas se barriesen de la América, quedarían las de tierra cortadas de todo apoyo, y de por sí se desharían como la sal en el agua. Las de mar no podrían volver a Europa en estado de reforzar considerablemente el armamento que por acá pudiese hacer la Corona británica. Desde luego, todos nuestros recelos de que los ingleses pudiesen caer sobre ninguno de nuestros puntos de América, quedaban desvanecidos, y España y Francia íntegras para todo lo que ocurriese.

Si se añadiese a esto la interrupción del comercio y los infinitos corsarios españoles, franceses y americanos que caerían sobre él ¿quién negará que con esto solo se inhabilitaría a la Inglaterra, que el rompimiento saldría a menos coste, y por consecuencia los fondos de su duración serían llevaderos para la Real Casa de Borbón? ¿Quién dejará de convenir de buena fe que con sólo el rompimiento caería el crédito inglés para empréstitos, y el fondo nacional se agotaría para suplemento de ellos?

Estas consideraciones solas pueden decidir de la posibilidad o imposibilidad de la Inglaterra, y de los riesgos o fortuna de la Casa de Borbón. Si ésta diese un golpe mortal a la Corona británica, queda dueña de la acción y su enemigo sin recurso de hombres, buques ni caudal. La nación inglesa atribulada, los partidos contrarios que la indisponen se comerían unos a otros, y por fuera y por dentro se hallaría en la mayor tribulación. Si se la deja en libertad sin aprovechar la ocasión, conservará la Inglaterra su crédito y hallará fondos con el más o menos beneficio que proponga. El orgullo nacional subsistirá, y mientras éste dura, se presta fácilmente a imposibles.

Con prevenir la acción se sale de cuidados para el pronto y para siempre jamás. Se abrevian los gastos y se puede conseguir no sólo el resarcimiento de ellos, sino la recuperación de alhajas que interesan a la España y a la Francia, la mejora de los tratados de comercio, el dominio de los mares, y una consideración respetable con todas las demás potencias para que las influencias Bourbonas[101] tengan aspecto de mandatos.

Con descuidar la ocasión, todo se pierde. Quedará un cuidado continuo, los gastos serán mayores y más duraderos, no habrá proporción de resarcirlos ni causa para reintegrarse de usurpaciones. El comercio, el uso de los mares, proseguirán con las trabas que sufren, y el concepto de Europa será consiguiente a la flojedad manifestada y a la incuria de sus Cortes.

La Francia con particularidad ha de pagar con el tiempo las resultas de dejar en pie su mayor enemigo. Ella, sobre año de diferencia, se ha de ver empeñada en tierra firme con todo su poder por las diferentes ocasiones en que indispensablemente se ha de comprometer. Entonces verá cómo, movido por otros y sin eso, por sí sólo el enemigo descuidado y ya restablecido, la cogerá con los brazos atados por sus demás contrarios. La España tendrá que salir a la demanda para cubrir las espaldas de su aliada, y a todo bien andar podrá hacerse tablas el fuego, quebrándose cada uno como estaba, hasta otra.

La España no puede dejar de prever este caso, porque va con el orden natural de las cosas. Y si lo ha de desviar, cuánto mejor fuera que aprovechase del día a medias con la Francia, acabándola de decidir para poner la Inglaterra en estado de que ni pudiese intentar interrumpir a la Francia, obligando entonces a la España a cubrir su aliado, ni tenerlas tampoco firme a la España sola, para que ésta no tenga que temerla ni depender de la voluntad de otro que, aunque fuese muy buena, podría estar embarazada al propio tiempo por diversos lados, y necesitándose toda para sí.

Si este enemigo común no queda incapaz de relevarse, la precaución en paz habrá de ser siempre como disposición para una guerra. Mal pueden florecer los reinos que vivan con estos ayes y con expensas continuadas, so pena de abandonarse a sus enemigos. Y ¿por qué? por haber malogrado la ocasión que no volverá en muchos siglos. Ya perdimos la de 1770, en que me han dicho repetidas veces, solos y juntos el señor príncipe de Masserano y el marqués Caraccioli, embajadores de España y Nápoles existentes entonces en la Corte de Londres, el mal estado en que se hallaba la Inglaterra en aquel momento, sin poder proveer de pronto a su urgencia. El mundo entero sabe que lo que gritaban para la satisfacción de las Malvinas era a fin de disimular su mal estado, y conociendo el modo de pensar de los ministerios de Madrid y Versailles, a quien impondrían con sus amenazas.

En el n° 1055 de la última expedición de 22 de junio, incluí a vuestra excelencia un papel del doctor Franklin sobre las cosas presentes. Ahora remito un 2° que ha hecho para disolver especies, que parece se le habían soltado bajo mano por este Ministerio para entretenerlo. Y éste no cree que yo lo tengo.

Dios guarde a vuestra excelencia muchos años. París, 20 de julio de 1777.
Excelentísimo señor
Beso la mano de vuestra excelencia
su seguro servidor
El conde de Aranda

Document 32
Legajo 3884, Estado, AHN
De los Comisionados de los Estados Unidos de América al conde de Vergennes y al conde de Aranda, Passy, Septiembre de 1777, no. 34[102]
[Memoria con un presupuesto, 9 páginas]
Original en inglés

Document 33
Legajo 3884, Estado, AHN
El conde de Aranda al conde de Floridablanca, París, 27 de septiembre de 1777, no. 1139 and no. 33
[Carta manuscrita con nota resumen, 3 págs.]
Original en español

El conde de Aranda (por extraordinario)[103]
Refiere su conversación con un agente de los diputados americanos sobre el modo de continuarse por nuestra parte las remesas a las colonias, pagando ellas en frutos de su país.

Excelentísimo señor

Muy señor mío:
Antes de ayer me vino a ver monsieur Grand, el banquero de esta Corte que corre con los diputados americanos, y a traerme el escrito adjunto que supuso ser el doble[104] del que pasaban al señor conde de Vergennes, para que yo lo dirigiese igualmente a Madrid. Con motivo de estar en inglés y no entenderlo yo, evité entrar en su lectura y contestación, y aunque monsieur Grand quería traducírmelo a voz, procuré que no lo hiciese asegurándole que el original lo [remitiría yo a Madrid en la][105] primera ocasión.

Diciéndome monsieur Grand que los términos de este papel eran precisados de que no se respondía por esta Corte a las proposiciones ventajosas que los diputados habían hecho el invierno pasado, ofreciendo varias cosas a la Francia en recompensa del partido que las Coronas de Bourbón[106] tomasen por ellas, y no pudiendo yo asegurarme de haberme hablado ninguno de estos ministros sobre el dicho particular, le insinué me alegraría ver su contenido, y habiéndome ofrecido y pasado una copia, la incluyo igualmente a vuestra excelencia.

Sobre ninguno de los dos escritos puedo discurrir porque carezco de la inteligencia de la lengua inglesa y para traducirlos, aunque habría infinitos en París y no sabría responder del secreto de los tales traductores.

Cuando vuestra excelencia se halle instruido por la versión segura que habrá mandado hacer, podrá decirme si de dicho papel de ofertas ha tenido conocimiento por mi correspondencia o por comunicación de ese embajador de Francia, o si se lo ha reservado este Ministerio.

>Dios guarde a vuestra excelencia muchos años. París, 27 de septiembre de 1777.
>Excelentísimo señor
>Beso la mano de vuestra excelencia
>su seguro servidor
>El conde de Aranda

Document 34
Legajo 3884, Estado, AHN
Una carta enviada por el conde de Aranda [al conde de Floridablanca], París, 27 de septiembre de 1777, y borrador de la respuesta,[107] sin fecha.
[Nota resumen, 1 pág.]
Original en español

El conde de Aranda (por extraordinario)
Refiere la visita que le han hecho los diputados americanos e incluye dos escritos que le han entregado, iguales a los que dieron a aquel Ministerio, sobre el estado actual de sus [negocios][108] y auxilios que necesitan.

[Borrador de respuesta de ¿Floridablanca? a la carta de Aranda resumida en la nota anterior]

[Carta manuscrista, 6 págs.]
Original en español

Excelentísimo señor
Refiere vuestra excelencia en su carta de 27 de septiembre señalada con el n° 1139, habérsele presentado monsieur Grand y entregádole un escrito igual al que habían puesto en manos de ese Ministerio los diputados americanos. Bien que, como estaba en inglés, se valió vuestra excelencia de esta circunstancia para excusarse a entrar en contestaciones o discursos sobre los puntos que en él se trataban.

Poco después de recibir la citada carta de vuestra excelencia, y cuando ya tenía yo traducido al castellano el mismo papel, me entregó el marqués de Ossun otra copia en francés con el extracto de lo que le escribían de su Corte con dicho motivo.

Como vuestra excelencia no pudo leerlo, empiezo por dirigirle su traducción para que desde luego se haga cargo de las solicitudes de los americanos, y de las razones con que procuran apoyarlas, las cuales se hallan explicadas con bastante arte y sagacidad.

El Ministerio de Versailles manifiesta mucha inclinación a adoptar las ideas de los diputados y a franquearles sumas crecidas de dinero, según aparece por el despacho escrito a este Embajador, y también incluyo a vuestra excelencia su copia a fin de que lo reconozca con mayor extensión.

Por parte de esa Corte no se nos han hecho más aberturas que las que a vuestra excelencia le constan, y se ve claro que lo han ejecutado en las ocasiones que lo ha[n] creído del caso, sin sujetarse a la prolijidad de instruirnos de cada incidente o conversación con los diputados, como tal vez habría convenido para nuestro gobierno.[109]

En mis despachos anteriores me he explayado bastante para persuadir el verdadero valor e importancia de los auxilios de todas clases que estamos dando de dos o tres años a esta parte a los colonos, y vuestra excelencia ha hecho de ello el uso correspondiente. Pero debe observarse que los diputados, y aún la Corte misma de Francia, no manifiestan en sus escritos estar convencidos de esta verdad, sin hacerse cargo que la mayor parte de los socorros que por nuestra mano se han dado a las provincias Americanas han llegado a convertirse en dádivas al comercio francés, como sucedió con los dos primeros millones de reales que regalamos por el conducto de ese Ministerio, los cuales se invirtieron en municiones y vestuario comprado en Francia, y se ha repetido con los socorros suministrados en letras a los mismos diputados.

Tampoco están muy hechos cargo del valor que se debe dar a nuestros armamentos, y por espíritu de moderación no nos toca detenernos mucho a compararlos con los que hasta ahora lleva hechos la Corte de Francia. Pero ha parecido conveniente llamar la atención de unos y de otros y hacerles comprender el modo de opinar del rey nuestro señor y de todo su Ministerio en las actuales circunstancias, así en el punto que va indicado de ayudar competentemente a las colonias, como en el de medir nuestros pasos y disposiciones de forma que no se precipite la guerra a pesar nuestro. Con esta mira se ha dispuesto el papel de que también acompaño copia, y se le ha entregado pocos días ha a este embajador en contestación del despacho que nos confió del señor conde de Vergennes.

Vuestra excelencia lo examinará cuidadosamente y con su acostumbrada exactitud arreglará a estas ideas sus discursos y persuasiones con los ministros de su majestad cristianísima.

Dios guarde etc.

Document 35
Legajo 3884, Estado, AHN
El conde de Aranda al conde de Floridablanca, París, 27 de septiembre de 1777, no. 1136 and no. 32
[Carta manuscrita, 3 págs.]
Original en español

Excelentísimo señor

Muy señor mío:
En el n° 4 de la expedición de 11 del corriente, contesta vuestra excelencia a mi oficio 1113 de 26 de agosto, en que participé la explicación de monsieur Grand de parte de los Diputados Americanos respecto a la demanda que les hacía el comerciante de Bilbao Gardoqui.

Arreglándome pues a lo que vuestra excelencia me comunica, he visto a monsieur Grand y díchole que los auxilios hasta aquí prestados, y de que Gardoqui exigía providencia de satisfacción,[110] quedaban generosamente acordados sin responsabilidad, como también varios otros que por diferentes vías se habían facilitado.

Le he hecho varias consideraciones sobre los excesivos gastos en que notoriamente había estado y aún estaba la España. Lo mucho que indirectamente contribuía en ventaja de los americanos con sus armamentos y preparativos, por cuya razón lo mejor sería formalizar un ajuste para continuar remesas conforme al que habían pacado[111] con los *fermiers*[112] generales.

Hecho cargo de todo monsieur Grand, hemos quedado en que los diputados responderán a Gardoqui diciéndole que respecto a tener esperanza de que los amigos[113] que lo comisionaron para el cargamento se prestarán a su satisfacción, quedando sólo el arreglar para lo sucesivo que el mismo Gardoqui se encargue de iguales envíos teniendo a bien el anticipar su coste. Que para el reembolso de las cantidades que supliere, será bueno ponerse de acuerdo en cuanto a los géneros que le conviniese recibir para su comercio, y sean producciones de las colonias, arreglando sus precios para proveer sus direcciones y entregas en pago de las anticipaciones.

He dicho a monsieur Grand que en consecuencia de esto se entiendan los diputados con Gardoqui como con un negociante su corresponsal. Que a él instruyan de los efectos que hubiere de remitir, que con él fijen sus precios, y que con él traten los géneros de pago y su valor, tiempos de su apronto y todo lo demás que en este asunto les pudiere ocurrir.

Éste me parece que es el espíritu de la carta de vuestra excelencia, reducido a que, como negociantes, haya terceros que intervengan en facilitar a las colonias los géneros que puedan conducirles en sus necesidades, y que se satisfagan las remesas que se hicieren.

Espero que monsieur Grand habrá comprendido sin equivocación cuanto le he dicho, y en vista de lo que traslado a vuestra excelencia, creo que sería bueno prevenir a Gardoqui para que siga su correspondencia arreglado a los expresados conceptos.

> Dios guarde a vuestra excelencia muchos años. París, 27 de septiembre de 1777.
> Excelentísimo señor
> Beso la mano de vuestra excelencia
> su seguro servidor
> El conde de Aranda

Document 36
Legajo 6998-9, Estado, AGS
Francisco Escarano al conde de Floridablanca, Londres,
3 de octubre de 1777
[Nota de presentación manuscrita, 1 pág.; carta manuscrita, 10 págs.]
Original en español

[1-Nota de presentación]
Inglaterra 1777
Carta reservada de Don Francisco Escarano
En Londres a 3 de octubre de 1777
Venida por navío español a Bilbao y recibida en 7 de noviembre cuyo aviso se le dio con voces simuladas.
Trata de su conversación con el Lord Mansfield relativa a los Americanos al estado actual de la Inglaterra y al modo de pensar del rey nuestro señor.

[2-Carta]

Excelentísimo señor

Señor:
   Doce días después de haber partido de esta Corte el señor príncipe de Masserano me entregó el cónsul Don Miguel de Ventades un pliego cerrado que había puesto en sus manos el Capitán de uno de nuestros navíos bilbaínos. Habiéndole abierto hallé en él una carta particular de vuestra excelencia escrita el 7 de julio de este año a aquel embajador, en que le prevenía la conducta que debía tener aquí con los ministros, o personas de su confianza relativamente a las circunstancias en que se halla esta Corte, y nos hallamos nosotros por lo respectivo a los negocios de América.
   La Instrucción de vuestra excelencia es tan precisa, tan clara, que nada me ha dejado que desear sino las luces del referido embajador, y sus conexiones, o amistad con los próceres de este país para desempeñarla bien. A falta de uno, y otro procure desde luego valerme de uno de los pocos medios que están en mi poder, y fue el del lord

Mansfield. Sabe vuestra excelencia que este magistrado, tan responsable por su edad, como por sus elevados talentos goza de muchos años a esta parte de toda la confianza de este monarca; que su majestad británica y sus ministros de Estado le consultan los asuntos políticos más difíciles; que su voto es preponderante en el Gabinete; y que raro, o ningún negocio se termina sin tomar antes su dictamen. Pareciome, pues, que si tenía la dicha de hacerle adoptar mis ideas habría logrado tuviesen efecto las de vuestra excelencia y así no tardé en pasar a su casa de campo pocas millas distante de la capital. No hallándole en ella vino antes de ayer mañana a mi habitación, y en un discurso de más de una hora se trató de lo que voy a referir a vuestra excelencia.

Empecé diciéndole que había estado a buscarle solo, para darle noticias de la felicidad con que iba haciendo su viaje el señor Príncipe de Masserano, constándome cuán gratas le serían. Manifestóseme muy agradecido; pidiome le avisase siempre que recibiese cartas de su íntimo amigo, e hizo los mayores elogios de su modo de proceder mientras había residido en Inglaterra.

Pasando después a darle la enhorabuena por los progresos del ejército que manda el general Bourgoyne, y contestándome que no se dudaba aquí fuesen en breve seguidos de otros aún más favorable por haber ya disensiones entre los rebeldes, que no podrían dejar de producir al fin su total ruina, le expuse parecerme no convenía se lisonjease demasiado, pues no era fácil el subyugar países tan vastos, y ganar los corazones de más de tres millones de habitantes guiados por el entusiasmo de la libertad, y resentidos vivamente contra las injurias que pretenden haber recibido; añadiéndole que según mi débil modo de pensar aumentarían, o disminuirían los esfuerzos de las colonias contra la metrópoli a proporción de las mayores, o menores esperanzas de un rompimiento de esta con aquellas potencias, de quienes esperan, tal vez en vano, asistencia y protección.

Díjome entonces que si todos los príncipes pensasen bien no se expondrían a una guerra por sostener a unos súbditos ingratos; a lo que le respondí ser casi de su opinión, persuadido de que las ventajas de la paz por pocas que sean eran siempre preferibles a todas las que pueden resultar de una guerra; pero que lo era también de que la suya no concluiría tan pronto, aunque los colonos rebeldes no tuviesen el menor auxilio de las provincias extranjeras, sino perdían toda la esperanza de ser empeñada la Inglaterra en un rompimiento con alguna de ellas. Deduciendo de su silencio que le hacía fuerza mi reflexión proseguí diciéndole: Milord: tal vez me engaño, pero estoy en la inteligencia de que si se encontrase modo de persuadir a aquellas Potencias con que se lisonjean los americanos que romperá esta Corte, que les aconsejasen a ceder a las proposiciones que de aquí se les hiciesen, sería un expediente tan eficaz que los veríamos muy presto rendirse a su deber. Díjome al oir esto que tenía mucha razón y que pensaba excelentemente, pero que en Francia estaban dando oídos a cuantos americanos se presentaban, y que últimamente habían llegado a París desde Berlín monsieur Lee, y monsieur Sayre, sujetos despreciables; añadiéndome con una especie de complacencia que el primero de ellos había perdido todos sus papeles en la última de estas dos Cortes. Por qué no se podría tantear la de Madrid, le pregunté entonces; a lo que me respondió estas formales palabras. El rey de España tiene un carácter: Sé que podemos fiarnos en él: Si, milord, le dije inmediatamente, y el mejor carácter del mundo: Su buena fe es bien notoria en todas partes. Dada una palabra sacrificaría todos sus intereses por cumplirla.

    Trájele pues a la memoria una conversación que había tenido con él tres años ha hallándome encargado de los negocios del rey, en la que habiéndome dicho que su majestad no olvidando nunca el atrevimiento que había tenido en Nápoles el capitán Martin no deseaba sino hacer la guerra a la Inglaterra en satisfacción de aquella injuria, le había demostrado evidentemente lo contrario, y que el rey anhelaba con ansia la continuación de la paz; que verdadero padre de sus vasallos no pensaba sino en los medios de hacerlos felices, aumentando la población, adelantando la agricultura, animando el comercio externo, y facilitando el interno con nuevos caminos, y canales en su Reino; obras que interesaban su noble corazón, y que cuando no cesasen del todo sufrirían siempre algún detrimento, si se viese su majestad en la precisión de invertir en una guerra parte de los muchos caudales que absorben. Asegurome tener muy presente mi conversación de entonces, y confesome que desde que le había sacado del error en que estaba vivía plenamente persuadido de que el rey era amante de la tranquilidad. Vínome en aquel instante muy al caso la sabia reflexión que he encontrado en la citada carta de vuestra excelencia de ser la España una heredad de que la Inglaterra saca el fruto, y apropiándomela le dije que teniendo este país un interés real en que floreciese el nuestro por el lucroso comercio que en él hacía debía contribuir a que se prolongase la tranquilidad que disfrutamos; lo que en mi entender dependía del rey británico. Mostrome creerlo firmemente sirviéndose de esta expresión.

A la Inglaterra traería cuenta de que por cada hombre que hay en España hubiese mil.

Después de una breve pausa me preguntó si sabía cómo pensaba vuestra excelencia en punto a los americanos, añadiéndome que ahora se decía por muy seguro que el doctor Franklin iba a Madrid, y que si se verificaba creería que un hombre tan astuto no emprendería semejante viaje sin la certidumbre de ser muy bien recibido.

Respondile que vuestra excelencia no anhelaba menos la continuación de la paz que el rey nuestro amo; que no dudaba le fuesen muy gratas qualesquiera proposiciones que tuviesen por objeto el prolongarla; que me constaba se proponía contribuir con todas sus fuerzas a que sus conciudadanos experimentasen los grandes beneficios que pueden resultar de ella; que casi podía asegurarle encontraría este Ministerio muy pronto a vuestra excelencia a trabajar a fin de que los colonos se rindiesen a la debida obediencia; y que por lo que miraba al doctor Franklin tal vez no se querría negarle la entrada en España sólo por ser un sabio, cuyas obras hacen tanto honor a la república literaria, y cuya reputación está tan establecida en ese Reino. Díjele además de esto que supuesto fuese cierto su viaje a Madrid podría la Inglaterra sacar partido de él, interesándose con nuestra Corte, para que por su medio llegase a conocer el Congreso general de Filadelfia cuán lejos estaba el rey de romper con esta nación, y cuánto celebraría la reconciliación entre las colonias, y la metrópoli; a lo que no me contestó sino con decirme que sentiría infinito se verificase la ida del expresado Franklin a Madrid, porque causaría una gran fermentación en este País, en donde no hay quien no tenga los ojos abiertos sobre nuestra conducta con los americanos.

Siguiose a esto el darle a entender que no se ocultaba al rey la actual situación de esta monarquía, el aumento de la deuda nacional, la interrupción de su navegación, y la sensible decadencia de sus manufacturas; a lo que me respondió que nadie conocía mejor que él los daños de la presente guerra; y mudando luego de asunto me confió le escribían de París, que estaba ya arreglado nuestro tratado con el Portugal; en virtud del cual cedíamos la Isla de Santa Cathalina, y conservábamos para siempre la colonia del Sacramento. Dile las mayores gracias por su confianza haciéndole al mismo tiempo la reflexión de que esto mismo debía servir a la Inglaterra de prueba de preferir el rey una mediana paz a todas las ventajas que puede sacar de una guerra, pues en el momento en que sus armas no encuentran obstáculo para llevar adelante sus triunfos renuncia a las prodigiosas utilidades que pueden procurarle por evitar la efusión de sangre del género humano, y hacer gustar a sus vasallos las de la tranquilidad; en lo que convino.

Al despedirse le dije que no hablaría de ninguno de los secretarios de Estado de las ideas que le había confiado por no tener orden de hacerles proposición alguna; y que sólo si alguna vez se me proporcionase ver al lord North le comunicaría mi pensamiento, acordándome que dos años ha me dijo en Palacio, que siguiendo las máximas del sabio ministro Walpole, quien opinaba siempre en el Consejo ser muy conveniente para este Reino alejar la guerra con la España, procuraría conservar la paz con nosotros cuanto pudiese. Puso fin a la conversación alabando el modo de pensar del lord North, y asegurándome partir persuadido de que el medio que yo le había propuesto seria eficacísimo para perpetuar la paz entre las dos monarquías, y quitar cualquier idea de desconfianza.

No dudo que el lord Mansfield habrá dado cuenta a este soberano de cuanto pasó entre nosotros, pero no me es fácil averiguar cuáles serán las resultas. Es verosímil que si fuesen como deseamos me busque para seguir el asunto. A mí no me queda qué hacer por ahora sino aguardar algunos días, e ir después a hacerle una visita de amistad a su casa de campo para ver cómo se explica.

Procuraré también hallar algún pretexto para abocarme con el lord North, a quien es muy difícil hablar despacio por los muchos, y graves negocios, que tiene a su cuidado. Es hombre de muy buena intención, bastante franco, y nadie tiene mayor interés personal en la conservación de la paz, ni en la sujeción de los insurgentes, pues sus embarazos de encontrar dinero para continuar la guerra crecen en razón de los pocos progresos que el ejército inglés hace en América. Con él era con quien trataba durante la escabrosa negociación de las Malvinas el ministro plenipotenciario de Francia monsieur Francés, y en sus talentos, y buen corazón hallaba aquellos recursos que no podía encontrar en el genio áspero, y poca abertura del Lord Weymouth.

Conociendo que no debo mostrar grande interés en hacer adoptar a estos ministros mis proposiciones y sobre todo que debo procurar las consideren puramente como efecto de mis buenas intenciones de que se continúe la actual armonía entre la España, y la Inglaterra iré con sumo tiento, y prudencia en esta negociación, pero no fundando su éxito sino en las superiores luces de vuestra excelencia le suplico se digne continuármelas con lo que aseguraré el acierto. Por explicar con claridad lo que ha pasado en la referida conversación he sido tan difuso en esta carta, que lleva a Bilbao el capitán del paquebote español San Sebastián, que no tardará en hacerse a la vela. Espero que vuestra excelencia lo disimulará atendiendo a mi buen deseo, y que vivirá persuadido de que me esmeraré en acreditar así en esta, como en cualquiera otra ocasión mi celo por el servicio de su majestad. Dios guarde a vuestra excelencia muchos años como deseo. Londres a 3 de octubre de 1777.

    Excelentísimo señor
    Beso las manos de vuestra excelencia su más humilde y rendido súbdito
    Francisco Escarano

🕮 Document 37
Legajo 2596, Santo Domingo, AGI
Roberto Morris and Guillermo Smith[114] a Bernardo de Gálvez, York en Pennsylvania, 24 October 1777, no. 169
[Carta manuscrita, 4 págs.]
Original en español

Señor:
    En 12 de junio último tuvimos el honor de dirigir a su Excelencia por el capitán Jaime Le Mere, igual a lo que se contiene en la copia anexa a ésta, a la que suplicamos sea su Excelencia referido, desde la que hemos sido felices en recibir su carta de 22 de junio último, pero es desgracia nuestra que en este paraje a el cual hemos sido precisados a retirarnos, no hay persona alguna bastantemente impuesto en la lengua española que puedan producir un trasunto corregido de ella, aunque hemos cogido de ella, y de la carta de Sr Polock, la parte de los efectos que se nos han avisado debían mandarse de España para nuestro servicio eran llegados al Nuevo Orleans y que mensualmente irían otros.
    Apercibimos que su Excelencia tiene el encargo de ellos, y que los entregará a nuestra orden, y por lo tanto nos tomamos la libertad de incluir a su Excelencia una certificación firmada por el presidente del Congreso, por la cual percibirá los negocios que se nos ha comisionado para que los administremos, y como quiera que no es nuestro pensamiento injuriarle su atención, con el motivo de evitarle en cuanto es posible el menor trabajo, hemos empleado al señor Olivero Polock, que reside en Nuevo Orleans, para nuestro agente, y le instruimos que flete o compre embarcaciones aparentes para el transporte de estos efectos costa a costa, hasta tanto que puedan llegar a algún puerto o estero nuestro donde ponerlos en tierra. Y se le previene consulte con su Excelencia sobre este asunto, y le suplicamos de su favorable atención la protección en él, dirigiéndolo en todo lo que convenga y protegiendo las embarcaciones y cargamentos etc., que Mr Polock tenga motivo de solicitar.
    Nos hallamos compelidos a extender más nuestras súplicas, pidiéndole que asimismo se sirva suplir a éste dinero en el caso de que

lo necesite para subvenir a los costos y gastos que puedan ocurrir en el transbordo de los géneros. Éste otorgará recibos de lo que se le entregare para estas erogaciones, y nosotros deberemos repagarlas en todo su valor por mano de nuestro agente en la Corte de España.

Nosotros no sabemos si tal vez se hallará impuesto de ella para hacer semejantes suplementos, pero de cualquier modo, estamos muy bien asegurados que de todo lo que ejecute en ellos tendrá su aprobación de allí. Bien pudiéramos no estar sujetos a esta ni otra necesidad, si nuestros puertos estuvieran abiertos para poder hacer remesas de harinas como antes, pero en la actualidad son tantos los navíos de guerra ingleses y tan fuertes en nuestra costa, que efectivamente han bloqueado todos los puertos donde se puede hacer el embarco de harinas. Sin embargo, hemos formado un plan (y lo estamos ejecutando) el que es muy probable hayan nuestros enemigos otro objeto en que emplear muchos de sus navíos. Y cuando esto se verifique, abrazaremos muy gustosos la proporción de remitir suplementos de harinas al Nuevo Orleans, impuestos antes que en él hay necesidad de estas.

La campaña se abrió así en esta como a el norte después de la que últimamente escribimos, y siguen con el mayor vigor. Muchas batallas se han ganado y perdido de ambas partes, pero al presente el general Howe y los realistas se hallan en posesión de la ciudad de Filadelphia, lo que ha ocasionado estar nosotros aquí, pero no han sido capaces de llevar sus navíos arriba a esta ciudad, pues tenemos en posesión las fortalezas y pasas del río.

El general Washington tiene cercada la ciudad, y presto los obligará por hambre a que la desamparen, y entonces los atacará, y tenemos las mayores razones para suponernos que saldrá muy victorioso. Al norte hemos tenido la fortuna más favorable, pues todas las batallas entre Bougoyne y nuestro general Gates han terminado en favor nuestro, y acabamos de recibir noticias que se oye de una total rendición de Bourgoyne con todo su ejército, prisioneros de guerra por capitulación, por lo que no tenemos ya enemigos que nos incomoden en aquellas partes. general Gates puede prontamente reforzar al general Washington, y como dejamos relacionado, hay muy poco que dudar que la campaña cerrará a nuestro favor, y que a la fin deberemos establecer aquella libertad que tan justamente nos corresponde disfrutar.

    Somos de su excelencia
    muy obedientes servidores
    Roberto Norris = Guillermo Smith
    PD = La noticia de la rendición de Bourgoyne está confirmada y tenemos en mano sus capitulaciones.
    Es copia traducida de su original
    Bernardo de Gálvez.

Document 38
Legajo 4612, Estado, AGS
El conde de Aranda al conde de Floridablanca, París, 26 de noviembre de 1777, no. 1178
Nota de remisión de documentos de [la Secretaría de Estado de España] al conde de Aranda. San Lorenzo el Real (El Escorial), 23 de octubre de 1777.
[Manuscrita, 1 pág.]
San Lorenzo el Real, 23 de octubre de 1777
(Por extraordinario)[115]

Con N° 11[116]

Remitiendo varios papeles que acreditan presas hechas por los americanos en perjuicio de los españoles; que el rey se ha disgustado mucho y suspende la remesa del dinero que iba a regalar; que hable él sobre esto seriamente.

Con N° 12

Que se le despacha este correo creyéndole de vuelta en Paris

[Carta manuscrita, 12 págs.]
Original en español

Excelentísimo señor

Muy señor mío:
En la expedición[117] de vuestra excelencia de 23 de octubre, que recibió Don Ignacio Heredia en mi ausencia, los números 2 y 11 tratan de asuntos de los Americanos; en aquel se manifiestan las intenciones del rey de ayudarlos competentemente; y en éste se explica su majestad justamente disgustado del exceso cometido por un corsario insurgente apresando la embarcación francesa *La Fortunée*, cargada con géneros para el comercio de Cádiz, por la sola razón de serlo ingleses y venir de aquellos puertos.

Mandábame su majestad hacer a esta Corte la explicación correspondiente, y la evacuó inmediatamente Don Ignacio Heredia, con copia que entregó del oficio de vuestra excelencia a monsieur

Devergennes. Igualmente quería el rey que yo hiciese entender a los diputados no sólo la restitución de la presa con total resarcimiento de los perjuicios causados, sino también unas eficaces providencias[118] para que en lo sucesivo se evitasen iguales atentados.

Para evacuar[119] esta parte, luego que me restituí llamé a monsieur Grand, el interlocutor reconocido como vuestra excelencia sabe. Le comuniqué cuanto debía, y desde luego él mismo me manifestó el sentimiento con que se hallaban Franklin, Deane y Lee, habiendo sabido por el señor conde de Vergennes el suceso y el sumo desagrado del rey católico. Quedó en trasladar a dichos diputados mi explicación y sus requisitos, y volvió en el siguiente día a manifestarme de parte de ellos la más sumisa disposición a cuanto pudiese satisfacer a su majestad, y contribuir a evitar que se repitiesen semejantes desórdenes.

Asegurome monsieur Grand que por primera ocasión escribirían al Congreso para la restitución de la presa y resarcimiento de sus daños, como también para que con el mayor rigor impusiese a los corsarios la continencia debida. Y aún para remediar de pronto en lo posible, comunicarían a sus corresponsales en los diferentes puertos de Europa una orden para hacerla saber a todos los bastimentos[120] americanos que arribasen, a fin de instruirlos y encargarles que a cuantos encontrasen de su nación en sus navegaciones, les previniesen la conducta que debían observar para no incurrir en acciones de esta naturaleza.

En uno de los días pasados me trajo monsieur Grand el borrador de una Memoria que pensaban pasarme los diputados para dirigirla a mi Corte, como en satisfacción de lo ocurrido, manifestando su sentimiento y ofreciendo practicar cuanto les fuese dable en prueba de su respeto por los soberanos de Borbón. Preguntele si la había visto Devergennes, y respondiéndome que no, le dije que practicase con su Excelencia el mismo paso de exponérsela, y que aquello que monsieur Devergennes aprobase o corrigiese, sería igualmente mi dictamen.

El 21 estuve en Versailles y pregunté a monsieur Devergennes si el banquero Grand había cumplido con mi encargo de hacerle ver la memoria dispuesta por los diputados, diciéndole al propio tiempo que yo me remitía a lo que su excelencia arreglase. Y me aseguró que sí, y haberle prevenido que suprimiesen la proposición que hacían de que entrasen en los puertos de ambas Coronas abiertamente sus corsarios con las presas, y que los almirantazgos juzgasen desde luego las que fuesen hechas en debida forma y las que practicadas fuera de las reglas corrientes, porque el admitir francamente los armadores con las presas hechas, era autorizar su corso. Y para que los almirantazgos de por sí tomasen conocimiento de las que se introdujesen, no necesitaban del permiso o consentimiento de los Insurgentes.

Volviome a ver monsieur Grand, y habiendo quedado en que yo recibiría la memoria que por monsieur Devergennes se hallase corriente, me ha traído la que acompaño a vuestra excelencia.

Ha estado a verme monsieur Lee, para hacerme saber que había recibido letras credenciales del Congreso que lo autorizaban directamente para España, y me indicó si pasaría personalmente a noticiarlo. Respondile que en ninguna forma, por subsistir las propias razones que anteriormente, y por ser suficiente que mi Corte lo supiese para algún caso necesario.

En las diferentes conversaciones que he tenido con monsieur Devergennes, se me ha explicado sobre que el rey no cortase sus auxilios como indica el n° 11, porque la Francia había acordado ya tres millones de libras en un año, y cuatro plazos a 750 mil cada tres meses. Y habiéndome dicho que lo había escrito ya a ese embajador de Francia, por él sabrá vuestra excelencia más precisamente los términos en que este Ministerio se explica.

Con este motivo hemos hablado del contenido del n° 2, y he subsanado la equivocación que en él he observado, y también en la memoria respuesta que en 17 de octubre pasó vuestra excelencia a ese embajador, de haber contribuido por nuestra parte con dos millones de reales, pues fueron cuatro, habiendo quedado persuadido el señor conde Devergennes de ser un descuido de pluma, pues su excelencia los percibió.

El 21, arrastrado de la conversación, me quiso confiar monsieur Devergennes que estaba ya sobre su partida el emisario que esta Corte envía a las colonias, haciéndolo pasar en un paquebote sin carga sospechosa como dirigido a la Isla de Miquelon, para que desde su ruta se deje caer al punto de la costa que pudiese arribar sin embarazo.

Monstrome las dos instrucciones que había de llevar, la una sobre su conducta con aquellos Estados Generales, la otra sobre el particular del comercio que convendría entablar para utilidad de la Francia, y me leyó la primera, pero no la segunda.

Dice en aquella que sólo se ha de dar a conocer a los principales del Congreso, encargándoles el mayor disimulo para con el público. Que ha de procurar persuadirles que en forma alguna lleguen a sugetarse a los ingleses, porque estos después los pondrían en una esclavitud. Que si por el medio de una pacificación consiguiesen que los ingleses reconozcan su independencia, nunca debe ser acordándoles privativa ni preferencias en el comercio, ni conviniendo en alianza alguna ofensiva ni defensiva con ellos, porque si así fuere, perderían las colonias el objeto interesante de traficar con las Coronas de Borbón, por cuyo medio indirecto quedarían reducidas y precisadas al solo comercio inglés, de modo que aunque reconocidas libres en el nombre, no lo quedarían en la sustancia. Que el grande interés de las colonias al tiempo de pacificarse con los ingleses será el de pedir la garantía de las Coronas de Borbón, porque quedando la Británica en posesión de la Florida, Nueva Escocia y Canadá, cogiendo por su dos costados aquel nuevo Estado, se verían cuando menos pensasen que resucitaban los derechos de la Inglaterra, y en ocasión que mano a mano volviesen a otro rompimiento, tomando mejor sus medidas la Inglaterra para conseguir su fin.

Esta es la sustancia de la instrucción general para el manejo del emisario, y observé al ojo que la otra de comercio era bien larga. Yo, por sacar algún rastro, introduje la discusión del género de comercio que podríamos hacer con ellos, y que el de España era más difícil de arreglar por estar sus posesiones contiguas a las colonias, cuando las Islas de Francia estaban en cierta distancia, que sólo servirían de escala o depósitos.

Díjome monsieur Devergennes que las colonias, según sus ideas y genio, se constituirían en Estado cultivador, sin dedicarse a la industria de fábricas y artes, más que las precisas para sus diarias necesidades. Que bajo este pie podría la España utilizar de ellas las producciones de la tierra de aquel vasto terreno y la provisión del bacalao, porque no tenía el goce de esta pesca como la Francia. Que en años de carestía de granos en España tendríamos aquel recurso para nuestra Península y para las provincias de América que lo necesitasen. Y como me percibí que huía el cuerpo a entrar en los artículos respectivos de la Francia, y aún en los de España hablaba por evadirse de los otros, desistí de embarazarlo.

En mi concepto privado me conformo con algunas de las proposiciones de monsieur Devergennes que dejo referidas.

En la instrucción de conducta y especies que ha de soltar el emisario, supone que la Corona británica pueda quedar en posesión de la Florida, Nueva Escocia y Canadá. Pues yo lo dificulto, si la Inglaterra no se apresurase en convenir con la independencia total y reconocimiento de Estados libres con el fin de retener dichos establecimientos, porque si los Americanos llegan a destruir las fuerzas inglesas de tierra, no dejarán de ocuparlos sin pérdida de tiempo, agregándolos a su confederación. Y deben practicarlo así por quedar para siempre libres de disturbios.

Tampoco convengo en que las colonias independientes se reduzcan a Estado cultivador, pues se han de poblar tanto de europeos, que se han de trasladar allá las artes introducidas desde su principio por buenos obreros de Europa.

No menos opino en el artículo de la pesca, que se lisonjea conservar la Francia en aquellos mares de Tierra Nueva[121] si los ingleses fuesen echados del Canadá, y sólo convendré en el caso de que subsistiesen, porque no estando ligadas las colonias de antemano por un tratado durante sus aprietos, y llegando a verse fuera de ellos, expelidos sus enemigos del continente y a la vista de un objeto tan interesante en las mares de su propia casa, puede ser que no se les haga tan apreciable el artículo de garantía creyendo no necesitarla más, y que prepondere el atractivo de un interés total en un ramo que la Europa, tarde o temprano, puede recibir de sus solas manos.

Tengo expresado en varios oficios de mi correspondencia que la Francia no piensa en otra cosa que en el incremento y extensión de su comercio, porque se cree tan poseedora y abundante de muchos artículos de industria, que han de superar siempre y vencer la balanza, no obstante los efectos que reciba por carecer de ellos, como tabacos, maderas, linos, cáñamos, añiles etc. Y a mi dictamen se confía en que con tratado y sin él ha de quedar corresponsal natural de las colonias, y necesario por el pronto para acostumbrarlas y radicarlas en su recíproco comercio.

Dios guarde a vuestra excelencia muchos años. París, 26 de noviembre de 1777.
Excelentísimo señor
Beso la mano de vuestra excelencia
su seguro servidor
El conde de Aranda

[Anexo A][122]
Legajo 4612-156, Estado, AGS[123]
Memoria de Franklin, Deane y Lee, al conde de Floridablanca, París, 23

de noviembre de 1777
[Manuscrita, 3 págs.]
Original en inglés

Anexo C
Legajo 4612-158I
Borrador de carta, sin fecha, firma ni destinatario. Se deduce que de Floridablanca al conde de Aranda, embajador en París, 9 de diciembre de 1777[124]
[Manuscrita, 5 págs.]
Original en español

Excelentísimo señor:
   Ha destinado vuestra excelencia la carta n° 1178 de 26 de noviembre a los puntos relativos a las colonias anglo-americanas, y voy a contestarla después de haber enterado al rey de las diversas especies que contiene, y tomado sus reales órdenes sobre cada punto.
   Ha parecido muy bien a su majestad cuanto vuestra excelencia ha tratado con monsieur Grand, interlocutor de los diputados americanos, sobre la restitución de la embarcación francesa La Fortunée, cargada para el comercio de Cádiz y apresada por un corsario insurgente por la sola razón de venir de puerto inglés con géneros ingleses.
   Mediante las ofertas hechas a vuestra excelencia por esos diputados, de escribir inmediatamente al Congreso para la restitución de la presa y resarcimiento de todos perjuicios, las medidas que iban a tomar para evitar se incurriese en adelante en otros atentados de igual naturaleza, el sentimiento con que se hallaban, su sumisa disposición a cuanto pudiese satisfacer a su majestad, y la confirmación de estas expresiones en la memoria que entregaron a vuestra excelencia y me remite, queda su majestad enteramente satisfecho, y aprueba admitiese vuestra excelencia la memoria puesto de acuerdo anticipadamente para ello con el señor conde de Vergennes.
   Ahora manifestará vuestra excelencia a los diputados para su consuelo, que su deferencia y disposiciones ha merecido el agrado de su majestad, así como el insulto del corsario le causó gran desagrado; que precisa recomienden al Congreso mucha firmeza en hacer ejecutar las órdenes que tienen sus armadores[125] de respetar el pabellón español y no inquietar en ninguna manera su comercio, pues no podrá tolerar su

majestad lo contrario, y que en el caso presente, prescindiendo de la
pronta restitución y resarcimiento completo de daños, de que no
desistirá su majestad, experimentarán como hasta ahora la continuación
de los efectos de la real liberalidad y compasión con que los mira su
magnánimo corazón, y de que verán pruebas efectivas y no escasas.

    Esto mismo en todas sus partes expresará vuestra excelencia para
su noticia al señor conde de Vergennes

    [El párrafo siguiente va escrito al margen izquierdo]:

    Para gobierno sólo de vuestra excelencia, le diré que la intención
del rey en cualesquier socorro que haga a los americanos es no ligarse
con promesas ni contratos, por muchas consideraciones que interesan
tanto su honor cuanto en política, combinando todas las circunstancias
actuales de Europa con nuestros intereses y la situación de nuestros
negocios. [Fin de la nota al margen]

    Queda enterado su majestad de haber recibido monsieur Lee cartas
credenciales del Congreso que le autorizan directamente para España, y
aprueba la respuesta que dio vuestra excelencia a su insinuación de si
vendría personalmente a noticiarlo, pues si hubiese venido, no sólo no
hubiera permitido su majestad se le escuchase ni admitiese a tratar
negocio alguno, sino que le hubiera hecho salir, no siendo en ninguna
manera necesaria la residencia aquí de ningún Diputado americano para
que su majestad continúe a los americanos su protección.

    Manifiesta vuestra excelencia su celosa exactitud en la relación
que hay de la instrucción que lleva el emisario que envía esa Corte a
las colonias, conforme se la leyó el señor conde de Vergennes en la
parte relativa a su conducta con aquellos Estados Generales, aunque no
le confió nada de la perteneciente al particular comercio que convendría
entablar para utilidad de la Francia. Su majestad estima las reflexiones
con que vuestra excelencia aclara esta noticia, y me manda
corresponderle con la de haberse enviado ya de aquí otro emisario,
cuyas instrucciones generales de conducta van bastante conformes con
las que lleva el emisario francés.

Document 39
Legajo 4612, Estado, AGS
Extracto de carta de Vergennes a Montmorin, Versailles, 2 de enero de 1778, no. 199
[Manuscrita, 2 págs.]
Original en francés
Extrait d'une lettre de monsieur le Comte de Vergennes à monsieur le Comte de Montmorin, écrite de Versailles le 2 Janvier 1778.

Je n'ai pas encore pu prendre, monsieur, les ordres du Roi sur la réponse de l'Espagne, ainsi je ne suis pas en état de vous faire connaitre la détermination de Sa Majesté, mais en attendant que je vous transmette le résultat de nos méditations, je crois devoir vous informer que la Cour de Londres redouble d'activité et d'instances au près des députés américains. Il vient d'arriver de sa part un chef Morave nommé Huston, homme de génie, ami intime de monsieur Franklin, et fort estimé du Roi d'Angleterre. Ce nouvel émissaire avant de partir de Londres, a eu un entretien secret de plus d'une heure avec Sa Majesté Britannique. Depuis son arrivée il a eu avec son ami une première conférence qui a duré plus de deux heures, et il doit en avoir une seconde demain. Le seul Docteur Franklin y a assisté, ses collègues n'y sont pas appelés. Ce n'est point par les Américaines que je suis instruit de ces faits, ils me sont parvenus par une voie indirecte sur la fidélité de la quelle je puis compter. Je vous prie, monsieur, de communiquer tous ces faits à monsieur le Comte de Florideblanche. Je m'abstiens de les accompagner d'aucune réflexion. Ce Ministre est trop éclairé pour ne point faire de lui-même toutes celles qu'ils présentent, et pour n'en point sentir tout le poids.

Document 40
Legajo 3884, Estado, AHN
(El conde de Floridablanca) al conde de Aranda, El Pardo (Madrid), 13
de enero de 1778, no. 69[126]
[Borrador de carta-instrucción manuscrita, con nota resumen al inicio,
22 págs.]
Original en español

Al conde de Aranda (por extraordinario) Con N° 1
ostensible[127]

Entrando en muchas reflexiones para deducir no hallarnos aún en tiempo de entrar en guerra y exponiendo varios casos y dudas, no sólo para aquel lance sino para las resultas o consecuencias.

Aquí están las 16 preguntas que el rey llamaba el Catecismo, y al fin de la 10 se pregunta expresamente sobre Gibraltar, Menorca, etc.

Búsquese la fría respuesta que nos dieron, y es la que falta.

Excelentísimo señor:

En mi carta de 23 de diciembre del año próximo pasado, dirigida a vuestra excelencia por el extraordinario que despachó este embajador de Francia, expuse difusamente a vuestra excelencia los modos de pensar del rey para que, sin abandonar ni disgustar a los colonos americanos, pudiésemos tomarnos algún tiempo en el cual viésemos el partido que iba adoptando la Inglaterra, tuviésemos más claridad sobre sus designios, y nos decidiésemos sin tropelía.

Por las noticias posteriores y por las que nos comunica vuestra excelencia en su última carta de 28 del mismo mes de diciembre, vemos que el Ministerio y el Parlamento inglés se ha tomado también tiempo para sus ideas, y que entretanto sus manejos y tentativas para ajustarse con las colonias giran sobre el presupuesto de salvar la soberanía de la metrópoli y el acto de navegación, endulzando estas pretensiones con palabras suaves y aún ambiguas.

En la misma carta de vuestra excelencia se refieren exactamente las maniobras de los dos partidos de Corte y oposición averiguadas por el doctor Bencroff, para ejecutar un ajuste con los americanos por medio de tres miembros de la misma oposición, con cuya especie coinciden los avisos directos que nos han llegado de Londres, de que asegurado el presente Ministerio de su permanencia por su majestad británica, trata sagazmente de comprometer a dichos miembros en un plano de ajuste, que no teniendo efecto desengañe a la Nación y la empeñe en otra campaña que aquel monarca desea hacer para tentar fortuna.

Sin embargo, pues, de todo esto, como su majestad quiere aprovechar el tiempo que opinó debemos tomar para estar prevenidos a todo lo que pueda suceder, y se acerca ya el del examen que se piensa hacer en Londres el día 2 de febrero del partido que convenga tomar a aquella Corte, ha juzgado su majestad indispensable que yo tenga por medio de vuestra excelencia algunas explicaciones con ese Ministerio sobre los varios casos que pueden sobrevenir si llegan a estrecharse las cosas en Inglaterra, a fin de que en todos procedamos de común acuerdo, formándose antes un plan y concertando los medios de llevarlo a debido efecto con las seguridades y preparativos que corresponde para prometerse un éxito feliz.

Como estos casos pueden ser muchos y lo son también los cabos que debemos atar, más o menos urgentes o posibles, es la voluntad de su majestad que yo los explique con natural franqueza sin recatar nada de nuestras ideas, objetos o recelos, pues así corresponde a la estrecha amistad y unión de las dos Cortes y a la mutua confianza[128] deben ambas descubrirse todos sus designios, situación y posibilidades, creyendo que nada se pierde con haberlo previsto y comunicado todo, aunque no todo se pueda hacer o remediar.

    1°. suponiendo que subsista el actual Ministerio inglés y que medite hacer otra campaña contra los colonos americanos, nos toca examinar y concertar si es conveniente distraerlo de tal proyecto con negociaciones y pasos anticipados, o por el contrario es mejor y más prudente dejarle que se empeñe, y reducir nuestras ideas a sostener a los mismos colonos con auxilios secretos, ofreciéndoles únicamente no desampararlos con tal que no nos den fundados motivos de recelar que traten de ajustarse sin nuestra noticia y de unirse con nuestros enemigos para obrar contra nosotros.

    2°. En mi citada carta de 23 de diciembre se tocó el caso en que viésemos mudarse el Ministerio británico y entrar en él personas enemigas de nuestras Cortes y de quienes, por su carácter, por las experiencias pasadas o por las medidas que se las vea tomar, deba recelarse un rompimiento. Y para tal lance conviene también concertar después de habernos explicado con decoro en la Corte de Londres, si deberemos empezar y seguir con viveza nuestras negociaciones para algún ajuste con las colonias.

3º. Para venir a este acomodamiento en el caso que acaba de citarse, serían necesarias las noticias e instrucciones que han pedido los diputados residentes en París a sus principales del Congreso, para no exponernos a tratar con sujetos que no tengan competentes luces, crédito ni facultades, según el estado actual de las mismas colonias. Y deseamos saber si esto puede dar tiempo a esperar, o si han enviado ya al Congreso proposiciones formales dichos diputados de París, como se ha divulgado.

4º. Debe considerarse si además de lo referido será también conforme a buena política esperar, cuanto permita la urgencia que hubiere, los avisos de nuestros emisarios que se hallan entre los colonos, a fin de tener por nosotros mismos un conocimiento moralmente seguro del estado de aquellos negocios y de lo que podremos contar con la fidelidad y fuerzas de aquellas provincias,[129] según las negociaciones que hayan entablado con su metrópoli los partidos y propensiones que allá prevalezcan, y las ventajas o intereses que esperen de unos y de otros.

5º. Como durante esta negociación puede romperse la guerra, o porque penetren o sospechen los ingleses nuestros manejos, o por otro motivo, es justo y necesario concertar las precauciones y el plan que haremos para defendernos y ofender a nuestros enemigos en cualquier acaecimiento anticipado, con medidas específicas que se habrán de tomar desde ahora. Sobre que esperamos ser iluminados, puesto que se debe recelar aquel caso, y que debemos en cuanto podamos evitar sus malas consecuencias.

6º. Debiendo comprender nuestra defensa el seguro retorno de la flota y de las fuerzas de tierra y de mar que vienen de Buenos Aires, se juzga preciso tomar alguna resolución para impedir que nuestros enemigos den un golpe fatal, concertando si hemos de hacer salir escuadras de mayor fuerza que las inglesas para cubrir dichos dos objetos, qué número de bajeles, y en qué tiempo y lugar se suministrará cada Corte, combinando y arreglando sus operaciones. O si será preferible otra idea que distraiga y ocupe a nuestros enemigos, de modo que les imposibilite atender a un mismo tiempo a defenderse y ofendernos.

7º. Hay otros objetos principales que deben desde luego ponerse a cubierto de toda invasión, como son las islas de Santo Domingo, la Martinica, Puerto Rico, Plaza de La Habana y costa de la provincia de Caracas, sin citar ahora otros muchos puntos en que pueden pensar los ingleses. Y así conviene acordar y saber desde luego cómo y con qué fuerzas marítimas y terrestres acudiremos a cubrir aquellos puestos de América o Europa, concertando las prevenciones que debamos hacer sin perder tiempo ni abandonar los demás objetos indicados en el artículo antecedente. Con la mira siempre puesta en el caso posible de que la Inglaterra quiera valerse de sus tropas y buques de guerra existentes en las colonias americanas para una invasión contra nosotros que empiece a tener efecto antes que hayan llegado por acá las noticias, cuyo fundado recelo obliga a tomar muy de antemano resoluciones activas y vigorosas para precaverlo.

8º. Por si tuviésemos tiempo para ajustar un Tratado con los colonos, y que no abusándose de su secreto pueda en aquel señalarse la época de su declaración o publicación, se hace necesario arreglar desde ahora cuando haya ésta de verificarse, haciendo al propósito un cálculo prudente del tiempo que se empleará en tomar y efectuar todas las medidas y precauciones conducentes a asegurar los retornos de Flota y expedición de Buenos Aires, juntamente con la defensa[130]

[Aquí el manuscrito vuelve a la letra original]

de las islas y puestos importantes de ambas naciones española y francesa. En el punto de Flota y fuerzas de nuestra América meridional, dudamos que hasta el mes de julio podamos contar con ellas en nuestros **puertos**.[131]

Consiguientemente, será preciso concertar y formar un plano sobre la sustancia y el modo de lo que se deba tratar con los colonos, en qué términos ha de ser su alianza, si puramente defensiva o también ofensiva; si será mejor y más decente llamarla protección y que las Coronas protectrices estipulen no abandonarlos mientras no sean reconocidos como Estado independiente; qué auxilios han de dar y recibir; si determinados o indeterminados, y qué ventajas ha de sacar la España o qué compensación de los daños y gastos que ha de sufrir, una vez que no puede servirla de nada el comercio con los colonos por nuestra situación, relaciones y tratados.[132]

10°. Para cuando llegue la época de la publicación o declaración, es igualmente preciso tener pensado lo que hemos de hacer y qué plan de guerra seguiremos que sea útil a las dos naciones, y que conserve o aumente si es posible la gloria de sus armas. La Francia podrá indicar los objetos que tiene para combinarlos con los nuestros y formar gradualmente la escala de las operaciones. La interrupción o extinción del comercio inglés puede ser un objeto de la mayor importancia para esa Nación, y este fruto lo sacará con sólo el acto de romper y hacer durar la guerra. Pero para nosotros es de ninguna utilidad tal interrupción, no pudiendo jamás disputar o competir en las ventajas del comercio con la Inglaterra ni con la misma Francia. Puede también esa potencia pensar en la conquista de las islas inglesas o en la mayor firmeza y libertad de su pesca de Terranova. La España por sí no tiene otro objeto que recobrar las usurpaciones vergonzosas de Gibraltar y Menorca, y arrojar del Seno Mexicano, bahía de Honduras y costa de Campeche unos vecinos que le incomodan infinito. Es menester, pues, concertar por dónde empezaremos y si convendrá que lo hagamos más bien separados que juntos, apoyando recíprocamente con la empresa y diversión de un aliado los designios del otro. En cuyo particular debe igualmente determinarse el número de fuerzas que cada uno ha de emplear y el tiempo o momento de obrar.

11°. Como todo aquel plano no se puede ejecutar en sus diferentes partes sin contar con los auxilios que estarán en estado de darnos los colonos, aunque sólo sea de diversión de fuerzas, conviene pensar si se les han de confiar o no con individualidad nuestras ideas, qué cosas se han de exigir de ellos específicamente para que ayuden a efectuarlas, y qué riesgos nos puede traer esta franqueza y comunicación de nuestros secretos a unas gentes que tienen tantas relaciones de nacionalidad, parentela y aún interés con la Gran Bretaña.

12°. Conviene asimismo a las dos Cortes saber, sobre una regulación prudente, el número de campañas que podrá hacer cada una y concertarse ambas, tanto sobre este punto como en lo que toca a hacer los respectivos esfuerzos para cumplirlo. Pues de otra manera no sería fácil lograr los designios que nos propusiésemos para la guerra que sobrevenga.

13°. Consiguientemente a lo referido, será justo decirnos si en el caso de que se verifique un rompimiento entre rusos y turcos, y que los primeros por sí solos o ayudados de otras potencias emprendan la conquista de la mayor parte del dominio otomano, especialmente en Europa, piensa la Francia hallarse en estado de acudir a todo y de no abandonar los empeños de la guerra que hayamos empezado con la Inglaterra, para que con esta previsión podamos evitar contingencias, pues podría la España verse entonces con alguna pérdida en sus posesiones y verse obligada a una paz perjudicial y vergonzosa. Lo que esperamos no querrá permitir una potencia tan amiga y aliada como la Francia, con quien contamos y contaremos siempre.

14°. Lo mismo decimos para el caso que la sucesión eventual de la Baviera u otros incidentes del continente, de Alemania y Flandes, obliguen a esa Corona a tomar parte en tales querellas, según lo que en alguna manera nos insinuó el Ministerio francés por abril del año próximo pasado, pues convendrá asegurar para tal lance el modo de conducirnos ambos aliados y no arriesgarnos a una paz intempestiva y perjudicial con ingleses.

15°. supuesto que la Corte de Londres no omitirá medio alguno de buscar distracciones a la Francia por la parte del continente, se desea saber si convendría anticipar algunos pasos en otras Cortes o tantear a los holandeses, que ya se muestran descontentos de la Inglaterra. A lo menos para hallar recursos y evitar daños contingentes aumentando a dicha Corte el número de enemigos.

16°. Últimamente, para este mismo fin desearíamos saber si convendría estimular a otros príncipes a hacer actos de reconocimiento de la independencia de las colonias, aunque sólo fuese por demostraciones y hechos de que se indujese. Y si estando el Gabinete británico disgustado con el rey de Prusia por haber impedido el tránsito de reclutas por el Rin, sería útil algún paso con aquel monarca, o si será dicho paso incompatible con otras relaciones y consideraciones que tenga que guardar la Corte de Versalles.

Adelantaríamos nuestro parecer sobre cada uno de los puntos que van insinuados si la desconfianza que tenemos de nuestras propias luces no nos detuviese; y así recurrimos a las de su majestad cristianísima y su ilustrado Ministerio para que nos comunique las suyas y podamos con ellas concertarnos para proceder de común acuerdo en una materia que es la más importante que puede ocurrir a las dos monarquías, por resultar de ella las mayores, más útiles o más fatales consecuencias.

Attachment: Legajo 4612-198, Estado, AGS
Le Comte De Montmorin a Comte de Vergennes, 13 janvier 1778
[2 págs.]
Original en francés

Monsieur
    J' ai l'honneur d'envoyer à votre excellence un extrait de la réponse j' ai reçue a l'expédition que j' ai envoyé à Versailles le 24 du mois dermier. Vous verrez, monsieur le Comte, que les circonstances deviennent chaque jour plus préssantes[133] et qu'il y a peu d'apparence qu'elles nous laissent le choix sur ce qu'il y a à faire. Il faudra vraisemblablement, ou prendre un parti ou renoncer à profiter du plus beau moment qui ait jamais été présenté à la maison de Bourbon.
    Quoique je sois à peu près toujours dans le même état, j'espère pouvoir aller jeudi matin vous renouveller, monsieur le Comte, les assurances de l'attchement et de la haute considération avec la quelle j'ai l'honneur d' être de Votre Excellence.

    Le très humble et très obéissant serviteur
    Le Comte[134] De Montmorin

Je joins ici una lettre de monsieur le Duc de Penthièvre pour Son Excellence monsieur le Comte de Floridablanca.

Sa Majesté Catolique[135] a le parquet que Vôtre Excellence a bien voulu me permettre de lui envoyer pour le faire partir par son courrier.

Document 41
Legajo 4616-87-I, Estado, AGS
El conde de Aranda al conde de Floridablanca, París
19 de marzo de 1778
[Carta manuscrita, 11 págs.]
Original en español

Excelentísimo señor

Muy señor mío:

Voy a continuar a vuestra excelencia las diferentes especies, que han mediado desde el número 1251 de 10 del corriente hasta la primera ocasión de extraordinario.

El jueves 12 me enseñó monsieur Devergennes el borrador de la carta que el rey cristianísimo había escrito con su correo del 10 al rey católico su tío, para apoyar la precisión en que se había hallado de la declaración a la Inglaterra sin tiempo para consultar a su majestad el paso que era indispensable practicar.

Me dijo monsieur Devergennes que en la misma hora habían partido tres correos, uno para Madrid, otro para Londres llevando la declaración, y otro para Viena con dos objetos, el uno comunicarle el referido paso con la Inglaterra, el otro darle cuenta de las solicitudes del rey de Prusia con esta Corte: especialmente la última de resulta de haber recibido el Barón Goltz el jueves 5 un correo de su Corte en virtud del cual pasó a Versailles el viernes 6 y dijo a monsieur Devergennes que su majestad prusiana considerando, que su alianza podía ser más segura, y útil a la Francia, que la de la Casa de Austria, deseaba formarla con esta Corona, tanto más propia para ella, cuanto no podía dejar de conocer la ambición de la Corte de Viena, y no querría la Francia apoyarla, antes bien cortarla en tiempo. Que el señor conde Devergennes le respondió, que como no se aguardaba semejante proposición, no estaba prevenido para responderle, y sólo podía decirle que habiéndose hecho la alianza entre París y Viena por las razones de prudencia, y beneficio recíproco que se consideró entonces, ahora a más fuerte razón era subsistente por la amistad, y estrecho enlace que se había seguido entre ambas familias, por cuya razón creía que sería intempestivo e inútil el hablar de semejante proposición.

Que el barón Goltz viendo que para su primer punto no hallaba disposición, pasó al de proponer que en el próximo altercado sobre la herencia del elector de Baviera, se declarase la Francia neutra; pues que la Corte de Viena no estaba en el caso de fundar que atacasen sus bienes hereditarios, porque si había guerra, el rey de Prusia nada quería para sí, sino salir a proteger un Príncipe considerable de la Alemania como el Palatino, a quien la violencia de Viena había impuesto, y amenazádole con riesgo de mayores daños, valiéndose de la superioridad de sus fuerzas. Que el señor Devergennes respondió, que aún no se veía claro sobre las pretensiones de Viena, que según fuesen podía asegurarle, que el rey cristianísimo profesaba una buena amistad a la Emperatriz Reina, y siempre estaría por la observancia de su alianza, a menos que no fuese una cosa muy extraña y voluntaria.
   Que el barón Goltz le manifestó como admiración de que la Francia contase tan poco con el rey de Prusia, y que no apreciase actualmente el estar con él, a más de las razones que habría contra la Casa de Austria, por la consideración de que la Francia iba a entrar en una guerra con la Inglaterra, la cual había buscado con muchas instancias al rey de Prusia, y este se había rehusado; pero que viéndose despreciado tomaría otro partido: que la Francia podía reflexionar, que una diversión de su majestad Prusiana sería embarazosa a la Francia: que también estaba en su mano la Corte de Petersburgo, la cual enredándose con el turco distraería a la Francia, quien se hallaría embarazada queriendo socorrer a este: que la czarina [*sic*] podía también dar auxilios a la Inglaterra, de que sólo el rey de Prusia podía distraerla, y lo mismo la Dinamarca. Que monsieur Devergennes le respondió, que su majestad prusiana era un Príncipe muy ilustrado para tomar parte en la disensión de la Francia, y de la Inglaterra; que esta se hallaba sin fondos con qué costear a su majestad prusiana los gastos que hiciese por auxiliarla, y que endeudarse su majestad prusiana por hacer un gusto, haciendo atravesar sus tropas por el Imperio para venir al territorio de la Francia donde no tenía ningún derecho de pretensión, no era creíble, poniendo de balde toda la pena que se diese para ello: Que no comprendía los auxilios que la czarina [*sic*] podría dar al rey británico, pues su ejército de tierra se necesitaba todo entero para contrarrestar al Turco.
   Que el barón de Goltz replicó, que la Rusia daría auxilios marítimos a la Inglaterra, y le respondió monsieur Devergennes que en cuanto a buques no le faltaban a esta, y no iría a valerse de los malos

rusos, teniéndolos buenos, y propios: que Goltz le replicó, sería en marineros, y monsieur Devergennes le rebatió que ni eran buenos los Rusos para la actividad de los Ingleses, ni los tenía la czarina [sic] bastantes para prestarlos, despoblando su país sobre lo que tendría en su mismo Imperio quienes clamasen contra ello: que en cuanto a Dinamarca venía tarde su reflexión, porque la Inglaterra ya había sacado de ella cuantos marineros era posible. Que le aumentó el señor Devergennes, que si su majestad prusiana buscaba la Francia como mediadora, para que en las disputas presentes de Alemania se prestase cada interesado a desistir en lo posible por el bien de la paz, en este caso la Francia haría todo su esfuerzo por contribuir al acomodamiento general.

Díjome monsieur Devergennes que tomando por pretexto esta declaración del rey de Prusia, la buena amistad de comunicarla a la Corte de Viena, y los embarazos en que la Francia se iba a hallar, si la Inglaterra llevase a mal la declaración que le hacía; añadía también, que el empeño de la Corte de Viena parecía por adquisiciones dudosas, que los principales príncipes del Imperio hacían ver en sus escritos dándolas por voluntarias, y forzadas; por lo que la Francia no se consideraba en el caso de prestarse a los auxilios estipulados, ni podría practicarlo como si se hallase desembarazada, cuando se necesitaba toda para defenderse.

Díjome monsieur Devergennes que por el primer correo ordinario iba a comunicar a la Holanda la declaración hecha a la Inglaterra porque allí se alegrarían mucho; pues a más de que en los términos que estaba concebida ponía la Francia a cubierto de ser agresora, y por consecuencia libertaba la Holanda de sus auxilios estipulados con la Inglaterra, deseaba la Holanda que empezasen otros a reconocer independientes las colonias, para facilitar el hacerlo ella también.

Díjome monsieur Devergennes, que apenas viniese la respuesta de Londres se presentaría Franklin a la audiencia del rey, que no sería en martes por la concurrencia del embajador de Inglaterra con los demás, ni tampoco iría las siguientes mientras Stormond [sic] estuviese; tomando otros días para hablar a los ministros sobre lo que se le ofreciese.

Fuí a ver a monsieur de Maurepas, lo hallé con el señor de Sartine, y mounsier Gerard: saliose este, hablamos del efecto que haría en Londres la declaración sobre Franklin me indicó lo mismo que monsieur Devergennes.

Díjome que Deane había recibido orden del Congreso para retirarse, creyendo serían chismes de desavenencia entre los diputados.

Que venía en su lugar uno de los Adams famosos partidarios de la independencia. Que apenas supo milord Stormond [sic] el retiro de Deane, creyéndolo disgustado, había empezado a trabajar por medio de terceros para ganarlo a fin que a su arribo fuese parcial a la Inglaterra para con el Congreso: pero que sobre que Deane estaba fino, se le regalaba el retrato del rey guarnecido, en prueba de la satisfacción de esta Corte durante su residencia, y que llevaría un oficio de monsieur Devergennes recomendándolo al Congreso.

Preguntome Mounsier de Maurepas si Don Francisco Escarano me había escrito, que el Lord Nugent uno de los que ahora hablaban más en el Parlamento, le había dicho que lo verdadero sería el hacer unión la España con la Inglaterra, pues esta sería amistad verdadera, y la de la Francia siempre costosa a la España por más parientes que fuesen. Respondile que nada me decía Escarano y repitió, pues así es, porque este se lo ha dicho a Noailles, quien nos lo escribe.

Hablando del nuevo aspecto que tomaban las cosas, y para captar el ánimo de monsieur de Maurepas, como también desenvolver sus ideas, dije yo, que si giraban bien según la apariencia, sería esta la época del mayor poder de la Francia; pues sobre haberse abierto un vasto comercio con las colonias, que antes tenía privado; con la separación de ellas quedaba muy bajo su enemigo natural, y con solo velar, que no se rehiciese, viviría la Francia sosegada, y con una influencia como nunca para con las demás potencias; que el señor conde de Maurepas podía concluir sus días glorioso en dejar la Francia como nunca había estado: Quedó muy lisonjeado de mi cumplido, y continuando el discurso me dijo, que se pondrían en las costas hasta 60 batallones, y formarían dos campos de invasión: Replicándole yo que a 30 por campo era poco, pues apenas harían 17 mil infantes cada uno, y así serían pequeños ejércitos para obrar solos por si donde desembarcasen: me replicó que la Inglaterra estaba desguarnecida; que para apariencia bastaban, y para el golpe que tenía premeditado, diez mil lo harían completamente. Preguntele, cuál era, me dijo que el echarse sobre la Isla de Wight que cubre el puerto de Portsmouth, con cuya toma este quedaría inutilizado, y se podría destruir aquel establecimiento: que era de tanta consecuencia para los Ingleses el rescatarlo, que al día siguiente estaba hecha la paz.

Esto es lo único interesante que se ha pasado en el intermedio de mi último correo del 7 de este mes hasta el de hoy, que despacho por el motivo que comprende el antecedente número.

Dios guarde a vuestra excelencia muchos años. París 19 de marzo de 1778.
Excelentísimo señor
Beso la mano de vuestra excelencia
su seguro servidor
El conde de Aranda

Document 42
Legajo 7000-71, Estado, AGS
Francisco Escarano al conde de Floridablanca, Londres,
14 de abril de 1778
[Carta manuscrita, 5 págs.]
Original en español

Excelentísimo señor

Señor:
Por si acaso paran en poder de nuestro vicecónsul de Calais las cartas de vuestra excelencia correspondientes al 30 próximo pasado me determino a despachar esta noche un criado a aquel puerto para que me las traiga, y por este medio seguro informaré a vuestra excelencia de lo poco que he podido saber y que me parece más digno de su atención.

Ha determinado el Ministerio hacer partir cuanto antes una escuadra de cinco navíos de guerra para las Indias Orientales, y dicen que la mandará el almirante Byron. En consecuencia de esta resolución ha dispuesto el almirantazgo que se empleen en componer el Burfort, que es uno de los cinco, doscientos carpinteros, a quienes se pagará doble jornal; y sin embargo no se cree pueda estar pronto en el término de tres semanas, como se quisiera.

El almirante Keppel ha ido a Chatam [sic] para acelerar el armamento del navío la Victory, y habiendo vuelto antes de ayer a Londres hizo partir inmediatamente todo su equipaje para Portsmouth, de lo que se infiere no tarde en ponerse a la vela.

En Spithead hay actualmente 31 bajeles de línea, comprendidas dos fragatas. Como diez de ellos tienen provisiones para ocho meses, y su tripulación completa se hallan aptos a ir a cualquier parte de América al primer aviso. El bastimento el Protheus ha marchado con municiones para Terranova.

Los duques de Devonshire, y de Dorset, como también estos señores de la primera Nobleza, entre los cuales hay algunos del partido de oposición, han solicitado que este soberano les dé el mando de los regimientos de milicias de sus respectivas provincias, y habiéndoselo concedido han besado ya la mano a su majestad británica.

Al mismo tiempo que se observan todos estos preparativos para obrar ofensiva, y defensivamente no hay la menor duda que los actuales ministros quisieran evitar una guerra con la Francia, si pudiesen salvar el decoro de la Nación, ya sea por puro patriotismo, o ya por su interés particular, porque ciertamente si se empieza una nueva guerra no conservarán sus empleos, siendo muy regular quiera dar su majestad británica el manejo de los negocios a personas en quienes tenga la nación alguna confianza. El Lord Chatam [sic] apenas se ha restablecido un poco ha vuelto a su casa de campo, diciendo a sus amigos que si el rey su amo piensa que a pesar de sus continuos achaques puede servir de algo en las presentes angustias de la Inglaterra sacrificará muy gustoso en beneficio de la Patria la poca salud que le queda.

Los Comisarios destinados a tratar con el Congreso se embarcarán luego que lo permita el viento, que en el día es muy contrario. Milord North ha dicho en la Cámara de los Comunes que esperaba desempeñasen con utilidad pública el encargo que llevaban, pero de esto no hay que hacer gran caso.

Sé que aún después de haber partido de aquí el embajador de Francia marqués de Noailles ha enviado este monarca secretamente a París un tal mister Pultney [sic] para tratar con el doctor Franklin, y que no ha vuelto muy satisfecho de sus entrevistas con aquel americano. Tienta esta Corte cuantos medios se le presentan para reconciliarse con las colonias, y aunque los ministros no quieran por ahora consentir públicamente en su independencia habrán de reconocerlas al fin por libres, sobre todo si ofrecen al comercio de la Inglaterra mayores ventajas que al de las otras naciones.

Ha habido la semana pasada varias juntas de los principales católicos, en que ha presidido el lord Peter [sic], y de resultas han resuelto ofrecer al rey sus vidas, y haciendas, y levantar a su propia costa, si su majestad británica gusta, un regimiento compuesto todo de gente de nuestra Religión. Si lisonjean de este modo que se les concederán algunos privilegios, y revocarán las leyes penales que hay contra ellos, pero ciertamente se lisonjean en vano, pues ni este monarca aceptará su oferta, ni habrá ministros que se atrevan a aconsejarles dar ninguna disposición en su favor, la que nunca podría tener lugar sin el consentimiento del Parlamento. Es el Lord Shelburne, conocido aquí por tan hábil como falso, quien ha persuadido al expresado Lord Peter, y a milord surry [sic], hijo primogénito del duque de Norfolk, ha juntarse para tratar de lo dicho, haciéndoles creer que el Lord Jorge Germain [sic], milord Mansfield, milord Butte [sic], y otros sujetos del Gabinete patrocinarían su instancia, pero este es un lazo que ha querido tender a los ministros para irritar contra ellos al pueblo, en caso de favorecer a los católicos.

Mañana empezarán las vacaciones del Parlamento, que durarán quince días con corta diferencia. Antes de separarse ha concedido la Cámara de los Comunes al ministro de Hacienda el permiso de buscar un millón, y medio de libras esterlinas sobre billetes del Echiquier [sic]: Aún esta suma agregada al nuevo préstamo de los seis millones no será suficiente para los gastos extraordinarios del año, si ocurre la guerra con la Francia, en cuyo caso se habrá de aumentar la deuda nacional, ya sea por medio de billetes de la Marina, o por el de alguna negociación secreta con los directores de la Compañía de Indias, a quienes ofrecerá el Lord North algunas ventajas con la esperanza de hacerlas aprobar en el Parlamento.

Dícese que saldrá en breve una proclamación para que cada parroquia del reino dé dos hombres, que servirán para formar nuevos regimientos, y completar los actuales, que no dejan de estar muy diminutos.

Es verosímil que los ministros vayan a pasar las Pascuas a sus casas de campo, como hacen todos los años, y que por este, u otro motivo se excuse milord Weymouth de conferir con nosotros pasado mañana.

No podrá dejar de parecer a vuestra excelencia esta mi única carta muy insubstancial, principalmente en un tiempo en que se deberían aguardar sucesos muy importantes, pero por más que haya procurado indagar si había algo digno de la curiosidad de vuestra excelencia no he podido saber más de lo que llevo referido.

Dios guarde a vuestra excelencia muchos años como deseo.
Londres a 14 de abril de 1778.
Excelentísimo señor
Beso la mano de vuestra excelencia su más humilde y rendido súbdito
Francisco Escarano

🟪 Document 43
Legajo 7001-12, Estado, AGS
Francisco Escarano al conde de Floridablanca, Londres,
29 de mayo de 1778
[Carta manuscrita, 5 págs.]
Original en español

Excelentísimo señor

Señor:
El martes pasado se propuso en la Cámara de los Comunes el examen de la conducta del general Bourgoyne en su expedición de Saratoga. Este general que asistió a la Cámara con el fin de satisfacer voluntariamente a varias preguntas que sabía le habían de hacer sus contrarios, habló por espacio de dos horas entrando en algunos puntos que le pareció exigían una satisfacción inmediata, y concluyó diciendo que él mismo deseaba se formase la Cámara en Junta particular para el referido examen, y justificación de su proceder. Al mismo tiempo se quejó de los ministros que habían aconsejado al rey le negase la entrada por ahora en Palacio: a que respondió milord Jorge Germain que se habían buscado casos iguales al suyo, para no darle este disgusto; pero que no se habían encontrado. Se opuso el lord Germain a la proposición del examen diciendo que el general Bourgoyne no estaba sujeto al juicio de la Cámara, hallándose como prisionero en Inglaterra; y aunque procuró Bourgoyne defender lo contrario, no pudo conseguirlo confesando él mismo que había venido de América con permiso del Congreso: y así se rechazó la proposición después de muchos debates. Durante ellos habló mister Lutrell en favor del general Bourgoyne, y no contento con elogiar su talento, valor y conducta, zahirió [sic][136] al Lord Germain comparando la suya en la batalla de Minden en que, dijo, había desobedecido las órdenes de sus superiores, y abandonado las banderas. Esta expresión picó a milord a tal extremo que tratando a mister Lutrell con palabras muy injuriosas le dijo que sabría vengarse de las que él había proferido.

Esta altercación conmovió a toda la Cámara, y a pesar de los esfuerzos que hizo el Orador para restablecer el orden imponiendo silencio a los ofendidos, no pudo lograrlo por algún tiempo. Señor Lutrell a quien amenazó sería arrestado dijo que pasaría por ello por no ceder del derecho de hablar en los términos que había ejecutado: que no había dicho cosa de milord que no fuese fundada en la opinión pública y en una sentencia dada en tiempo de Jorge II después de un juicio formal: y que milord había usado contra él de epitectos [sic][137] que ofendían su carácter y que no quería sufrir. Por fin obligó el Orador a señor Lutrell, que quiso en este intermedio salirse de la Cámara, a que volviese a su puesto, y exigió de él y de milord que se desdijesen de todas las expresiones inmoderadas, e insultantes en que habían prorrumpido. Lo hicieron así, siendo milord el primero que empezó a disculparse. No había sido sólo milord Germain el provocado. Señor Lutrell en su arenga echó algunas indirectas algo picantes a milord North: y este, cuando señor Fox gritaba orden, dijo que era el más desordenado de todos: pero estos desahogos no tuvieron ningunas resultas.

Por el impreso que incluyo a vuestra excelencia verá las ventajas que van a experimentar los católicos de este reino y la forma del juramento que deberán prestar al rey; aunque puede ser que antes que se publique el *bil* [sic][138] se mude en éste alguna expresión que no será muy esencial. Estas ventajas son muy grandes por lo que mira a la seguridad de los bienes de los católicos, a las adquisiciones de otros que pueden hacer en este país, y al orden regular de la subcesión [sic][139] en las familias, evitando las desgracias que provenían de que un segundo pudiese, haciéndose protestante, privar al primogénito de su natural herencia. Mas por lo que toca a las leyes penales, aún existen en su vigor (en cuanto no están revocadas) las más horribles contra los católicos: y sólo celebran hoy estos las ventajas citadas, porque dichas leyes no se ejecutan en el día, y porque se hallan esperanzados en que la sesión próxima del Parlamento obtendrán una revocación a lo menos implícita de las más fuertes.

Se ha propuesto en la Cámara de los Comunes que se suplique a su majestad que en atención a la necesidad que hay de concluir muchos negocios pendientes en el Parlamento, no lo prorrogue según el uso, sino que continúe por ahora citándose de unos días a otros hasta que aquellos se terminen: pero ha sido rechazada esta proposición.

Otra se ha hecho en la misma Cámara, y la ha retirado el que la expuso por la contradicción que hallaba en sus compañeros: y fue la de una súplica de la Cámara al rey manifestando a su majestad los deseos de que se verifique cuanto antes la reconciliación con los americanos, y que la Cámara ayudará a su majestad en todas las medidas que juzgue oportunas a este fin. Sostuvo esta proposición el partido de la Corte; pero sospechó el de la oposición que podría de esta suerte el ministerio de declarar independientes a las colonias si les pareciese necesario para la reconciliación; y en este supuesto se manifestó contrario a la súplica.

El miembro de la Cámara de los Comunes que ha hecho estas dos proposiciones es un tal señor Hartley que está en el partido de oposición (no extrañe vuestra excelencia la del dictamen de la Corte respecto a la independencia de las colonias, pues en este punto difieren muchos individuos de ambos partidos) y ha vuelto poco ha de París adonde fue, no sé si llevado de su celo, o por comisión del Ministerio para tratar con señor Franklin de un medio de reconciliación con los Americanos. Franklin le dijo que no la lograría la Inglaterra si no concedía a estos la independencia.

Ha propuesto el Parlamento al rey mande librar por una vez a la familia de milord Chatam [sic] 200 libras esterlinas para pagar las deudas del difunto; cuya suma satisfará a su majestad la nación.

> Nuestro señor guarde la vida de vuestra excelencia muchos años como deseo. Londres 29 de mayo de 1778.
> Excelentísimo señor
> Beso la mano de vuestra excelencia su más humilde y rendido súbdito.
> Francisco Escarano

Document 44
Signatura 121, AHPTF/AZC.
Graciano Sieulanne a Franklin, Santa Cruz de Tenerife,
30 de julio de 1778
[Carta manuscrita, 4 págs.]
Original en francés

Copie d'une lettre du monsieur Sieulanne à monsieur le Docteur Franklin.

À Sainte Croix de Ténérife, le 30 Juillet 1778.

Monsieur:
    J'ai l'honneur de vous informer que le capitaine G. Cunningham, commandant le bateau américain La Revenge, armé en course, ayant pris et mené à l'île de Palme une des Canaries, le brigantin anglais la Comtesse de Moreton, il me proposa de le conduire à la Martinique. Après avoir obtenu l'agréement de mon Consul dans ces îles et avoir fait mes conventions avec le capitaine Cunningham, je me transportai à la Palme où je pris possession du dit Brigantin. Mais, monsieur, comme j'étais à appareiller[140] le 19 de ce mois, le Gouverneur de la Palme envoya une chaloupe armée à mon bord pour m'obliger d'aller lui parler, ce qu'ayant fait, il me dit qu'il venait de recevoir l'ordre de monsieur le Marquis Tavallosos, Commandant Général des Canaries, d'arrêter mon bâtiment et il fit en conséquence descendre à terre les voiles et les boussoles. Je lui demandai les raisons d'un procédé aussi violent, il me répondit que non seulement il avait ordre de m'arrêter, mais même le capitaine Cunningham. Celui-ci avait appareillé un peu avant moi et il était encore à la vue du port. Le Gouverneur ajouta qu'il fallait que je m'adresse au Général. Je passai en conséquence à Ténérife et m'étant présenté au dit Général, il m'accabla d'injure, moi et le capitaine Cunningham, nous traitant de brigands. Je lui répondis que j'ignorais ce qu'il pouvait avoir contre ce capitaine, que ma ¿mission?[141] le bornait à conduire la prise dont il s'agit à la Martinique, et que je venais savoir la raison pourquoi il m'avait fait arrêter aussi ignominieusement. Il me dit

alors d'aller trouver un négociant anglais établi au port de l'Oros, appelé monsieur Thomas Cologhan. Ne scrutant à quoi cette démarche aboutirait, je fus rendre compte à mon Consul de ce qui se passait. Il me conseilla d'écrire au dit Seigneur Cologhan, qui me fit la réponse dont je joins ici la copie.

Cette lettre, monsieur, développe tout le mystère et il parait que c'est par représailles que j'ai été arrêté et que le capitaine Cunningham devait l'être. Je ne réfléchirai point sur un procédé aussi violent de la part du Général des Canaries. Je me bornerai seulement à vous supplier de vouloir bien employer vos bons offices pour que la Cour d'Espagne oblige ce Général a me payer tous les frais que ces retards m'ont occasionné, et qui peuvent être évalués en cinq cents piastres, attendu que mon marché avec le capitaine Cunningham est par traversée, avec huit hommes d'équipage et que je serai obligé de vendre à perte une portion de mon chargement à la Palme, lequel consiste en vin de Catalogne. Cette somme pourra être remise à monsieur le Consul de France qui me la fera passer où je me trouverai, selon les prières que je lui en fait et les avis que je lui donnerai. Je pense aussi, monsieur, qu'en bonne justice ce Général devrait être tenu de répondre de tous les événements jusqu'à mon arrivée à la Martinique, puis qu'il m'a provoqué un retard de près de trois semaines.

Le chargement et le navire sont estimés seize mille piastres ou soixante- quatre mille livres.

Pour ce qui regarde, monsieur, l'insulte fait au pavillon, je suis persuadé que vous en obtiendrez satisfaction et qu'il ne sera plus exposé dans ces parages à des semblables attentats. J'espère aussi que vous excuserez mon importunité, mais j'aurais cru manquer aux égards que je dois au capitaine Cunningham, qui a bien voulu me confier ses intérêts, si j'avais omis de vous faire part de cette circonstance.

J'ai l'honneur d'être avec respect monsieur votre etc
Sieulanne

✷ Document 45
Legajo 4618-52, Estado, AGS
B. Franklin a mister Grand, Passy, 3 de noviembre de 1778
[Carta manuscrita, 2 págs.]
Original en francés

(Nota manuscrita de presentación, media página)
El conde de Aranda, París, 9 de noviembre de 1778
Original en español

Incluye la respuesta de los Diputados Americanos sobre las quejas dadas del corsario Conyngham.

Se queja por su parte el Diputado Americano de que por vía de represalia apresamos un Americano y lo condujimos a Canarias.

Respuesta en 23 con n° 2
Franklin to Grand, Passy, 3 de noviembre de 1778
Original en francés

Enterado, y que no se contesta sobre el segundo punto hasta tomar noticias de este antecedente del navío que se llevó a Canarias.
 Nous devons des remerciements, monsieur, à la personne qui nos a fait remettre para votre canal, la note que nous avons reçu contre Cunningham, et nous devons l'assurer de nouveau qu'étant pénétrés de respect pour Sa Majesté Catholique, rien ne nous peine plis que des plaintes de sa part contre nos gens. Elle aura vu par les papiers que vous avez remis dans le temps de notre part a Son Excellence monsieur le Conte d'Aranda, toutes les mesures que le Congrès avait prises pour prévenir même toute inconduite de la part de nos armateurs et gens de mer, et rien ne prouve mieux sa sollicitude a cet égard que la proclamation qu'il vient de rendre, dont voici la copie N° 2 a la quelle nous joignons celle de sa résolution pour conserver la propriété d'un navire, quoique appartenant à une Puissance dont nous n'avons pas lieu de nous louer.
 Mais si l'on fait attention aux procédés atroces des anglais envers toutes les Nations indistinctement, en ne sera pas surpris que leur

fâcheux exemple ne trouve des sectateurs dans quelques individus d'une nation qu'ils ont si fort outragée. Mais cela ne disculpe pas Conyngham. C'est un crime à nos yeux d'avoir déplu à une Puissance pour la quelle le Congrès est pénétré de respect et quoiqu'elle ce soit fait justice elle-même en faisant saisir par représailles la prise anglaise que Conyngham avait conduite à Ténérife pour la faire passer à la Martinique. Nous n'en informerons pas moins le Congrès des sujets de plainte que cet armateur a donné à Sa Majesté Catholique. Ce sera certainement un nouveau motif pour faire rendre à son pavillon tous les égards et le respect qu'il lui porte. J'ose espérer de la sagesse ainsi que de la justice de Sa Majesté qu'elle ajoutera foi a cette expression de nos sentiments pour Elle, et qu'Elle daignera à son tour nous en faire éprouver les effets.

J'ai l'honneur d'être, monsieur, Votre très humble et très obéissant serviteur
B. Franklin
À Passy ce 3 Novembre 1778
M. Grand

Document 46
Legajo 4618-51, Estado, AGS
El conde de Aranda al conde de Floridablanca, París, 9 de noviembre de 1778
[Carta manuscrita, 2 págs.]
Original en español

Excelentísimo señor

Muy señor mío:
En carta de 14 de septiembre número 3 me informa vuestra excelencia de los excesos que el corsario americano Cunningham estaba cometiendo continuamente sobre nuestras costas; y señaladamente de la presa que acababa de hacer de un navío sueco, cargado en Londres por cuenta de españoles; y me previno vuestra excelencia de orden del rey, lo hiciese entender por segunda mano a los diputados americanos, exigiendo que providenciasen lo conveniente para la restitución debida; y para el arreglo de la conducta de Cunningham.

Así lo ejecuté por medio del banquero mounsier Grant, según dije a vuestra excelencia en carta de 2 del pasado número 1348. Y en su consecuencia me ha traído el mismo Grant la carta que sobre este particular le ha escrito el doctor Francklin [sic], acompañada de la proclamación del Congreso sobre el trato de los pabellones neutros; y la resolución del mismo, sobre una presa portuguesa, con sus traducciones en francés. Todo lo cual paso a manos de vuestra excelencia para que pueda enterar al rey de la respuesta de estos diputados sobre nuestra queja, y del estado en que se halla este asunto.

Dios guarde a vuestra excelencia muchos años. París 9 de noviembre de 1778.
Excelentísimo señor
Beso la mano de vuestra excelencia
su Seguro Servidor
El conde de Aranda

Document 47
Legajo 4620-126, Estado, AGS
El conde de Aranda al conde de Floridablanca, París,
19 de julio de 1779
[Carta manuscrita, 3 págs.]
Original en español

Excelentísimo señor

Muy señor mío:

Las cartas de Inglaterra vienen muy irregulares tanto por la dilación del pasaje de Downes a Ostende, bien diferente de lo estrecho del de Calais para practicarlo en moderado tiempo, como por el riesgo de los corsarios que corren los paquebotes correos, los cuales se detienen en Downes mismo, siempre que entienden hallarse en el Canal alguna embarcación sospechosa. Por eso las últimas cartas que han llegado a este comercio son del 9, y sólo dicen que la Flota del Almirante Hardy había estado en la bahía de Torbay, de donde había vuelto a salir reforzada hasta 40 navíos de línea.

Con fechas de 2 y 17 de mayo me escribió vuestra excelencia sobre insultos atribuidos al pabellón americano contra el paquebote correo español, que venía de Tenerife a La Coruña, y una saetía catalana sobre las aguas de la isla de Santo Domingo, para que lo hiciese saber al Diputado de los americanos en esta Corte, en los términos que juzgase conducentes. En consecuencia llamé al banquero señor Grand, y le entregué los simples relatos de dichos sucesos traducidos al Francés, para que los hiciese entender al doctor Francklin [sic]; y en el día de hoy me ha traído por respuesta la que ha dado el Comisionado Americano en Nantes, que incluyo a vuestra excelencia.

Igualmente me ha entregado señor Grand la otra copia que acompaña de un recurso que ha hecho al mismo Francklin [sic] un comerciante establecido en Alicante llamado Montgomery, el cual supone ser americano, y que con todo ha sido tratado como inglés en las disposiciones que se han tomado después del rompimiento; pidiéndome lo pasase a vuestra excelencia con aserción de que era individuo partidario de los Estados Unidos.

Se dice que las disposiciones del embarco prosiguen con actividad en Saint Malo, y el Havre de Gracia [sic];[142] y que el campo de Dunkerque se aumenta de infantería, y caballería.

Acuso a vuestra excelencia el recibo de sus cuatro números del 5 del corriente que no exigen contestación particular.

Dios guarde a vuestra excelencia muchos años. París 19 de julio de 1779.
Excelentísimo señor
Beso La mano de vuestra excelencia
su seguro servidor
El conde de Aranda

Anexo A
Legajo 4620-127, Estado, AGS
The Count de Aranda, Paris, 19 de julio de 1779
[Nota manuscrita de presentación, media pagina
Original en español

Montgomery a B. Franklin, Alicante, 26 de junio de 1779
[Copia de carta manuscrita, 3 págs.]
Original en francés

Incluye la respuesta que le ha dado al diputado americano sobre nuestras quejas contra tres corsarios nombrados la Resolution, el Plimouth y la Petite Resolution, asegurando que no cree existan tales armadores ni que hayan salido, como se supone, de los puertos de Francia pues tendría informes.
Acompaña el recurso de un americano llamado Montgomeri establecido en Alicante que se queja de tratársele en todo como inglés y quererle echar del reino.Respondida en 2 de agosto con Número 2
Que se tomarán informes por lo tocante a Montgomeri para saber si hasta ahora ha pasado por inglés y ahora intenta se le mire por americano. Que por lo respectivo al embargo fue una providencia general que tomó el soberano en Alicante partiendo de un principio equivocado y se puso remedio luego que se supo aquí.

Copie d'une lettre de monsieur Montgomery d'Alicante à monsieur B. Franklin, 26 Juin 1779
[Original en français]

Je me trouve dans la cruelle nécessité d'importuner Votre Excellence pour l'informer que, non obstant mon exactitude à me déclarer et è me souscrire sujet des 13 États-Unis de l'Amérique Septentrionale, toutes les fois que les négociants étrangers établis ici ont été sommé pour le Gouvernement pour venir déclarer de quel pays ils étaient, hier, sur une déclaration de guerre faite contre l'Angleterre, on est venu s'emparer de ma personne, de mon bien, et un soldat [sic] que nombreuse est venu remplir ma maison. Je présentai immédiatement le certificat et le passeport que vous m'aviez donné conjointement avec Messieurs Lee et Adams, lorsque j'ai eu l'honneur de vous aller faire ma cour en Août dans mon passage pour cette ville. Mais ces pièces ne m'ont procuré aucun redressement, ce qui me fit demander si l'Espagne avait déclaré la guerre contre l'Amérique. Quoiqu'on m'a répondu négativement, je n'en ai pas été mieux traité et je ne sais pas même la parance [sic] du devenir.

Ayant la conscience de la plus parfaite innocence et n'ayant contre moi qu'un extérieur aussi anglais que j'en suis opposé quant aux sentiments, je supplie Votre Excellence de vouloir bien écrire immédiatement au Comte de Ricla, le Ministre de la Guerre, pour qu'en conséquence de ma qualité de sujet des alliés, il veuille bien ordonner qu'on me restitue ce qu'on m'a saisi, et que je sois réintégré dans tous mes droits. Veuillez aussi me dire qui es le Chargé des Affaires à Madrid, s'il y en a déjà de nommé, afin que j'ai à m'adresser à lui à l'avenir en cas de récidive.

Je me repose entièrement sur votre bienveillance et sur votre équité pour me tirer de l'état de détresse où je me trouve.

Je ne doute nullement que vous ne m'honorez d'une réponse sans laquelle il me serait bien difficile de me tirer de cette pénible situation et de sauver le crédit et d'éviter la perte de celui etc etc

Anexo B
Legajo 4620-129, Estado, AGS
J. Williams a Franklin, Nantes, 13 de julio de 1779
[Carta manuscrita, 2 págs.]
Original en francés[143]
Traduction d'une lettre de monsieur J. Williams de Nantes du 13 Juillet 1779 à monsieur le Docteur Franklin.

En réponse aux deux papiers contenus dans votre lettre du 9 courant. Le premier un détail des insultes faites au pavillon espagnol par trois vaisseaux de guerre américains; la Résolution, Le Plymouth et La Petite Résolution, qui ont dû mettre à la voile de Nantes. Le second un Mémoire des insultes faites au même pavillon par d'autres vaisseaux américains aux Antilles.

Je dois vous assurer que je n'ai jamais eu vent de l'existence de vaisseaux de guerre américains des noms ci-dessus, et que je n'ai pas connaissance qu'il en soit jamais sorti de ce nom d'aucuns ports de France. Ces circonstances et plusieurs autres me portent à croire que des corsaires anglais ont abordé des vaisseaux espagnols sous pavillon américain, en se déclarant sujets des États-Unis, dans le dessein de nous faire envisager par cette nation et tout autres comme des pirates.

Je n'épargnerai rien pour me procurer les informations les plus exactes à ce sujet et si jamais je découvre l'exemple de pareille conduite de la part d'aucun américain, je croirai de mon devoir de la dénoncer et de faire ce qui dépendra de moi pour le livrer à la rigueur des lois. L'honneur et la réputation de mes vertueux compatriotes s'y trouvant fortement intéressés.

Document 48
Legajo 4620-130, Estado, AGS
J. Williams a Franklin, Nantes, 22 de julio de 1779
[Copia manuscrita de traducción de carta del inglés, 1 pág.]
Original en francés

Traduction de la lettre de monsieur J. Williams à monsieur le Docteur Franklin en datte du 22 Juillet 1779

Depuis que j'ai eu l'honneur de vous écrire le 13 de ce mois, pour vous informer que les corsaires dont la Cour d'Espagne portait plainte, ne pouvaient être américains, j'ai fait de plis amples recherches et à fin de déraciner chez monsieur l'Ambassadeur jusqu'à la plus petite incertitude, je vous renvoie les papiers que vous m'aviez fait passer, accompagnés d'une attestation des courtiers d'ici, qui déclarent que jamais corsaires de ces noms n'ont parus en France.

Je ne puis rien affirmer relativement à celui aux Antilles, mais je suis intimement convaincu que toutes ces insultes ont été faites par les anglais et non par les américains.

Je suis avec respect.

Legajo 4620-131, Estado, AGS
Nantes, 20 de julio de 1779
[Certificado firmado por los traductores, 1 pág.]
Original en francés

Nous, interprète juré des Langues Étrangères et courtiers royaux soussignés, certifions que tous les bâtiments, frégates ou corsaires appartenant aux États-Unis de l'Amérique qui ont mouillé dans cette rivière, ont été servis et assistés par nous en qualité d'interprète et courtier soudits, et que depuis la guerre actuellement existante entre les dits États et le Royaume de la Grande Bretagne, il n'a mouillé dans cette rivière aucuns bâtiments, frégates ou corsaires de la dite nation ou appartenant aux dits États portant les noms et commandées par les dénommées-ci après Scarain (?) la frégate La Résolution monté de 26 cannons et 120 hommes d'équipage, commandé par le capitaine Jean Gran. Le Plymouth de 20 cannons et 100 hommes d'équipage, commandé par le capitaine Ning. Le corsaire La Petite Résolution de 14 cannons, 40 hommes d'équipage, et la frégate La terrible, capitaine Samuel Syers. Monsieur Jon (sic) Williams de cette ville nous ayant représenté un mémoire portant plaintes contre les dites frégates et corsaire qui auraient insulté le 30 Mars dernier sous pavillon des États-Unis, se disant venir de Nantes, le paquebot courrier espagnol nommé le ¿Pájaro?[144] faisant veille de Santa Cruz de Tenerife pour la Corogne, a requis de nous un certificat pour justifier que les dites frégates et corsaire ne sont jamais venus en cette rivière et que depuis le mois de Janvier de la présente année jusqu'à l'époque sousdite, il n'est sortie de ce port ou rivière qu'un seul bâtiment corsaire américain nommé Le Général Washington d'Alexandrie en Virginie, commandé par le Sieur François Speake, qui montait 16 ou 18 cannons, qui a appareillé d'ici vers la fin de Mars dernier et c'est rende à Brest pour y joindre un convoy, qu'en conséquence il est à présumer que l'insulte faite au paquebot espagnol a eu lieu par des anglais, masqué sous pavillon des États-Unis de l'Amérique. En foie de quoi nous vous délivrons le présent pour servir et valuer ce que de raison.

À Nantes, le 20 Juillet 1779.
Odielle de la Bauche, Duchesne, F.M. Van Neunen.

Document 49
779-75-IR, AHPTF/AZC
Juan Còlogan a Tomás Cólogan, 27/31 de deciembre de 1780
Original en inglés

🌸 Document 50
Legajo 4624-71, Estado, AGS
El conde de Aranda al conde de Floridablanca, París, 9 de abril de 1781, no. 1930
[Carta manuscrita, 3 págs.]
Original en español

                Excelentísimo señor

Muy señor mío:
    Ayer me envió el doctor Franklin el pliego de vuestra excelencia que trajo el correo de ese representante de las colonias americanas, monsieur Jay, con fecha del 28 de marzo, e inclusa la carta del administrador del correo de Burgos sobre el correo francés a quien había sorprendido un delirio bastante fuerte. Y como por la posterior de vuestra excelencia del 30 por el correo de Cabarrú veo que ya habían parecido los pliegos retardados, me limitaré a informar mañana al señor conde de Vergennes de tan accidental suceso, siendo regular que se halle ya noticioso de todo por ese Embajador de Francia.
    Corren por aquí noticias favorables de la India Oriental, suponiéndose que Hyder Ali Kan haya batido a los ingleses. Y también del lado de Nueva York de que Washington haya maltratado a Clinton. Y aunque alguna gaceta de las de Holanda lo trae también como PD[145] de las cartas de Londres del 30, suspendo mi juicio hasta las primeras de Inglaterra.
    Monsieur de Grasse despachó una corbeta el 27 desde los 42 grados de latitud y 16 de longitud occidental, meridiano de París, considerándose a 60 leguas oeste del Cabo de Finisterre. Y el dicho bastimento ha asegurado que desde su separación había reinado por tres días el viento nordeste favorable a la navegación del convoy, de modo que no dudaba hubiese llegado con él a entrar en las brisas o vientos alisios, y que haría una navegación pocas veces vista.
    Don Matías de Gandasegui,[146] en su última del 30, me dice que había llegado a Limerick en Irlanda una presa francesa llamada el *Sartine*,[147] procedente de La Habana con pliegos para las dos Cortes. Pero que se habían echado a la mar con tiempo los paquetes de que venía encargada, y me pide lo participe a vuestra excelencia.

Dios guarde a vuestra excelencia muchos años. París, 9 de abril de 1781.
Excelentísimo señor
Beso la mano de vuestra excelencia
su seguro servidor
El conde de Aranda

Document 51
Legajo 4624-73, Estado, AGS
El conde de Aranda al conde de Floridablanca, París, 12 de abril de
1781, no. 1931
[Carta manuscrita, 2 págs.]
Original en español

                                          Excelentísimo señor.

Muy señor mío:
    Recibí la de vuestra excelencia del 28 de marzo por un correo del señor Jay al doctor Franklin, el cual me la remitió con persona de su casa, conteniendo el suceso del correo francés a quien se trastornó la cabeza en las cercanías de Burgos. Instruí de ello al señor conde de Vergennes antes de ayer martes, haciéndole leer el aviso del Administrador del Correo de Burgos a los directores de Madrid, y quedó comprendido de todo, a más que también había recibido igual noticia por ese embajador.
    Al salir de mi Audiencia me dijo el doctor Franklin que hoy devolvería el mismo correo, y si yo quería escribir le enviase el pliego para las 10 de la mañana, lo que acepté para poder prevenir a vuestra excelencia que hoy le escribo 3 cartas. A saber: ésta, otra por correo francés que me dijo monsieur de Vergennes despacharía a la noche o mañana temprano, y la principal por Don Francisco Cabarrú, que partirá a medianoche y la llevará a Irún, previniendo yo al administrador de aquel correo que si la mala ha de pasar en horas de diferencia, envíe por ella a vuestra excelencia mi pliego, y no siendo así despache una estafeta.
    El asunto es el que contenía el despacho de vuestra excelencia por el correo de Cabarrú en 30 de marzo. En la que irá por el correo francés lo tocaré superficialmente, y va extenso en la de Cabarrú, pero naturalmente será la última de las tres que llegue, por lo cual convendrá que, aunque ese embajador entere a vuestra excelencia por su parte, procure vuestra excelencia no contestarle en nada hasta haber recibido mi narrativa, y a título de que mi carta se remitirá a lo que él dijere, ponerlo en el caso de que exprese a lo largo cuanto se le comunique. Creeré que para el 21 bien pueda llegar mi pliego de Irún a vuestra excelencia.

Dios guarde a vuestra excelencia muchos años. París, 12 de abril de 1781.
Excelentísimo señor
Beso la mano de vuestra excelencia
su seguro servidor
El conde de Aranda

Document 52
Signatura 121, AHPTF/ACZ
Tomás Cólogan Valois a Juan Cólogan Valois, Tenerife,
6 de junio de 1781[148]
[Libro de copias de 1777 a 1782, carta extracto, 2 páginas]
Original en inglés

Document 53
Signatura 121, AHPTF/ACZ
Tomás Cólogan Valois to Robert Morris, Tenerife, 7 June 1781[149]
[Libro de copias, 1777 to 1782]
Original en inglés

Document 54
Signatura 121, AHPTF/AZC
Tomás Cólogan a Juan Cólogan de Cólogan, Pollard & Company, Tenerife, 1 de agosto de 1781.[150]
[Libro de copias de 1777 a 1782, extracto de carta manuscrita, 4 págs.]
Original en inglés

Document 55
Legajo 4626-179, Estado, AGS
El conde de Aranda al conde de Floridablanca, París, 18 de mayo de 1782, no. 2191
[Carta manuscrita, 2 págs.]
Original en español

                Excelentísimo señor

Muy señor mío:
    En el N.2 del 5 del corriente por correo francés, me dice vuestra excelencia la voz esparcida de que los americanos iban a expedir patentes de corso contra el pabellón portugués, bajo el cual, creyéndolo seguro hasta aquí, tenían los españoles aventurados muchos caudales y efectos. En cuyo supuesto averiguase yo con maña y reserva si fuese cierta semejante providencia, y en tal caso instase a monsieur Franklin para que solicitase al Congreso las órdenes de salvar los efectos españoles pertenecientes a los españoles.
    De algunas preguntas que fui haciendo nada saqué en el asunto, ignorándolo todos. Por lo cual, el martes 13, hallándonos en el cuarto del señor Delfín aguardando la entrada para hacerle la Corte el cuerpo diplomático, aproveché el momento para acercarme de monsieur Franklin, y preguntarle qué había sobre tal corso contra la bandera lusitana. Y me respondió con naturalidad que ni lo sabía ni lo creía, que bastante enemigo tenían con la inglesa para buscarse otros. Preguntele con esta ocasión si el pabellón americano entraba en los puertos de Portugal, y me dijo que desde el decreto de su majestad fidelísima que se les prohibió, no usaban de ellos. Que después se les había dado a entender que con pabellón francés no serían despedidos y, que aunque bajo mano se había hecho saber a los navegantes por estos mares, ninguno había usado de tal medio hasta ahora. Díjome que dicha especie sobre los portugueses había salido de Londres para enredar no más, y me repitió no saber ni creer tal cosa.

    Dios guarde a vuestra excelencia muchos años. París, 18 de mayo 1782.
    Excelentísimo señor
    Beso la mano de vuestra excelencia
    su seguro servidor
    El conde de Aranda.

Document 56
El conde de Aranda al conde de Floridablanca, París,
6 de julio de 1782
[Carta manuscrita, 2 págs.[151]]
Original en español
París, 6 de julio de 1782

Excelentísimo:
    Anda por aquí tal mudanza de tiempo, que habiendo precedido algún calor excesivo de dos o tres días por tres alternativas, hemos caído en un fresco de octubre que hace seis u ocho que dura, y es una infinidad de resfriados la que reina, en que es menester cuidar mucho del pecho. Yo me hallo con él, y no me ha venido bien el tener que escribir ni andar a derecha o izquierda, pero vaya el servicio del rey, que es lo que importa. Veo que vuestra excelencia también se resiente de su salud, y como su vida sedentaria y de tavolino[152] ha de ser más continuada que la mía, es menester que vuestra excelencia procure minorarla en lo posible, porque es fuerte enemigo de la salud la señora[153] pluma.
    Ya respondo de oficio sobre lo comunicativo de la instrucción que se me envió, y quedo comprendido de la particular de vuestra excelencia que recibí ayer, de 27 del pasado.
    Hoy comerán conmigo Jay y Franklin, a la moda de este país pero sin convite en forma, y por el sólo fin de irlos acostumbrando a vernos la cara para cuando empecemos a hablar familiarmente.
    Va un paquete gordo para el conde de Lacy, que son unos tratados de Artillería que le envía un oficial general de aquí y pueden convenirle en Gibraltar. Con que pido a vuestra excelencia que cuando haya correo se lo envíe, y si acaso por el ordinario, que sea franco de porte.
    Mande vuestra excelencia a su verdadero servidor
    Aranda
    He salido ya con hallar el dinero de mi facultad, en que vuestra excelencia ha concurrido con facilidades para ello. Y así le repito gracias.
    Excelentísimo señor conde de Floridablanca.
    [Al dorso]
    París, 6 de julio de 1782
    El conde de Aranda
    (por correo nuestro)
    Confidencial.

Document 57
Legajo 4630-187, Estado, AGS
El conde de Aranda al conde de Floridablanca, 23 de Julio de 1783, no. 2487
[Carta manuscrita, 1 pág.]
Original en español

Excelentísimo señor

Muy señor mío:

Hoy sin papel ni más que recado de su parte y nombre de su dirección, me ha pasado el señor Franklin dos ejemplares de la Constitución de los 13 Estados unidos,[154] uno en $4°$[155] para el rey Nuestro señor, y otro en $8°$ para mí. Con lo cual dirijo aquel a vuestra excelencia por esta ocasión.

Dios guarde a vuestra excelencia muchos años.
París, 23 de julio de 1783.
Excelentísimo señor

[Anexo]

El señor conde de Aranda
Remite un ejemplar de la Constitución de los 13 Estados Unidos, que el señor Franklin le entregó para el rey Nuestro señor.

Recibida en 23 de agosto. Que he presentado al rey este ejemplar y ha mandado se guarde en el Archivo de la Secretaría. Y que mediante se vendan, convendrá que para el uso común envíe tres o cuatro ejemplares en $8°$.

Que ayer presentó el señor conde al rey, como encargado de los negocios de los Trece Estados, a monsieur Caymarquel.[156]

Document 58
Legajo 4630-234, Estado, AGS
El conde de Aranda al conde de Floridablanca, París, 3 de septiembre de 1783, no. 2523
[Carta manuscrita, 1 pág.]
Original en español

                                                Excelentísimo señor

Muy señor mío:
    Remito a vuestra excelencia dos ejemplares de la Constitución de los Estados de América, y por otro extraordinario irán los demás que vuestra excelencia me pide en el N.8 de la expedición del 23 pasado.

    Dios guarde a vuestra excelencia muchos años. París, 3 de septiembre de 1783
    Excelentísimo señor
    Beso la mano de vuestra excelencia
    su seguro servidor
    El conde de Aranda

Franklin de la Posguerra

Document 59
Actas de Sesiones de la Real Academia de la Historia, Madrid, 9 de julio de 1784, RAH
[Manuscrito, 3 págs.]
Original en español

Academia de 9 de julio de 1784

El señor Don Ramón de Guevara hizo presente que el doctor Benjamín Franklin, ministro plenipotenciario de los Estados Unidos de la América Septentrional en la Corte de París, había regalado un ejemplar de la colección de sus obras, especialmente políticas, al ilustrísimo señor director, escribiéndole con este motivo una carta en inglés que por orden de su ilustrísima ha traducido el mismo señor Guevara, y que se traerá a la academia con copia del original y la minuta de la respuesta que le diese su ilustrísima. Añadió el propio señor Guevara que a la carta y ejemplar de las obras de Franklin acompañó el señor Don Guillermo Carmichael, encargado de los negocios de los mismos Estados Unidos en esta Corte, un billete de su puño cuya copia leyó a la academia, en el cual participa a su ilustrísima que la academia de ciencias establecida en Filadelfia bajo el título de Sociedad Filosófica había nombrado por uno de sus individuos al mismo señor ilustrísimo con las circunstancias honoríficas noticiadas en la Gaceta de Madrid de ----[157] del presente mes, capítulo de Londres.

En atención a lo expuesto y a la fama justamente adquirida generalmente por el doctor Franklin de célebre político y sabio, y a ser miembro de las principales academias de Europa, y por corresponder a la demostración que ha hecho la Sociedad Filosófica de Filadelfia, le propuso su ilustrísima a la academia para individuo honorario. Y se acordó por aclamación admitirle en la clase de tal.

Se acordó convidar al Excelentísimo señor marqués de Santa Cruz, director de la Real Academia Española, y a los individuos de ella, por su hermandad con la nuestra.

Por el señor secretario
José de Guevara Vasconcelos

[Al margen: relación de académicos asistentes a la sesión]:

Director, Murillo (censor), Huerta, Casiri, Sánchez. O. de la Roca, Sedano, Ortega, Capmany,[158] Cerdá, Viera, Guevara de Vasconcelos, López, Jovellanos, Cuesta, Rivero, duque de Almodóvar, Marqués de la Lapilla, Palomares, Ayala, Castelló, Miranda, P. Banqueri, Guevara (por el señor Secretario).

Document 60
Legajo 8141-33, Estado, AGS
Misceláneas de despachos y otras notas, miercoles, 12 de octubre; y viernew, 14 de octubre de 1785
(Borrador manuscrito, 5 págs.)
Original en español

Miércoles 12 de octubre
    El lunes recibió señor Adams despachos de América.[159]
    Muchos aventureros irán con los primeros navíos a la India para establecer una factoría nueva en Negapatnam [sic][160] en la Costa de Coromandel; dándose por supuesto que no se restituirá ya a los holandeses los que al presente no tienen equivalente para dar en cambio.
    El navío de su majestad Asurance de 44[161] ha mandado equiparse inmediatamente en Chatham para un destino distante. Se cree que irá a la India.
    <u>Gravesend 11 de octubre</u>. Han dado a la vela los navíos mercantes Belisario por la costa de Mosquitos, y el nombrado Juana y Isabel, capitán Fraser por Piscataqua.
    El Navío Impregnable de 90 cañones que debía botarse en Deptford este mes, permanecerá según nueva orden en sus gradas hasta la primavera próxima.
    <u>Nevis 30 de julio</u>. La fragata *Boreas* ha apresado 4 bastimentos americanos con sus cargas, que hacían tráfico clandestino con esta isla, fueron confiscados inmediatamente por este expedito Tribunal de Almirantazgo.

Viernes 14 de octubre
    Por muy deseosa que esté su majestad Católica de cerrar los puertos de sus dominios a toda clase de géneros de las manufacturas británicas y irlandesas; no ha llegado aún la nación española a estado suficiente de madurez para poder sostener tal providencia. El vasto consumo que se hace en sus dominios de América de efectos de lana y

de otros géneros de fábrica Inglesa (sin contar los surtidos indispensables en España misma) debe impedir la expedición de una cédula de dicha naturaleza; pues no se hace en aquel Reino la vigésima parte de telas de lana que necesitan, aún en su recinto solamente, ni podrían proveerse en otra parte de Europa tampoco de otros muchos objetos: Así pues debe mirarse el párrafo publicado días pasados en algún Impreso nacional "de que un caballero recién llegado de Cádiz había traído dicha noticia" como una de aquellas invenciones hechas meramente para inquietar a la nación sin fundamento.

El miércoles a la tarde se recibieron cartas de Gibraltar, traídas en el Navío Ana, Capitán Heachan [sic][162] que llegó a Queensborough. Contienen aviso de haber arribado allí de Cádiz el navío Peace & Plenty, capitán Robertson, después de haberle detenido un corsario Argelino, y quitádole algunas barricas de vaca salada y otros varios artículos.

Habrán de regresar todos los bastimentos de su majestad del destino de Mediterráneo en el mes de Marzo próximo y serán reemplazados por otros, excepto el Trusty de 50 cañones, en que ha partido el comodoro Cosby.

Mientras los holandeses estuvieron en amistad con esta nación han disfrutado por una serie larga, no interrumpida, de mucha paz y prosperidad. Estaban dichosos en sus casas y respetados fuera de ellas; pero apenas formaron nuevas conexiones y se separaron de sus antiguas se ha apoderado la Casa de Austria de una parte de sus territorios, obligándoles aún a pagar los gastos de tal revolución. Ya la Prusia ha manifestado sus pretensiones, las que se supone seguirán nuevas condescendencias: Y así han perdido por su ambición y perfidia en dos años, todas aquellas ventajas en cuya adquisición se habían empleado casi por dos siglos enteros.

En carta de Copenhague se observa que había llegado allí una partida de carpinteros de Rivera de los astilleros de Génova, habiéndose visto precisados a separarse de aquella República en consecuencia de algunas desavenencias que tuvieron con algunos Magistrados relativamente a sus pagas. El rey los empleó inmediatamente continuando en su empeño de poner su Marina en el pie de las más respetables de Europa.

Los avisos que tenemos de Portsmouth en la Nueva Hampshire informan de haber botado al agua los americanos en aquel puerto en el mes de agosto último un navío nuevo de 50 cañones, nombrado el

Defensor y que seguían allí la construcción de otros de 74 que parece ha de venderse a los Franceses.

<u>Filadelfia 25 de junio</u>. Se sabe de cierto que la intención de Don Franklin en visitar a la América a esta época es con el fin de contribuir con sus luces a la formación de un nuevo código de leyes para el mejor gobierno de los Estados diversos: Se parecerá de algún modo al de Inglaterra y se pondrá particular atención en hacerlo conciso y bien inteligible. También contribuirá este segundo Newton a conciliar los ánimos de todos los partidos y a poner en perpetuo olvido las distinciones odiosas de Whigismo [sic] y Torismo [sic]. Se cree que se le dará la presidencia del Congreso en la próxima elección pues no hay persona más bien calificada para ello.

Se sabe de Nueva Escocia que habiendo.[163]

<u>Nueva York 28 de julio</u>. El Estado de Frankland ha concluido un tratado de paz y amistad perpetua con los Indios Cherokeses [sic] y hay negociación pendiente de dar a aquella nación un lugar entre los representantes del mismo Estado y se espera que los comisionados de los Estados Unidos conseguirán apaciguar así mismo a los Indios Creeks y otras tribus del occidente que nos molestan como también a los de Kentucky [sic].

<u>13 de Agosto</u>. No son favorables los avisos de la negociación de nuestros comisionados con las 6 naciones de los Indios [illegible] insisten en varias concesiones de territorios que suponen pertenecerles refiriéndose a las estipulaciones de los oficiales británicos del estrecho de Niágara.

Document 61
Archivo privado de la familia Gasset (Madrid)
Benjamín Franklin a Pedro Rodríguez, conde de Campomanes,
Filadelfia, 4 de Diciembre de 1786
[Documento principal, 1 página]
Original en inglés

Document 62
Legajo 55-138, Archivo del conde de Campomanes
Documentos referentes al nombramiento del conde de Campomanes como miembro de la Sociedad Filosófica de Filadelfia, año 1787. Incluye dos notas de presentación y un borrador de carta.
[1- Nota de presentación manuscrita, 1 pág.]
Original en español

Título de individuo de la Sociedad Filosófica de Filadelfia.
Nota–
Adjunta se halla la carta con que le dirigió el Sr. Benjamín Franklin y la contestación de su Ilustrísima
[2- Nota de presentación manuscrita (1 pág.).]
Original en español

Madrid 24 de mayo de 1787

Al señor Benjamín Franklin:
 Respondiendo a la suya de 4 de diciembre último que está inclusa, y enviándole el tomo primero del Diccionario Español Latino y Árabe del padre Cañes, entre otros libros que le remite la Academia de la Historia, cuya lista acompaña.

[3- Borrador de carta manuscrito, 3 págs.]
Original en español

Excelentísimo señor

Muy señor mío:
 He recibido por mano del señor Guillermo Carmichel la estimada carta de vuestra excelencia de 4 de diciembre próximo pasado, juntamente con el apreciable título de individuo de la Sociedad Filosófica Americana, y el tomo segundo de sus Transacciones, que contiene los estatutos del cuerpo, la lista de socios y varios experimentos, observaciones y escritos sobre asuntos relativos por la mayor parte a las ciencias naturales y exactas.
 Por todo estoy muy reconocido, así a vuestra excelencia como a nuestra Sociedad, en cuyas obras, que me interesan ya como propias por

la honra que me ha dispensado incorporándome a su gremio, voy viviendo con indecible satisfacción tal juicio, sana crítica e inteligencia en las respectivas facultades de que tratan, que juzgo contribuirán efectivamente a promover mucho los conocimientos útiles objeto del loable instituto de nuestra Academia de Filadelfia, y a igualarla, consiguientemente después de la renovación de sus trabajos a beneficio de la paz, con las más antiguas y célebres de su clase establecidas en Europa.

En medio de las continuas ocupaciones del gobierno del Consejo puesto de algunos años a esta parte a mi cargo, me hallará ese cuerpo y su ilustre Presidente pronto siempre a contribuir no sólo a su servicio y obsequio, sino también a sus tareas, no desaprovechando oportunidad de ayudarlas en cuanto lo permitan las circunstancias, el tiempo y [ilegible] me ocurran especies o noticias que crea propias para los fines de la Sociedad.

Acompaña a los libros que envía a vuestra excelencia nuestra Academia de la Historia el tomo primero del Diccionario Español Latino Arábigo, impreso aquí bajo mi dirección; a principio del cual puse un discurso sobre la utilidad del estudio de la lengua arábiga, especialmente para los españoles, considerando [ilegible] dedicar a su [ilegible] los ratos que me dejaban libres en la juventud los estudios y negocios de mi profesión. Quedo en remitir apenas salgan los tomos restantes para complemento de la obra, que están bajo la prensa.

La carta de vuestra excelencia y su nuevo don [sic] han renovado los afectos de gratitud a sus anteriores favores y la estimación y amistad que me profesa su recomendable persona; cuya vida pido a Nuestro señor guarde dilatados y felices años.

Madrid, 24 de mayo de 1787.

NOTES

Introduction

1. Benjamin Franklin, "The Autobiography," in *Benjamin Franklin: The Autobiography and Other Writings*, ed. L. Jesse Lemisch (New York: Signet Classic, 1961), 107.
2. Lemisch, ed., *Benjamin Franklin*, xiii; Gordon S. Wood, *The Americanization of Benjamin Franklin* (New York: Penguin Books, 2004), 7.
3. Lemisch, "Introduction," in *Benjamin Franklin*, x–xi.
4. See Celia López-Chávez, "Benjamin Franklin, España y la diplomacia de una armónica," *Espacio, Tiempo y Forma: Revista de la Faultad de Geografía e Historia* Serie IV, no. 13 (2000): 319–27. *Infante* is a title given to all the sons and some of the nephews of the king of Spain, except the heir apparent to the Crown. Don Gabriel was King Carlos III's third son. *Armónica* is the word used in the documents and is used here with its English spelling to differentiate it from the harmonica, which is played with the mouth.
5. The details of Franklin's mission and activities in France are given in any number of secondary sources. Some of the details of his work with the Spanish government can be found in Thomas E. Chávez, *Spain and the Independence of the United States: An Intrinsic Gift* (Albuquerque: University of New Mexico Press, 2002), 49–57, 61–63. Some of the original documentation, located in Spain, was used in this book.
6. Carlos III, as quoted in Joaquín Oltra and María Ángeles Pérez Samper, *El Conde de Aranda y los Estados Unidos* (Barcelona: Promociones y Publicaciones Universitarias, S. A., 1987), 60.
7. Vergennes, as quoted in Oltra and Pérez Samper, *El Conde de Aranda*, 96.
8. "Congressional Appointment," signed by John Hancock, president of the Congress, 2 January 1777, Archivo Histórico Nacional (hereafter AHN,) Estado, legajo 3884, exp. 3, folio 21 (attachment to Document no. 23 herein).

9. Franklin to Aranda, Paris, 1 April 1777, AHN, Estado, legajo 3884, no. 23; see Document no. 23 herein.

10. Expedientes Personales de Correspondientes Extranjeros (Actas), 9 July 1784, Real Academia de la Historia, Madrid (Document no. 59 herein). While still in France, Franklin sent some of his published works to the Real Academia before his admission into the organization. Don Pedro Rodríguez Campomanes y Pérez Sorriba, the Count of Campomanes, proposed his membership.

11. For the best review of a Benjamin Franklin who is different in important ways from the Franklin of our inherited common understanding, see Wood, *Americanization*.

12. Quoted in Lemisch, *Autobiography and Other Writings*, 279.

13. For example, see Sophus A. Reinert, "The Way to Wealth around the World: Benjamin Franklin and the Globalization of American Capitalism," *American Historical Review* 120 (February 2015): 61–97.

14. See Wood, *Americanization*, 231–32.

15. For a recent study, see Larrie D. Ferreiro, *Brothers in Arms: American Independence and the Men of France and Spain Who Saved It* (New York: Alfred A. Knopf, 2016).

16. Carlos Cólogan Soriano, *Tenerife Wine: Historias del Comercio de Vino. Siglo XVIII (1760–1797)* (Islas Canarias, Autor-Editor de Obra Prop., 2017); and Cólogan Soriano, *Un Corsario al Servicio de Benjamin Franklin* (Islas Canarias; Gaviño de Franchy Editores, 2013).

17. Roberto Pérez, "El legado aragonés de la Duquesa de Alba," and "Los títulos aragoneses de la Casa de Alba pasan al segundo hijo de Cayetana; Alfonso Martínez de Irujo concentra los títulos de duque de Hijar, duque de Aliaga y conde de Aranda," *ABC Aragón*, 21 November 2014.

18. Chávez, *Spain and the Independence of the United States*.

19. See, for example, H. W. Brands, *The First American: The Life and Times of Benjamin Franklin* (New York: Doubleday, 2000); Walter Isaacson, *Benjamin Franklin: An American Life* (New York: Simon & Schuster, 2003), 344–46, 408–09; Stacy Schiff, *A Great Improvisation: Franklin, France and the Birth of America* (New York: Henry Holt, 2005); and Wood, *Americanization*. Brands, *First American*, 521, mentions Franklin's letter to the Infante Don Gabriel. See document no. 11 herein. A more recent exception is Ferreiro, *Brothers in Arms*.

20. For example, Leonard W. Labaree, William B. Willcox, et al., eds., *The Papers of Benjamin Franklin*, 24 vols. (New Haven, CT: Yale

University Press, 1959); William Chauncy, ed., *The Journals of the Continental Congress*, 2 vols. (Washington, DC: US Government Printing Office, 1904); Paul H. Smith, ed., *Letters of Delegates to Congress, 1774–1789* (Washington, DC: Library of Congress, 1976–91); and Francis Wharton, ed., *The Revolutionary Diplomatic Correspondence of the United States*, 6 vols. (Washington, DC: US Government Printing Offices, 1889).

21. Hayward Keniston, "Carta de nuestra correspondiente en Michigan," and Ambassador John Davis Lodge, notes for his speech, "Expedientes personales de correspondientes extranjeros," (legajo marked) "B. Franklin," Real Academia de la Historia.

22. Pantaleón Aznar, *Vida del Dr. Franklin sacado de documentos auténticos* (Madrid: 1798), "… ofrezco la vida de Benjamin Franklin, quien no se debe olvidar entre los genios en Europa que se han distinguido en este siglo en Europa."

23. Juan Francisco Yela Utrilla, *España ante la independencia de los Estados Unidos* (1925; repr., Madrid: Colegio Universitario de Ediciones Istmo, 1988). For example, see 2:26–39, 2:94–95.

24. Labaree and Willcox, *Papers*.

25. *Documentos relativos a la independencia de Norteamérica existente en archivos españoles*, 11 vols. (Madrid: Ministerio de Asuntos Exteriores, 1977–85).

26. Oltra and Pérez Samper, *El Conde de Aranda*.

27. Reyes Calderón Cuadrado, *Empresarios españoles en el proceso de independencia norteamericana: La casa Gardoqui e hijos de Bilbao* (Madrid: Unión Editorial, S. A., 2004); Vicente Rivas, *Don Juan de Miralles y la independencia de los Estados Unidos* (Valencia: Generalitat Valenciana, 2003).

28. *Enciclopedia general ilustrada del País Vasco* (San Sebastián, Spain: Editorial Aunamendi, 1983), 15:296–97.

29. Carmen de Reparaz, *Yo Solo: Bernardo de Gálvez y la toma de Panzacola en 1781* (Barcelona: Ediciones del Serbal, S.A., 1986), 232. Herein that document is listed as John Hancock, "Congresional Commission," attachment to document no. 23.

30. See López-Chávez, "Benjamín Franklin, España"; and Juan Martínez Cuesta, "Relaciones culturales entre la corte de Carlos III y los Estados Unidos de América," in *Madrid en el contexto de lo hispano desde la época de los descubrimientos* (Madrid: Universidad Complutense de Madrid, Departamento de Historia del Arte, 1994), 2:1063–70.

31. Aranda to the Marqués de Grimaldi, Paris, 13 January 1777, AHN, Estado, legajo 3884, exp. 2, folio 4, no. 938. Document no. 19 herein.

32. Labaree and Willcox, *Papers*, 23:177.

Chapter 1

1. Francisco Escarano was the Spanish secretary and chargé d'affaires in the Spanish embassy in London, who was sent to England to mediate the Anglo–French dispute and negotiate a peace before France and then Spain declared war.

2. Victor Amédée Philippe Ferrero Fieschi, Prince of Masserano (1713–77), was the Spanish ambassador to England. At the time, he was in Madrid recuperating from the gout. The title *Prince of Masserano* refers to his connection to the Principality of Masserano, near Biella, Italy, which was made a princedom in 1598 by Pope Clemens VIII. The House of Ferrero Fieschi ruled the principality until 20 March 1767, when it came under the rule of the House of Savoy. The Spanish ambassador apparently kept the title after he and his family lost its authority over the principality. He died on 26 October 1777 while returning to Spain from London.

3. This is a note documenting that the government's reply was sent from El Pardo on the given date. El Pardo was a royal hunting preserve about ten miles north of Madrid. In the sixteenth century, King Felipe II built a royal palace in the town that Carlos III refurbished and used as a royal retreat a century and a half later.

4. Don Luis de Ventades was a Basque merchant, Spanish bureaucrat, and a relative of Miguel de Ventades. See note 8.

5. Johannes (or John) Pohlman, who was a noted fabricator of pianos in London between 1768 and 1790.

6. The eleventh Duke of Villahermosa, Juan Pablo de Aragón-Azlor (1730–91), inherited the title from his uncle, José Claudio de Aragón, in 1761. His uncle died single and without children. Juan Pablo served as an attaché to the Spanish embassy in Paris until 1772, when he traveled to London and then Madrid. He was appointed ambassador to Turin from 1779 to 1783. While in Turin he married the young María Manuela Pignatelli, who was born around 1765; she was the daughter of Spain's ambassador to France, whom Juan Pablo worked under. His father-in-law was the Count of Fuentes, Joaquín Atanasio Pignatelli de Aragón y Moncayo. Escarano

either is in error or making an assumption in this letter, for there was no Duchess of Villahermosa in 1774. Apparently, the Count of Fuentes's young daughter was betrothed to Juan Carlos, but the wedding would not take place for at least another five to six years.

7. A guinea is British money equal in value to one pound, one shilling or twenty-one shillings.

8. Miguel de Ventades, a relative of Luis de Ventades and a Basque merchant and minor diplomatic official who spent most of his career as a consul in London. He transferred to Paris when Spain declared war in 1779.

9. Don Gabriel de Borbon, third son of the Spanish king Carlos III.

10. Marianne Davis, a friend of Franklin and a famous musician, who was giving concerts on the glass armonica throughout Europe, many times accompanied by her sister Cecilia, who sang. See Celia López-Chávez, "Benjamin Franklin y la realeza española: Una conexión musical," in *Norteamérica a finales del siglo XVIII: España y los Estados Unidos*, Eduardo Garrigues López-Chicheri, coordinator (Madrid: Marcial Pons, 2008), 131.

11. Davis's claim that her father was the instrument's inventor is not corroborated in the known literature about the glass armonica. See López-Chávez, "Benjamin Franklin y la realeza española," 129, 130, 134n38.

12. Frederick, Lord North, the chief minister of Great Britain from 1770 to 1782.

13. Henry Fox, 1st Baron Holland (1718–74), held the posts of secretary of war, secretary of the Southern Department, and paymaster of the forces. He was considered to be a future prime minister and became a rival of William Pitt. He never became prime minister. At the time of this letter he was retired and would die seven months later, on 1 July 1774.

14. The official response to this letter came from Madrid.

15. For Miguel de Ventades, see note 8.

16. The correct spelling is probably *Constate* or *Costante*, a noble family's name in the region of Languedoc, France.

17. Prince William Henry (1743–1805), grandson of King George II and the younger brother of King George III, who made him the Duke of Gloucester and Edinburgh and Earl of Connaught in November 1764. His secret marriage to Maria Walpole, the illegitimate granddaughter of Sir Robert Walpole, estranged him from his older brother.

18. Henry, the younger brother of the Duke of Gloucester and of King George III.

19. Joaquín Atanasio Pignatelli de Aragón y Moncayo, father of the future Duchess of Villahermosa, ally of the Duke of Aranda, who replaced him as ambassador to France in 1773. See note 37.

20. William Murray, 1st Earl of Mansfield, chief lord justice, and member of the Parliament. He would come to be considered the most powerful British jurist of the century.

21. Simon Harcourt, 1st Earl Harcourt (1714–77), the British ambassador to Paris from 1768 until 1772, when he was promoted to general. He accepted the appointment of lord lieutenant of Ireland in October.

22. This cannot be the poet Pushkin because he was born in 1799.

23. Silesia is a region that is now in southwest Poland. In the eighteenth century, it was a rich area with a flourishing mining and textile industry. Prussia took it from the Austrian Hapsburgs in 1745.

24. Jerónimo Gioeni y Valguarnera, who died in 1774, the year of this letter.

25. At this place in the document the transition between paragraphs is not logical. The following paragraph seems to refer to the earlier paragraph concerning Masserano's back pay.

26. Thomas Robinson, 2nd Lord Grantham, was Great Britain's ambassador to Spain from 1771 until Spain declared war in 1779. He served as president of Britain's Board of Trade from 1780 into 1782, and from July 1782 to April 1783 he was foreign secretary.

27. Bernardo del Campo was a Spanish operative who worked under Spain's secretaries of state, Grimaldi and Floridablanca.

28. Giambatista Beccaria, an Italian scientist and priest with whom Franklin corresponded while perfecting the glass armonica. See López-Chávez, "Benjamin Franklin y la realeza española," 131, 135.

29. Both Bilbao and San Sebastián are on the northern coast of Spain, which means they are the Spanish ports closest to England.

30. These appear to be some kind of a foreign guide in booklet form.

31. Jean Juste Ferdinand Joseph de Croy, Prince of Croy-Havré and Count of Priego, who was born in Brussels in 1716 and died in Córdoba in 1790. Carlos III of Spain made him a knight of the Spanish Fleece.

32. George Hervey, 2nd Earl of Bristol (1721–75), the British ambassador to Madrid from 1758 until 1761. He died in March 1775.

33. William Henry Nassau, 4th Earl of Rochford (1717–81), a valued advisor of foreign affairs for King George III. He had been ambassador to France as well as northern secretary. He became southern secretary in

December 1770. After his retirement in November 1775, he became the king's secret emissary to the French, trying to stop them from giving secret aid to the Americans.

34. Count of Sernafis, or Searnafis, the ambassador of Sardinia. After a short illness, he died in Paris as ambassador to France on 24 April 1788.

35. Pablo Jerónimo Grimaldi y Pallavicini, the Marquis of Grimaldi (ca. 1720–89). Born in Genoa, Italy, and the former Spanish ambassador in Paris from 1761 to 1763, he was the Spanish minister of state for foreign affairs from 1763 until 1776, when he was made ambassador to Rome until 1785. He was replaced as a minister of state by José Monino, the Count of Floridablanca.

36. Frederick II (Frederick the Great, 1712–86), the king of Prussia from 1772 until his death.

37. "Poniatuski" in the original document.

38. This might be in reference to Joachim Alexander Kasimir, born in Warsaw in 1764.

39. "Change-Alley" in the original, which can be interpreted as "change of devises."

40. Adrien-Louis de Bonnières, Count of Guines (1735–1806), was a French army general and diplomat. He was a favorite of Queen Marie Antoinette as well as France's ambassador to the Court of St. James (Great Britain) from 1770 to 1776, when he returned to France after a scandalous case involving the misuse of embassy funds. He was acquitted and remained in favor in France.

41. The original Spanish is *Jefe*, which translates to "boss," an odd word for the seventeenth century. This has raised a question, for Escarano's boss is Masserano, to whom he is writing. The other possibility is that Escarano is referring to Masserano's boss, who would be the secretary of state, the Count of Grimaldi. Nevertheless, the use of the term *boss* is very odd for its informality in the very formal world of the eighteenth century.

42. Francis Seymour-Conway (1718–94), 1st Viscount Beauchamp and 1st Earl of Hertford. He had been Great Britain's ambassador to France and viceroy of Ireland.

43. In Spanish, a *sinecura* applies to an employee or worker who has little or no work.

44. Thomas Osborne, 4th Duke of Leeds, a lawyer and former justice, was deputy lieutenant of West Riding, County Yorkshire, which included the city of York.

45. The heir apparent to the Duke of Leeds was styled the Marquis of Carmarthen. Osborne's only surviving son, Francis, inherited the title in 1789.

46. "Fluxión": *Flujo* in Spanish, is a pathological accumulation of liquids in an organism. In this case the eyes.

47. Or "visitor's guide."

48. This probably refers to a communication or letter.

49. "[A]qua de Celse" in the original document. This is confusing as celse, or seltzer water, supposedly had not been invented at this time. As will be noted, quinine had been discovered in Peru. The Natives there mixed it with sweetened water. This might be in reference to the development of quinine in liquid form in Europe.

50. This might be in reference to Alured Clarke, who Franklin sarcastically called "general" when in reality he was a "major," at the time in which this letter was written. Three years later he was sent to America, where he was put in command of the British forces until the end of the war.

51. Words in italics appear in French language in the original document.

52. This could refer to a style of wig in the eighteenth century that looked like something "wooded," or it could refer to a type of wig whose manufacturer had the surname Foresta or Forestá. This is the surname of a family of Italian origin that settled in France in the sixteenth century; during the eighteenth century the surname still existed among families based in the south of France.

53. The Count of Searnafis had received his credentials as ambassador of Sardinia in London in the year 1773.

54. Joaquín López de Zúñiga y Castro, the 12th Duke of Bexar, or Bejar, was in charge of the infante's education and his mentor. The Duke of Bexar died on 10 October 1777.

55. "Jefe" in the original. See footnote 41.

56. The words in italics are in French in the original Spanish version.

57. Henry Howard, 12th Earl of Suffolk, Great Britain's Secretary of State for the North Department. He died on 7 March 1779. The title passed posthumously to his son, who was born on 8 August of the same year. His son died two days later on 10 August.

58. "Vagaries of the winds": in Spanish is *ventadas*, which refers to the difficulties of navigation. However, in letter dated 18 March 1774,

Escarano makes reference to Luis de Ventades, who was going to pay the transportation fee to Bilbao or his relative Miguel de Ventades, at the time a Spanish consul in London. It is a mystery whether the word *ventadas* in the context of this letter is in reference to the winds or to "Ventades" the person(s).

59. This is in reference to Harcourt's proposals, which are left unsaid in this letter.

60. For a prolonged period Haslang was sent from Bavaria to London. His son became the Prime Minister of Bavaria.

61. *Bill* in the original. It should be *proyecto de ley* in Spanish.

62. Charles Pratt, Primer Count Camden (1714–94): English lawyer, judge, and politician who sided with Pitt the Elder with respect to the independence of the thirteen British colonies.

63. The use of the word *interested* here could mean that they were carrying this amount of money or they were pursuing business that was profit-seeking for the amount mentioned in the document.

64. David Murray, 2nd Count of Mansfield, Viscount Stormont, was the British ambassador to France during the first years of the war. He was transferred to secretary of state for the Northern Department in Great Britain. Franklin used his title (Stormont) in reference to lies or falsehoods. Over time *Stormont* became a euphemism for a lie. Aranda constantly incorrectly wrote Stormont with a *d* as in "Stormond."

65. Willliam Butler XVIth Count of Ormonde and IXth Count of Ossory, who died in 1783. "License" in the sense of "authorization."

66. This and the following letter were copied by the same person. They have the same incorrect or badly scribbled date that appears to be 1779 but in reality is 1775. The two letters are numbered consecutively and belong together.

67. This refers to a French naval port and base on the Mediterranean coast.

68. *Dey* is the title of the ruler of the Regency of Algeria.

69. This refers to a French nobleman.

70. This is a major port on the northern coast of France. It is the French town closest to England, which is twenty-one miles across the English Channel.

71. The Spanish is *A la buelta*, which usually means *on the reverse side of the same page*. In this case, it refers to Document 12, which belongs with this one.

72. A copy of this letter, unsigned, is in legajo 7016-53, no. 470, Estado, AGS.

73. Henry Howard, the 12th Earl of Suffolk, Great Britain's secretary of state for the Northern Department, died on 7 March 1779. The title passed posthumously to his son, who was born on 8 August of the same year. The son died two days later, on 10 August.

74. Melilla, as it is spelled in Spanish, is a Mediterranean port on the north coast of Africa to the east of Ceuta and opposite Spain.

75. Written as *Bill* in the original.

76. A copy of this document was published in Leonard W. Labaree, William B. Willcox, et al., eds., *The Papers of Benjamin Franklin*, 24 vols. (New Haven, CT: Yale University Press, 1959), 22:298–99. The published document is a letterpress copy held in the Library of Congress. The editors note that a second copy, in the Yale University Library, has some minor differences. What is published here is the original letter, and the original spelling is maintained.

77. Cayo Salustio Crispo, *La conjuración de Catilina y la guerra de Jugurta* (1772). Salust was a Roman writer, and Don Gabriel translated *La conjuración* into Spanish. Commonly known as Salustio (86–34 BC), he was one of the most important Roman historians of the first century BC. His original work was never published but survived the years in complete form. The English title is *The Conspiracy of Catiline and the War of Jugurtha*. Franklin received a copy of the prince's translation as a personal gift. The prince had the book printed in limited edition and never sold it, but gave it to friends and colleagues. See Martínez Cuesta, Juan. "Relaciones culturales entre la Corte de Carlos III y los Estados Unidos de América," in *Madrid en el contexto de lo hispano desde la época de los descubrimientos* (Madrid: Universidad Compultense, Departamento de Historia de Arte, 1994), 2:1067. Franklin received the book in Philadelphia in the middle of August. He described it as "beautifully and magnificently printed." Typographically superior to the best printing in Paris, the volume is now housed in the Beinecke Library of the Yale University Library.

78. General Thomas Gage, commander of all the British forces in North America, had moved to Boston from New York.

79. This refers to the 10th of the previous month.

80. The two successful American commanders were Ethan Allen and Benedict Arnold. Masserano has confused the information, for he neglects to mention the latter while using the two names of the former, changing "Ethan" to "Easton," to indicate two people. Fort Ticonderoga and its garrison of forty-eight men was captured on 10 May 1775.

81. Text is underlined in the original.

82. Under the command of Henry Knox, the cannons were transported overland through forests and snow to reinforce the rebel siege of British-occupied Boston. The existence of additional armaments was one reason the British vacated the town on 17 March 1776 under Sir William Howe, who succeeded Gage.

83. Text is underlined in the original. "Skenesborough" is probably Kingsborough.

84. The ships' names are underlined in the original.

85. Lord Dartmouth is Lord North's stepbrother, with whom he was very close.

86. The British government appointed Franklin postmaster of all the colonies. When Franklin's actions and criticisms contrary to the British government became more pronounced, he was removed from the position. However, after his return to America, the Continental Congress appointed Franklin Postmaster General.

Chapter 2

1. Published in Spanish in Juan Francisco Yela Utrilla, *España ante la independencia de los Estados Unidos* (1925; repr., Madrid: Colegio Universitario de Ediciones Istmo, 1988), 562–64.

2. The Château de Marly, also known as *Marly-le-Roi*, a small royal residence 11 1/2 miles west of Paris, became famous as the leisure residence of Louis XIV and was destroyed after the French Revolution.

3. Underlined in the original. Dr. Jacques Barbeu du Bourg (1709–79), a French scientist, writer, and translator who translated into French and published many of Franklin's works, including Franklin's testimony before the British House of Commons in 1766. He worked as a secret agent for the colonies. Aranda interviewed him about Franklin. See Joaquín Oltra and María Ángeles Pérez Samper, *El Conde de Aranda y los Estados Unidos* (Barcelona: Promociones y Publicaciones Universitarias, S.A., 1987), 137–38. As with "Devergennes," Aranda condenses du Bourg into one name, "DuBourg," which has been retained in this translation. Various historians have conveyed his name as DuBourg, Dubourg, du Bourg. In English the majority seem to agree with Aranda's simplified "DuBourg." See, for example, H. W. Brands, *The First American: The Life and Times of Benjamin Franklin* (New York: Doubleday, 2000); and Carl Van Doren's Pulitzer Prize-winning 1941 edition, *Benjamin Franklin* (New York: Garden City Publishing, 1941, copyright 1938 by Carl Van Doren).

4. Actually, he traveled with two boys, his grandsons William Temple Franklin, who was around seventeen years old, and Benjamin Franklin Bache, who had just turned seven.

5. These are mercenary troops from the German state of Hesse-Kassel recruited by Great Britain.

6. Aranda consistently spelled the name "Devergennes" instead of the correct "de Vergennes." The Count of Vergennes was the French foreign minister, with whom Franklin and other diplomats dealt.

7. Jean-Frédéric Phelypeaux, Count of Maurepas (1701–81), the elderly, essentially French minister of state (1774–81). He lacked interest and experience in foreign affairs and thus protected de Vergennes while allowing him great independence in foreign affairs.

8. Catherine II, czarina of Russia, also known as Catherine the Great, who ruled from 1762 to 1796.

9. This refers to Joseph II of Austria, Holy Roman Emperor, who in 1777 traveled incognito to France, where he visited his sister Marie Antoinette, the queen of France. He also visited Vergennes with the hope of getting aid for his plan to reclaim Bavaria. The emperor used the Count of Fulkenstein as a pseudonym. In London, Masserano heard a slightly different name but identified the correct person.

10. David Murray, 2nd Count of Mansfield, Viscount Stormont, the British ambassador to France during the first years of the war. He became the secretary of state for the northern department of Great Britain. Franklin used his title of Stormont to refer to a lie or falsehood. In time, a *lie* was commonly called a *Stormont*. Aranda constantly incorrectly wrote Stormont with a *d*, as in *Stormond*.

11. This refers to the House of Commons, or Lower Chamber, of the British Parliament.

12. This refers to both the House of Lords, and Upper Chamber, of the British Parliament.

13. Misspelling of *Ticonderoga*.

14. "Has caused a decrease in the funds": the original in Spanish says "ha causado una baja en los fondos." We cannot do more than speculate here regarding the meaning of this phrase. It could mean that the arrival (and presence) of Franklin in France was causing expenses that decreased the funds that the country or the court had set aside for Colonial aid.

15. *Paquebote*: Refers to a packet or mail boat.

16. John Murray, Lord Dunmore, was the last British governor of Virginia. He was forced to leave the colony after trying to resist the rebellion.

He became unpopular and is known for his November 1775 proclamation that offered freedom to any slave who left his master to ally and fight with the British. Dunmore was forced to leave Virginia in 1776. He returned to England, where he took a seat in the House of Lords.

17. This and a subsequent letter (no. 20) with the same date were written after Grimaldi received his appointment to Rome. However, Grimaldi continued in Madrid until his successor, José Monino, the Count of Floridablanca, could physically replace him.

18. This letter was published in Spanish in 1925 by Spanish historian Yela Utrilla, *España*, 582–91.

19. Correctly written in Spanish, "el Conde de Vergennes," which translates to "the Count of Vergennes." For some reason Aranda always wrote "Devergennes" as one word.

20. Franklin's ship, *Reprisal*, was diverted from its destination at Nantes and had to put in at Quiberon Bay, situated on a French Peninsula of that name in the region of Brittany. Franklin, with his grandsons, rented a fishing boat that took them to Avray; he then took a coach to Nantes, where he arrived on 7 December. He left for Paris eight days later, stopped over in Versailles on the 20th, and entered the French capitol the next day. Thomas E. Chávez, *Spain and the Independence of the United States: An Intrinsic Gift* (Albuquerque: University of New Mexico Press, 2002), 53.

21. Refers to María Francisca I, the queen of Portugal and niece of Carlos III. She was the daughter of his sister.

22. The French *livres* were the monetary medium of exchange between 1701 and 1795, when the franc replaced it. Various livres existed, such as the *tournois*, minted in Tours, or the *parisi*, minted in Paris. The most common and accepted were the *livres tournois*.

23. Refers to Carlos III, the king of Spain.

24. Silas Deane, who along with Arthur Lee and Franklin formed the Committee of Secret Correspondence in France. Their charge was to negotiate support and alliances with the European countries.

25. Refers to Conrad Alexandre Gerard, a senior foreign minister official, who was sent to the rebelling colonies as France's diplomatic representative. Spain, at the time maintaining strict neutrality, used him to convey its positions to the Continental Congress.

26. The first commissioner in the French bureaucracy is the right-hand man to the secretary of state.

27. Pierre-Augustin Caron de Beaumarchais was a French writer who worked with Arthur Lee before the American Commission was formed. In

1766, he was named to run the fictitious company of Roderique (Rodríquez) Hortalez et Cie, which funneled munitions and supplies to the colonies. Franklin became suspicious of him and kept him at a distance.

28. Underlined in the original.

29. A, B, and C are attachments to this document. They are translated and included herein.

30. Refers to Louis XVI, the king of France.

31. This is Carlos III, the king of Spain.

32. *C* is underlined in the original.

33. This is in reference to the flag of a ship that indicates its country of origin. In this case the "United Colonies of America," which had declared their independence.

34. This refers to wagons and weapons pulled by horses, mules, or oxen.

35. This appears to be Aranda's convoluted way of expressing his belief that the Irish Catholics would side with Catholic Spain if they did not feel under siege from the latter.

36. The Algarve is the southern coast of Portugal.

37. Refers to the English Channel.

38. This sentence is written in French in the original.

39. Written in French and underlined in the original.

40. Written in French and underlined in the original.

41. Mahón is a city on the Mediterranean island of Menorca, held at the time by Great Britain.

42. In Spanish, "primera abertura" indicates the first written document of the colonies' intentions presented by Franklin.

43. Yela Utrilla published this document in Spanish translation (*España*, 578); Yale published it in English (Labaree and Willcox, *Papers*, 23:89–90). Yale notes that a draft exists in Harvard Library.

44. The attachment has written at the top "Traduido del Yngle," or translated from the English. Whoever did the English to Spanish translation was probably French as indicated by some of the expressions that were used.

45. Published in Spanish by Yela Utrilla, *España*, 591–600; and in Spanish and in an abbreviated form in English by Yale (Leonard Labaree and William B. Wilcox et al., eds. *The Papers of Benjamin Franklin*, 24 vols. [New Haven: Yale University Press, 1959] 23:173–80). Yale appears to have copied the Yela Utrilla edition (see the Introduction to this book).

46. Refers to Saint Petersburg, Russia. Francisco Antonio de Lacy, the Count of Lacy, was a native of Ireland who distinguished himself in the service of Spain in military campaigns in Italy and Portugal. He was

an enlightened man who was appointed Spanish ambassador to Sweden and Russia, and after the outbreak of war participated in the siege of Gibraltar. His relationship to the more famous Peter Lacy (1678–1751), who became a Russian imperial commander, and his son, Franz Moritz von Lacy (1725–1801), an Austrian field marshal and close advisor to Joseph II, the Holy Roman emperor, presents an intriguing question.

47. Franklin is probably referring to Roderique Hortalez et Cie, a dummy company set up in France and managed by Beaumarchais. Both France and Spain laundered money through the company in support of the rebelling colonies. Franklin's acknowledgment in this letter is coy, to say the least.

48. This could refer to the *Gaceta de Madrid*, a newspaper that published such news from around the world. *Gaceta* might be used here as a reference for whatever paper, including those of England and France.

49. An interesting point here is that the Continental Congress sent a cargo of American products to Cádiz in Spain and this cargo was sent to pay for the purchase of ships and arms in France but officially was to be received by an English company that would pay for the shipment.

50. In Spanish, it is "*Libra tornesa.*" This was the French pound minted in the city of Tours, France.

51. The expression is *giro de seis*, which means that a net gain of six million can be made. For example, if the Americans have two million pounds to purchase goods from merchants, because of the many merchants competing for the business, they can drive the prices down. In this way, two million pounds can be stretched into six million pounds.

52. This probably refers to meetings held before the signing of the treaty during which the delegates discuss the details that would become part of the treaty.

53. The Rock of Gibraltar is connected to Spain by land and sits in the narrow strait that connects the Atlantic Ocean and the Mediterranean Sea. It was captured by an Anglo–Dutch force in 1704 during the War of the Spanish Succession and ceded "in perpetuity" to England under the Treaty of Utrecht in 1713. Under protest from Spain, it remains a territory of Great Britain today. The British occupied Mahón on the Island of Menorca in the Balearic Islands in the Mediterranean Sea in 1708. England converted both enclaves into strategic naval bases where, additionally, massive contraband trade took place that harmed Spain's interest. Spain always considered the occupation of these possessions by Anglo–Dutch forces to be illegal and nothing more than usurpation, hence the "deserved forfeiture" of their

restoration to Spain. Spain subsequently forcibly occupied Menorca after it declared war on Great Britain in June 1779.

54. Dunkirk is a city and port on France's northern coast a little over six miles (ten kilometers) from the Belgium border. Because it became a base for privateers (pirates), France was forced to destroy and close the harbor, as stipulated in the Treaty of Utrecht in 1713. Louis XV started to restore it, but the English destroyed it during the Seven Years' War. Louis XVI planned to repair the harbor to its previous glory.

55. This is *fiebres tercianas*—malaria—in the original Spanish, or *paludismo* in Spanish. The general symptoms are three days of fever, headache, bone pain, and general weakness.

56. Quinine, made from the bark of trees growing at high altitude in Peru, was used in Spain long before US historians gave them credit for it. One historian claimed that quinine was not in use until 1820, when the French figured out how to extract the active ingredient from the bark. Obviously, this is wrong, for Spain was providing quinine to the American colonists during the War of Independence. Charles Lee, the second in command of the Continental Army, requested quinine as early as 1776. See Luis de Unzaga y Amezaga to José de Gálvez, 30 September 1776; and Bernardo de Gálvez to José de Gálvez, 12 May 1777, both in legajo 2596, Santo Domingo, AGI. In the second letter, Bernardo de Gálvez repeats his orders to supply the "British Americans [with] quinine," among other items. Also see Jack Weatherford, *Indian Givers: How the Indians of the Americas Transformed the World* (New York: Crown, 1988), 77–78. In the original document the Spanish word is *quina*; the *Real Academia de la Lengua Española* dictionary defines *quinina* (quinine) as the organic compound (alkaloid) of the *quina*, from the bark of the tree. Simply put, *quina* is the medicine, and *quinine* is the compound.

57. The Treaty of Paris, signed on 10 February 1763, which ended the Seven Years' War. Spain ceded Florida to Great Britain for the return of Manila and Havana. Great Britain kept Canada.

58. Appears as "Panzacola" in the original document.

59. This refers to the letter from Count of Aranda to Grimaldi: Paris. January 13, 1777. See Document 20.

60. This refers to Vergennes and his apparently secretive attitude.

61. Published in Spanish in Yela Utrilla, *España*, 622–23.

62. The words capitalized in this letter are as they appear in the original.

63. The original *document* lists a number 1 but no following numbers.

64. The British West Indies in the Caribbean Sea; it is significant that Jamaica is included. At the time, sugarcane was an important cash crop on the islands.

65. Published in English in Yela Utrilla, *España*, 578–79, with some differences. A partial Spanish translation is included in a footnote. Yale published the document in English; Labaree and Willcox, *Papers*, 23:108–109. Yale sites a copy in the American Philosophical Society and a draft in the United States National Archives. Yale notes that the American commissioners sent a copy of this document to the Spanish and French governments. They note that the Spanish document has the words *whereas a friendly and commercial connection*," while the French document has *whereas a trade with equal terms*. Of course, the French document names Franklin a commissioner to France. The French document is in Yale; Labaree and Willcox, *Papers* 22:634–35.

66. Not capitalized in the original.

67. Charles Thomson, or Thompson, the secretary to the Continental Congress, assigned Timothy Matlack to pen the document. Matlack was the scribe who wrote the Declaration of Independence. Like Hancock, Thompson's was one of the signatures on the first publication of the Constitution of the United States. He was a friend of Franklin's and a founding member of the American Philosophical Society. He could read and translate Greek and Latin.

68. The Count of Floridablanca replaced the Duke of Grimaldi as Spain's minister of state on 19 February 1777. Floridablanca remained in that position until 1788. Yela Utrilla published this letter in Spanish, *España*, 651–54.

69. The long, legal-size pages of this letter were folded in half. The blank backside addressed the letter "To His Excellency the Count of Floridablanca." The opposite corner has a note in minuscule writing that states, "Plenipotentiary and Proposals of Franklin."

70. The authors are aware that Aranda has called the Marquis of Grimaldi the *Duke of Grimaldi*. Grimaldi was a duke during a part of his life.

71. The American Commission, with Franklin's approval, decided to send Arthur Lee to Madrid, the capital of Spain, without Spain's approval. He was encountered in the town of Vitoria-Gasteiz, northeast of Burgos.

72. Refers to the Congressional Commission and Franklin to Aranda, 1 April 1777, Document no. 23 with its attachment herein.

73. Apparently Messarano sent Floridablanca the memorial in English with a Spanish translation. Both are kept together in AGS.

74. The capitalized words are kept as in the original document.

75. Bernardo de Gálvez was governor and commander of land forces in Spanish Louisiana from 1776 until 1783.

76. This is a version of a translation from English into Spanish that exists in the archive. The English version has not been located.

77. Oliver Pollock, a native of Ireland and a West Indies merchant based in Havana then New Orleans, who became a patriot fighting under an American flag alongside Bernardo de Gálvez. He became an agent for Virginia and subsequently the Continental Congress in securing Spanish aid through New Orleans.

78. Underlined in the original. *Gastos* translates to *expenses*. The Americans and possibly Lee somehow forgot or could not pronounce the actual name, which is Vitoria-Gasteiz. Lee left Paris on 7 February 1777. See Document no. 24, note 187, herein.

79. The Marquis of Grimaldi, at the time being replaced by the Count of Floridablanca, assigned the Basque banker and businessman Diego de Gardoqui to intercept Lee before he got to Madrid, causing a scandal and violating Spain's neutrality, which provided a cover for that country's secret aid. Gardoqui apparently met Lee at Burgos and escorted him to the town of Vitoria-Gasteiz, where a series of secret meetings with Grimaldi was held. Gardoqui translated. Lee learned that Spain had stockpiled supplies in Havana and New Orleans and that more aid would be shipped that winter through Gardoqui's company. He also learned that Spain would approach Holland about extending credit for the Colonial cause.

80. British General William Howe and his brother, Admiral Richard Howe, were given command of the British forces in the colonies and were authorized to end the war as soon as the colonists submitted.

81. Adjutant General Horatio Gates retired as an officer in the British army and joined the Colonial cause when the rebellion broke out. He took command of the American troops at Ticonderoga, where he avoided defeat in the first battle before British general John Burgoyne's advance, only to win an important victory at the second battle. At the time Sir Guy Carleton was the captain general and governor in chief of Quebec. He was not at Saratoga.

82. José I, the king of Portugal, died on 22 February 1777.

83. Sebastião José de Carvalho e Melo, the Marquis of Pombal, was the Portuguese minister of state and the strongman who actually ran the Portuguese government. He was anti-Spanish and pro-English. With José

I's death, he fell from power. Aranda adds that both the Portuguese king and his minister "disrespected" King Carlos III of Spain.

84. Queen María Francisca I ascended to the throne on the death of her father, King José I of Portugal, on 22 February 1777. Her mother was King Carlos III's sister, who helped negotiate a treaty with Spain that was signed on 11 October 1777. See Chávez, *Spain*, 64.

85. This refers to the king of France.

86. The quote is underlined in the original.

87. Refers to Antoine-Raymond-Gualbert-Gabriel de Sartine, the minister of the Navy of France.

88. In part based on Aranda's assertion that Great Britain could not afford to risk war with Spain because of their Colonial problems, Spain sent one of the largest fleets ever to travel to the Americas. Placed under the command of Don Pedro de Cevallos, the fleet sailed in November 1776 and, in 1777, successfully attacked Portuguese and British settlements down the Brazilian coast to the Río de la Plata. At the same time, another Spanish fleet sailed up the Tajo River and anchored in front of Lisbon to make a point with Pombal. See Chávez, *Spain*, 43.

89. Refers to Spain and France.

90. The Duke of Choiseul was Vergennes's predecessor as France's Minister of Foreign Affairs. They were rivals.

91. Annotation in Spanish, perhaps written by Spain's secretary of state.

92. William Pitt (the Elder), 1st Earl of Chatham, was a British statesman and politician, the father of the more famous William Pitt, who became Great Britain's prime minister. Lord Chatham supported the Colonial position during the run-up to the war.

93. This is Lord George Germain, 1st Viscount of Sackville. He was known as Lord Sackville until 1770, and as Lord George Germain from 1770 to 1782. He was a British soldier and politician who served as Secretary of State for America in the British cabinet during the war.

94. In Latin: "But in its time, no one dared to act."

95. Underlined in the original.

96. Underlined in the original.

97. Underlined in the original.

98. The word in Spanish is *fusiles*, which technically means *rifles*. *Escopeta* definitely translates to *musket*.

99. This line is in different handwriting and in Spanish in the original.

100. In Latin this means *resist the beginnings*, or *nip it in the bud*. Underlined in the original.

101. This note is in the original document at the top.

102. This is Thomas Thynne, 3rd Viscount of Weymouth, the British secretary of state of the Southern Department. He resigned in 1779.

103. This copy was sent by the Count of Vergennes to Franklin and Deane, Versailles, 16 July 1777. This note was written in the same handwriting, in French, as the main letter.

104. L'Orient, or Lorient, is a seaport in northwest France. It became a full-scale naval base in 1769, and by 1775 the port had become a center for privateers.

105. Lambert Wickes was a corsair officially sailing under the authority of the colonies. He was one of the most notorious and successful captains at capturing British ships. He was the captain of the *Reprisal*, which transported Franklin to France.

106. Water leaks or other types of damage, such as broken planks or the lack of sails, were used as an excuse by ship captains, who were forbidden to enter certain ports due to a declared war or for other reasons unless they were expressly authorized to do so by treaties. The damage served as an excuse to enter these ports for repairs and safety. In most cases, the need for repairs was a fabrication that was accepted by the port officials as a way of dealing in contraband. In the case of *La Représaille*, or *Reprisal*, it is clear that the ship did not have permission to enter the port but did so with the excuse of needing repairs.

107. The original document misspells his name as Stormond, with a *d*.

108. This could refer to Stormont considering the possibility of war, as a result of which the embassy in Paris would be closed and he would be withdrawn from France. In reality, Stormont was soon replaced and, most likely, surmised that his term was up.

109. Food, water, and repairs was a legal excuse for allowing warring ships into port but it also was a front commonly used by the American captains to get in port and offload their booty.

110. Dominique Caracciolo, Marquis of Villamaina, was born in Spain. He became a diplomat and politician for the Kingdom of Naples. He was ambassador to London (1764–71) and France (1771–81). He later became viceroy of Sicily.

111. The Malvinas Islands, also known as the *Falkland Islands*, are an archipelago in the southern Atlantic Ocean, three hundred miles off the Argentinian coast. The islands had been and would continue to be contested by Great Britain and Spain. In 1774 the British abandoned the islands,

leaving a plaque claiming them for George III. The Spanish Viceroyalty of the Río de la Plata (Argentina) was the only governmental entity in the islands until 1811, when the British returned.

112. Passy was an upscale suburb of Paris where Franklin lived, mostly as a lodger, in the home of Monsieur de Chaumont.

113. Yela Utrilla published this letter in its original English with a Spanish translation in a footnote (*España*, 682–87); the attached requests are listed as a separate document with a disjointed translation in Spanish in a footnote. Yela Utrilla dates the document September 1777. Yale published the document; Labaree and Willcox, *Papers*, 22:555–63.

114. The et ceteras are in the original. The odd form of capitalizing certain words, as written in the original document, has been retained in this rendition.

115. This is Rodolphe-Ferdinand Grand, the French banker for American funds. He lived in Paris. As the American commission's banker, he worked closely with Franklin. His wife, Marie, was a friend of both Franklin and, later, John Adams. Franklin and Grand became good friends and continued writing to each other after the war.

116. This is a notation on top of the main letter that was written in Floridablanca's office.

117. Some words are missing from the original document because of a fold. The phrase might also read: "I contrived that he not do it by assuring that I should send it in its original form to Madrid at the first opportunity."

118. This is a note written that refers to the main letter.

119. Here the writing is illegible. *Negocios* or *businesses* is a guess that makes sense.

120. See Document no. 33 herein.

121. This refers to the Marquis d'Ossun, the elderly French ambassador to the Spanish court, who would be promoted to the Council of State in the summer of 1778 and then quickly replaced.

122. Neither of these letters is included herein.

123. This refers to Diego María de Gardoqui Aniquibar, a successful heir to a prominent Bilbao banking and merchant family that traded with the colonies. He spoke English and accepted assignments from his government. He used his company and connections to help Spain send aid to the colonies as well as to clandestinely outfit American privateers. After the war he was appointed Spain's first ambassador to the United States.

124. The "fermiers generales," Les Fermiers généraux, or farmers-general, was a highly unpopular and corrupt customs, excise, and indirect tax operation in France. The collectors, known as *fermiers généraux*, enriched

themselves and married or bought themselves into the aristocracy. *Fermeirs* is in French in the original.

125. Underlined in the original.

126. *Surreptitiously* (in the original in Spanish *con voces simuladas*) is used in the sense of announcing that the letter was secretly received, something that was common to do with letters of high significance, sensibility, or importance.

127. Major General John Burgoyne was in command of the British forces in Canada. He devised the strategy to invade the colonies from Canada through Lake Champlain and Ticonderoga to the upper Hudson River Valley. His plan came to naught when he was met and defeated by the Colonial forces at Saratoga. The result of this battle is considered by many historians to be the turning point of the war.

128. Refers to *mother country*, which, in this case, is England.

129. Stephen Sayre was a member of the American community living in London at the time of the outbreak of the Revolutionary War. Accused by Lord Rochford, Sayre was arrested for high treason and then released. As a firm patriot to the Colonial cause, Sayre left England in the summer of 1777 to serve the rebelling colonies as a diplomatic agent. Lee returned from his failed negotiations with Frederick the Great. While in Berlin, a member of the British embassy broke into Lee's quarters and pilfered his papers. That act created a scandal. See note 46 herein.

130. This is probably Étienne-François, Marquis of Stainville, 1st Duke of Choiseul, the retired French Minister of Foreign Relations and Ambassador to Rome. He was very influential in the Treaty of Paris that ended the Seven Years' War.

131. This letter is a translation from English. In the translation process, the names were translated as well. The correct names are Robert Morris and William Smith. Morris was a merchant based in Philadelphia involved in legal as well as illegal businesses throughout Spanish America. He became an associate of Juan Miralles, Spain's observer in the colonies. Together they sent ships with merchandize to Cuba and later to Spain. He signed the Declaration of Independence and as a member of the Continental Congress was part of the Secret Committee of Correspondence that sent Franklin to Spain. From 1781 to 1784 he was Superintendent of Finance for the colonies and as such was in charge of the Colonial navy. An ally of Alexander Hamilton, he is credited with creating the Bank of North America after the war. It was the first bank in the United States.

132. This letter was translated along with "Committee for Commerce by the Congress to Bernardo de Gálvez, 12 June 1777," which is included as Document no. 26 herein.

133. The British, with a huge force of 267 ships and 18,000 troops, sailed out of New York on 22 July 1777 and occupied Philadelphia on 26 September after winning a bloody battle at Brandywine Creek on 11 September. Despite suffering heavy losses, under Washington the Continentals survived the battle intact. This British strategy also backfired, for this same force was supposed to meet Burgoyne pushing from the north. In part, their absence resulted in the Colonial victory at Saratoga. The Continental Congress fled to York, Pennsylvania. As a side note, soon thereafter, in November 1777, John Adams received an appointment to replace Silas Deane on the committee in France.

134. Oliver Pollock, a native of Ireland and American patriot, was a merchant in the Caribbean trade. He spoke Spanish, became an agent for Virginia, and with Bernardo de Gálvez arranged for Spain's covert aid to move through New Orleans. He also fought alongside Spanish troops against the British.

135. On 17 October 1777, the Continental forces under the command of Horatio Gates defeated a British attempt to move south from Canada down the valley of Lake Champlain to the Hudson River and separate New England from the rest of the country. This, the first major victory for the Americans, was a blow to British strategy.

136. This refers to San Lorenzo del Escorial, the royal palace and mausoleum that was built in the sixteenth century by King Felipe II and was the inspiration for Versailles, in France. El Escorial is approximately fifteen miles northwest of Madrid.

137. As usual, *de Vergennes* is misspelled throughout this letter as *Devergennes*.

138. Aranda is referring to Spain's neutrality, which allowed it to give clandestine aid to the colonies.

139. Miquelon and St. Pierre are two islands off the southern coast of Newfoundland at 47° N latitude, 56° 40' W longitude.

140. This refers to an agreement in which Great Britain would give up the colonies, which would not be beholden to Great Britain in any way.

141. The first of the three documents is a rough French translation of the English memorial, which is the second document. The French document was translated for the convenience of Spanish and French officials.

In it, words and whole paragraphs are crossed out and rewritten. The French translation is in legajo 4612-155, Estado, AGS. Because the original English memorial is reproduced in its entirety herein, the French is not included in translation here.

142. Yale (Labaree and Willcox, *Papers*, 25:184–87) published this document with a citation for Archives des Ministères des Affaires Étrangères and a draft with the date of 21 November.

143. The reader should note that anomalies of the time have not been edited out of the document. Some sentence structure, words apparently capitalized for emphasis, and the spelling of *favour* have been retained.

144. This is Attachment B, the next document in this book.

145. This was a printed formal document used to name and commission captains of ships in the Colonial navy. Franklin kept a file of this document to issue at his discretion. The printed form included blank spaces to be filled in with the names of the ships, owners, commanders, tonnage (size), number of cannons, and the size of the crew.

146. The hyphenated names and uppercase words are repeated here, as they are in the document.

147. Yela Utrilla published this document in English; *España*, 712–14.

148. The word *armadores*, or *shipbuilders*, is written in a different hand over a crossed-out word that begins with *c*.

149. In the original manuscript, this sentence continues with "in order that His Majesty continue [providing] his protection to the Americans." However, the line is crossed out.

150. Armand Marc, the Count de Montmorin Saint-Hérem, was thirty-two years old when he replaced the aging Marquis d'Ossun as France's ambassador to Spain in 1777.

151. Moravians were exiled Protestants from what is now the Czech Republic, a sect of which established itself in western North Carolina in 1752. Franklin had long-standing relations with the Moravian community. "Huston" is James Hutton, a representative of the Moravian Church and Franklin's friend, whom he met in London when Hutton was a leader of the Moravian community.

152. His actual name was James Hutton. The king thought that Hutton might prevail upon Franklin to agree to a peace without independence. Hutton probably knew better, yet tried and failed to convince him anyway. However, a more probable motive was Hutton's request that Franklin write a letter to the Colonial leaders asking them not to persecute the Moravian community, whose members were pacifists.

153. This is a draft, written by at least two people, that apparently was being prepared under the auspices of Floridablanca. Whether it was ever sent in this form is questionable. Subsequent research may turn up the final version.

154. Upon receiving Aranda's long diatribes expressing his sentiments regarding how Spain should react to the American colonies and his thoughts on war against Great Britain, the king of Spain, through Floridablanca, sent a list of sixteen questions to his major advisors. The following draft is a summary of the answers compiled by Floridablanca's office.

155. These are the laws that restrict foreign maritime trade between Great Britain and its colonies; they were one of the reasons the colonies rebelled.

156. Refers to Dr. Edward Bancroft (1745–1821): a scientist, writer, and a double spy during the Revolution. He befriended Franklin, who paid him a secretary's salary to spy on the British. The British also paid him, and he supplied them with intelligence about the doings of the American commissioners. The Spanish and French, like the Americans, were unaware of his betrayal. Some historians believe that Franklin suspected him in 1777.

157. The British government, led by Lord Frederick North, was having doubts about the conflict in its American colonies. King George III's accession itself created instability at a time when troubles with the Americans were going from bad to worse. The king wanted to maintain what he had inherited but was a mediocre ruler. Great Britain's unstable government was marked by constant changes, changing attitudes toward the colonies, intrigue, squabbling ministers, and a time of transition. The king and Parliament hoped for a quick victory, but with Saratoga, they realized that their aspirations were misplaced. The Colonial sympathizers were vociferous and financially influential but were not part of the traditional Parliament.

158. This was a fleet of seven ships-of-the-line, eight frigates, four smaller ships, and many transports that carried fourteen infantry battalions and four cavalry squads. In all, the fleet had nine thousand men under the command of Don Pedro de Cevallos, who was sent to South America to eradicate illegal British and Portuguese smuggling. The fleet embarked from Cádiz on 13 November 1776 and was a brilliant success as it moved down the Brazilian coast, smashing British smuggling operations, and then took Uruguay from the Portuguese, thus securing the Río de la Plata and Buenos Aires. One justification for this gambit was Aranda's argument that Great Britain could not afford war because of their Colonial problems.

Another reason was that, at the time, Portugal was allied with Great Britain, and Spain wanted to eliminate Portugal as a player in any upcoming conflict.

159. Appears in bold in the original document.

160. A short, half-cutoff marginal note appears here on the left side. It is impossible to read.

161. There is no number 9, which is the missing point referred to in the opening statement of this document.

162. Genoveva Enríquez, "Guillermo Terry, armado en Cádiz y su navio "Soberbio': Guerra y comercio en la prima mitad del Siglo XVIII." PhD dissertation, University of Seville, 2023. Enríquez postulates that, the sentiment being raised here is based on the knowledge that Spain had been abandoned by France in the past, notably in the 1744 battle of Toulon while fighting against the English, and that France was as covetous of Spain's colonies as England.

163. That is, Spain cannot absolutely trust France, for there exists the possibility that France could turn on Spain during the war, ally with Great Britain, and go after Spain's possessions in the Americas.

164. Frederick the Great hated England and refused to allow mercenary troops slated for the colonies to pass through his territories.

165. Refers to Louis Jean Marie de Borbon (1725–93), the grandson of Louis XIV and his mistress, Madame de Montespan. He had a stressed relationship with Louis XV. Known as the *Duke of Penthièvre*, he was one of the richest men in France and lived far from Versailles. By this time he had devoted his life to dispensing charity, which saved him during the French Revolution.

166. This is an odd sentence because of the French word *parquet*, which literally translates to a type of wooden floor. The inclination is to see the word as *packet*, which would make more sense. However, the word is clear on the original document and is translated as is.

167. Baron Goltz was Frederick the Great's minister to France. At the time, Arthur Lee had returned from an unsuccessful trip to Berlin to secure Frederick's alliance. Frederick hated England but wisely avoided war with the more powerful country. Also, at the time, Frederick had become distracted with preventing a hostile takeover of Bavaria by the Austrian prince. Goltz sought France's assurances it would not interfere. See Paul Leland Haworth, "Frederick the Great and the American Revolution," *The American Historical Review* 9, no. 3 (April 1904): 466–71.

168. *Palatino* in Spanish, meaning *one who belongs to the palace*; in this case the *Palatine* refers to one who deserved the position or the crown.

169. Refers to Emmanuel Marie Louis de Noailles, a career diplomat. He was the French ambassador to London from 1776–83, after which he was assigned to Vienna.

170. Refers to William Pulteney, a member of Parliament who believed that with Franklin's help war could have been avoided and peace maintained.

171. Robert Petre, 9th Baron Petre, a member of the Catholic nobility who avoided politics.

172. Charles Howard, 11th Duke of Norfolk and Count of Surrey from 1777 to 1786. He was an active member of the conservative Tory Party. He supported King George III but opposed the war with the colonies. He served in the Parliament from 1780 to 1784.

173. George Germain, 1st Viscount of Sackvile, was the Secretary of State for America during the war of American Independence. He was severely criticized and blamed for the loss of the colonies.

174. Refers to John Stuart, 3rd Count of Bute, born in Scotland and a confidant of King George III, who named him Prime Minister (1762–63). He was forced to give up his position and because of his influence on the king and his efforts to circumvent the Constitution, he became immensely unpopular in both Great Britain and America.

175. *Rope* is used to mean *trap*.

176. This is the British government department responsible for collecting and distributing public funds. Also referred to as *His Majesty's Exchequer*.

177. *Abandoned the flags* is a literal translation, which means *surrendered*.

178. *AHPTF/AZC* is the acronym for *Archivo Histórical Provincial de Santa Cruz in Tenerife/Archivo Zárate-Cólogan*.

179. This letter was published in Carlos Cólogan Soriano, *Tenerife Wine: Historias del Comercio de Vinos, Siglo XVIII (1760–1797)*, 306–7. The translation presented here is slightly different.

180. Gustavus Conyngham or Cunningham, a native of Ireland, was an American corsair officially commissioned in the Colonial navy by Benjamin Franklin. His surname appears in the documents with both spellings.

181. That is, the Marquis of Tabalosos: Luis Eugenio Fernández de Alvarado y Perales, Sixth Count of Cartago and First Marquis of Tabalosos. He was governor and commanding officer of the Canary Islands from 1775

to 1779. A few months after leaving this post he died in Poitiers (France) from unknown causes.

182. Refers to the Marquis of Tabalosos.

183. *Piastra* may refer to a type of money that is particular to a region that in times past was a part of Italy.

184. Great Britain had prohibited its own countrymen from leasing ships to the American rebels, a prohibition it extended to countries allied with it.

185. Refers to Havre de Grâce.

186. This introductory document includes the note indicating receipt of the documents sent by the Count of Aranda, the synopsis of the same, and the response that has been given in Spain. Following the introductory note, the letters are ordered backwards, from the latest (letter dated 19 July 1779 from Aranda to Floridablanca,) to the earliest (copy of letter from Montgomery to Franklin, dated 26 June 1779.)

187. Spelled *Montgomeri* in the original introductory note.

188. This document has been translated from French into Spanish as well as into English. The original version, of which there is no available copy, most assuredly would have been in English.

189. Jonathon Williams was Franklin's grandnephew. He was stationed at Nantes to oversee shipments to America. The British ambassador to France claimed that this name was used as a cover in correspondence written by Nicholson. After the war, Williams returned to America with Franklin. He would become the first Superintendent of West Point (Van Doren, *Franklin*, 576, 601, and 727).

190. The word *insult* was a term used during this period to signify those attacks for which it was thought no reason or motive existed. The word could also be translated as *attack*.

191. Note the use here of the name *United States*.

192. It is not clear whether this is the name, because an ink stain on the manuscript covers the word.

193. In France, men occasionally had first names that seem feminine in Spanish, as in this case of *Marie Pierre Charles* or the name that appeared earlier, *Odiette*.

194. In this context this means *consulting lawyer* or *legal adviser*.

195. *Maître* in the original French. It is the title that is given in France to lawyers, attorneys, and notaries. It does not translate similarly in Spanish, so it has been translated literally, as *master*, although that is not correct. The title is tantamount to the Spanish *licenciado*, which would not be an exact translation, because in this case it involves sworn translators and

commercial agents. It can be said that *maître* referred to someone who in the exercise of his profession had an official title.

196. *Sol* (also called *sou*) refers to French currency.

197. Ostend, Belgium, was an important fortified town and port on the North Sea approximately 70 kilometers east of Dunkirk. In 1780 it came under the authority of Austrian Emperor Joseph II, who controlled its international trade, which was limited to the British and the Dutch.

198. As noted later in this document, the *Province of Flanders* was a brig, a merchant ship.

199. This is in reference to the Cólogan cargo taken to Philadelphia as a prize on board the *Golden Rose* that was captured by an American captain.

200. Refers to the large, enclosed body of water fronting Ostend. "Basin" in English.

201. This refers to a dry white wine produced in Tenerife.

202. This is a semi-independent British island located between England and Ireland

203. Refers to an island in the British Channel off the coast of Normandy.

204. Refers to Juan Cólogan Blanco (or White), who ran the company until his death in 1771. The war referred to here is the Seven Years' War (1756–63).

205. For more details on what happened regarding the mental breakdown, see document no. 51.

206. Francisco Cabarrús (1752–1810) was a native of France who moved to Spain in 1771 and became a Spanish subject. He was a financier and economist who became an advisor to the government of King Carlos III.

207. Hyder Ali Khan was a military leader and ruler of Mysore, in southern India, who resisted the British occupation. From 1762 until his death in 1782, he joined with France in fighting the British in India. He was succeeded by his son Tipu Sultan. With the help of a French armada, the wars ended with the defeat of the British.

208. Refers to François-Joseph Paul, Marquis de Grasse Tilly, the Count of Grasse, commonly known as *Admiral de Grasse*. An admiral in the French navy, he is most famous for his command of the French fleet that contributed to the allied victory at Yorktown.

209. Cape Finisterre is a major landfall that juts into the Atlantic Ocean on the route between northern Europe and the Mediterranean on the western coast of northern Spain.

210. Refers to the Spanish vice-consul in London.

211. Underlined in the original.

212. Refers to the letter that will be sent through the mail provided by Franklin.

213. Irun is a Spanish town and thoroughfare on the border with France. Due west of Bilbao, it served as a kind of distribution point where the letters that were sent regularly between France and Spain were accumulated and sent on.

214. Refers to the letter sent through the mail provided by Franklin.

215. Apparently, this refers to the French ambassador in Madrid, who would receive and pass on to Floridablanca the letter sent through the French mail service. Basically, Aranda is instructing Floridablanca to wait until he receives all three letters. Apparently, the two sent via Franklin and Cabarrús were to be gathered in Irun and forwarded together. They had different, more sensitive information for Floridablanca.

216. Mail between Spain and France could be sent through different venues, which points to the common practice of opening and intercepting letters, for there were spies everywhere. This was common practice in every country. Sometimes letters were sent knowing that they would be opened and therefore contained misleading information, which forces the historian to consider the letter's content with a jaundiced view, especially if nothing of importance is written; for there might be another, similar letter with the same date, or one close to it, in which the valuable and true information is conveyed.

217. This is a copy of an original written in a bound letter book. This letter was published in Spanish and appears in part in Cólogan Soriano, *Tenerife Wine*, 244. A larger portion of the letter is published here.

218. This could refer to Bernard T. See Cólogan Soriano, *Tenerife Wine*, 244. If so, this is most likely Bernard Texier, who, with his brother Jacques was a merchant based in Saint Eustatius in the Caribbean Sea who was involved in the slave trade. His commercial network was used to pass correspondence from the colonies to Spain, including secret correspondence sent by Juan de Miralles y Traham, who was Spain's "observer" in the colonies. See Light Townsend Cummins, *Spanish Observers and the American Revolution, 1775–1783* (Baton Rouge: Louisiana State University Press, 1991), 128.

219. Refers to a lawyer in Madrid who worked on behalf of the Cólogans; Cólogan Soriano, *Tenerife Wine*, 336–37.

220. The passage beginning with "Once you are in Paris" and ending with "obtain from there" has been paraphrased due to the bad syntax and low command of the English language. For transparency's sake, what follows

is taken directly from the document. "Once you was in Paris we believe it was very easy in you to have a letter from the Count of Aranda and the Viscount de la Herería, that cannot but have some friends in the Council of War, even from Doctor Franklin yet must have connections in the Spanish Court but nothing secure to you in the essential point we request from this we believe we forwarded about 20 letters of recommendation, and none could go from such high stationed people as you could easily obtain."

221. This line is drawn in the copy made in the letter book.

222. This letter is published in Spanish in Cólogan Soriano, *Tenerife Wine*, 344–46.

223. This document was published in a little more abbreviated form in English in Cólogan Soriano, *Tenerife Wine*, 346. The Cólogan family had offices in London and their preferred monetary exchange appeared to be shillings. That they did business with the rebelling colonies and Great Britain from their Spanish base in Tenerife is an interesting scenario in which international business tried not to be hindered by political rivalries.

224. Text presented here is a small part of a long, rambling letter dealing with various business matters.

225. The *Golden Rose* was a merchant ship captured by American privateers and taken to Philadelphia. The Cólogans claimed half the proceeds from the cargo's sale. They maintained that the ship was neutral and illegally taken.

226. Refers to available money.

227. This refers to the British government, where Juan Cólogan is based; he ran the family offices in London.

228. Refers to insurers. One result of wartime privateering was the steep increase in insurance coverage for merchant ships and cargoes.

229. *Vintage* refers to a type of wine, and *pipe* is a unit of measurement. In this case 125 wine gallons stored in wooden barrels. See Cólogan Soriano, *Tenrife Wine*, 29.

230. *Dauphin*, or *delfín*, is the title of the firstborn child of the king of France, in this case probably the daughter and not the son.

231. Aranda uses *Lusitania* for *Portuguese*.

232. Written in different handwriting on the backside of the fold is, "Paris, 6 July 1782, the count of Aranda (by my mail) Confidential." Because of its lack of formalities, this letter appears to be a personal note to Floridablanca.

233. Aranda uses the word *cameran*, which he misspelled and conjugated in the third person from the noun *cámara*, which means *a chamber, hall*, or *parlor*. Literally he wrote, "Today I parlayed with Jay and Franklin."

234. Aranda writes "Estados unidos," meaning states that are united, not the name of the new country.

235. Refers to a note directed to Aranda in reference to the copy of the Constitution that Franklin has sent.

236. William Carmichael, whose name is spelled phonetically here as *Caymargual*, was a native of Maryland and fluent in Spanish. The Continental Congress sent him to France as a secret agent and assistant to Silas Deane. He returned to America to represent Maryland in the Continental Congress in 1778–79. After Spain declared war in June 1779, he was sent to Spain as John Jay's secretary. He and Jay did not get along. In April 1782, he replaced Jay as US minister to Spain. He remained in the position until illness forced him to leave in 1794. Late in life George Washington appointed him to negotiate with Spain in what became known as *Pinckney's Treaty*.

Chapter 3

1. This is a section of the minutes taken on the above date by acting secretary Josef de Guevara Vasconcelos.

2. Directors Murillo (Censor), Huerta, Casiri, Sánchez, C. de la Roca, D. Sedano, Ortega, Capmani, Cerdá, Viera, Guevara de Vasconcelos, López, Jovellanos, Cuesta, Rivero, Duke of Almodóvar, Marquis of La Lapilla, Palomares, Ayala, Castelló, Miranda, P. Banqueri, Guevara (as secretary in place of the regular secretary, Mr. Flores).

3. Any reference to *Illustrious Person* or *Director* refers to the president of the Board of Directors of the Royal Academy of History, Don Pedro Rodríguez Campomanes y Pérez Sorriba, the Count of Campomanes. Campomanes was a Spanish statesman, economist, and writer with over thirty publications to his name. He studied law and ancient languages, including Arabic, and was a colleague of the Conde de Aranda. He was an adherent of the position that the state had supremacy over the Church, a position sometimes referred to as *Erastianism* after the Swiss physician and theologian Thomas Erastus.

4. Refers to the American Philosophical Society, founded by Franklin.

5. This sentence is crossed out on the draft but is legible. Mister Adams is John Adams, who in 1778, along with John Jay, replaced Silas Deane and Arthur Lee as the Colonial diplomatic representatives in Europe. He arrived via Spain in December 1779. See David McCullough, *John Adams* (New York: Simon & Schuster, 2001), 225–28.

6. Refers to Negapatam or Negapattinam. A seaport on the east coast of India that the British East India Company took from the Dutch in 1781.

7. As in many instances with these dispatches, there are expressions or sentences that are only understood in a context that the reader may not have. As a result, the meaning is very difficult to understand even in Spanish, much more to translate to English. The translators, in these cases, include in brackets possible words or concepts that can make sense, given the lack of details.

8. This refers to 44 cannons.

9. Possibly refers to Haechan.

10. Appears as *Copenhague* in the original.

11. The Gasset Family Private Archive contains the papers of Pedro Rodríguez, the Count of Campomanes.

12. On 16 January 1784, the Count of Campomanes was the first Spaniard to be invited to join the American Philosophical Society. Two years later, the Society began issuing certificates of membership. The certificate dated 20 January 1786 was enclosed with the letter that Franklin wrote on 4 December 1786. In 1784 Campomanes, as director of the Royal Academy of History, extended membership to Franklin. For reproductions of Franklin's letter to Campomanes and the Certificate, see Carolyn Kinder Carr et al., eds., *Legacy: Spain and the United States in the Age of Independence, 1763–1848* (Washington, DC: Smithsonian Institution, 2007), 182.

13. This archive is currently housed in the library of the *Fundación Universitaria Española* in Madrid (Spain). The Gasset family are descendants of the Count of Campomanes.

14. This list is not found in the archive of the Count of Campomanes.

Chapter 4

1. This is a note documenting that the government's reply was sent from El Pardo on the given date.

2. The official response to this letter came from Madrid.

3. At this place, the transition between paragraphs is not logical. The following passage seems to refer to the earlier paragraph concerning Masserano's back pay.

4. Written as "Becaria" in the original.

5. This is a tourist guide booklet.

6. In wealthier houses, this is the person in charge of mentoring and educating children.

7. Written "Poniatuski" in the original document.

8. *Sueldo*: Refers to currency; a coin with different values depending on time and country.

9. *Change-Alley*; this can be interpreted as "change of divises."

10. *Encerado* = This refers to waterproof fabric; in this case, probably covered in wax.

11. Contralor = this is a person who monitors accounts.

12. In Spanish, a *sinecure* applies to an employee who has little or no work.

13. *Fluxión: flujo*. Refers to a pathological accumulation of liquids in an organism. In this case, the eyes.

14. This probably refers to Constante or Costante, a noble family name from the region of Languedoc, France. The particular person referred to has not been identified.

15. Phrase is written in French in original.

16. This could refer to a style of wig worn in the eighteenth century that looked like something "wooded," or it could refer to a type of wig whose manufacturer had the surname Foresta or Forestá.

17. Phrase is written in French in original.

18. The original is *ventadas* or *ventades*. Aunque también podría ser una referencia a "Ventades" (Miguel de) cónsul. "Vagaries of the winds:" In Spanish *ventadas* refers to the difficulties of navigation. This also could refer to Luis or Miguel de Ventades.

19. Written "Bill" in the original document; in Spanish, the term is *proyecto de ley*.

20. This and the following letter were copied by the same person. They have the same scribbled date, which appears to be 1779, but in reality is 1775. The two letters are numbered consecutively and belong together.

21. *Dey* is the title of a Muslim ruler of Algieria.

22. The Spanish *a la vuelta* usually means *on the reverse side of the same page*. In this case, it refers to Document 12, which belongs with this one.

23. A copy of this letter without a signature is kept in legajo 7016-53, no. 470, Estado, AGS.

24. Written "Bill" in the original document.

25. As spelled in the original document.

26. Refers to the tenth of the previous month.

27. Phrase is underlined in the original document.

28. The ships' names are underlined in the original document.

29. Yela Utrilla published this document in Spanish in *España*, 562–64.

30. Name is underlined in the original document.

31. The verb *injerir* (with *j*, not with *g*): entrometerse, introducirse en una dependencia o negocio.

32. Aranda consistently spelled the name "Devergennes" instead of the correct "de Vergennes."

33. Refers to a one-way trip to Santo Domingo.

34. The correct spelling is *Ticonderoga*.

35. Published in Spanish in Yela Utrilla, *España*, 582–91.

36. In the text, the word appears to be *relativamente* in abbreviated form.

37. The correct word should be *habérseme*.

38. This refers to regular mail.

39. Aranda writes Spanish with common French expressions, such as saying *la Francia, la España, la Inglaterra*, which in French are *la France, l'Espagne, l'Angleterre*," probably because French was the most used language.

40. In the original text the word is *Commis*. This refers to the first commissioner of the French bureaucracy, who worked at the right hand of the secretary of state.

41. Letter is underlined in the original document.

42. A, B, and C are attachments to this document. C is underlined in the original document.

43. The expression *mediaron sus trabajos* probably is intended to mean *it was difficult* or *it was complicated*.

44. *Pabellón* refers to the flag on a ship that identifies its country. In this case the "United Colonies of America," which had declared its independence.

45. A *traslado* is a copy of a document.

46. This refers to wagons that transport cannons, which are pulled by horses, mules, or oxen.

47. *Exequible*: What can be done or carried out.

48. This refers to the English Channel.

49. In this case the word *sobrehueso* is used to refer to *work* or *troubling*.

50. Written in French in the original document.

51. Written in French and underlined in the original document.

52. Written in French and underlined in the original document.

53. The expression *desde luego* signifies *now* or *rapidly*.

54. *Desjarretada* = weakened and without force.

55. *Primera abertura* indicates the first written document of the colonies' intentions presented by Franklin.

56. This refers to Franklin.

57. Yela Utrilla published this document in Spanish translation in *España*, 578; Yale published it in English; Leonard Labaree, William B. Wilcox et al., eds. *The Papers of Benjamin Franklin*. 24 vols. New Haven, CT: Yale University Press, 1959) 23:89–90. Yale notes that a draft exists in the library at Harvard.

58. At the top of this attachment is written *traduido del Yngle*, meaning *translated from the English*. Whoever did the English-to-Spanish translation was probably French, as indicated by some of the expressions that were used.

59. *Bastimento* means *provision*.

60. This refers to Spanish translation.

61. *Terreneuve* is in French in the original document.

62. *Traslado*, which means *to copy from a document*.

63. This refers to another copy.

64. *Fiebres tercianas* refers to malaria, or *paludismo* in Spanish. The general symptoms are three days of fever, headache, bone pain, and general weakness.

65. This translates as *your pay*.

66. This refers to something that takes away substance, weakens.

67. This refers to *Quakers*.

68. "*Aumentará a pérdida de vista*" *significa que aumentará muchísimo su población. Se engrandecerá hasta más allá de lo que alcanza la vista*. Means "it will greatly increase its population; it will become large and richer than we can tell."

69. Yela Utrilla published this document in English and with some differences, *España*, 578–79. Yale published the document in English, Labaree and Willcox, *Papers*, 23:108–9. Yale cites a copy in the American Philosophical Society and a draft in the United States National Archives. Two copies were made: one in Spanish and one in French. A French copy has been published by Yale, Labaree and Willcox, *Papers*, 22:634–35.

70. The long, legal-size pages of this letter were folded in half. The blank backside addressed the letter "To His Excellency the Count of Floridablanca." The opposite corner has a note in minuscule writing that states, "Plenipotentiary and proposals of Franklin."

71. The word should be *a*.

72. This surely refers to a letter of exchange.

73. This word should be *con*.

74. This version of the document is the Spanish translation from English that ended up in the archive. The original in English has not been located.

75. This is underlined in the original document. *Gastos* translates to *expenses*. The Americans, most likely Lee, forgot or could not pronounce the town's actual name, which is Vitoria-Gasteiz.

76. This means *having given up, renounced*.

77. This is underlined in the original document.

78. Should be *Se me ocurrió*.

79. Capitalized as in the original document.

80. *Conformes* means *everyone is of the same opinion*, or *unaminous*.

81. "Y si ellos mismos hubiesen visto estos progresos [la paz y alianza entre España y Portugal] habrían dicho a España que iba a resolver todos los problemas, y causar una guerra general cuando no tenían gana de ningún ruido." This is a complicated phrase. It probably indicates that Spain is allied with France and with Portugal, and does not have any other European enemy besides England and will be able to solve whatever problem may arise because of its power, thereby avoiding a war. Nevertheless, the Spanish have no desire to go to war [*no tenían gana de ningún ruido*].

82. *Chanceando* means *joking*.

83. This note was written in Spanish, probably by Spain's secretary of state.

84. This phrase is underlined and written in Latin in the original document.

85. This is underlined in the original document.

86. This is underlined in the original document.

87. *Asenso* means *veracity, truthfulness*.

88. Written in Spanish in the original document.

89. This is written in Latin and underlined in the original document. It means to *be patient* or *resist at the beginning*.

90. Written *Affiche* in the original document. In Spanish, *pasquín* refers to a poster or announcement that is posted in public places.

91. As written in the original document. Probably signifies *number*. This does not appear to be a French abbreviation because there is no such word that ends with an *a*.

92. In the original document this note is written on top.

93. This refers to legally captured ships or *legitmate presses*.

94. Refers to a break in diplomatic relations, which would mean war.

95. *Echadizas* refers to exaggerarted threats meant to scare or intimidate.

96. Significa pedir entrada en un puerto al que no tuvieran derecho a entrar, pidiendo socorro alegando avería o necesidad de víveres y agua. Esto. Como se dijo, era motivo común usado por los corsarios y capitanes navales americanos.

97. *Calentarse de cascos* means *the head warms up*, in the sense of getting excited about an idea or to persist in pursuing an idea.

98. In this context the word *enervada* can be interpreted as *before you lose your nerve*, or *strength*.

99. As written in the original document. It should be *aventurada* or *venturosa*.

100. Related to *altercado*, meaning *fight* or *confrontation*.

101. Appears as *Bourbonas* in the original document.

102. Yela Utrilla published this letter in its original English with a Spanish translation in a footnote; *España*, 682–87; the attached requests are listed as a separate document with a disjointed translation in Spanish in a footnote. Yela Utrilla dates the document September 1777. Yale published the docuent; Labaree and Willcox, *Papers*, 24:555–63.

103. This is a note written on the border of the main letter by someone in Floridablanca's office.

104. *El doble* means *the copy*.

105. The words in brackets do not appear in the original document. It seems the words were lost in a fold of the document. These added words are a guess deduced from the context.

106. Written *Bourbon* in the original document.

107. Supposedly this letter is from Floridablanca.

108. Illegible in the original. From the context and what can be inferred from the letters below an ink stain, it appears that the word could be *negocios*.

109. This is meant to indicate how the government governs or manages this business.

110. Refers to *method of payment*.

111. This should be *pactado*.

112. Written in French in the original document.

113. Word is underlined in the original document.

114. This letter is translated from English. In the process, the names were also translated. The correct names are Robert Morris and William Smith.

115. This means *sent by urgent mail.*

116. The answer that is summarized in the main letter below goes with letter number 11, also with letter number 12.

117. This means *in the letter.*

118. *Providencias*; this means *provisions to prevent or remedy damage.*

119. *Evacuar* means *to complete a procedure.*

120. This can be understood as *embarkations.*

121. This refers to *terranova.*

122. The first of three attachments is a rough French translation of the memorial written in English, which is the second document. The French document was translated for the convenience of Spanish and French officials. It has words and whole paragraphs crossed out and rewritten. The French translation is in legajo 4612-155, Estado, AGS. Because the original English memorial is reproduced in its entirety here, the French is not included in transcription.

123. In Labaree and Willcox, *Papers*, 25:184–87, Yale published a version of this document that mentioned the archive of Spain's Asuntos Exteriores (foreign affairs) and a draft dated 21 November.

124. Yela Utrilla published this document translated into Spanish in *España*, 712–14.

125. The word *armadores* or *shipbuilders*, is written in a different hand over a crossed-out word that begins with *c*.

126. This is a draft written by at least two people that was apparently being prepared under the auspices of Floridablanca. Whether it was ever sent in this form is questionable. Subsequent research may turn up the final version.

127. This word appears detached in the original, just as it appears here. It does not have any relation with anything else in the other pages.

128. A word appears to be missing between the words *confianza* and *deben*.

129. Until this point, the text is in draft form and the page ends with the original document. The following page begins with "según las negociaciones ..." or "according to the negotiations" and the writing is more careful and clearer.

130. *Defensa* appears in bold in the original document. The rest of the original document is blank with a note that says *continue* on page four. The text countinues in the following page and appears in the same handwriting as before.

131. An illegible note appears here in the margin.

132. There is no number 9, which is the missing point referred to in the opening statement of this document.

133. The word *pressantes* probably should be read as *presents* and translated as *acucientes* in Spanish, which means *pressing* in English.

134. The writing appears to be *le et*. It should be written *le ete*, an abbreviation for *le Comte*. Montmorin was a count.

135. Refers to the king of Spain.

136. Should be *Zaherió* = humilló.

137. Should be *Epítetos* = juicios.

138. *Bill* in English.

139. Should be written as *sucesión*.

140. *Appareiller* means *to prepare the rigging for departure, set sail*.

141. Part of the word is missing in the original document.

142. This refers to Havre de Grâce.

143. This document has been translated from French into Spanish, as well as into English. The original version, of which there is no available copy, most assuredly would have been in English.

144. This word is not clear in the original document as it is covered with an ink stain.

145. Appears as *PD* in the original document. This could mean *post dated*.

146. Name is Gandásegui, with an accent.

147. Text is underlined in the original document.

148. This is a copy of an original written in a bound letter book. This letter was published in part and in Spanish in Carlos Cólogan Soriano, *Tenerife Wine: Historias de Comercío de Vinos, Siglo XVIII (1760–1797)*, 244. A larger portion of this letter is published here.

149. This letter has been published in Spanish translation in Cólogan, *Tenerife Wine*, 344–46.

150. This is a part of a much larger and confusing document that includes various business dealings.

151. Because of a lack of formalities, this letter appears to be a personal note from Aranda to Floridablanca.

152. *Tavolino* is an Italian word that means *table*.

153. Appearas as *S* in the original document.
154. *Estados unidos* means *states that are united in a cause* and does not refer to the name of the new country.
155. This refers to the full sheet, which was folded into four parts.
156. This refers to William Carmichael.
157. This is blank in the original document.
158. Written *Capmani* in the original document.
159. This phrase is crossed out in the draft but is legible.
160. This refers to Negapatam.
161. This refers to 44 cannons.
162. This may refer to Haechan.
163. This phrase is incomplete and crossed out, but is legible.

BIBLIOGRAPHY

Aznar, Pantaleónrn. *Vida del Dr. Franklin sacada de documentos auténticos.* Madrid: Editorial, 1798.

Brands, H. W. *The First American: The Life and Times of Benjamin Franklin.* New York: Doubleday, 2000.

Calderón Cuadrado, Reyes. *Empresarios españoles en el proceso de independencia norteamericana: La casa Gardoqui e hijos de Bilbao.* Madrid: Unión Editorial, S.A., 2004.

Carr, Carolyn Kinder et al., eds. *Legacy: Spain and the United States in the Age of Independence, 1763–1848.* Washington, DC: Smithsonian Institution, 2007.

Chauncy, William, ed. *The Journals of the Continental Congress.* 2 vols. Washington, DC: United States Government Printing Office, 1904.

Chávez, Thomas E. *Spain and the Independence of the United States: An Intrinsic Gift.* Albuquerque: The University of New Mexico Press, 2002.

———. *Doctor Franklin & Spain: The Unknown History.* Santa Fe, NM: The Press at the Palace of the Governors, 2016.

Cólogan Soriano, Carlos. *Un Corsario al Servicio de Benjamín Franklin.* Canary Islands: Gaviño de Franchy, Editores, 2013.

———. *Tenerife Wine: Historias del Comercio de Vinos. Siglo XVIII [1760–1797].* Canary Islands, Autor-Editor Obra Prop, 2017.

Cummins, Light Townsend. *Spanish Observers and the American Revolution, 1775–1783.* Baton Rouge: Louisiana State University Press, 1991.

de Reparaz, Carmen. *Yo Solo: Bernardo de Gálvez y la toma de Pensacola en 1781.* Barcelona: Ediciones del Serbal, S.A., 1986.

Documentos relativos a la independencia de Norteamérica existentes en archivos españoles, 11 vols. Madrid: Ministerio de Asuntos Exteriores, 1977–1985.

Enciclopedia General Ilustrada del País Vasco, vol. 5, 296–97. San Sebastián, Spain: Editorial Aunamendi, 1983.

Ferreiro, Larrie D. *Brothers in Arms: American Independence and the Men of France and Spain Who Saved It.* New York: Alfred A. Knopf, 2016.

Franklin, Benjamin. "The Autobiography." In *Benjamin Franklin: The Autobiography and Other Writings*, edited by L. Jesse Lemisch. New York: Signet Classic, 1961.

Haworth, Paul Leland. "Frederick the Great and the American Revolution." *The American Historical Review* 9, no. 3, (April 1904): 460–78.

Isaacson, Walter. *Benjamin Franklin: An American Life*. New York: Simon & Schuster, 2003.

Labaree, Leonard, and William B. Wilcox et al., eds. *The Papers of Benjamin Franklin*. 24 vols. New Haven: Yale University Press, 1959.

Lemisch, L. Jesse, ed. *Benjamin Franklin: The Autobiography and Other Writings*. New York: Signet Classic, 1961.

López-Chávez, Celia. "Benjamín Franklin, España y la diplomacia de una armónica." *Espacio, Tiempo y Forma: Revista de la Facultad de Geografía e Historia* IV, no. 13 (2000): 319–27.

———. "Benjamin Franklin y la realeza española: Una conexión musical." In *Norteamérica a finales del siglo XVIII: España y los Estados Unidos*, E. Garrigues López-Chicheri. Coord. Madrid: Marcial Pons, 2008.

Martínez Cuesta, Juan. "Relaciones culturales entre la Corte de Carlos III y los Estados Unidos de América." In *Madrid en el contexto de lo hispano desde la época de los descubrimientos*, vol. 2, 1063–70. Madrid: Universidad Complutense de Mardrid/Departmento de Historia de Arte, 1994.

McCullough, David. *John Adams*. New York: Simon & Schuster, 2001.

Oltra, Joaquín, and María Ángeles Pérez Samper. *El Conde de Aranda y los Estados Unidos*. Barcelona: Promociones y Publicaciones Universitarias, S.A., 1987: 60.

Reinert, Sophus A. "The Way to Wealth around the World: Benjamin Franklin and the Globalization of American Capitalism." *American Historical Review* 120 (February 2015): 61–97.

Rivas, Vicente. *Don Juan de Miralles e independencia de los Estados Unidos*. Valencia: Generalitat Valenciana, 2003.

Schiff, Stacy. *A Great Improvisation: Franklin, France and the Birth of America*. New York: Henry Holt, 2005.

Smith, Paul H., ed. *Letters of Delegates to Congress, 1774–1789*. Washington, DC: Library of Congress, 1976–1991.

Van Doren, Carl. *Benjamin Franklin*. New York: Viking Press, 1938; reprinted New York: Garden City Publishing, 1941.

Weatherford, Jack. *Indian Givers: How the Indians of the Americas Transformed the World*. New York: Crown, 1988.

Wharton, Francis, ed. *The Revolutionary Diplomatic Correspondence of the United States,* 6 vols. Washington, DC: United States Government Printing Office, 1889.
Wood, Gordon S. *The Americanization of Benjamin Franklin.* New York: Penguin Books, 2004.
Yela Utrilla, Juan F. *España ante la independencia de los Estados Unidos.* Lérida: Gráficos Academia Mariana, 1925; reedición: Madrid: Colegio Universitario de Ediciones Istmo, 1988.

INDEX

A

Act of Confederation, 77
Adams, John, 3, 5, 171, 186, 209, 353, 368, 386, 413, 415, 424
Allarme, 38, 238
Allen, Ethan, 402
Alvarado y Perales, Luis Eugenio Fernández de, 6th Count of Cartago and 1st Marquis of Tabaloso, 179, 419
America, 2, 16, 36, 40, 41, 43, 44, 46, 54, 66, 69, 75, 77, 78, 83, 85, 88, 89, 95, 100, 107, 108, 111, 113, 114, 117, 127, 132, 139, 154, 163, 173, 176, 191, 198, 201, 210, 400, 403, 411, 419, 420, 424; *see also* American colonies, 13 United States of North America, United Provinces of America, United States of America
American cause, 44
proposed treaty with France, 84
American colonies, 1, 3, 25, 29, 38, 40, 41, 44, 46, 48, 74, 77, 80, 82, 83, 84, 93, 94,

American colonies (*continued*) 98, 109, 120, 152, 156, 162, 163, 193, 238, 417; *see also* American Revolution, War of Independence
aid received, 77, 109, 112, 127, 128, 129, 130–32, 162, 398, 405, 410
assistance from France, 48, 61, 74, 77, 81, 104, 106, 108, 109, 112, 117, 121, 128, 133, 151, 162, 170, 171, 407
as British colonies, 7, 36, 47, 48, 57, 59, 61, 62, 78, 79, 98, 156, 401
declaration of war against England, 82, 88, 113, 115, 168, 186, 306, 368
dependency on England, 105, 107, 122
emissaries to, 158, 193, 403, 414
English Colonies of America, 70
government of, 211
independence of, 67, 166, 170, 174, 178
maritime trade, 40, 80, 129, 417
naval capabilities, 48, 79, 94, 112, 129, 163, 188–90 414, 416, 419

440 • Index

American colonies (*continued*)
    American warships, 185, 187
    rift between England and, 6, 57, 79, 84, 89, 94, 106, 107, 111, 114, 142, 152, 178, 202, 299
    and Spain, 47, 48, 71, 84, 85, 86, 95, 97, 142, 407
        aid from, 57, 60, 66, 74, 77, 81, 109, 127, 128, 133, 136, 137, 141, 164, 415
    possessions in America, 79
    United Colonies of America, 64, 66, 67, 84, 406, 427
American colonists, 41, 48, 94, 136, 141, 160, 162, 163, 164, 165, 408
American Commission, 3, 405, 409
American corsairs, 119, 122, 124, 419
    Cunningham, 183
    The Delfin, 118, 30
    The Lexington, 118
    and refuge in French ports, 118, 119
American flag, 184, 187, 409
American Philosophical Society, 5, 207, 208, 212, 213, 214, 391, 408, 409, 424, 425, 428
    certificates of membership, 212, 213, 425
    Transactions, 212, 213
American privateers, 4, 115, 153, 185, 413, 423
American Revolution, 8, 105, 111, 112, 115, 119, 121, 122, 123, 126, 128, 129, 130,

American Revolution (*continued*)
    141, 143, 144, 153, 188, 408, 418; *see also* War of Independence
American warships, 82, 187
The Amphitrite, 59, 60, 74, 77, 109, 257, 271, 273, 302
Ana, 210, 314, 387
Anglo-American Colonies, 156, 340
Antilles, 187, 188, 368, 370
Aragón, José Claudio de, 396
Aragon, province of, 8, 19, 219
Aragón y Moncayo, Joaquín Atanasio Pignatelli de, Count of Fuentes, 19, 219, 396, 397
Aragón-Azlor, Juan Pablo de, Duke of Villahermosa, 396
Archive of the Secretariat, 204
archives of Spain, 1, 9, 10, 13
Archivo de la Fundación de Alba de Tormes, 8
Archivo de Simancas (AGS), 7
Archivo del Ministerio de Asuntos Extereores (MAE), 8
Archivo del Real Academia de la Historia (RAH), 7
Archivo General de Indias (AGI), 7
Archivo General del Palacio Real (AGP), 7
Archivo Histórico Nacional (AHN), 7
Archivo Zárate-Cólogan in the Archivo Histórico Provincial de Santa Cruz (AHPTF/AZC), 7
The Aretusa, 44, 244
Argentina, 5, 412

armaments, 36, 40, 53, 112, 124, 136, 137, 143, 402
armonica, 2, 3, 5, 16, 18, 20, 21, 25, 31, 32, 397, 398; *see also* harmonica
Army of the Danube, 29
artillery, 20, 44, 48, 55, 94, 203
artillery trains, 65
artillery treatises, 203
Austria, 52, 68, 210, 251, 265, 404; *see also* House of Austria
Ayers, Samuel, 189
  Terrible, 189

B

Bache, Benjamin Franklin, 403
Bache, Sarah Franklin, 5
Bahamas Channel, 84
Baltimore, MD, 92
Bancroft, Dr. Edward, 161, 343, 417
Barbeu-DuBourg, Jacques, 47, 48, 50, 62, 249, 260, 403
Battle of Minden, 176
Bayona, 29, 229
Beaumarchais, Pierre-Augustin Caron de, 62, 260, 405, 407
Beccaria, Father Giambatista, 21, 221, 398
Beethoven, Ludwig van, 5
Belisario, 209, 386
Biblioteca Nacional (BN), 7
Bilbao, 11, 21, 25, 27, 109, 139, 144, 221, 225, 227, 302, 325, 327, 332, 398, 400, 413, 421
the *Bird*, 189
Blanco, Juan Cólogan, 7; *see also* Juan Cólogan e hijos

Blaquier, 36, 236
Bolea, Pedro Pablo Abarca de, Count of Aranda, 3, 11, 39, 181, 197, 408, 420, 422, 423
  private papers of, 8
  Spanish ambassador to Paris, 6, 11
Bonnières, Adrien-Louis de, Count of Guines, 29, 34, 35, 223, 228, 234, 399
Borbon, Louis Jean Marie de, Duke of Penthièvre, 418
Boreas, 209, 386
Boston, 29, 41, 43, 44, 46, 109, 154, 229, 241, 243, 244, 245, 302, 402
Bourbon Crowns, 85, 133, 151
British Cabinet, 166, 411
British Crown, 48, 79, 81, 85, 94, 106, 122, 124, 151, 152; *see also* British Majesty, George III, 2, 397, 398, 412, 419
British Isles, 82
British Majesty, 20, 22, 27, 28, 37, 41, 44, 46, 140, 159, 161, 173, 174
British Sugar Islands, 89
Buenos Aires, 163, 164, 345, 346
Buick and Company, 76, 272
Burfort, 173, 355
Burgos, Spain, 93, 94, 95, 193, 195, 286, 287, 373, 375, 409, 410
Burgoyne, General John, 55, 100, 140, 146, 176, 293, 414, 415
Butler, William, 16th Count of Ormonde and 9th Count of Ossory, 37, 401

Byron, Admiral John, 173, 355

C

Cabarrús, don Francisco, 195, 421, 422,
Cádiz, 65, 66, 76, 153, 154, 156, 191, 200, 210, 263, 272, 335, 340, 387, 407, 417, 418
Calais, 36, 39, 41, 53, 173, 184, 236, 239, 241, 252, 355, 366
Cambridge, MA, 43, 243
Campo, Don Bernardo del, 20, 23, 220, 223, 398
Canada, 55, 75, 78, 83, 84, 88, 151, 152, 253, 272, 274, 279, 280, 338, 339, 408, 414, 415
  and British forces, 4514
  and France, 78, 84
cannons, 44, 48, 74, 94, 370, 371, 402, 416, 425, 427, 433
  bronze, 48, 74
Cape of Finisterre, 193, 373, 421
Caraccioli, Louis-Antoine, 126, 318
Caracciolo, Dominique, Marquis of Villamaina, 412
cargo, 115, 180, 201, 407
  seized, 148, 149, 150, 183
Carleton, Guy, 1st Baron of Dorchester, 55, 100, 253, 293, 410
Carlos III, King of Spain, aka Carlos VI of Naples, 3, 4, 7, 91, 101, 141, 393, 395, 396, 397, 398, 402, 405, 406, 410, 417, 421, 423

Carmichael, Don Guillermo, 204, 207, 213, 382, 384, 424
Carolina, 50, 249; *see also* North Carolina, South Carolina
Carvalho e Melo, Sebastião José de, Marquis of Pombal, 56, 101, 254, 294, 410, 411
Catherine II (Catherine the Great), aka "the czarina," 20, 23, 24, 51, 169, 170, 351, 352, 404
Catholics, 174, 175, 177, 406
Cevallos, don Pedro de, 103, 295, 411, 417
Chamber of Lords, 106, 107
Cherokee Indians, 211
Choiseul, Étienne-François de, Marquis of Stainville, 1st Duke of Choiseul, 296, 411, 414
Coast of Campeche, 165
Cólogan, Tomas, 180, 200
Cólogan Blanco, Juan, 421, 423
Cólogan Valois, Juan, 197, 199, 377, 378
Cólogan Valois family, 7, 200
Cólogan Valois e hijos, 7, 423
  Golden Rose, 421, 423
Colonial allied foces, 80, 114, 165, 420, 421
Committee of Secret Correspondence, 3, 405, 414
Congress of Philadelphia, 46, 47, 53, 55, 142
Constant, Josef, 19, 22, 28, 219, 222
Constitution of the States of America, 205, 409
Constitution of the Thirteen United States, 204, 409

Constitutional Convention, 4
Continental Congress, 3, 4, 6, 9, 11, 403, 405, 407, 409 410, 414, 415, 424
contraband, 155, 407, 412
Conyngham [Cunningham], Captain Gustavus, 18, 179, 180, 181, 182, 183, 361, 362, 363, 364, 365, 419
Comtesse of Moreton, 179
correspondence, 76, 99; see also Committee of Secret Correspondence
   secret, 3, 13, 38, 75, 382, 405, 414, 422
corsairs, 7, 64, 118, 124, 148, 149, 150, 156, 179
   American, 119, 120, 122, 124, 149
Cosby, Commodore Phillips, 210, 387
Trusty, 210
Council of War, 197, 423
Count of Aranda, see Bolea, Pedro Pablo Abarca de
Count of Campomanes, see Rodríguez Campomanes y Perez, Pedro
"Count of Devergennes," 57, 58, 168, 258, 336, 337, 338, 350, 351, 352, 353, 403, 405, 415, 427; see also Gravier, Charles, Count of Vergennes
Count of Floridablanca, see Moñino, José, 1st Count of Floridablanca
Count of Fuentes, see Aragón y Moncayo, Joaquín Atanasio Pignatelli de

Count of Haslang, see Haslang, Joseph Franz Xaver Graf von
Count Lacy, see Lacy, Francisco Antonio de
Count of Maurepas, see Phélypeaux, Jean-Frédéric
Count of Priego, see Croy, Jean Juste Ferdinand Joseph de, Prince of Croy-Havré and Count of Priego
Count de Ricla, see Funes Villapando Ambrosio de
Count of Sernafis (Searnafis), 22, 29, 222, 229, 398, 400
Count de Vergennes, see Gravier, Charles, Count of Vergennes
Court of Lisbon, 53, 101, 141, 197
Court of Madrid, 74, 75
Court of Paris, 69, 75, 120, 207
Court of Petersburg, 169
Court of Versailles, 166
Court of Vienna, 169, 170
Courts of Admiralty, 153
Courts of Spain and France, 71, 90, 153
Cox, Steven, 17
Creek Indians, 211
Croy, Jean Juste Ferdinand Joseph de, Prince of Croy-Havré and Count of Priego, 22, 398

D

Danube, 20
Davis, Marianne, 16, 216, 397
Deane, Silas, 3, 6, 61, 63, 73, 77, 81, 93, 98, 130, 149, 171, 336, 352, 353, 405, 411, 415, 424

debt
  England's national, 67, 80, 105, 115, 142, 175
Declaration of Independence, 3, 4, 48, 414
Defender, 210
d'Ossun, Pierre Paul, Marquis d'Ossun, 57, 87, 120, 135, 313, 413, 416
dragoons, 121
Duke of Alba, 8
Dunkirk, 81, 1119, 85, 192, 407, 420
The Dutch, 166, 191, 209, 210, 407, 421, 425
  and discontent with England, 166

E

East India Company, 29, 37, 175, 425
East Indies, 173, 193
El Ferrol, 65, 66, 263
England, 36, 44, 51, 55, 105, 113, 165, 188, 407, 415, 418, 419, 423
  Colonial rebellion, 67, 79, 142, 143, 151, 152
  Court of, 129
  doubts about American conflict, 417, 420
  as an enemy, 107, 202
  fighting forces, 8, 53, 63, 67, 80, 85, 94, 109, 124, 130, 152, 163, 171
  financial effects of war, 82, 105, 107, 108, 123, 125, 126, 130
    national debt, 67, 80, 105, 115, 142, 175

England (*continued*)
  French opposition, 66, 80, 81, 85, 107, 112, 113, 114, 122, 125, 164, 168, 169, 170, 174, 175
  king, 107, 159, 397, 398, 417, 419
  maritime trade with colonies, 108, 417
  naval forces, 114, 122, 124, 155, 175, 210, 403
  and North America, 78
  and Portugal, 102, 103
  Russian support for, 76
  and Spanish opposition, 69, 80, 81, 83, 85, 96, 142, 144
  Treaty of Paris, 4, 408, 414
  undefended, 171
  war with colonies, 1, 4, 90, 91, 98, 103, 105, 106, 107, 109, 111,112, 114, 115, 417, 419
    minority supporting peace, 107, 419
  war with Holland, 191
  war with Spain, 171, 411, 417
English Colonies of America, 36, 47, 57, 59, 70, 78, 189; see also American colonies
English privateers, 7, 74, 184, 187, 407
English Sugar Islands, 88, 90, 128
English warships, 66, 67, 74, 80, 94, 105, 146, 163, 173
Enlightenment, 3
Escarano, Don Francisco, 30, 31, 171, 231, 353, 396, 399, 400
Europe, 5, 10, 42, 53, 77, 78, 79, 83, 89, 112, 113, 124, 125,

Europe (*continued*)
127, 152, 199, 208, 210, 214, 298, 305, 308, 397, 400, 421, 424
aid and support for colonies, 130, 157, 163, 199, 210
powers of, 113, 114, 115, 165
war in, 88, 95, 105, 118

F

Ferrero Fieschi, Victor Amédée Philippe, Prince of Masserano, 30, 126, 139, 140, 230, 318, 327, 328, 396, 399, 402, 404
Spanish ambassador to England, 6, 11, 42, 396
fishing, 36, 41, 81, 84, 151, 152, 165
Florida, 50, 81, 84, 88, 151, 152, 249, 277, 280, 338, 408
Foresta, 29, 229, 426
Fortune (La Fortuné), 148, 153, 154, 156, 340, 355
Fountainbleau, 61
Fox, Charles, 25, 225
Fox, Henry, 1st Baron of Holland, 17, 177, 397
France, 3, 10, 52, 84, 85, 403, 405
as ally to American colonies, 57, 58, 60, 61, 67, 74
armaments of, 48, 67, 370, 371, 425
correspondence, 73, 422, 425
military positions, 65, 66
navy, 69, 81, 113, 114, 124, 404, 411, 421
ports, 54, 75, 77, 82, 97, 116, 117, 118, 119, 121, 122,

France (*continued*)
146, 148, 150, 185, 193, 202 309, 401, 412
and relationship with Spain, 48, 67, 89, 98
and war with England, 81, 82, 112, 113, 114, 165
Franklin, Benjamin, 2, 47, 61, 70, 73, 159, 178, 199, 200, 201, 394, 404, 413, 416, 424
and the American Philosophical Society, 5, 208, 213, 424
The Autobiography of Benjamin Franklin, 5
correspondence, 8, 63, 181, 407, 411, 421, 422, 425, 427
correspondence with the Count of Vergennes, 76, 77, 117, 411
correspondence with Don Gabriel de Borbon, 3, 13, 30, 402
correspondence with the Marquis of Grimaldi, 73
correspondence with Spain, 1, 3, 6, 7, 8, 9, 75, 81, 91, 96, 97, 197, 414, 422
and the Count of Aranda, 3, 4, 11, 87, 104, 109, 126, 193, 195, 203, 423, 424
early accomplishments, 2–3, 211, 388
early life, 5, 6
as Founding Father, 1, 5
The Franklin Papers, 12, 104, 126
and glass armonica, 2, 3, 16, 18, 21, 25, 397, 398

Franklin, Benjamin (*continued*)
  as member of Pennsylvania legislature, 2, 6, 93, 95, 149, 192, 202, 204, 406, 427
  as member of Spanish Royal Academy of History, 7, 213, 214, 394, 425
  memorials, 63, 64, 68, 77, 82, 96, 97, 98, 111–16, 127–32, 149, 153–54, 415
  as Minister Plenipotentiary of France, 4, 53, 90, 144, 207–8, 408, 409, 428
  as minister to Spain, 4, 13, 61, 71, 90
  in Paris, 50, 52, 53, 55, 56, 59, 60, 61, 62, 63, 70, 170, 174, 178, 404, 405, 409, 412
  and Philadelphia, 2, 3, 6, 36, 41, 44
  Poor Richard's Almanac, 1, 2, 5
  as postmaster, 46, 403
  as president of the Executive Council of Pennsylvania, 4
  relationship with Spain, 6, 9, 10, 11, 13, 34, 81
  subscription libraries, 2, 5
  treaty with France, 57–58
Franklin, Francis, 5
Franklin, William Temple, 403
Frederick II, King of Prussia, 23, 52, 168, 169, 170, 399, 414, 418
French court, 61, 68, 105, 107, 119, 120, 158
French language, 11, 63, 183, 184, 400, 406, 418, 427
French sugar islands, 107
French trade, 97, 136
frigates, 36, 38, 44, 50, 89, 90, 94, 104, 173, 188, 189, 209
Fundación Universitaria Española, 7, 425
Funes Villalpando, Ambrosio de, Count of Ricla 186, 368

G

Gage, General Thomas, 43, 46, 243, 245, 402
Gandásegui de, Don Matías, 193
Gardoqui, Diego Maria de, 11, 137, 325, 326, 410, 413
Gardoqui family, 11
Gardoqui e Hijos, 7, 137–38, 325–26
Gates, General Horatio Lloyd, 100, 146, 293, 334, 410, 415
General Washington, 189
George II, 177, 397
George III, 2, 107, 156, 159, 397, 398, 412, 419
Gerard, Conrad Alexandre, 62, 77, 170, 260, 273, 352, 405
Germain, George, 1st Viscount of Sackville, 106, 176, 177, 356, 358, 359, 411, 419
Germany, 115, 166, 169, 170
Gibraltar, 38, 51, 66, 69, 80, 85, 160, 165, 203, 210, 238, 249, 250, 263, 266, 277, 281, 343, 347, 381, 387, 406, 407
  Rock of, 407
Gioeni y Valguarnera, Jerónimo, Duke of Montealegre, 20, 220, 398
glass armonica, *see* armonica, harmonica

Golden Rose, 199, 200, 201, 421, 423
Goltz, Baron August Friedrich Ferdinand von der, 169, 170, 350, 351, 352, 418
Gonzaga, Don José, Marquis of Mora, 19, 27, 219, 227
Good Boor, 197, 198
Good Fortune, 27
gout, 17, 19, 20, 56, 396
Gran Malvina, 33, 233
Grand, Rodolphe-Ferdinand, 133, 135, 137, 138, 149, 150, 156, 181, 182, 184, 191, 192, 198, 199, 201, 321, 323, 325, 326, 336, 337, 340, 363, 364, 366, 413
  audit, 130–32
Gravier, Charles, Count of Vergennes, 3, 50, 59, 60, 61, 62, 63, 64, 65, 76, 77, 86, 96, 101, 102, 104, 119, 120, 121, 133, 136, 148, 149, 150, 151, 152, 157, 158, 168, 169, 170, 171, 193, 195, 257, 258, 259, 260, 261, 262, 263, 273, 282, 289, 294, 295, 296, 312, 313, 314, 321, 324, 336, 340, 341, 373, 375, 403, 404, 405, 408, 411, 415, 427
Great Britain, *see* England
Grimaldi, Jerónimo, 1st Duke of Grimaldi, 23, 27, 93, 94, 95, 222, 227, 286, 287, 288, 396, 398, 399, 404, 408, 409, 410
Guerra, Don Ramón de, 207, 219, 276

Gulf of Mexico, 84, 165

H

Hamilton, Alexander, 414
Hancock, John, 4, 81, 92, 156, 277, 393, 395, 409
Harbour of Pensacola, 90
Harcourt, Simon, 1st Earl of Harcourt, 19, 22, 25, 28, 34, 219, 222, 226, 228, 234, 398
harmonica, 27, 30, 33, 393; *see also* armonica
Haslang, Joseph Franz Xaver Graf von, 22, 35, 234, 400
Havana, 99, 163, 193, 408, 409, 410
Havre de Gracia, 185, 366, 420, 432
Henry, William, Duke of Gloucester and Edinburgh, 19, 37, 397
Heredia, Don Ignacio, 148, 335
Hervey, George, 2nd Earl of Bristol, 22, 27, 37, 222, 227, 398
H. M. S. *Assurance*, 209
Holland, 93, 95, 170, 193
House of Austria, 168, 169, 210
House of Bourbon, 124, 167
House of Buick, 76
House of Commons, 29, 106, 111, 174, 175, 176, 177, 178, 403, 404
House of Lords, 36, 404
Howard, Charles, 11th Duke of Norfolk, 174, 356, 419
Howard, Henry, 12th Earl of Suffolk, 33, 40, 41, 56, 240, 241, 254, 400, 401

Howe, Admiral Richard, 146, 251, 293, 334, 410
Howe, William, 5th Viscount Howe, 52, 100, 146, 251, 293, 334, 402, 410
Hutton, James ("Huston"), 159, 342, 416
Hyder Ali, 193, 373, 421

I
India, 209, 373, 386, 421, 425
Infante Gabriel of Spain, aka Gabriel de Borbón, 3, 11, 13, 16, 18, 21, 25, 30, 31, 33, 42, 216, 218, 221, 225, 230, 231, 233, 393, 394
  death of, 33, 233
Insurgents, 48, 50, 60, 61, 70, 82, 94, 104, 109, 119, 120, 121, 122, 123, 124, 144, 150, 267; see also American colonists
Ireland, 36, 65, 66, 112, 193, 398, 399, 406, 409, 415, 419, 421
Irun, Spain, 195, 196, 421, 422
Island of Miquelon, 150, 415
Island of Santa Catalina, 143, 330
  Colony of Sacramento, 143
Isle of Man, 192
Isle of Wight, 172, 353

J
Jay, John, 5, 193, 195, 203, 373, 375, 381, 423
  as Minister Plenipotentiary of Spain, 424
Jefferson, Thomas, 3
Jones, John Paul, 11

Joseph II of Austria, Holy Roman Emperor, 404, 406, 421

K
Keniston, Hayward, 9, 395
Keppel, Admiral Augustus, 1st Viscount Keppel, 173, 355

L
L'Orient, 117, 310, 412
La Palma, Canary Islands, 179, 180
Lacy, Francisco Antonio de, Count of Lacy, 73, 203, 270, 381, 406
Lacy, Franz Moritz von, 73, 203, 270, 381, 406
Lake Champlain, 55, 253, 414, 415
Lake Erie, 83, 279
Lake Huron, 83, 279
Lake Ontario, 83, 279
Law of Nations, 88, 115, 153
Le Havre, 59, 77
Le Mere, Captain Jaime, 145, 333
Lee, Arthur, 3, 71, 72, 73, 88, 93, 94, 95, 130, 141, 150, 153, 154, 157, 186, 256, 261, 268, 269, 270, 273, 284, 286, 287, 288, 329, 336, 337, 341, 368, 405, 409, 410, 414, 418, 424
Lee, General Charles, 95, 288, 408
Leicester, 46, 245
letter book, 7, 422, 423
Lexington, 118, 311
liberty, 89, 146
Limerick, Ireland, 193, 373

Lisbon, 53, 56, 103, 411
Liverpool, 46, 192, 245,
Lodge, John Davis, 9, 395
London, 2, 6, 16, 19, 20, 29, 31, 34, 38, 44, 74, 76, 111, 121, 122, 126, 154, 159, 161, 162, 168, 171, 173, 183, 193, 202, 208, 396, 397, 400, 404, 412, 414, 416, 419, 421, 423
López de Zúñiga y Castro, Joaquín, 12th Duke of Bexar, 385, 400
Louis IV, 122
Louis XIV, 114, 307, 403, 418
Louis XV, 407, 418

M

Madrid, 4, 7, 8, 11, 20, 26, 29, 30, 33, 62, 70, 75, 93, 103, 142, 168, 197, 220, 226, 227, 229, 230, 231, 233, 234, 253, 256, 260, 261, 262, 267, 286, 296, 318, 321, 330, 368, 375, 396, 398, 404, 409, 410, 413, 415, 422, 425
Madrid Gazette, 208
Malvinas Islands (Falkland Islands), 126, 144, 318, 331, 412
Manchester, 46, 245
Marc, Armand, Count de Montmorin Saint-Hérem, 416, 432
María Francisca I, 405, 410
Martínez Cuesta, Juan, 11
Martinique, 104, 121, 163, 179, 180, 182, 361, 362, 364

Matlack, Timothy
 and Declaration of Independence, 4, 409
Memorials, 189, 409
 Franklin's, 57, 63, 64, 68, 77, 82, 96, 111
 Franklin, Deane, and Lee's, 153–54
 Stormont's, 98, 120 415
 with US budget, 127–32
 Vergennes's, 57, 85, 97, 149, 150, 157
Menorca, 160, 165, 343, 347, 406, 407
Middleton, 37, 237
Miralles y Traham, Juan, de, 11, 422
Mississippi River, 83, 84, 90, 99, 279, 280
Moñino, José, 1st Count of Floridablanca, 159, 167, 398, 399, 404, 409, 410, 416, 417, 420, 422, 423, 428, 430, 431, 432
Morris, Robert, 191, 197, 198, 201, 414, 430
Mozart, Wolfgang, 5
Muniain, Don Fermín Sánchez de, 197
Murray, David, 2nd Earl Mansfield, 7th Viscount Stormont, 37, 53, 101, 119, 120, 170, 171, 252, 294, 353, 401, 404, 412
 memorial, 98, 120
Murray, John, Lord Dunmore, 404
Murray, William, 1st Earl of Mansfield, 19, 140, 143, 175, 398

muskets, 48, 109

N
Nantes, 48, 50, 53, 60, 119, 184, 187, 189, 247, 249, 252, 258, 312, 366, 368, 371, 405, 420,
Nassau de Zuylestein, William Henry, 4th Earl of Rochford, 19, 22, 25, 27, 33, 38, 45, 219, 222, 226, 227, 233, 238, 244, 398, 414
Negapatam (Negapattinam), 209, 386, 425, 433
New Jersey, 2, 91, 100
  Brunswick, 100, 293
  Princeton, 100
  Trenton, 100, 293
New Orleans, 83, 84, 99, 145, 146, 409, 410, 415
Newfoundland, 36, 41, 81, 88, 152, 165, 173, 415
Noailles, Emmanuel Marie Louis de, Marquis of Noailles, 171, 174, 353, 356, 419
North, Frederick, 2nd Earl of Guilford, aka Lord North, 16, 19, 21, 28, 29, 143, 174, 175, 177, 331, 357, 397
North Carolina, 91, 155, 416
Nova Scotia, 88, 151, 152, 211

O
Ohio River, 83
Oltra, Joaquín
  El Conde de Aranda y los Estados Unidos, 10, 393
Osborne, Francis, 5th Duke of Leeds, 25, 225, 399
Osborne, Thomas, 4th Duke of Leeds and Marquis of Carmarthen, 25, 399
Ottoman Empire, 165

P
packet boat (*paquebote*), 150, 184, 254, 332, 337, 366, 404
Pantaléon Aznar, 9, 395
Paris, 3, 6, 11, 19, 27, 28, 34, 35, 37, 47, 50, 52, 53, 57, 59, 60, 95, 102, 104, 119, 120, 134, 141, 143, 162, 168, 178, 192, 193, 197, 199, 200, 219, 227, 228, 234, 237, 246, 249, 251, 252, 256, 258, 259, 261, 271, 276, 288, 295, 297, 312, 314, 321, 329, 330, 345, 350, 356, 360, 373, 396, 397, 398, 399, 402, 403, 405, 410, 412, 413
  Court of, 58, 64, 69, 75, 80, 120, 122, 207, 266, 313, 384
  Franklin in, 61, 62
  Treaty of Paris, 4, 408, 414
Parliament, 17, 25, 29, 41, 161, 171, 174, 175, 177, 178, 398, 404, 417, 419
Paul, François-Joseph, Marquis de Grasse Tilly, the Count of Grasse, 193, 373, 421
Pennsylvania, 2, 4, 6, 46, 91, 100, 155, 333, 415
Pensacola, 11, 84, 90
Pérez Samper, María Ángeles, 10
  El Conde de Aranda y los Estados Unidos, 10

Petite Resolution, 185, 187, 189, 367, 368, 371
Petre, Robert, 9th Baron Petre ("Lord Peter"), 174, 356, 419
Phelypeaux, Jean-Frédéric, Count of Maurepas, 51, 67, 102, 170, 171, 249, 264, 295, 353, 403
Philadelphia, 2, 44, 142, 146, 191, 198, 201, 207, 208, 210, 244, 330, 384, 388, 402, 414, 415, 421, 423
  Congress of, 46, 47, 52, 53, 55, 245, 246, 251, 252, 253
  Franklin's life in, 2, 3, 6, 36, 41, 236, 241
Pignatelli, María Manuela, "Duchess of Villahermosa," 15, 19, 20, 24, 28, 215, 216, 219, 220, 224, 227, 396, 397
pirates, 7, 187, 369, 407; *see also* privateers
Pitt, William, 1st Earl of Chatham, 106, 174, 178, 355, 356, 360, 397, 401, 411
Plymouth, 185, 187, 189, 368, 370
Pollock, Oliver, 99, 145, 146, 409, 415
Portsmouth, New Hampshire, 44, 172, 173, 210, 244, 353, 355, 387
Portugal, 51, 53, 66, 69, 85, 89, 103, 183, 202, 250, 258, 263, 266, 410, 417
Pratt, Charles, 1st Earl of Camden, 107, 300, 401

privateering, 150
  wartime, 423
privateers, 4, 7, 74, 115, 116, 117, 184, 185, 187, 407, 412, 413, 423; *see also* Conyngham (Cunningham), Captain Gustavus
  vessels, 185, 188, 189
Proceedings of our American Congress, 42
Protheus, 173, 355
Province of Aragón, 8, 19, 219
Province of Flanders, 191, 192, 421
Prussia, 68, 115, 210, 398, 399; *see also* Frederick II
Pulteney, William, 174, 356, 419

Q
Quakers, 83, 279, 428
Queen of Portugal, 60, 101, 405
Quiberon Bay, 60, 258, 405

R
Real Academia de la Historia, 5, 7, 9, 384, 394
La Représaille (Reprisal), 117, 310, 405, 412,
La Revenge, 179, 361
Revilla, Antonio de, 15, 215
  San Bernardo, 15, 215
Revolutionary War, 7, 11, 414; *see also* American Revolution, War of Independence
Robinson, Thomas, 2nd Lord Grantham, 220, 294, 398
Roderique Hortalez et Cie, 405, 407
Rodríguez Campomanes y Perez, Pedro, Count of Campomanes, 207, 394, 424, 425

Royalists, 146
Russia, 39, 68, 113, 191, 404, 406
   and aid to England, 51, 76, 113, 170
   "The Partition of Poland," 23

S

Saavedra, Francisco, 8
Saint Malo, 119, 185, 366,
Salust, 42, 402
San Sebastián, 21, 144, 221, 332, 398
Santa Cruz de Tenerife, 189, 371, 384
Santo Domingo, 27
Santo Domingo, 50, 75, 104, 121, 163, 184, 227, 249, 272, 297, 314, 346, 366, 427
Saratoga, 176, 358, 410, 414, 415, 417
Sarmiento, Domingo Faustino, 5
Sartine, 193, 373
Sartine, Antoine-Raymond-Gualbert-Gabriel de, 102, 104, 170, 295, 297, 352, 411
Sayre, Stephen, 141, 329, 414
Second Continental Congress, 3, 4, 6
   Secret Committee of Correspondence, 3, 405, 414
Seven Years' War, 408, 414, 421
   Treaty of Paris, 4, 408, 414
Seymour-Conway, Francis, 1st Viscount Beauchamp and 1st Earl of Hertford, 25, 225, 399
ships of the line, 80, 104, 109, 173, 184, 417
ships of war, 94, 127, 132, 155, 173

Silesia, 20, 223, 398
Spain, 1, 64, 83, 409, 421
   alliance with France, 68, 69, 85
   consumption of British goods, 209
   national archives, 4, 10
   natural enemies of, 83
   naval forces, 51, 65, 66, 82, 124
   and peace with England, 79, 80, 96, 144, 160, 171, 396
   ports, 40, 64, 128
   reconciliation with Portugal, 78, 81, 101, 102, 103, 122, 123, 143, 418
   and support of American Revolution, 11, 60, 61, 83, 84, 91, 94, 95, 109, 125, 127, 145, 146, 157, 186, 407, 410, 413, 414, 417
   trade with England, 142, 151, 54, 160, 164, 209, 414
   war with Great Britain, 36, 83, 90, 143, 165, 192, 396, 397, 398, 411, 417, 424
Spanish court, 3, 71, 77, 141, 153, 157, 180, 188, 197, 207, 405, 406
Spanish and French relations, 6, 57, 67, 68, 69, 89, 98, 115, 124, 125, 416, 418, 422, 429
Spanish Royal Academy of History, 7, 207, 213, 214
Speake, Francis, 189, 371
Stuart, John, 3rd Count of Bute, 175, 356, 419
Sugar Islands,
   English, 90, 128
   French, 88, 107

"Suits of Clothes," 127, 128, 130, 132

T
Tenerife, 7, 182, 184, 189, 361, 364, 366, 371, 421, 423
Terrible, 189, 371
13 United States of North America, 186, 204
Thomson [Thompson], Charles 4, 92, 156, 409
Thynne, Thomas, 3rd Viscount of Weymouth, 116, 144, 175, 309, 331, 357, 411
Ticonderoga, 43, 55, 100, 410, 414, 427
Treaty of Friendship and Commerce, 57, 58, 65, 81
Treaty of Navigation and Commerce, 122
Treaty of Paris, 4, 408, 414; see also Seven Years' War
Trusty, 210

U
United Colonies of America, 64, 84, 406, 427
United Provinces of America, 71, 84, 94
United States of America, 84, 88, 89, 90, 91, 105, 127, 128,153, 155, 188, 189, 207, 211, 261, 269, 280, 420
  and aid from France, 89, 107, 109, 112, 130, 154
  independence from Great Britain, 88, 99, 105, 111, 112, 113, 114, 115, 129

US Senate, 5

V
Ventades, Don Luis de, 15, 21, 25, 27, 215, 219, 221, 222, 225, 227, 228, 396, 397, 400, 426
Ventades, Don Miguel de, 21, 22, 28, 139, 215, 327, 396, 397, 400, 426
Versailles, 58, 60, 61, 62, 63, 65, 70, 71, 75, 77, 101, 102, 126, 135, 149, 167, 168, 256, 258, 259, 260, 261, 262, 267, 271, 273, 294, 295, 318, 323, 336, 349, 350, 405, 411, 415, 418
  Court of, 166
Victory, 173, 355
Vienna, 52, 168, 419
  Court of, 169, 170

W
War of Independence, 408; see also American Revolution, Revolutionary War
Washington, General George, 100, 146, 189, 193, 293, 334, 371, 373, 415, 424
Westminster Abbey, 37, 237
Wickes, Lambert, 117, 412
Williams, Jonathon, 420
Windsor Cathedral, 37, 237
wool, 209, 210

Y
Yale University, 10, 12, 402, 406, 408, 409, 413, 416, 428, 430, 431
Yela Utrilla, Juan Francisco, 10, 405, 406, 408, 409, 413, 416, 426, 427, 428, 430, 431

Acknowledgments

A book, any book, is the culmination of the effects of people and events, even more so when a team and support group are formed to work toward the finished product. This book originated with the research for an earlier book, *Spain and the Independence of the United States: An Intrinsic Gift*. Thanks to the support of a Fulbright Research Grant and a second grant from the Dirección General de Relaciones Culturales y Científicas of the Spanish Foreign Ministry (Ministerio de Asuntos Exteriores), the research for that earlier book uncovered many documents dealing with Benjamin Franklin. To facilitate the project as well as assure its quality, I was encouraged to do two things. First, form a team of scholars—historians, translators, and archivists. The second suggestion came from Ray Dewey, a long-time friend, who assured me that money could be raised to pay for a team. Franklin, he insisted, would be a popular topic.

Two other friends, Rob and Patricia Kurz, quickly agreed with Dewey and established a support group to begin raising the necessary funds. Without the efforts of the Kurzes, especially Partricia, who *enthusiastically* chaired the committee, and major leading gifts from Kevin and Leonore Daniels, the act of compiling the documents needed for this volume could not have begun, much less been completed.

The research needed to create this book was completed through the scholarly efforts of myself, Dr. Russ Davidson, Dr. Genoveva Enríquez, Patricia Kurz, and Dr. Celia López-Chávez. The team worked out a system of cross-checking each transcription and translation. This work was tedious, sometimes perplexing, but always interesting. Special thanks go to Celia López-Chávez for her detailed final edit of the manuscript before it was submitted. Tom Ireland of Santa Fe did an initial edit of the manuscript. Tom gets credit for the book's title. Clem Whelan helped with some early French translations. Alan William Adame worked on some Spanish translations. Guillermo Gallego Muñoz of Granada, Spain, helped select some of the final documents included in this book. Some credit must go to Fray Angélico Chávez (now deceased) and Dr. Donna Pierce, who completed initial translations of more than a few of the documents cited in *Spain and Independence* that were subsequently included here.

Everyone involved in this project, from the support group, the fifty-plus donors, and the academic team, sincerely believes this volume will be a new source to consult on the history of the birth of the United States as well as the beginning of its diplomatic relations with the Hispanic world.

The American Philosophical Society Press was the logical organization to publish this work. Franklin was a founder of the Society, which is mentioned herein in connection with the Real Academia de la Historia in Spain. Naturally, then, the publication of documents relative to Franklin in the archives of Spain should be published by his own organization. We are especially grateful to Mary McDonald, former Director of Publications, whose proactive approach resulted in a perfect association made even more so with the collaboration of the University of Pennsylvania Press. Thanks to Ms. McDonald's recommendation, this edition includes transcriptions of all the Spanish and French documents. For the more serious-minded reader, these are an invaluable resource. Peter Dougherty, the new Director of Publications at APS, has been of infinite help to me in preparing this volume to become the first publication of APS's collaboration with the University of Pennsylvania Press. Kate Tyler Wall, APS's Managing Editor, along with Alison Swety Beninato, helped with the manuscript after the decision was made to include the documents in their original language. Kathie Jiang, the Marketing and Client Management Assistant for the University of Pennsylvania Press, has been of invaluable help as we figured out the cover design and planned how to market the book. Pamela Lankas, of International Graphic Services, was tasked with being the lead editor, or as she put it, "the person to usher the manuscript through publication." By its nature, this manuscript is much more complicated than a straight narrative. I have enjoyed and been impressed with her attention to detail. As stated earlier, this book is the result of the work of many people and I, whose name will be most associated with the final product, cannot be thankful enough for all the good people who have been a part of this project from its inception to this publication.

The Instituto Franklin of the Universidad de Alcalá naturally agreed to publish a Spanish version of these documents without transcriptions. Led by Dr. Julio Cañero Serrano, the staff there enthusiastically worked to produce the Spanish edition that facilitated this multi-lingual edition. I am

Acknowledgments • 457

very grateful for their support with the Spanish documents. Special thanks go to Irene Moreno Acevedo, the first editor assigned to this book, and to her successors, Ana Serra and Ana Lariño. Francisco Sáez de Adana, recently elected the Instituto's new director, helped to coordinate and support this effort.

Very special thanks go to Dr. Susan Tiano, Dr. William Stanley, and Vickie Madrid Nelson of the Latin American and Iberian Institute (LAII) of the University of New Mexico. The LAII played a key role in the success of this work as it coordinated and managed the donations raised in support of this project.

Historian Carlos Cólogan Soriano introduced us to family archives housed in the Archivo Histórico Provincial de Santa Cruz in the Canary Islands. He generously provided us with his books and then followed up by sending documents to us. We count him a good friend as well as a scholar.

Spanish Consul General Enric Panés's enthusiasm for our work resulted in his help in raising awareness and providing financial support. John Espinosa, also of Houston, and the Granaderos y Damas de Gálvez opened doors that led to offers of very important support. Their combined enthusiasm for what we were doing was infectious.

This resource of archived information is intended for historians and any person curious about learning more about Benjamin Franklin, the independence of the United States, and Spain's connection to both. It is our hope that many of the documents included here will be the basis for new historical interpretations.

What follows is a list of major donors to this project. Each contributed $1,000 or more and/or hosted a fundraiser in their home. One contributor donated $20,000. These are a few of the fifty-plus donors who contributed to the project. All are true heroes; they not only understand the value of history, they support it. These are special people who see a future in sharing the past.

Thomas E. Chávez
Albuquerque, New Mexico, USA

Kevin and Leonore Daniels
Rob and Patricia Kurz
Sarah Hunt Espinosa
Miguel and Maria Estela Rios
Susan Conway and Pat Oliphant
Davis and Christine Mather

Ray and Judy Dewey
Allen Sprowl
Dan and Nancy Lori
Armin and Penny Rembe
Ambassador Ed Romero

www.ingramcontent.com/pod-product-compliance
Lightning Source LLC
Chambersburg PA
CBHW021231300426
44111CB00007B/504